*This is an annual. That is to say,
it is substantially revised each year, the
new edition appearing each November.
Those wishing to submit additions,
corrections, or suggestions for the
1995 edition should submit them prior
to February 1, 1994, using the form
provided in the back of this book.
(Forms reaching us after that date will,
unfortunately, have to wait for the
1996 edition.)*

What Color Is Your Parachute?

Other Books by Richard N. Bolles

The Three Boxes of Life,
  And How To Get Out of Them

Where Do I Go From Here With My Life?
  (co-authored with John C. Crystal)

1994 Edition

What Color Is Your Parachute?

A Practical Manual for Job-Hunters & Career-Changers

by

Richard Nelson Bolles

Ten Speed Press

PUBLISHER'S NOTE

This publication is designed to provide accurate and authoritative information in regard to the subject matter covered. It is sold with the understanding that the publisher is not engaged in rendering professional career services. If expert assistance is required, the service of the appropriate professional should be sought.

The drawings on pages 26, 159, 160, 164, 172, 188, 266, 278, 298, and 310 are by Steven M. Johnson, author of *What The World Needs Now.*

Library of Congress Catalog Card No. 84-649334
ISBN 0-89815-568-1, paper
ISBN 0-89815-584-3, cloth
Published by Ten Speed Press, P.O. Box 7123, Berkeley, California 94707

Type set by Haru Composition and Hannah Associates, San Francisco, California
Consolidated Printers, Inc., Berkeley, California
Printed in the United States of America

Contents

This is dedicated to the one I love
(my wife, Carol)

Preface

This is my personal space, the place where I get a chance every year to say something new about this book and the changing world out there.

My concern and my obsession is helping every bewildered job-hunter or career-changer out there, in the midst of all the bewildering changes that are happening in the workplace.

For, the vast restructuring of the workplace that is going on in the '90s continues apace, throughout the world -- and consequently the need for this book continues apace, throughout the world. *Parachute* continues to be translated into new languages every year. During this past year, the Italian edition was introduced in Italy, quickly sold out, and had to be reprinted, thanks to the stunning translation work of Giuseppe Mojana, and the hard work of his associates: Fabrizio Luzzatto-Giuliani, Francesco Bogliari, Peppo Mojana, and that of such distinguished Italian journalists as Antonio Fortichiari, of the leading family weekly GENTE.

We need many different languages -- even in the U.S., where one out of seven speaks a foreign language at home. That's 31.8 million people, and they speak 329 different languages.[1]

However, the most signal discovery for me this past year was how much this book -- even in its U.S. edition and English/ American language -- gets read in so many different countries around the world: namely, *the U.S.* (of course), *Canada* (one out of every ten copies of this book are sold there), *England* (a growing readership), *New Zealand* (where over fifteen thousand copies have been sold), *Australia,* and so on. Letters sitting on my desk at the moment are from readers of the U.S. edition who reside in *Thailand, Brazil, Mexico, Saudi Arabia, Poland, Japan, Hong Kong, India, Bulgaria, Estonia, Germany, Switzerland, Belgium, The Netherlands,* and many other countries.

---

1. *USA Today,* 4/28/93.

I visited Australia and New Zealand this year, for the first time, and this visit impressed upon me in a new way that I must write every year with a deep awareness of how many of the readers of this U.S. edition do *not* reside in the U.S. I have taken some steps toward that with the edition you now hold in your hands, wherein I have tried to talk about U.S. statistics and resources with a heightened consciousness that these are being read in other countries than the U.S.

I get letters every year inquiring why there is not a national edition of *Parachute* for each different country, with a listing of resources, counselors, and books peculiar to that country alone -- instead of the generic U.S. edition with U.S. resources. The answer is that of course I wish there were such, but the work of producing a national edition for each country is so stupefying in its scope, that it precludes its accomplishment. We did produce a special version of the book for England, some years ago, but it languished on the shelves, since it could only be done but once, given its limited distribution and sales -- and readers in England quickly showed an overwhelming preference for the U.S. edition, which was equally available there in England, and which -- unlike the England edition -- is updated and revised each new year, sometimes dramatically.

I should mention that it takes me the better part of nine months to stay up to date with the U.S. resources alone. It is easy enough to get a *list* of the resources, both books and people, but *evaluating* which ones are useful and which ones are not is a much more difficult and time-consuming venture.

Were this easy to do in other countries, I would recommend (to my publisher) that we do it. But alas, the task boggles the mind. So, I have tried to rewrite *Parachute* so that it is pretty-much *self-contained*, with most of the stuff that readers will need, contained within these large borders.

Personally, I yearn for the earlier years, when *Parachute* was a thin little book. But alas, the times have gotten more compli-cated -- and so has job-hunting.

Let me recite, once again, the major themes of this book. There are five:

(1) The average person has to go job-hunting eight times in his or her life. Some job-hunts are successful. Some are not.

(2) The major difference between successful and unsuccessful job-hunters is not some factor *out there* (such as a 'tight' job-market), but the way they go about their job-hunt.

(3) It is important for you to learn how to go about your job-hunt yourself, rather than expecting someone else to rescue you. An ancient proverb says: "Give me a fish, and I will eat for today; teach me to fish, and I will eat for the rest of my life." This book is an attempt to teach you how to fish, with respect to the most difficult task any of us faces in life: the job-hunt -- whether it be a hunt for the same thing you've always done, or for something new and different, in the way of a career. In other words, this book is an attempt to *empower* you as job-hunter or career-changer so that no matter how many times you may have to go about this task during the rest of your life, you will know how to do it, and do it well.

(4) Beneath all the 'practical tips' and strategies in this book, lies the underlying conviction that you are really good (at what you do), that you have important, marketable talents, and that you probably have great difficulty in truly believing this, because of our national totally-irrational inferiority complex.[2]

(5) For career-changers the message is: there is a whole world out there, and you might as well leave your 'security field' and enter it.[3]

This is a thick book, but you are not expected to read it all, at once. You do not need to read Chapter 7 if you are not interested in moving. You do not need to read Chapter 6, if you have no interest in starting your own business, etc.

But, knowledge which you don't seem to need at all *this year,* may turn out to be knowledge you need very badly *next year.* So, I spend five months each year rewriting the whole book, to sharpen it for the '90s, and explain all that I know, as carefully and thoroughly as I can. I do want to emphasize, however, that the ideas discussed in this book are *not* my bright ideas, but are culled from the experience of *successful* job-hunters and career-changers -- thousands of them -- over the years.

---

2. I am indebted to my friend, Roger Parker, author of many desktop publishing manuals, including *The Makeover Book,* for summarizing these learnings from the time that he first used *Parachute* back in 1974.

3. *Ibid.*

And now, in closing this preface, my annual litany of heartfelt thanks. In order that this book could be written in the first place, endless travel and interviewing was conducted originally around the whole U.S. covering some 65,000 miles. Then, and since, I want to thank:

• The countless victims of our country's outdated, outmoded and Neanderthal job-hunting apparatus, who shared with me their problems and difficulties, and finally their triumphs.

• Everyone who continues to take time to write and tell me how they used this book to effect meaningful changes in their life and work, and especially those who tell me *which* ideas in the book were particularly helpful to them.

• Those creative souls, who first pointed out to me what was wrong with this country's whole job-hunting and career-changing *system,* and gave me documentary evidence of the same -- in particular Dick Lathrop, Sidney Fine, the late Bob Wegmann, Daniel Porot, Tom and Ellie Jackson, Howard Figler, Arthur Miller, Bernard Haldane, Nathan Azrin, Carol Christen, John Holland, Peter Drucker, and -- above all -- the late John Crystal, who gave me the framework, now preserved in Chapters 9, 10, and 11 in this book, of *What, Where and How.* God bless you, John, in your heavenly rest.

• Bev Anderson, who has done the layout of this book *(and all my other written works)* year after year, since 1972. I love working with her; she is a delight.

• Haru Watanabe for the great care he gives to the typesetting each year.

• Phil Wood, my publisher, for his unfailing support in my work.

• His associates George Young, Hal Hershey, and Jackie Wan who each year help this book to get done and get done right.

• My office staff, who over the years have taken a great burden off my back, so that I might devote my time to research and writing.

• The Lord God, our Great Creator, who is the One who has given me the talents and the inspiration to write this book -- and the will to revise it each year.

• My dear ninety-year-old aunt, Sister Esther Mary, of the Community of the Transfiguration (Episcopal) in Glendale,

Ohio, who has taught me from my youth up.

• And -- above all others -- my dear wife, Carol, for her wit, wisdom, encouragement, and love over the years. As my four grown children, Stephen, Mark, Gary, and Sharon, and my 17-year-old stepdaughter, Serena, will attest, she is a *wonderful* woman. It is my greatest achievement in life to be her husband.

Now, on with the book. My friend, I wish you good luck. I wish you persistence. I wish you success, not only with your job-hunt or career-change, but -- even more -- with your life.

Dick Bolles
P. O. Box 379
Walnut Creek, California 94597
July 31, 1993

A Grammar Footnote

I want to explain three points of grammar, in this book: pronouns, commas, and italics. My unorthodox use of them invariably offends unemployed English teachers so much that they write me to apply for a job as my editor.

To save us unnecessary correspondence, let me explain. Throughout this book, I often use the apparently plural pronoun "they," "them," or "their" with singular verbs or antecedents - - such as, "You must approach *someone* for a job and tell *them* what you can do." This sounds strange and even wrong to those who know English well. To be sure, we all know that there is another pronoun - - "you" - - that may be either singular or plural, but few of us realize that the pronoun "they," "them," or "their" was also once treated as both plural and singular in the English language. The latter usage changed, at a time in English history when agreement in number became more important than agreement as to sexual gender. Today, however, our priorities are shifting once again. Now, the distinguishing of sexual gender is considered by many to be more important than agreement in number.

The common artifices used for this new priority, such as "s/he," or "he/she," are tortuous and inelegant. Hence, Casey Miller and Kate Swift, in their classic *The Handbook of Nonsexist Writing,* argue that it is time to bring back the earlier usage of "they," "them," and "their" as both singular and plural - - just as "you" is/are. They further argue that this return to the earlier historical usage has already become quite common out on the street - - witness a typical sign by the ocean which reads "Anyone using this beach after 5 p.m. does so at their own risk." I have followed Casey and Kate's wise recommendation.

As for my commas, they are deliberately used according to my own rules - - rather than according to the rules of historic grammar (which I did learn - - I hastily add, to reassure my old Harvard English teachers, who despaired of me then and now). My own rules about commas are: write conversationally, and put in a comma wherever I would normally stop for a breath, were I speaking the same line.

The same conversational rule applies to my use of italics. I use italics wherever, were I speaking the sentence, I would put emphasis on that word or phrase. Rarely, I also use italics where there is a digression of thought, and I want to maintain the main thought and flow of the sentence.

And I saw my ship
Carried on the great sea,
Safely, I thought,
Until suddenly I realized I was
In the belly of the great whale.
                    Jonah

CHAPTER ONE

A
Cup of
Hope

The other day,
I was fresh out,
Of work,
Of luck,
Of hope; and so
I knocked on every door
There was, with cup in hand,
And pleading look,
To see if someone
Anywhere
Could spare
A cup
Of hope.
It's like it was,
In days of old,
If you were baking
And suddenly found
No sugar, you went next door
And asked them to lend you
What you had not,
And they had plenty of,
So now, I knock:
And does my neighbor have
Some hope (I hope)
Some hope that they could spare?
I only need a cup
This time,
To get me through the week.

Why have I run out?
I think you know.
I think you know it well;
But just in case you really don't
My story goes like this:

The world is in a sorry
Shape.
The crises keep on
Coming.

Coming one right after
    Another,
        Until our capacity
        To respond
            Falls down exhausted on the ground.
            Nations are exhausted, too,
                By new problems, new
                Challenges
                    Every day:
                    We've felt a kind of
                    Shaking
                    In the ground
                    Beneath our feet,
                    We've felt a kind of
                    Earthquake
                    In the ground
                    Beneath our feet,
                The kind where bridges fall
                Into the shaking sea,
                And buildings develop
                Cracks
                That make them suddenly
            Unsafe.
                Yes the nations are exhausted
            By the *Workquake*
            Where
        The earth without warning,
    Opens up,
And jobs are swallowed, as though
They'd never been.
With many businesses declared unsafe
Except for fewer employees.

    In former times, we knew, of course,
        The workers would
        Eventually
        Be called back, for
        That was the way
            It always had been

And always would be,
World without end. Amen.
But that's not the way
It's turning out,
In the '90s; this time
The *temblor* came as though to announce
The Day
That Jobs Began to Vanish,
And in every industrialized country
And land
The whole workplace is learning
To be
Or not to be,
A leaner, meaner
Economy.
Learning to *downsize*,
Tight'ning the belt
Without warning
Or mercy --
As they learn how to live
Poorer.

And we,
Well we
Are dividing
In each nation
Into those who grow
Poorer
And those who grow
Richer,
Two societies
Side by side,
With those who cannot sleep
For fear
Of those who cannot eat.
Yes, two
Societies
And we may be
Members of one, one morning,

And members of the other
By night
Fall.
We suffer these days
A fear of falling,
As half of those who still
Have jobs
Fear they will lose
Them
Tomorrow.
"There is a deep-seated concern
Out there,"
Said Alan Greenspan,
Chairman of the Federal Reserve,
"That I have not seen
In my lifetime.

Life seems
So uncertain
Now,
And so -- to tell the truth -- are we.
In yesterdays
We had a rescuer,
Labor, government,
Captain Midnight,
Superwoman,
To save us in the nick of time.
But now the world is more complex
And so much power
Seems to lie
In someone else's hands,
Which feels no compassion
For our plight --
Nature, Fate, or destiny.

We need a job,
In this new world,
Work that is
Meaningful,

We need a nod,
A friendly hand
Up
To the top of
The mountain;
We need a rope,
We need
Fresh hope.

Still down here in the valley, now,
We knock on any door:
'Sir or Lady, can you spare
Some hope
For me?
I've run fresh out.
I need to know tomorrow
Will not be
So bleak as now it seems;
I need to know
There's something I can do
To figure out
A way around
All obstacles.

I need to know
That in the overwhelming sea,
There's somewhere I can
Swim,
Some life-preserver I can
Grasp.
Until at last I get to shore
Of this new world,
Where
Hopefully
I will not only learn
How to survive, in body,
But even learn
To prosper, in my soul.
Oh, do you have some hope to spare,

To fill my cup?
My heart?
My life?'

Well, friend, that is the point, you see,
Of why I wrote this book,
The one you're holding in your hand,
In which you've chanced to look.
You do have power, in your life,
There are things you can do,
You do not have to tread this path,
Without a single clue.
We'll tell you how to still find hope,
E'en in life's darkest night
And where to look that you may see
The first rays of the light.
If you have faith -- believe in God --
We'll talk about that, too.
How faith applies, as Source of Hope,
Whatever you may do.

There's exercises in this book,
You'll find that they are fun,
They fit together, each of them,
Until they form but one
Design -- a tapestry you'll weave,
On loom of Time, from Memories,
Your Wishes, and your Goals; they'll yield
A pattern you can see.

We'll teach you how, e'en in this Age
Of shrinking jobs -- and fear --
You can find work you truly love,
A meaningful career,
So let us set out now, with hope
Together, me and you,
Upon our journey, through this book --
It's time for Chapter Two.

I've tried to be content
With my lot in life.
But, boy, I hate all this soot,
And seeing my sisters get out,
While I stay here, cleaning the hearth.
Come on, now, where
Is that glass slipper
You promised?

Cinderella

CHAPTER TWO

The Workquake
of The '90s

Chapter 2

THERE'S A WHOLE LOT
OF SHAKIN' GOIN' ON

In Earth's crust, there are two kinds of **earthquakes.** One is the *single sharp jolt,* with aftershocks barely felt. Once that earthquake's come and gone, for all practical purposes it's over.

The other is the *mammoth earthquake* that is followed by one major aftershock after another, one day after another, so that almost as soon as you have gotten back up on your feet, you are knocked to the ground again, the next day. And it goes on, and on.

Likewise, there are two kinds of **'workquakes'** that may occur beneath the surface of the world's marketplace. The first, like the single sharp earthquake jolt with aftershocks barely felt, we call **'a Recession.'** The second, where one major aftershock occurs after another, is more than a Recession. It involves **a major and profound restructuring of the whole workplace.**

In the 1990s we are not simply in a prolonged Recession -- though many so-called *experts* keep talking as though we were. *"Well, our recovery from the Recession ground to a halt again last month."* And so on, and so forth.

No, no, no. We are experiencing something much more profound in the '90s. We are in the midst of **a mammoth 'workquake'** -- a major ongoing restructuring of the world's whole workplace. This mammoth 'workquake' of the '90s has these characteristics:

- **Debt Everywhere.** Major debt exists throughout the world due to the excesses of the '80s, which is hamstringing governments, corporations, organizations, banks, and individuals, with a resultant downsizing of government, aid, bank loans, corporation size, and individuals' ability to buy.

- **Downsizing Everywhere.** A downsizing of organizations, from the largest and best-known corporations, to the smallest two-employee office, is occurring, resulting in one major wave of layoffs after another, year after year after year.

• **Pessimism.** Increased anxiety in the workforce exists among those who still have their jobs, with resultant consumer pessimism.

• **More Hours.** A dramatic increase in the hours that established full-time employees have to work, now is widespread, because employers want to hold down their *benefits* costs (medical care, etc.) by using workers who already have these benefits -- rather than hiring new workers who would raise those costs for the employer.

• **Lower Paychecks.** The increasing disappearance of well-paying jobs (particularly in the manufacturing sector), is all around us, leading to decreasing paychecks for families, hence a drop in their standard of living.

• **Lower Standard of Living.** This lower pay, plus the increased costs of living -- particularly housing, medical care, and the like -- has dramatically lowered the standard of living of a great many workers.

• **More Part-time Work.** There has been a dramatic increase in the number of people who are acting as *temporaries,* or are involved in *part-time work* -- often involuntarily.

• **Less Job Security.** The consequence is that nobody's job is safe anymore. You may find yourself thrown out of work at any time, *due to another 'workquake' aftershock.* Your firing or termination may be precipitated by: a 'downsizing,' or a 'rightsizing,' or a 'restructuring,' or by your employer going out of business, or by a personality conflict with your supervisor or boss, or by some form of prejudice: age discrimination, racial discrimination, sex discrimination, and the like. In many cases, you can be laid-off or fired *totally without warning.* You are *out of there.*

Also, with so many unemployed people, many employers have new and higher standards for employee performance, and if you don't measure up, there are plenty of others they can find to take your place. Even CEOs of large corporations -- General Motors, IBM, etc. -- can be suddenly out on the street, these days.

It means nothing that you may have worked at that place for *years,* and have given that organization the best years of your life. You are 'history,' caught in the 'workquake.' And very likely you will be depressed, or angry or even livid.[1]

These days, the major shocks keep coming one after the other, with very little interval in between.

What has resulted, is that here in the '90s, 2 out of every 14 workers are unemployed *(to one degree or another),* 6 out of the 14 are employed but worried about losing their job, and 6 out of every 14 workers are employed and not worried about losing their job.[2] Nonetheless, the latter may be thinking about chucking it, anyway.

THE RULES
ABOUT HIRING AND FIRING
IN THE '90s

If you get fired in the '90s, you may be seized by a whole host of feelings -- ranging from disappointment, to bitterness, to absolute rage. But most of all, you will likely be aghast at what this experience has shown you about the way the World of Work

---

1. Getting fired is no fun. I've been fired twice, myself, once when I was 22, and once when I was 41 years old. In the world of work today, you can get fired for 'screwing up' on the job OR you can get fired even when you're doing a simply excellent job. If your next employer asks *why* you were fired, it is sufficient if you merely say, "Usually, I get along well with everyone, but in this particular case the boss and I just didn't get along with each other. Difficult to say why." You don't need to say any more than that.

2. These figures were put together, by me, from various government sources. They are for the U.S., and are for the month of February, 1992. However, I think they are pretty generally true of any country in the world affected by this vast 'workquake' of the '90s, and I believe they will remain true as long as this mammoth 'workquake' we are in, continues.

functions. Most of us don't understand the nature of the world of work, until we bump our head or stub our toe on that nature.

"I don't have a parachute of any color."

High school or college doesn't prepare us for this. Only in the hard school of life do we begin to slowly and painstakingly piece this information together. Eventually we realize there are twelve 'rules' in the world of work about Hiring and Firing. They are these:

1. Nobody owes you a job.
2. You have to fight to get a job. *("Fight" means "persevere," "use ingenuity," "compete.")*
3. You have to fight to keep a job. Loyalty, years of service, or personal friendship with the boss, do not in any way guarantee you a job at that place for the rest of your life.
4. You may quit anytime you want to.

5. Your employers may lay you off, or fire you, anytime they want to. They may do this because they have run out of money, and can't afford you anymore. They may do this because they have to decrease the size of their business, or are going out of business. They may do this because they find your skills do not match the work that they need to have done. Or they may do this because they have a personality conflict with you.

6. You may quit without any warning or much notice at all to your employer, leaving them high and dry.

7. Your employers may fire you, or lay you off, without any warning or much notice at all to you, dumping you unceremoniously out on the street.

8. If you quit, you may do everything you can to help your employer find a suitable replacement, or you may do nothing.

9. If you are fired, your former employer may do everything in the world to help you find other employment, or may do nothing.

10. As you look back, you may feel that your employers treated you very well, in accordance with their stated values -- or you may feel that your employers treated you very badly, in total contradiction of their stated values.

11. If *you* were the only one who was fired or let go, the other employees may promise they will fight to save your job, but you need to be prepared for the fact that when the chips are down, they may actually do nothing to help you. You will feel very alone.

12. Nonetheless, you remain a rare and unique individual, no matter how the world of work treats you. Your worth is not defined simply by your work, but by your spirit, your heart, and your compassion toward others.

If you are reading this *before* you are out of work, paste these on your mirror, and memorize them until you know them by heart. That way, there won't be any surprises for you, no matter how hard the times. You will be mentally prepared, for anything.

THE SKILLS NEEDED
TO SURVIVE THE
'WORKQUAKE' OF THE '90s

It is clear that there are three basic skills you must master, in the '90s if you are going to survive:

A. **You need to know how to survive while you are unemployed.** Survival, in this case, means both economic and spiritual. *(Appendix C, Chapter 5, Chapter 7, and the Epilogue in this book deal with this.)*

B. **You need to know how to go about job-hunting in some original ways** when jobs are scarce. *(Chapters 3, 4, 6, 12, 13, and 14 deal with this.)* And,

C. **You need to know how to go about identifying and landing a new career,** without going back to school for retraining -- if possible. *(Chapters 8, 9, 10, and 11 deal with this.)*

Once upon a time, in a sunnier decade, these were *optional* skills which you could choose to pick up, or not, as you pleased. That's no longer true. Now, these are necessary *survival* skills -- crucial to your making it through the '90s. Ideally, you need to master these three survival skills *before* you land *in the soup*.

It would be nice if our high schools and colleges had taught these skills to you, before you had even embarked upon the rough seas of The Workplace. But no such luck. You will have to pick these survival skills up on your own. Sometimes -- *in fact, most times* -- right in the midst of the crisis, internal or external, that you are in. That, of course, is why you are reading this book, isn't it? You have become acutely aware of the fact that you need these skills. Now.

And, my friend, since the average person does 6–8 job-hunts in his or her life, and three career changes, these are skills that you will need not just now, but *for the rest of your life.*

JOB-HUNTING
OR CHANGING CAREERS
EVEN WHEN
YOUR JOB IS SAFE

Of course, just because your job is safe, currently, doesn't mean that these skills have no relevance for your life.

You may be getting ready to change jobs or careers *voluntarily.* Even if the economy is in a major upheaval, and this would seem to be a really bad time to leave the security of your present job, you may still be ready *to chuck it.* You may be tired of it, bored, fed up, and hungry for something better in life -- something new, more exciting, and more challenging.

Or, if your work has been exciting, and challenging -- beyond measure -- it may be that you're stressed, burnt out, exhausted, and hungry for something smaller, more peaceful, calm, and secure.

Either way, you're ready to go job-hunting, perhaps even to change careers. Of course everyone tells you you're crazy, and that this is no time to be making any such kind of move. But you don't care. Your internal time clock has just struck midnight. *Bong!*

If you feel this way, you have lots of company. In the U.S., which is probably typical of most developed countries today, a recent survey[3] found that 33% of all workers in the U.S. had thought seriously about chucking their jobs the previous year, and 14% actually did -- over a two-year period. Given the fact that in the U.S. 119 million are working, *as I write,* that means 39 million toyed with the idea of seeking something better, and over 16 million actually went through with it, during last year and the year before.

WHO WILL RESCUE YOU?

So, you're ready. You were fired, or you're ready to quit. And now what?

Why of course! You're waiting for someone to rescue you.

Isn't that what we've always been taught: that if ever we are thrown out of work, or voluntarily quit, someone out there will

---

3. Conducted in 1991.

come to rescue us, come to our aid, steer us in the right direction, and hook us up with a proper job? Voila! Our troubles will be short-lived.

We are, of course, unclear about **who** that someone will be: the union, or the federal government, or the state, or private agencies, or newspapers -- but we believe it will be **someone.** Alas, when our time comes, and we are completely out of work, instead of someone coming to rescue us, there usually is only the sound of silence.

Many unemployed people have sat at home for months, waiting for God to prove that He loves them, by causing a job to just walk in the door. *It does happen.* But not often enough for you to ever count on it. Settle it in your head, from the outset:

WHO WILL RESCUE YOU

No one else on earth cares as much about what happens to you, when you are unemployed, as you do. Therefore it is you who must take over the management of your own job-hunt or career-change, if it is to be successful.

No one else is going to be willing to lavish as much time on it, as you will.

No one else will be so persistent, as you will.

And if you decide to change careers, no one else will have so exact a picture of what kind of job you are looking for, as you will.

It is you who needs to learn, and master, for all the years to come, the process of creative job-hunting and effective career-change. You will need this knowledge desperately.

Job-hunting, after all, is a repetitive activity in most of the countries of the world. This isn't likely to be the last time you're going to be doing this. Do remember that.

Says one job-hunter: *"As a mid-level executive, I've lost my job two times in less than ten years, and used* Parachute *both times to help me through the re-employment process. This book helped me through the roughest months of my life."*

Twice in less than ten years is not remarkable. Jobs in the U.S. last an average of 4.2 years -- and probably a similar length in other countries.[4]

That's why surveys reveal that **the number of times you will have to go job-hunting during your lifetime will likely be around eight.** Eight! Therefore, the time you spend on mastering your job-hunt or career-change *now* will stand you in good stead for the rest of your life.

On the other hand, if you do it haphazardly now, you are just going to have to master it all over again, next time.

No one can do it *as well* as you.

No one can do it *as often* as you.

YOU must go about doing the things you need to do, by way of budget planning, seeking unemployment benefits if you are eligible for them, etc.[5]

---

4. Of course a particular job you have may last longer than that -- especially as you grow older.

5. If you are totally unfamiliar with unemployment, there are these resources to help you:

Tom Morton, *The Survivor's Guide to Unemployment: How to prepare yourself, Taking care of yourself and your family, How to file for unemployment insurance benefits, What to do when you're facing extreme hardship, etc.* Piñon Press, P.O. Box 35007, Colorado Springs, CO 80935. 1992.

Also: Emily Koltnow and Lynne S. Dumas, *CONGRATULATIONS! You've Been Fired: Sound Advice for Women Who've Been Terminated, Pink-Slipped, Downsized, or Otherwise Unemployed.* Fawcett Columbine, published by Ballantine Books, 201 E. 50th St., New York, NY 10022.

Jill Jukes and Ruthan Rosenberg, *I've been fired, too! Coping with your husband's job loss.* Stoddart Publishing Co., Ltd., 34 Lesmill Rd., Toronto, Canada M3B 2T6. 1991.

Richard Layard, *How To Beat Unemployment.* Oxford University Press, Walton St., Oxford, OX2 6DP, U.K. 1986.

YOU must deal with the despair or depression which so often comes with this time of life. (*How to do this* is described in Chapter 5.)

YOU must learn how to carry out your own job-hunt or career-change. (Which is what the rest of this book is about.)

You may do it with support from others.
You may do it with coaching from others.
You may do it with God's help.
But, in the end, the one who must most immediately rescue you, is

YOU . . . YOU . . . YOU.

I saw, of course, the cliff,
I saw the turbulent ocean blue;
But everyone else was going that way,
So I thought that I would, too.

Larry Lemming[1]

1. A lemming is defined by Webster's as any of several short-tailed furry-footed rodents that are notable, in their European forms, for their recurrent mass migrations which often continue into the sea where vast numbers are drowned.

CHAPTER THREE

The Least Effective Job-Hunting Methods: Resumes, Agencies and Ads

Chapter 3

REJECTION SHOCK

When we are out of work, or have decided to go looking for a new job, we know that we dread it, before it even begins. And no wonder.

We *know* what lies ahead. We know we are going to have to approach one place after another, in one way or another. We know that we are going to get turned down, at a lot of those places. We know there is a lot of truth in my friend Tom Jackson's description of the typical job-hunt. In his *Guerrilla Tactics in the Job Market* he pictured it this way:

NO NO NO NO NO NO NO NO NO NO NO NO NO NO NO
NO NO NO NO NO NO NO NO NO NO NO NO NO NO NO
NO NO NO NO NO NO NO NO NO NO NO NO NO NO NO
NO NO NO NO NO NO NO NO NO NO NO NO NO YES.

It's a difficult process to approach with any enthusiasm or joy. All of our lives we are taught to hate being rejected. We learn at least fifty delicious ways to avoid rejection. We'll do anything to avoid being rejected, and I mean **anything.** The history of human dating, for example, is littered with such tactics as "I'll reject him (or her) before they have a chance to reject me." And then, along comes the job-hunt. Eight times in our lifetime (on average) we have to go through this painful process. And, except at its very end, it is **nothing but** a process of rejection. The very thing we've spent our life trying to avoid.

There's got to be a better way. And, fortunately, there is. It's called 'the creative process of job-hunting' -- for want of a better name. It minimizes this type of rejection by having you approach your job-hunt as though it were a career-change, and carefully choosing the places *you* want to work at -- ignoring whether or not they have a vacancy. It is explained at length in Chapters 9–11, should you want to leap to there *right now.*

OUR NEANDERTHAL JOB-HUNTING SYSTEM

Otherwise, since you are taking management of your own job-hunt, you need to spend some time looking at, and understanding, the job-hunting process that we normally fall into -- you know: resumes . . . classified ads . . . agencies . . . and the like.

The first idea to get clear about, is that **this so-called 'job-hunting system' as it is normally practiced in this country** (and most countries of the world) **is no system at all.** It is so ineffective that for decades now, personnel experts have privately called this *system* 'Neanderthal' and 'the Numbers game.'[2] It is loosely

---

2. In any given city, there's an employer wandering around trying to find somebody with particular experience and skills, while at the same time there is in that same city a job-hunter wandering around who has that experience and those skills; *and neither of them knows how to find each other. That's* Neanderthal, believe me.

composed of about twenty different job-hunting *methods,* from which you choose. It's sort of like a smorgasbord.

So, when you go job-hunting you take your pick among the twenty. *Naturally,* it would be helpful to know -- out of the twenty -- which ones are most effective, so that you could put your energy and your time into *those* methods. Lucky you. They've been studied a lot, over the years, and the findings can be summarized as follows:

The five most effective methods of finding a job *(according to various surveys, including one of ten million job-hunters)* turn out to be:

1. Applying directly to an employer, factory, or office in person (this leads to a job for 47 out of every 100 job-hunters who try it).

2. Asking friends for job-leads (this leads to a job for 34 out of every 100 job-hunters who try it).

3. Asking relatives for job-leads (this leads to a job for about 27 out of every 100 job-hunters who try it).

4. Using the placement office at the school or college that you once attended (this leads to a job for 21 out of every 100 job-hunters who try it).

5. And, in contrast to all of these, as I mentioned earlier, there is **the creative approach to job-hunting** -- *see Chapters 9–11* -- (which leads to a job for 86 out of every 100 job-hunters who try it).

Now, except for the last, none of these percentages are very inspiring, are they? But wait until you see the figures for the least effective.

The five least effective methods of finding a job are:

1. Using Computer Bank listings or 'registers' (this doesn't lead to a job for 96 out of every 100 job-hunters who try it).

2. Answering local newspaper **ads** (this doesn't lead to a job for between 76 to 95 out of every 100 job-hunters who try it -- *depending on the level sought; the higher the level, the less effective).*

3. Going to private **employment agencies** (this doesn't lead to a job for 76 to 95 out of every 100 job-hunters who try it -- *again, depending on the level sought).*

4. Answering ads in professional or trade **journals** within your field (this doesn't lead to a job for about 93 out of every 100 job-hunters who try it).

5. Mailing out **resumes** by the bushel (this doesn't lead to a job for 92 out of every 100 job-hunters who try it).

For those who like diagrams, I have summarized all of this on the next page.

SPENDING THE MOST TIME ON THE LEAST EFFECTIVE METHODS

Now, common sense would suggest that you give each of the above methods exactly the amount of time its effectiveness deserves. By this logic, you should spend six times as many hours going directly, face-to-face, to places where you would like to work, as you spend on resumes, *because going directly to places where you would like to work is six times more effective in finding a job.*

But what do we do, when it's our time to go job-hunting? Well, you know. Left to our own instincts, and the kind of information about how to go job-hunting that we've picked up *on the street,* we instinctively devote our time to 'the big three': resumes, agencies, and ads. And what's so strange about that? Just this: every single one of these is found on the list of the five *least* effective methods of job-hunting, above. Not a one of them is on the list of the five *most* effective ways of finding a job.

THE
NUMBERS
Our Wonderful Job Hunting

DESPAIR CITY

Failure rate: 77.8%	Failure rate: 85%
Going to A Union Hiring Hall (if you belong)	Contacting An Executive Search Firm

Go back to start (Move to the left this time)

CONGRATULATIONS!

YOU FOUND THE JOB YOU WANT!

Following The Creative Minority's Prescription (Chapters 9, 10, 11) — Success rate: 86%

Using Personal Contacts — Success rate: 68%

Applying Directly to An Employer In Person — Success rate: 47.7%

Asking Friends for Job Leads — Success rate: 34%

Asking Relatives for Job Leads — Success rate: 26.7%

Using Your School's Placement Service — Success rate: 21.4%

Asking A Professor or Teacher for Job Leads — Succeeds in finding a job for 12.1% of those who use this method.

OR MAY BE PLAYED WITH 67 PLAYERS

You
1   Coach (a book or counselor)
10 People you do a Practice Field Survey on
15 People you do informational interviewing with
40 Employers you contact in person

Failure rate: 86.3%	Failure rate: 87.1%	Failure rate: 87.5%	
Using the Federal/State Employment Service	**Placing Ads Yourself ("Available")**	**Taking Civil Service Test To Get A Job**	**Answering Ads from Elsewhere In The Country**

Failure rate: 90%

GAME
(Neanderthal) System

Going to Job Fairs, etc. Where Employers Are

Failure rate: 91.8%

MAY BE PLAYED WITH 722 PLAYERS

You
- 5   Newspapers
- 7   Private employment agencies
- 2   Registers
- 700   Resumes sent to employers
- 2   Job Fairs
- 4   Executive Search Firms

Mailing Out Resumes By The Bushel

Failure rate: 92%

Answering Ads in Journals for Your Field

Failure rate: 92.7%

Using Computerized Listings or "Registers"

Failure rate: 96%

START

YOUR JOB-HUNT

Answering Local Newspaper Ads

Going To Private Employment Agencies

Fails to find a job for 95–76% (depending on level sought) for those who use this method.

Failure rate: 95–75.8%

This is why our job-hunting system is so Neanderthal. Even in the worst of times, jobs fall vacant at an amazing rate. People die, people retire, people get disabled, people get restless and switch jobs, etc. So our problem in hard times isn't that there are no job vacancies out there. It's that **we have instinctively chosen the least effective ways of discovering those vacancies.**

But, if you're going to use these least effective methods of job-hunting (and many of you probably are, aren't you?) you might as well know how they work -- or how they *don't* work -- and how you can best use them.

OUR FAVORITE WAY OF AVOIDING REJECTION:
RESUMES

> **RÉ-SU-MÉ rez-ə-mā** n [F. *résumé* fr. pp. of *résumer* to resume, summarize] SUMMARY *specif:* a short account of one's career and qualifications prepared typically by an applicant for a position. —Webster's

Yes, I know. You've heard -- since the day you were born -- that *the* way to go job-hunting is to prepare a decent resume *(or 'curriculum vitae')* and then send it out by the bushel baskets to every prospective employer you can think of, or find listed in your field in the local library. That's why experts call our Neanderthal job-hunting system 'the numbers game.' The greater the numbers, the better your chances. Blanket the country, if necessary -- the more, the merrier.[3] So the mythology goes.

O my! What a passionate belief in resumes there is among job-hunters, and how out of proportion it is to how often resumes actually work! Consider the following:

---

3. To help you, there are even organizations which will publish your resume *(along with a lot of other job-hunters')* in a small booklet, and circulate it to employers. Forty-Plus Clubs do this, through their *Executive Manpower Directory.* So do some of the State Job Service/Employment Development Departments *(California, for example, has such a system, called PROMATCH, with 23 offices, which does this for experienced professionals).* It sounds as if *it couldn't hurt,* but do remember (if this sounds appealing to you) that you're in that booklet with a *lot* of other people.

1. Resumes have a lousy track record. A study of employers done a number of years ago discovered that there was one job offer tendered and accepted, for every 1470 resumes that employers received, from job-hunters. Were such a study repeated today, I believe the figures would be worse. Resumes have fallen into even greater disrepute among employers today, due to so many job-hunters lying about their qualifications -- *and being found out.* Employers do check resumes, these days. So how do the odds of *one out of 1470* sound to you? Well, let me put it this way: would you take a plane flight if you knew that only one out of every 1470 planes ever made it to their destination? Then, why so much faith in resumes, which are just as fragile? When you send out bushel baskets of them, and that doesn't get you a job, well, resumes are just doing what they normally do: *nothing.*

2. If you are presently employed, you can lose your job by sending out a resume. I know someone this actually happened to. Let's call him Jim. Jim was the manager of a bank. He was happy where he was, but he also was looking down the road to think of where he might eventually go next. So, he sent out one copy of his resume in answer to an ad from another bank, 'just to test the waters.' The employer to whom Jim sent that resume, however, was (unbeknownst to him) a friend of his current employer, so they talked, "Did you know one of your managers is looking for a new job?" Jim was called in and fired on the spot, despite his explanation that he was only looking way down the road. "You don't have the right attitude for working here," he was told. (They meant *loyalty until the death -- on* his *part, not theirs.*)[4]

---

4. By the way, speaking of hunting for a job while you are presently employed: *don't* use your present employer's stationery or envelopes for your resume, or send your resume from your employer's fax machine. Remember, that company's name appears at the top of every page when transmitted to a potential employer. The question this raises in the mind of the employer who *receives* your resume, is: "This person is obviously using materials taken from that place without permission. If I were to hire this person, what materials or services would they take from *my* place, without asking?" Ethics *are* becoming more important in business and politics (or hadn't you noticed?). We know you don't want to get turned down just because your resume looks sloppy. Neither do you want to be turned down because your *resume ethics* look sloppy.

3. Most of all, you can devastate your self-confidence by depending on resumes as your primary job-hunting strategy. Why? Because of the mythology about resumes that I alluded to, earlier, which causes a large number of job-hunters to believe that resumes *almost always* work, for everyone. Here's how that mythology gets fueled:

a) With at least nine million job-hunters out there hunting for a job during Hard Times, the odds are that *some* job-hunters will actually get an interview, and subsequently a job, *because* they sent out resumes.

FRANK AND ERNEST · by Bob Thaves

© 1987 Newspaper Enterprise Association, Inc. Used by permission.

b) But many, many more job-hunters do not get a job by means of a resume. In fact, an *incredible* number do not even get *one* invitation to an interview, in spite of sending out 800 or 900 resumes.

c) The ones who do get a job thereby, talk a lot about it; the ones who find that resumes didn't work for them, usually keep quiet about that. So, if you hear people discussing their experience with resumes, it's usually only those for whom it worked. Hence, the widespread impression that 'this is a method which works for almost everyone.'

If you believe that, and you send out loads of resumes, and you don't even get a nibble, what are you going to think? It is not that another job-hunting method has been tried, and failed. It is that a method which you *think* works for almost everyone else, has failed for you. So you're going to think that something is wrong with *you*. Hence, plummeting self-esteem, and thence depression, emotional paralysis, and worse symptoms often follow. This has happened to tens of thousands of job-hunters. It has even happened to me. Don't let it happen to you. You have to get back to point #1, above: resumes have a lousy track record. As I said earlier, if you decide to send out bushel baskets of them, and that doesn't get you a job, well, that's how resumes are. They're just doing what they normally do: nothing. If you don't get even a nibble, that doesn't mean that anything's wrong with you. Something's desperately wrong with resumes . . . as a job-hunting technique.

THERE IS NO MAGIC

But, of course, you're probably going to prepare a resume anyway, aren't you? And, to be practical, if you're talking to some employer who is halfway across the country, you *may* need a resume. (Though oftentimes a long individual letter, summarizing the same stuff, is preferable -- since so many employers these days are highly allergic to resumes -- period -- and break out into a rash, if they even see one in their mail.) Or, if you're having a series of interviews with an employer in the same city as you are, you may want to *leave* a resume behind you, *after* the first interview.

The first rule (also the last rule) about preparing your resume or c.v. is that there is no such thing as a *right* format or form for a resume or c.v. I used to have a hobby of collecting resumes that had actually gotten someone an interview and, ultimately, a job. Being somewhat mischievous, I delighted in showing them to employers whom I knew. Many of them didn't like the winning resume at all. "That resume will never get anyone a job," they would say. Then, I would tell them, "Sorry, you're wrong. It already has. What you are saying is that it wouldn't get them a job *with you*."

The resume reproduced on the next page is a good example of what I mean. *(You did want an example of what I mean, didn't you?)* Jim Dyer, who had been in the Marines for twenty years, wanted a job as a salesman for heavy construction and mining equipment thousands of miles from where he was then living. He devised the resume you see, and had fifteen copies made. "I used," he said, "a grand total of seven before I got the job in the place I wanted!"

E.J. DYER   Street, City, Zip   Telephone No.

I SPEAK
THE LANGUAGE
OF
MEN
MACHINERY
AND
MANAGEMENT

...

OBJECTIVE: Sales of Heavy Equipment

QUALIFICATIONS   * Knowledge of heavy equipment, its use and maintenance.

                  * Ability to communicate with management and with men in the field.

                  * Ability to favorably introduce change in the form of new
                    equipment or new ideas... the ability to sell.

EXPERIENCE   * Maintained, shipped, budgeted and set allocation priorities for
                    85 pieces of heavy equipment as head of a 500-man organization
Men and   (1975-1977).
Machinery
                  * Constructed twelve field operation support complexes, employing
                    a 100-man crew and 19 pieces of heavy equipment (1965-1967).

                  * Jack-hammer operator, heavy construction (summers 1956-1957-1958).

  Management   * Planned, negotiated and executed large scale equipment purchases
                    on a nation to nation level (1972-1974).

    Sales   * Achieved field customer acceptance of two major new computer-
                    based systems:
                    - Equipment inventory control and repair parts expedite system
                      (1968-1971)
                    - Decision makers' training system (1977-1979).
                  * Proven leader ... repeatedly elected or appointed to senior posts.

EDUCATION   * B.A. Benedictine College, 1959. (Class President; Editor
                    Yearbook; "Who's Who in American Colleges").

                  * Naval War College, 1975. (Class President; Graduated "With
                    Highest Distinction").

                  * University of Maryland, 1973-1974. (Chinese Language).

                  * Middle Level Management Training Course, 1967-1968
                    (Class Standing: 1 of 97).

PERSONAL   * Family: Sharon and our sons Jim (11), Andy (8) and Matt (5)
                    desire to locate in a Mountain State by 1982, however, in
                    the interim will consider a position elsewhere in or outside
                    the United States ... Health: Excellent ... Birthdate: December
                    9, 1937 ... Completing Military Service with the rank of
                    Lieutenant Colonel, U.S. Marine Corps.

SUMMARY   A seeker of challenge ... experienced, proven and confident of
                  closing the sales for profit.

Like the employer who hired him, I loved this resume. Yet, when I've shown it to other employers, they have criticized it for using a picture, for being too long (or too short), etc., etc. In other words, had Jim sent his resume to *them,* they wouldn't have been impressed enough to invite him in for an interview.

So, don't believe anyone who tells you there's one right format for a resume, or one style that's guaranteed to win. It's still a gamble, where you're hoping that the employer(s) you like will also like your resume. Generally speaking, the most endearing quality needed in it, besides completeness, neatness and clarity, is that *you* shine through it all. If you decide you *do* want or need a resume, you will want more guidance than this. A number of books are listed in the footnote below.[5]

---

5. Let me say at the outset of this listing that the most popular of the books on resumes, by a long shot, is Richard Lathrop's *Who's Hiring Who,* wherein he describes and recommends "a qualifications brief" -- an idea akin to that which John Crystal used to propose: that in approaching an employer you should think of offering him or her a written proposal of what you *will* do in the future, rather than "a resume" of what you did do in the past. Of course there are those who say, "No matter what you try to call it, it's still a resume in the end." Yana Parker, who has written the other most popular resume book (according to our mail) agrees, and has titled her book simply *The Damn Good Resume Guide.* Now, the more complete list:

Richard Lathrop, *Who's Hiring Who?* 12th Edition. Ten Speed Press, Box 7123, Berkeley, CA 94707. 1989, 1977, 1976, 1971, 1967, 1966, 1961, 1960, 1959. First-class, highly recommended. A simply excellent resource, best by a long shot on the subject of resumes (or qualifications brief, as Dick calls them). Used more often by our readers than any other book, except *Parachute.*

David Swanson, *The Resume Solution; How To Write (and Use) A Resume That Gets Results.* JIST Works, Inc., 720 North Park Ave., Indianapolis, IN 46202-3431. 1991. This is a relatively new book on resumes, with tips not to be found in other books. It is very popular. (Dave has been my staff at my workshops since 1978.)

Yana Parker, *The Damn Good Resume Guide.* New edition. Ten Speed Press, Box 7123, Berkeley, CA 94707. 1989, 1986, 1983. Describes how to write a functional resume. All new resumes in this new edition. Employers' comments upon resumes which actually got people jobs, are especially helpful. A very popular and useful book.

Yana Parker, *The Resume Catalog: 200 Damn Good Examples.* Ten Speed Press, Box 7123, Berkeley, CA 94707. 1988. The title says it all. A supplement to the book above.

Yana Parker, *Damn Good Self-Teaching Resume Templates.* Damn Good Resume Service, P.O. Box 3289, Berkeley, CA 94703. 1991. This is a computer disk, and manual, for both MAC and DOS computers. It is another supplement to the book above.

Tom Jackson, *The Perfect Resume.* Anchor Press/Doubleday, Garden City, NY 11530. 1981. This is Tom's best-selling book, and with good reason.

William S. Frank, *200 Letters for Job Hunters.* Ten Speed Press, Box 7123, Berkeley, CA 94707. 1993, revised.

The end of the matter is this: resumes will be around as long as people go job-hunting, in spite of resumes' terrible track-record. First of all, though you *can* send out 800 resumes and not get a single nibble, *sometimes* they do work. Secondly, they *seem* like such a nice way to avoid rejection. Your name gets out there, and even if it doesn't lead to a job, at least you're not standing there in front of a would-be employer, staring into his or her face while you hear the bad news. With resumes, it's rejection all right. But it doesn't feel so . . . *personal*. I mean, there's so many *hundreds* of them that lead nowhere. Finally, resumes offer a nice way out for those of us who are just afraid --

Robert Hochheiser, *Throw Away Your Resume* (2nd ed.). Barron's Educational Series, Inc., 250 Wireless Blvd., Hauppauge, NY 11788. 1990, 1982. Well, of course I like the title, even if he doesn't fully mean it, as the body of the book makes clear. Nonetheless, he has some interesting perspectives if you are going to present yourself in writing to an employer.

Di Inchley, *Résumés for Results: A Complete Guide to Preparing Resumes and Written Applications*. The Business Library, Information Australia, A.C.N. 006 042 173, 45 Flinders Lane, Melbourne, VIC 3000, Australia. 1992. A book on resumes for Australian readers.

Carl McDaniels, *Developing a Professional Vita*. Revised Edition, 1990. Garrett Park Press, Box 190, Garrett Park, MD 20896. 1990. Especially for candidates for academic positions.

Peggy Schmidt, *The 90 Minute Resume*. Peterson's Guides, P.O. Box 2123, Princeton, NJ 08543. 1990. Written by the career columnist for The New York Post. Contains interesting sections, such as "How to Make an Ordinary Job Sound Important."

Tom Washington, *Resume Power: Selling Yourself on Paper*. Mount Vernon Press, 1750 112th N.E. C-247, Bellevue, WA 98004. 1990, 1988, 1985.

Donald Asher, *The Overnight Resume*. Ten Speed Press, P.O.Box 7123, Berkeley CA 94707. 1991.

J. I. Biegeleisen, *Job Resumes*. Perigee Books, The Putnam Publishing Group, 200 Madison Ave., New York, NY 10016. 1991. The author has been writing resume books since 1969 at least. This is revised and updated.

There are more books on resumes than you can shake a stick at. If the above sampling is not enough for you, see your local bookstore. It should also be noted that there are a number of software packages available, to help job-hunters prepare a resume. Some of these are listed on page 382.

afraid to get out, afraid to go face-to-face, afraid to risk. Resumes are a nice way to kid ourselves, so that we *feel* we are doing
something about our job-hunt, even if -- so far as effectively
finding a job is concerned -- we are actually doing next to
nothing.[6]

USING EMPLOYMENT AGENCIES

The second job-hunting strategy that we instinctively turn to,
in our Neanderthal job-hunting system, is agencies.

Agencies seem like a wonderful idea, when you are unemployed. *My goodness, there's actually someone out there who can link
employers looking for jobs with very-qualified me.* We all like to think
that somewhere out there is just such a *switchboard*, where all the
employers and all the job-hunters, in an area, can come to find
each other.

Unhappily **no place** in this country has even a clue as to
where all the jobs are. The best that *any place* can offer you is a
kind of sampling, a sort of smorgasbord, if you will, of some of
the jobs that are available, out there.

So, if you want a sampling, you will naturally want to visit an
agency. Agencies are of several types: private, federal/state, and
those retained by employers. Let's look at them in turn, beginning with the private agencies.

PRIVATE EMPLOYMENT
AGENCIES

What we need here is a rundown in some methodical fashion:

Types: Employment agencies are either for long-term work,
or for temporary work. The latter are called 'temporary agencies.'

---

6. Except, of course, the paper, printing and postage . . . and your high hopes. Speaking of high hopes, there is a Catch-22 situation here. Every expert in the world will tell
you that if you're going to send out resumes, send out as many as you possibly can. But,
human nature being what it is, the more you send out, usually the higher your hopes
get. Therefore, the more those hopes get dashed, when *even all those hundreds* don't get
you a job. It's that old adage, 'The higher you go, the harder you fall.' Send out five
copies of your resume, you don't care if they don't work; send out 800, *you care.*

Specialization: Some agencies list all kinds of jobs. Most specialize. Typical specialties, among long-term as well as temporary agencies: accountants, office services, data processing, legal, insurance, sales/marketing, underwriting, industrial (assemblers, drivers, mechanics), construction, engineering, management/executives, financial, data processing, nannies (for young and old), and health care/dental/medical, *among others.* You can find them listed in the Yellow Pages of your local phone book, under such headings as *Employment Agencies; Employment Service–Government, Company, Fraternal, etc.; and Employment–Temporary.* If they specialize, their listing or their ads will usually indicate what their specialties are.

Fees: Most often, the fees are paid by employers, but sometimes it is the job-hunter who pays.[7] Be sure to ask which is the case. *Naturally,* you want agencies that make no charge to the job-hunter, if you can find them.

Loyalty: The first lesson to learn about agencies is that while they claim to represent employer and job-hunter equally, when push comes to shove (like, when the job listing they have doesn't quite match you) their loyalty will lie with those who pay the bills (which in most cases is the employer), and those who represent repeat business (again, employers). This means that some agencies may try to talk you into taking a job that doesn't fit you at all, just so they can get the employer's business (and fee).

Effectiveness: And now we come to the biggie: how well do agencies serve you, the unemployed job-hunter? Well, some time back, a spokesman for the Federal Trade Commission announced that the average placement rate for employment agen-

---

7. If you go to an agency where you, not the employer, are going to have to pay the fee, there are several things you should know. One is, the application form that you fill out is a legal contract. Be sure you understand all its implications. For example, with many agencies, if the contract states that you give them *exclusive* handling, and then you go out and find a job independently of them, you may still have to pay *them* a fee. Beware. Secondly, fees vary from state to state. Ask what it is, and if there's a limit. In New York, for example, a fee cannot exceed 60% of one month's salary, i.e., a $15,000-a-year job will cost you $750. The fee may be paid in weekly installments of 10% (e.g., $75 on a $750 total). In 80% of executives' cases, it is the employer who pays the fee. Thirdly, fees that you pay to find a job are usually tax deductible. But check it out with some tax expert beforehand, to see if that is the case, before you agree to the contract.

cies was only 5% of those who walked in the door.[8] That means a 95% failure rate, right? *Tilt.* Incidentally, you should know that some agencies play games with their figures, so they can *claim* a high placement rate. They boast something like: "95% of all our clients find jobs through our agency." The trick is in whom they consider to be clients. They don't mean all those who come through that door. No, no, no. They make this game work, by accepting as 'clients' only a small percentage of those who walk in the door. And who might these be? You guessed it. The job-hunters that the agency thinks will be easiest to place. *Cute.* Of course they can place 95% of *them!*

APTITUDE
TESTING

"Let's put it this way — if you can find a village without an idiot, you've got yourself a job."

8. I was once at a meeting with a former head of an agency. Because he no longer worked there, he seemed like a good person to find out the truth from. So, I quoted this 5% success rate, to which he replied, "Oh no. That's not right. I'd say it was more like 1%."

Usefulness to career-changers: Very limited. Agency business is primarily a volume business, requiring rapid turnover of clientele, little time given to the individual job-hunter, with their primary focus on the most-marketable job-hunters, especially those on whom they can make a handsome fee. Career-changers, who have no previous track record in a particular industry or job, represent huge problems for agencies, which most of the time they are not willing to waste time on. Exception: *some* agencies are run by the most caring human beings in the world. If you are *lucky* enough to fall into *their* hands, you may get a lot of attention, even if you are new in the field where you are looking. This kind of care is most likely to be found at a new, or suddenly expanding agency, which needs names of job-hunters badly if it is ever to get employers to 'list' with them. But overall, agencies represent long-shot odds for you the job-hunter. They only know where a comparatively *few* jobs are, and none of them may fit you.

Well, so much for the private agencies. Now, to the other kind of employment agencies:

THE FEDERAL/STATE EMPLOYMENT SERVICE

Here's the rundown:

Name: The local State employment office in your town or city is actually part of a nationwide Federal network, called "The United States Employment Service," or USES for short. USES has seen its staff and budget, nationwide, greatly reduced in recent times.

Services: About one-tenth of these offices offer job-search workshops, from time to time -- depending on the demand, and whether or not a counselor is available who knows how to teach such a workshop. Beyond that, they have listings of *some* of the jobs available in your geographical area -- usually ones that employers have already tried to fill in every other way they can.

Out-of-State Jobs: Because it is part of a nationwide network, your local USES or Job Service office should have access to the Interstate Job Bank listings, which will tell you about job opportunities in other states or cities that may be of interest to you. The normal number of these listings runs around 6,000 at any one time; 98% of the USES offices have these listings on micro-fiche, and 20% of the offices *also* have a computer hookup. The listings are typically two weeks old before you see them, but many of them are for 'constant hires,' so that may not matter.

Effectiveness: Behind all the statistics, lies the all-important question: how much help are they going to be to you? Well, according to one study, USES placed only 13.7% of those who sought a job there. This means of course that they failed to find a job for 86.3% of the job-hunters who went there to find a job.[9] So, *if* you go there, *be realistic* about your chances of finding a job thereby. Your chances are 13 out of a 100. *Don't* put all your job-hunting eggs in this one basket.

AGENCIES ORIENTED TOWARD EMPLOYERS

One of the things that job-hunters rarely understand is the fact that employers are as baffled by our country's Neanderthal job-hunting 'system' as we are, and **don't know how to find decent employees, any more than job-hunters know how to find decent employers.** Therefore, they have certain agencies which *they* pay to find employees for them. *Naturally,* such agencies know about vacancies. They're being paid to *fill* them! Well, let's do our usual rundown:

Nicknames: Headhunters, body snatchers, flesh peddlers, tal-ent scouts.

Actual Names: Executive search firms, executive recruiters, executive recruitment consultants, executive development spe-cialists, management consultants, recruiters. It's a hazy category. For one thing, *yesterday's* employment agencies *today* often pre-fer to call themselves Recruiters or Executive Search firms. *(Em-ployment agencies typically have to operate under more stringent state or federal regulations, hence the appeal of a different, less-supervised, genre such as Executive Search.)* Anyway, there are places that will sell

---

9. Another study claimed that approximately 30% of those who search the job listings at USES find a job thereby. Many of these are only for temporary jobs, however. Still another survey revealed that 57% of those who found jobs at USES were not working at that job just 30 days later. This, of course, reduces the 30% claimed by the first study, to just 17%, after one month, which is pretty close to the 13.7% cited above.

you lists of executive search firms. For example:

Directory of Executive Recruiters, published by Consultant News, Templeton Rd., Fitzwilliam, NH 03447. Published yearly. Lists several hundred firms and the industries served.

Directory of Personnel Consultants by Specialization (Industry Grouping). Published by the National Association of Personnel Consultants, Round House Square, 3133 Mt. Vernon Ave., Alexandria, VA 22305, 1-703-684-0180.

Effectiveness: *Very effective* from the employers' point of view. *Very ineffective* from the job-hunters' point of view. That's because the mission these firms have been given by employers is *to hire away from other firms or employers,* workers who are already employed, and rising -- executives, salespeople, technicians, or whatever. *(In the old days, these firms searched only for executives, hence their now-outdated title.)*[10] If you read this mission statement over, you will notice it says *nothing* about their wanting to hire the *unemployed.*

Usefulness to Job-Hunters: Well, *if* you currently make $75,000 or more per year, and *if* your resume and cover letter look *thoroughly* professional and well thought out, and *if* you send your resume to one of the larger executive search firms in this country, experts say you have a one in ten chance that they will contact you. Anyone else, the odds are *much* worse. In other words, most experts say to the unemployed: *Forget it!*

AGENCIES SET UP
BY EMPLOYERS

Every job-hunter's dream is of a marketplace where employer and job-hunter can come to meet face-to-face. It's like an agency, except there's no job-order lying there on the desk. Instead, there's a live hiring (or at least, interviewing) person on the other side of the desk. Recruiters who come on campus, at some colleges, seem to embody this dream. Also, 'job-fairs' set up by business, industry, or private parties, embody the same dream.

---

10. If you want to know more, there is: John Lucht, *Rites of Passage at $100,000+.* Viceroy Press (1-800-VICEROY, for ordering). Review by one of our readers: "This book describes in depth the methods of headhunters, what to expect and how to deal with them on an on-going basis. Highly recommended for anyone in middle-management or above. . . ."

People *do* find jobs from talking to recruiters, and people *do* find jobs from going to job-fairs. But it should be an auxiliary strategy, at best, since most often it leads absolutely nowhere.

But that's true of *all* employment agencies: whether private, federal/State, employer-oriented, or whatever.

GOING TO EMPLOYMENT AGENCIES

A study called *The Job Hunt: Job-Seeking Behavior of Unemployed Workers in a Local Economy* was made by A. Harvey Belitsky and Harold L. Sheppard some years ago. By studying blue-collar workers in West Virginia, they discovered that the greater the number of job-hunting avenues used by a job-hunter, the greater his or her job-finding success.

Therefore, it makes sense to use as many of these different job-hunting avenues as you can, but not spending more time on them than their track record warrants. In the case of employment agencies, that would mean one or two hours a week at most.

WANT ADS IN NEWSPAPERS

The third job-hunting strategy that we instinctively turn to, in our Neanderthal job-hunting system, is want ads.

Where ads are found: In the business section, sports section, education section, or Sunday edition, of your local newspaper. Also, for management or financial job-hunters, in the *Wall Street Journal* (especially Tuesday's and Wednesday's editions).

Type of jobs advertised: Usually those which have a clear-cut title, well-defined specifications, and which the employer is having a hard time filling. If they can fill it by word-of-mouth, they don't advertise. It should also be noted that people play all kinds of games with ads, besides looking for job-hunters.[11]

Phrases Designed to Lure You In, But Conceal the Mundane Duties of That Job:

"Energetic self-starter wanted" (= You'll be working on commission)

"Good organizational skills" (= You'll be handling the filing)

"Make an investment in your future" (= This is a franchise or pyramid scheme)

"Much client contact" (= You handle the phone, or make 'cold calls' on clients)

"Planning and coordinating" (= You book the boss's travel arrangements)

"Opportunity of a lifetime" (= Nowhere else will you find such a low salary and so much work)

"Management training position" (= You'll be a salesperson with a wide territory)

"Varied, interesting travel" (= You'll be a salesperson with a wide territory)

Phone numbers in ads: many classified ads include the employers' phone number, because they want to see if they can *screen you out* without ever having to take the time to see you in person. It is in your best interest that you don't get screened out over the phone, but use it only to get a chance to meet the employer face-to-face. Therefore, regarding whether or not to use the phone that the ad has *so helpfully* listed, most experts say, "don't say anything over the phone, except that you want to set up an appointment."[12] Period.

Effectiveness: Within 48–96 hours after an ad appears (the third day is usually the peak), an employer will typically receive

---

11. If, out of sheerest curiosity, you want further information about the games that employers play with ads, I refer you to the chapter called "Blind Ad Man's Bluff" in David Noer's book, *How to Beat the Employment Game*. Ten Speed Press, Box 7123, Berkeley, CA 94707. Or at your local library.

12. One way to avoid being drawn into conversation, designed to screen you out over the phone, is simply to say: "I'm sorry I can't talk now; I'm at my current job."

Suite 700 North
San Francisco, CA 94107
Attention: Fin/TMC
NO PHONE CALLS PLEASE
EOE F/M/H/V
MINORITIES ARE ENCOURAGED
TO APPLY

FINANCE

ACCOUNT REPRESENTATIVE

Security Pacific Credit Corporation, a subsidiary of Security Pacific Corporation, seeks a leasing/equipment finance professional to assist in developing, implementing and managing a client's MILPITAS OFFICE. Requires lease/finance experience in areas of vendor leasing contract administration, lease program management and training. Ideal candidate is currently an Account Representative with a vendor lessor or is involved in sales finance program management with a major capital equipment manufacturer. Excellent salary and flexible benefits program.

GRAPHIC ARTIST – A work exp. in graphic, marketing, desktop publishing/skills in Mac, & computer electronic graphics (PaintBox/Aurora Systems). Artist will work w/promotion, production, news, & sales. Send resume to: Matt Chan, Creative Services Director, KXTV, 400 Broadway, Sacramento, CA 95818 EOE

GRAPHICS – Leading software manufacturer seeks full-time Macintosh production artist skilled in illustration 3.0 and familiar with other leading Macintosh programs. Fast-paced, fun, attractive environment.
Health Care

Health Plan/ Hospital Outside Services

Department Coordinator

Contracting department in growing managed health care company located in Foster City has an immediate F/T position for an experienced individual to coordinate workflow and provide support to contractors and department director.

Position reports to director and requires excellent WordPerfect skills, phone skills and ability to organize and coordinate departmental activities. Min. 3

---

from 20 to 1000 or more resumes, and will proceed to systematically *screen out* 95 to 98 out of every 100.

Usefulness to job-hunters: *(Better sit down.)* A study conducted in two "typical" cities -- one large, one small -- revealed, and I quote, that "85% of the employers in San Francisco, and 75% in Salt Lake City, did not hire any employees through want ads" during a typical year. Yes, that said *any* employees, *during the whole year.*[13] In other words, if you use ads, they only give you access to (at most) 25% of the employers in that city, during the entire year, and even then, 95–98% of the time you're going to be screened out without ever getting in to see even those employers!

As if all of this weren't bad enough, your job-hunting career with ads is further compromised by the fact that some of the ads you see are fakes. For example, there are fake ads run by unscrupulous con men (and women), masquerading as employers, who place ads solely in order to get your Social Security number, and the number of your driver's license, over the phone. With these two numbers alone, from you, they can often take you to the cleaners behind your back, with some of the con games they've invented. (Yes, you've got it right: they don't have any jobs to offer; they just want to do a job on you. I know people this has actually happened to.) Legitimate employers

---

13. Olympus Research Corporation, A Study to Test the Feasibility of Determining Whether Classified Ads in Daily Newspapers Are an Accurate Reflection of Local Labor Markets and of Significance to Employers and Job Seekers. 1973. From: Olympus Research Corporation, 1670 East 1300 South, Salt Lake City, UT 84105.

never ask for such personal information, over the phone. *So, don't ever give your Social Security number and your driver's license number, over the phone, or in a letter, please -- except to State or Federal government agencies such as IRS, welfare, etc., or when you're dealing face-to-face with employers, banks, or hospitals.*

Then there are fake ads with 900 numbers. They are usually listed in the Help Wanted sections of the newspapers, and promise you information about jobs, for a fee. Their common denominator is that they all give you a 900 area code phone number to call. (They give no address -- just the phone number.) In 499 out of 500 cases, these ads are to be avoided like the plague. Their offer of help is *too good to be true.* (Read that again.) They will take your money, and offer nothing of value in return, except *maybe* some old, very outdated ads. (Naturally, some of you won't believe me; but don't say I didn't warn you.)

Finally, there are fake ads run by employment agencies, in order to lure you to write or come in, the better to fatten their "resume bank" for future clout with employers. Sometimes these are *real* ads for jobs *that have already been filled* (run to get you in there, so they can manipulate you with the old *"bait and switch"* trick). In January of 1990 the Department of Consumer Affairs of the City of New York charged *50* Manhattan employment agencies with running deceptive ads that did not disclose they had been placed by employment agencies *(to do so is in violation of the New York City Consumer Protection Law)*.

Nevertheless, despite all these warnings, if you're *desperate* I'm sure you'll be tempted to try to answer some ads -- at least the ones you *think* are not fakes. In that case, here are some tips (but, *puh-leeze* don't get your hopes up!)

ANSWERING ADS

- Keep your answer brief. All you're trying to do, in answering the ad, is to be invited in for an interview. Period.
- Whether you get hired or not is the task of the interview, not the task of the answer you first send in.
- In answering, just quote the specifications that the ad asked for; nothing else. Then list what qualifications you have that exactly match each of those qualifications. That's the end of your answer.
- List your qualifications as a series of points, with maybe a 'bullet' (as it is called) in front of each -- as appears on this card.

- If there's a specification you don't meet (like, "experienced with motor boats"), you may wish at least to say something like "interested in motor boats." That is, if it's true.
- If there's anything else you're dying to tell them, save it for the interview. All they're looking for, among the answers they receive to their ad, is "who meets our specifications." They'll go on from there, with those that get invited in for an interview.
- Mail it in. Don't expect much. Remember, only 2 out 100 survive.

HOW TO ANSWER SALARY REQUESTS IN ADS

- If the ad requests, or even demands, that you state your salary requirements, beware. Employers often use this to screen out job-hunters who would otherwise qualify.

- Therefore, experts will give you contradictory advice here. Some say: ignore the request, don't even mention it. This leaves the employer free to think that maybe you just overlooked it.

- Other experts say: employers are not so easily fooled. Make some comment, at least, like: "I have enjoyed my career, because each new position has been increasingly challenging. I have been promoted regularly, with increasing authority, and commensurate increases in my salary."

- Still other experts say: Answer the request. But meet it head-on with a range, rather than a single salary figure. State a range, they say, of at least three to ten thousand dollars variation -- e.g., $15-20,000 -- and then add the words "depending on the nature and scope of my responsibilities," or words to that effect.

- The overarching rule is: if the ad doesn't mention salary, don't you either, in your response to that ad.

YOUR RESPONSE

- Be sure to include your phone number, in case that's the way the employer prefers to contact you.
- Consider sending your response by Federal Express; until everyone is doing this (and they're not, yet) your response will stand out in the mind of the employer, or receptionist.

CHECKING YOUR RESPONSE BEFORE YOU MAIL IT

- You must make certain that the spelling in your letter (and resume if you include it) is absolutely errorless. Show it to at least two members of your family, or friends, or workmates, whom you know to be excellent spellers.
- If a spelling error is found, redo the entire letter. (White-Out is a no-no.)
- Check to make sure that the final sentence in your letter speaks about the next step, and that it leaves the control in your hands, not theirs. Not "I hope to hear from you," but "I look forward to hearing from you, and will call you next week to be sure you received this letter -- the mails being what they are."

Some experts counsel other strategies -- *such as*, putting "Personal and Confidential" on your envelope; *and/or* mailing your letters so as to *arrive* in mid-week (that's Tuesday, Wednesday, or Thursday); *and/or* following up with a phone call seven days later -- at either the beginning of the employer's workday, or near the end of it. The trouble is, some employers are weary of these strategies (*especially, putting "Personal and Confidential" on an envelope containing a resume*) and just grow irritated with people who use it. You don't want an employer irritated with you.

There is another strange strategy which often *does* work, however, and it goes like this. Read your local newspaper every day, and make note of ads which you would like to respond to,

except that you don't have all the credentials, qualifications or experience that the ad calls for. You may send your response in, anyway. But, because it falls short, it will usually be ignored.

Naturally, in time, the ad will stop running, so watch during succeeding weeks to see if that ad *starts running again.* It usually won't, because the employer found the person they were looking for. But if it *does* start running again, that's usually a sign that the employer couldn't find a person with the qualifications he or she was looking for. Now you have a chance to bargain.

Here's how one job-hunter reported her success with this strategy: *"The particular ad I answered the first time it ran required at least an associate degree, which I did not have. What I did have was almost ten years' experience in that particular field. When the ad reappeared a month later I sent a letter saying they obviously had not found what they were looking for in the way of a degree, so why not give me a chance; they already had my resume. Well, it worked. I got the interview, I made them an offer that was $6,000 less than they were going to pay a degreed person, but still a $6,000 increase for me, over my prior position. I got the job. Needless to say, everyone was happy. I have recommended this same procedure to three of my friends, and it worked for two out of three of them, also."*

A GROUP LISTING OF ADS

The idea of finding some place which publishes summaries of employers' ads -- particularly for your field -- is a *twist* on ads, and sounds very attractive. Such places go under a variety of names: journals, registers, clearinghouses, etc. It's even more attractive, *of course,* if they promise they will list *you* or *match* you up with the listings of vacancies they have.

The major problem with such places: how old the listings may be by the time you receive them, and how likely it is that an employer will wait for you to send in your response many days, or even weeks, later, when typically for most ads -- as we saw -- an *avalanche* of responses comes in within 96 hours.

Anyway, you who like to live dangerously, here are *some* of these journals, magazines, registers, and clearinghouses:

The Wall Street Journal's *National Business Employment Weekly:* a weekly compilation of "career-advancement positions" from its four regional editions. Available on some newsstands, or order from: 420 Lexington Ave., New York, NY 10170, 1-212-808-6792. Each issue is $3.95.

Job Ads USA: a monthly summary of ads, which they have culled from 100 newspapers that month. You can order it from Militran, Inc., Box 490, Southeastern, PA 19299-0490, 1-800-426-9954.

Journals: There is a list of such journals: see S. Norman Feingold and Glenda Ann Hansard-Winkler, *Where the Jobs Are: A Comprehensive Directory of 1200 Journals Listing Career Opportunities.* Garrett Park Press, Garrett Park, MD 20896. 1989. As you can tell by the title, this book lists more than 1200 journals, which all together describe (allegedly) over one million available jobs each year.

For Non-profit Organizations Doing Public or Community Service: ACCESS, Networking in the Public Interest, 50 Beacon St., 4th Floor, Boston, MA 02108, 1-617-720-5627. Fax No.: 1-617-720-1318. Listings of job opportunities, ranging from entry level to Executive Director positions, are disseminated through three publications: (1) *Community Jobs: The Employment Newspaper For The Nonprofit Sector,* which has a monthly section called *Opportunities in Nonprofit Organizations;* (2) A College Edition of *Community Jobs,* published in the Spring and Fall; and (3) *Opportunities in Public Interest Law,* published twice a year – in the Spring and Fall. Typically, each will list 700 positions or less.

For Jobs Outdoors: Environmental Opportunities, Box 1437, Keene, NH 03431, publishes a monthly listing of environmental jobs, internships, and positions-wanted notices under the same name. Each issue contains twenty-four to forty full-time positions in a variety of disciplines. 1-603-357-8410. The Association for Experiential Education, 2885 Aurora Ave. #28, Boulder, CO 80303-2252, 1-303-440-8844, publishes a nationwide jobs clearinghouse list ($5 per issue, $40 for 12 issues).

For Teachers: *The NESC Jobs Newsletters* are published by the National Education Service Center, P.O. Box 1279, Dept. PB, Riverton, WY 82501, 1-307-856-0170. Between April and August, this weekly series of newsletters lists about 58,000 job openings annually. Each week's edition contains only new listings, none repeated. The newsletters are published year 'round, with fewer listings in the months August to April. You select one or more of fourteen different job categories, and receive listings of jobs in those categories only.

For Executives: *The Executives Network,* 131 State St., Suite 424, Boston, MA 02109, 1-617-227-1155, is a nationwide database, though concentrated in the eastern half of the U.S., listing both job-hunting candidates and job-openings, primarily in financial services, and primarily for executives making $25,000 to $100,000 a year. As with all such registers, there are *many more* candidates (8,000 currently, of whom approximately 30% are likely to be in the range of about 100 per month). Nonetheless, if being kept abreast of these listings (through Newsletter and mailings) interests you, the charge for you, as candidate, to get your resume listed with them, is $50. (Until recently, there was no charge.)

For Government Jobs: *Federal Career Opportunities,* published biweekly by Federal Research Service, Inc., 370 Maple Ave. W., Box 1059, Vienna, VA 22180, 1-703-281-0200. Each issue is 64 pages, and lists 3,200+ currently available federal jobs, in both the U.S. and overseas.

For Jobs in Criminal Justice: The *NELS Monthly Bulletin,* National Employment Listing Service, Criminal Justice Center, Sam Houston State Univ., Huntsville, TX 77341, 1-409-294-1692. A nonprofit service providing information on current job opportunities in the criminal justice and social services fields.

For Jobs in The Christian Church: Intercristo is a national Christian organization that lists over 18,000 jobs, covering hundreds of vocational categories within over 1,000 Christian service organizations in the U.S. or overseas. Their service is called Christian Placement Network. In 1992, 12,500 people used the Christian Placement Network; one out of every twenty-five job-hunters who used this service found a job thereby. (That, of course, means twenty-four out of twenty-five didn't.) But if those odds don't bother you, you can be listed with them for three months for $41.50. Their address is 19303 Fremont Ave. N., Seattle, WA 98133, and their phone number is 1-800-426-1342, or 1-206-546-7330. Jeff Trautman, Executive Director.

For The Blind: Job Opportunities for the Blind, 1800 Johnson St., Baltimore, MD 21230, 1-301-659-9314, or 1-800-638-7518. Exists to inform blind applicants about positions that are open with public and private employers throughout the country. Maintains a computerized listing. Also, they have cassette instructions on everything for the blind job-seeker. Operated by the National Federation of the Blind in partnership with the U.S. Department of Labor.

For Jobs Overseas: *International Employment Hotline,* a monthly newsletter which lists international employment opportunities. *International Employment Hotline,* Box 3030, Oakton, VA 22124.

Remember, with any or all of these listings, all you can hope to find is a sampler or smorgasbord, if you will. The number of jobs that are available, but are *not* listed anywhere, is *astronomical.* How you find *those,* is described in Chapters 11 and 12.

With ads, as with all the sad strategies in this chapter, the mischief is not in using the strategy. The mischief is in counting on it, or spending a great deal of time on it.

AND IN NOT HAVING
ANY OTHER PLAN

Well, Mr. or Ms. Job-Hunter, that just about covers the favorite job-hunting system of this country: resumes, agencies and ads.

The Neanderthal system which 'experts' call the Numbers Game.

If you send out that resume, or visit that agency, or scour those ads, and then find that it works for you, great! *Congratulations on your new job!*

But if it doesn't, you may be interested in the other plan -- you know, the one they had saved up for you, in case our normal Neanderthal job-hunting system didn't work for you? Small problem: with most of the personnel experts in our country (and in most of the countries of the world), there is no other plan.

And that . . . is that.

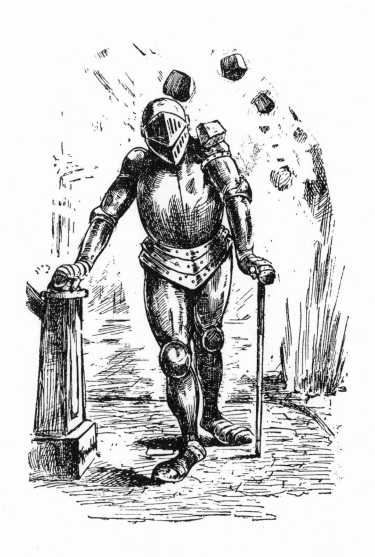

*Pray, as though everything
depended on God;
then work, as though everything
depended on you.*

CHAPTER FOUR

More Effective Ways of Job-Hunting

Chapter 4

THE MYTHOLOGY: 'THERE ARE NO JOBS'

When we rest our job-hunt completely on resumes, agencies, and ads, and those methods don't work for us, you would suppose we would then say, "Well, obviously *these* methods don't work." But that is not what we say.

What we say is: "There are no jobs out there."

Our unspoken logic runs something like this: "I can't find any jobs using these methods; therefore, there must not be any jobs."

Wrong!

Suppose you moved to a big city, where you found a really nice apartment, but you decided you didn't want (or need) a telephone. And now let us suppose that someone over on the other side of that city is asked if you exist. They've never heard of you, so their first response is, "I dunno." Being resourceful, however, they go and look in the telephone book; they assume that *anyone* who lives in the big city *must* have a telephone. But when they look, there is no mention of you. They call information to ask if you have an unlisted number. Nope. So in this city, they conclude: you don't exist.

Now, you know what's wrong with their conclusion. You do exist! And, in that city! But you can see from this simple illustration that if someone can't find you through *normal* channels, it *does not mean* that you don't exist. It only means that he or she can't find you using those channels.

So it is with you and jobs, during hard times or easy. The fact that you can't find any jobs you want through the so-called 'normal job-hunt channels' -- resumes, agencies, and ads -- *doesn't* mean that the jobs don't exist.

It only means you can't find them using those methods.

THE JOBS *ARE* OUT THERE

Evidence #1: A Survey. In the U.S., there have been nine Recessions since World War II, occurring as regularly as clockwork, every few years. During one of them, the National Federation of Independent Business conducted a survey to discover how many vacancies there were among small businesses. They discovered there were one and a half million, right during that Recession. And that was just for *small* businesses, never mind *large* businesses.

That's why job experts will tell you that even during the hardest of times there are two million vacancies out there, at any given moment. Probably more.

Evidence #2: Logic. It's not hard to understand why the vacancies number two million. Even during the worst of economic times, say during the U.S.'s Great Depression of the '30s, the unemployment figure was 37% at its worst, which means 63% of all workers at that time still had jobs.

Were the '90s to have such a time, 79 million workers would still have their jobs. Among them, vacancies would inevitably develop. Workers would still get fed up and quit, never mind how hard the times, and need to be replaced. Workers would still get fired for incompetence, and need to be replaced. Workers would still get disabled on the job, and for some time need to be replaced. Workers would still die before reaching their sixties, and need to be replaced. Workers would still retire, and need to be replaced. It's easy to see why two million vacancies would still exist. That's a vacancy rate of just 2.5% among active workers, in such a time.

Incidentally, since times aren't that tough currently, there are 119 million currently employed in the U.S. A vacancy rate of 2.5% among *them* would equal three million vacancies, not just two.

Evidence #3: Government Statistics: For the last three years, the U.S. government has published each month an unemployment count of about 9,000,000 people. That's the *monthly* figure. If that's the case, what's the *yearly* figure, you may ask. The answer, at least in 1991, turns out to be 25,000,000. That is, one out of every five workers in the U.S. was out of work, unemployed, at some time during the year.[1]

Okay, you do the arithmetic: 25,000,000 were unemployed, not by their own choice, sometime during the year. By the beginning of the following year, 'only' 9,00,000 unemployed were still left. On the dark side, that's still a *depressingly* large number. But, on the bright side, it means that:

16,000,000 of the unemployed found jobs, *during the year.*

That works out to 1,333,000 job vacancies found and filled *each month.*[2]

---

1. For 1991 the Conference Board said this was the correct figure. The government claimed it was lower -- 17% -- though during a previous Hard Time, the government came up with the 20% figure also. One poll put the 1991 figure even higher: a Time/CNN poll put it at 23% ("23% of American workers were unemployed, not by their own choice, at some time in 1991"; *Time,* January 13, 1992).

2. Each month, on the first Friday of the month, the U.S. government reports the *net* gain in jobs the previous month. It is arrived at, by taking the total number of jobs one month, and subtracting the total number of jobs for the next month. Why this figure is in sharp contrast to the figure I have reported above is easily illustrated. Suppose in a given month 1,300,000 jobs were lost or eliminated, but in that same month some 1,250,000 vacancies got filled. That means 1,250,000 job-hunters found a job that month. However, the government will subtract 1,300,000 from 1,250,000 and report that the *net* figure for that month was 50,000 jobs lost, implying that *no* job-hunters found a job that month -- or, to be more blunt, that "there are no jobs out there."

And since our earlier studies suggested there are at least two million vacancies each month, that also means at least 750,000 vacancies went undiscovered and unfilled, *each month.*

These three evidences, cited above, explain why experts say "Of course, there are job vacancies out there -- even during the hardest of times."

The latest self-help book for pessimists.

If you can't find those jobs, that means you're using the wrong methods to look for them.

> You will discover that the major difference between successful and unsuccessful job-hunters is not some factor out there (such as a tight job-market), but the way they go about their job-hunt.

HOW TO IMPROVE YOUR
JOB-HUNTING SUCCESS

If you play tennis, and you wanted to learn how to improve your game, you would go talk to *good* tennis players, to learn how they do it. If you run, and wanted to improve your running, you would go talk to *good* runners, and learn how they do it. If you paint, and wanted to learn how to paint better, you would go study under *master* painters, to see how they do it.

It is the same with job-hunting. If you are job-hunting, and you want to learn how to do it better, you go talk to *successful* job-hunters, people who *were* out of work, and since then have found a job they really love.

SHORTCUT
FOR NON-READERS

If you don't feel like finishing this book, then put it down, and go out there into the world, and talk to successful job-hunters among your neighbors, friends, relatives, and social groups: ask them how they did it, what they feel in retrospect they did wrong, what they feel in retrospect they did right, and so on. Then, go copy what the majority of them did.

Over the past twenty years, thousands and thousands of successful job-hunters have shared with us what made their job-hunt work. As it turns out, there are ten 'secrets' to successful job-hunting, regardless of what country you're in, regardless of what line of work you're in, regardless of how difficult a time we are in.

During the remainder of this chapter, we will look at each of these, in turn.

THE FIRST SECRET OF
JOB-HUNTING SUCCESS

Now, some of these 'secrets' for increasing your job-hunting success will sound remarkably silly, elementary and obvious to you. "Well, any fool would know *that!*" you will say. Unhappily that's not true, as our mail clearly reveals. We look for *complex* secrets to success, when most often it is the *simplest* of truths that hold the key.

And now to the first one:

For some reason, when we are unemployed we often shoot ourselves in the foot. I don't know exactly why, but without any rhyme or reason we often come up with some *unspoken* mental quotas in our head. It goes something like this: *this should take me about 30 phone calls, 15 calls in person, and then I'll have a job.* We go about our job-hunt, fill those quotas, and then -- whether we have a job or not -- we give up. At least one out of every three of us does.

BE PREPARED FOR A LONG JOB-HUNT

One job-hunter out of every three becomes an unsuccessful job-hunter, simply because they abandon their search before a job is found. Why? Because "I didn't think it was going to take this long."

Know this: the job-hunt in the U.S. (and many other countries) typically lasts from eight to twenty-three weeks -- or longer -- depending on the state of the economy, where you are, how old you are, and how high you are aiming.

Mentally prepare for your job-hunt to last longer than you think it will.

Don't count on the 'eight weeks.' Assume it is going to take the twenty-three weeks, at a minimum.

Don't give up! Jobs do not walk in the door while you're lying on the couch!
Persistence is the name of the game. Be gently, lovingly, stubbornly persistent.

Persistent also means being willing to go back to places that interested you, at least a couple of times in the following months, to see if by any chance their 'no vacancy' situation has changed.

Successful job-hunters have kept records. This was one man's experience, which is fairly typical:

> *107 places identified in his chosen geographical area as "interesting"*
> *126 phone calls placed to them*
> *45 interviews conducted in person*

Another job-hunter, a woman in New Zealand, cited her experience:

> *"I have been job-hunting for the past twelve months. I'm now writing to tell you of my great success in finding a full-time job after my 205th job application. The job is a fulfillment of my lifetime ambition. I start this week and will be earning $20,384 a year."*

These two job-hunters' records give you a realistic picture of how persistent a successful job-hunter *may* have to be. You need to keep up your job-hunt for as long as it takes.

Of course, sometimes lightning strikes. Here's another job-hunter's experience:

> *"After reading Parachute, and completing the homework, I wrote ONE letter to ONE corporation resulting in ONE fabulous job. From logo design to licensing to lesson plans, I was able to help a corporation establish its own on-site child care center. Amazing things happen when mind, heart, and soul are focused on the right task."*

The conclusion of the matter, is this: the job-hunt is completely unpredictable, as to its length. *The first secret* of success is to be mentally prepared for *whatever* it takes.

THE SECOND SECRET OF JOB-HUNTING SUCCESS

SPEND MORE HOURS A WEEK ON YOUR JOB-HUNT

Two-thirds of all job-hunters spend 5 hours or less on their job-hunt each week. Considering that the job-hunt may take 30 weeks or longer, you can see that what this adds up to: 150 hours of job-hunting, before their job-hunt is successful.

While it is true that some factors, such as how long a committee takes to make up their mind to hire you, are independent of the time you put in on your job-hunt, it makes sense to suggest that if a job-hunt takes 150 hours, spend more time on it, per week, and you should be able to shorten the number of weeks it takes for you to find employment.

Spend 20 hours a week, at least, on your job-hunt. 30 hours a week if you are desperate. This should cut down the number of weeks it takes you to find work, dramatically.

THE THIRD SECRET OF
JOB-HUNTING SUCCESS

GO VISIT THE PLACES WHERE YOU WOULD LIKE TO WORK

You must go face-to-face with employers, whenever possible.

"Face-to-face" means that you physically go to the places where you would like to work, rather than sending a piece of paper, such as a resume or covering letter.

"With employers" means that you try to see the boss, and not some in-between. Generally speaking you should try to avoid the personnel or human-resources department; only 15% of all organizations even have such departments, so with 85% of all companies, it's easy to talk to the boss.

Going face-to-face with employers leads to a job for 47 out of every one hundred people who try it.

If the companies or organizations that interest you, are far-away, going face-to-face is of course more difficult. But there are still ways to keep this *personal*. See the next chapter, and Chapter 12, for details about using your vacation and your personal contacts in that faraway city.

So far as companies or organizations here in your geographical area are concerned, there are, of course, places where it is absolutely *impossible* to get in to see 'the boss,' i.e., the one who has the power to hire you. He or she is surrounded by a castle, with a moat, and eight large over-sized hungry alligators in the moat. You of course will hurl yourself against its ramparts a half-dozen times, anyway, furious that you can't get in to see that person. But, could I ask you a question: "*Why* do you want to work for *a place like that?*"

I mean, never mind that you're taking this *very personally*. Rejection, rejection, rejection, flashes on and off in your brain. But, haven't they *(by these actions)* told you something about themselves that is important information for you to have? And having gained that information, isn't it time for you to reassess *whether you really want to work at a place like that?*

THE FOURTH SECRET OF JOB-HUNTING SUCCESS

Job-hunters who have no experience in job-hunting tend to make large organizations *'the measure of all things'* going on in the job-market. If the newspapers are filled with the news of companies like Sears, General Motors, and others laying off thousands of workers, most job-hunters *assume* that this means 'there are no jobs out there.' This is a very common, and very costly, mistake. Just because the Fortune 500 are downsizing, rather than expanding, does *not* mean they accurately reflect the whole marketplace. It only means that, within that marketplace, large companies are *not* the place to go when times are tough.

GO AFTER SMALL COMPANIES

Approach smaller businesses, companies, and organizations rather than large firms. Generally, small firms are much more likely to be expanding, but the 'big guys' are likely to be contracting. Since 1970, two out of every three new jobs have been created by organizations with one hundred or less employees. You therefore need to concentrate on every small firm in your town or city that is within commuting distance, and has one hundred or less employees. (I would start with those that have twenty or less employees, personally.) Small firms are easier to approach, the boss there is easier to talk to, and there are no forbidding personnel or human resources departments to screen you out.

As a job-hunter you are looking for *steady* or *expanding* companies, in these difficult times. These are most likely ones which
are *relatively* small now, but on their way to *bigger.* Hence, you
need to focus your job-hunting efforts on small companies because somewhere among them *are* companies like Apple Computer which started out in a garage, or ASK Group, of Mountain
View, California, which started out in a spare bedroom.

Big companies are racking up record-size deficits, and they
are attempting to get out of the red ink by dramatically cutting
their workforce. Of course, many small companies are also racking up deficits, and attempting to get out of the red by dramatically cutting *their* workforce. But overall during the 1980s while
the Fortune 500 companies were *cutting* 3.7 million jobs from
their payrolls, smaller companies *created* 19 million new jobs.[3]

If you would improve your job-hunting success, *be sure* to
concentrate your energies on small companies (with 100 or less
employees, better yet, 20 or less employees) in your town which
are stable, or on their way to becoming larger companies.

---

3. *The San Francisco Chronicle,* 2/1/93.

THE FIFTH SECRET OF JOB-HUNTING SUCCESS

SEE MORE EMPLOYERS EACH WEEK

In the U.S., and likely in other countries as well, job-hunters only visit six employers a month, on average; that's one reason nine million job-hunters still can't find work. As job-hunter, you may need to see seventy employers or more, before you are through. You should determine to see at least two employers a day, one in the morning, one in the afternoon, every weekday, at a minimum, for as many months as your job-hunt may last.

REMEMBER THERE ARE TWO KINDS

In approaching employers during a job-hunt it is crucial to remember that there are two kinds of employers out there:

- those who won't hire you because they will be put off by whatever job-hunting handicap you may have -- age, race, inexperience, physical or mental handicap, etc.;
- and, those who will hire you, if you are otherwise qualified to do the job, and won't care what kind of job-hunting handicap you might have.

During your job-hunt, you are not interested in the former kind of employer, no matter how many of them there are. You are only looking for those employers who are not put off by your job-hunting handicap, and therefore will hire you, if you can do the job.

THE SIXTH SECRET OF
JOB-HUNTING SUCCESS

USE EVERY CONTACT YOU HAVE TO HELP YOU LOOK

It takes about seventy eyes and ears to find a job. Tell everyone you know that you are job-hunting and would appreciate their keeping their eyes and ears open.
Ask your friends if they know of openings where they work. Ask your relatives if they know of openings where they work. Ask them if they know of openings where other members of their family work or where their friends work. Don't just tell them that you're 'looking for a job.' Tell them exactly what kind of a job you're looking for. The more specific you can be, the more they will be able to help you. Have as many other eyes and ears out there looking on your behalf, as possible.

If you happen to own a telephone answering machine, you might even consider putting this on that machine, as part of your opening message.

It is *not* sufficient to tell your friends, relatives, and working acquaintances, "Hey, I'm looking for a job. Let me know if you hear of *anything*." What does "anything" mean? Are you willing to take a job as a dishwasher in a local restaurant? Are you willing to work off a garbage truck? Are you willing to be a typist in a typing pool? Are you willing to sweep chimneys? All of these are honorable jobs for people who can do them with a sense of integrity and pride in their work. But do you really mean *anything*?

If you would enlist your friends, relatives, and working acquaintances to help you with your job-hunt, you've got to give them better information than *anything*. You've got to spell out specifically what kinds of work you're looking for, and what kinds of skills you like to use. Figure out whether you're best with People, or Things, or Information. It makes a difference. A big difference. Get as specific as you can (*"I'm good with my hands,"* or *"I like to help organize events and carry out planning to the last detail."*) You must know which are your best and most enjoyable skills.[4]

And, incidentally, since you never know *when* you may bump into a contact -- someone who could lead you to a job -- don't get *real sloppy* in your appearance while you are out of work. Be comparatively neat, clean, and nicely-dressed whenever you go out into the world -- even if it's just downtown, or out to the mall, for grocery shopping. You don't want any *contact* thinking, because of your sloppy dress, that you are 'on the skids.' No, oh no you don't.

4. If you don't know how to describe in detail what you do best, then please see Chapter 9. Read it. Do it. It may seem to describe paper and pencil exercises that you only need if you are contemplating a career-change. But in actual fact, those exercises are useful to anyone who needs to describe what kind of work they are looking for, in more detail.

THE SEVENTH SECRET OF
JOB-HUNTING SUCCESS

HAVE A PLAN B

Don't expect that you will necessarily be able to find exactly the same kind of work as you have done in the past.

Take the job-label-from-your-past off yourself ("I am an auto-worker," etc.). Think of yourself instead as "a person who..."

Define some other line (or lines) of work that you could do, can do, and would enjoy doing, using the same skills and experiences.

Figure out what would make you different from nineteen other workers who can do the same thing.

You may be able to describe right off the top of your head some other kind of work that you like to do, and know you are good at; perhaps something you've done in your spare time *(like: make dresses, repair sailboats, etc.)* However, if you can't think of anything off the top of your head (or the tip of your tongue), then run do not walk to Chapters 9 and 10. Read *and do* the exercises there, thoroughly.

ARLO & JANIS reprinted by permission of NEA, Inc.

THE EIGHTH SECRET OF JOB-HUNTING SUCCESS

SETTLE ON MORE THAN ONE 'TARGET'

What this means is that you don't 'put all your eggs in one basket' -- to coin a phrase. You don't decide to go after a job at just one factory, one government agency, one secretarial office, one volunteer organization, one library, one church, etc.

Years ago, it was entirely unnecessary to highlight this rule, since it was obvious to most people that *this way lies madness.* But of late, more and more job-hunters seem to be settling on one place as *"the ideal place where I would like to work,"* and having absolutely no plan B as to what they will do if that place obstinately refuses to hire them (as seems to be the case more often than not).

Don't do it. Have at least five target organizations or companies that you're going after.

Let me say it again. No matter how appetizing your *first choice* looks to you, no matter how much it makes your mouth water at the thought of working there, *you are committing job-hunting suicide* if you don't have some alternative targets. I mean, maybe you'll get that dream-come-true. But -- *big question* -- what are your plans if you don't? You've *got* to have other plans **now** -- not when that first target runs out of gas, three months from now. If you wait, you've wasted three months.

THE NINTH SECRET OF
JOB-HUNTING SUCCESS

GET A SUPPORT GROUP TO HELP YOU

The job-hunt is one of the loneliest experiences in all of life. Partly, that's a matter of how we play it. Me, myself and I are about to go job-hunting. No, no, no! Rethink that strategy. You need somebody, or a bunch of somebodies, to steer you and cheer you on, and cheer you up.

You need a sounding-board to bounce ideas off of, and you need a brainstorming group to help you identify places to visit, possible contacts, and so on.

In the jargon of today, such a group is called 'a support group,' and such a person is called 'your best friend' or 'partner.'

Suggestions as to who can serve this function for you, are listed below. Don't...do it...alone!

Here's how you can find support groups:

a. Job-hunting groups that already exist in your city or town, such as "Forty Plus" clubs, "Experience Unlimited" groups, job-hunt classes at your local Federal/State employment offices, or at the local Chamber of Commerce, or at your local college or community college, or at your local Adult Education center, etc.[5] The likelihood that such help is available in your community increases dramatically for you if you are from certain groups held to be disadvantaged, such as low income, or welfare recipients, or youth, or displaced workers, etc. Ask around.

---

5. A sample listing of these kinds of places is to be found in the *National Business Employment Weekly*, on its pages called "Calendar of Career Events." It's available on some newsstands, or you can order an issue directly from: National Business Employment Weekly, 420 Lexington Ave., New York, NY 10170, 1-212-808-6792 or 1-800-JOB-HUNT.

b. A job-hunting group that doesn't currently exist, but that you could help form with other unemployed people -- at your local church, synagogue or religious center. (Often your priest, minister, rabbi, or leader can put you in touch with such people.) Some enterprising job-hunters, unable to locate any group, have formed their own by running an ad in the local newspaper, near the "help wanted" listings. *"Am currently job-hunting, would like to meet weekly with other job-hunters for mutual support and encouragement."*

c. Your mate or partner, grandparent, brother or sister, or best friend. A loving 'taskmaster' is what you need. Someone who will make a regular weekly appointment to meet with you, check you out on what you've done that week, and be very stern wtih you if you've done little or nothing since you last met. You want understanding, sympathy, and discipline. If your mate, brother or sister, or best friend, can offer you all of these, run -- do not walk -- to enlist them immediately.

d. A local career counselor. I grant you that career counselors aren't usually thought of as 'a support group.' But many of them do have group sessions; and even by themselves they can be of inestimable support. If you can afford their services, and none of the above suggestions have worked, this is a good fallback strategy. Before choosing such a counselor, however, *please* read Appendix A, in the back of this book, thoroughly. That Appendix also tells you how to locate such counselors.

THE TENTH SECRET OF
JOB-HUNTING SUCCESS

USE AS MANY AVENUES AS YOU CAN

A study called *The Job Hunt: Job-Seeking Behavior of Unemployed Workers in a Local Economy* was made by A. Harvey Belitsky and Harold L. Sheppard some years ago. By studying blue-collar workers in West Virginia, they discovered that the greater the number of job-hunting avenues used by a job-hunter, the greater his or her job-finding success.

There are, in fact, seventeen different job-hunting avenues. The average job-hunter uses less than two of them during his or her entire job-hunt.

You can increase your job-hunting success by using as many of them as possible.

And what are the seventeen job-hunting avenues that constitute our job-hunting system in this country (and most other countries)? Well, we've already seen almost all of them, in this chapter or the last; but let's tick them off again, with the most effective first, and the least effective last. Here goes: using personal contacts, asking friends for job-leads, asking relatives for job-leads, applying directly to an employer, using your school's placement service, asking a professor or old teacher for job-leads, going to a hiring hall (if you belong to a union), contacting agencies retained by employers *(executive search firms)*, using the Federal/State employment service, placing ads yourself, taking civil service tests, answering ads from elsewhere in the country, mailing out resumes by the bushel, answering ads in journals for your field, using computerized listings or registers, going to private employment agencies, and looking at newspaper ads.

I want particularly to emphasize *using your school's placement service*. Some job-hunters never think of going back to the college, community college, or high school that they once attended, to visit the placement/career-planning office there. Perhaps they don't even know it has one. Yet most of the 3,280 institutions of higher education in this country do, however informally.[6] So do many high schools, these days -- if they weren't hit by budget-cuts. In the placement or career-planning office there, look for bulletin board notices of jobs, vacancies, and even more importantly, look for lists of graduates who live in your geographical area. If you don't see that information, ask for it.

Well, that finishes our ten secrets.[7] And now, how shall we summarize it all? This way:

> The essence of successful job-hunting is having alternatives. Alternative avenues of job-hunting. Alternative ways of describing what you do. Alternative ways of approaching employers. Alternative leads to jobs. Alternative 'target' organizations that you're going after. The problem with unsuccessful job-hunters is that often they pursue a plan that has no alternatives. You must not follow in their footsteps, if you want your job-hunt to be successful.

6. A directory listing many of these offices is published, and is available for perusal in most Placement Offices. It is called the *Directory of Career Planning and Placement Offices,* and is published by the College Placement Council, Inc., 62 Highland Ave., Bethlehem, PA 18017, 1-215-868-1421.

7. If you want more than these ten job-hunting strategies, I refer you to *The Complete Job and Career Handbook: 101 Ways to Get From Here to There,* by S. Norman Feingold and Marilyn N. Feingold. Garrett Park Press, PO Box 190B, Garrett Park, MD 20896. 1993. This $15 book lists many other strategies for you to explore, should your job-hunt reach a dead end. Chapter titles include: "Infrequently Used/Non-traditional Job and Career Search Techniques," "Check List of 177 Ways to Help Get A Job and Advance Your Career," etc. Very helpful, and detailed. Dr. Feingold is a pioneer in the career counseling field, and he and Marilyn really know their stuff.

WHEN NONE OF THIS IS WORKING

Now, naturally, you want to know what to do if you try all ten of these strategies, and you still don't have a job. *Whoa! You haven't had time to try all ten of those strategies; you just finished reading this chapter.*

But suppose this is *later*, and you *have* done them all; what then? Well, check to be sure you have done them *as written*. We have been astounded to discover how many people *think* they have done all of these ten strategies, when in reality they have unintentionally *cut corners*.

And do remember that these ten secrets are not a "smorgasbord," where -- out of the ten -- you choose two or three ideas that you like. You need to take *all ten* seriously.

As the old saying has it, "It is not that great ideas have been tried, and found inadequate; it is that they have been prejudged as inadequate, and never even tried."

But if you *have* done them all -- faithfully and thoroughly -- and *nothing is working,* then there is a simple life-preserver for you: flee to Chapters 9, 10, and 11, read them, and do the exercises there. These paper and pencil exercises may *seem* to be necessary only if you are contemplating a career-change. But in actual fact, those exercises are *essential* for anyone who is floundering. They are there precisely for the times when these ten secrets don't work, for you.

I decided not to wait a long time,
To wait for the mercies of God;
I simply took a broom in my hand,
And started sweeping.

> A Russian Jew, an aeronautical
> engineer, upon emigrating
> to Israel.

CHAPTER FIVE

If It Looks Like It's Going To Be 'A Long Haul': How To Avoid Getting Depressed

Chapter 5

U.S. Statistics

At least one out of every five workers in America is unemployed at *some* time during the year. And it can last quite a spell. During the 1990s thus far, at any given moment:

35 out of every 100 unemployed persons have been out of work less than five weeks, thus far;

28 out of every 100 have been out of work between five and fourteen weeks, thus far;

13 out of every 100 have been out of work between fifteen and twenty six weeks, thus far;

24 out of every 100 have been out of work twenty-seven weeks or longer; and/or have stopped looking altogether.[1]

If you are out of work, there is obviously a chance that you could be in the 35% who find work within five weeks; in which case, the concerns raised in this chapter can be, for the most part, ignored.

But, the odds are twice as great -- 65% -- that your job-hunt will take longer, maybe *much* longer. So, it could be "a long haul" before you find work. Therefore, we need to talk.

---

1. Statistics based, in part, on the February 1992 issue of the *Monthly Labor Review,* published by the U.S. Department of Labor, Bureau of Labor Statistics; and, in part, on the figures for discouraged workers for that same time period; and, in part, on a paper by the late Bob Wegmann, entitled, "How Long Does Unemployment Last?"

IF THERE'S JUST NO MONEY ON YOUR TABLE

Why people get depressed when unemployed is no great mystery. They have no money. Typically, during Hard Times, over 30% of all adults -- working or not -- describe their financial situation as "shaky." An even higher percentage of unemployed people would thus describe their situation. Many have been living from paycheck to paycheck.

So, the first thing you're going to have to do, when unemployed, is figure out how to survive financially. If you don't know how, because this is a new experience to you, Appendix C in the back of this book describes some helpful strategies.

UNEMPLOYMENT AS A DEPRESSING TIME

There are three additional reasons why we find unemployment such a depressing time in our life:

(1) It is the end of an era. For months, years, maybe decades, we were used to thinking of ourselves in terms of *that job* at *that place*. It gave our life its coherence, it gave us our daily routine, it gave us our identity. "Who are you?" *"Oh, I'm a foreman at the General Motors plant down the road."* But when we are laid-off or fired, that era comes to an end. What do we say now? "Who are you?" *"Well, I don't really know, any more."* That's depressing.

(2) It goes on too long. Most of us are good at doing difficult things, as long as we only have to do it for a short time. We can walk (quickly) through an area with a bad stench. We can put up with a three-day cold. We can stand to miss one meal. We can hold our breath for thirty seconds. We can run a hundred-yard dash. We can endure a bad relationship, as long as it doesn't last more than one week. But we don't like it when things go on too long. That starts to get us down.

This of course is our situation when we are unemployed. A period of unemployment that lasts only two weeks -- hey, *no problem!* But if it drags on and on and on, we get weary just thinking about it. "Enough, already," we cry. Yet, there is no end in sight. That's depressing.

(3) It makes us feel powerless. We like it when we can make a difference. In our household. In our neighborhood. In our community. At our workplace. We do something, something happens or changes, as a result. That makes us feel good. But we don't like it when we face the opposite situation. This is why unemployment is often about as welcome as a rattlesnake at a picnic. When we're out of a job, we try this. Sometimes it works like a charm. But other times, nothing happens. We try that. Nothing happens. We are still out of work. We still can't find a job. We still are unemployed. It goes on and on, and *nothing* we do seems to make any difference. We begin to feel absolutely powerless. That's depressing. *Very* depressing.

THE MEANING OF 'DEPRESSION'

---

de•pres•sion \di-Ëpresh-fln\ n (1): a state of feeling sad : DEJECTION (2): a psychoneurotic or psychotic disorder marked esp. by sadness, inactivity, difficulty in thinking and concentration, a significant increase or decrease in appetite and time spent sleeping, feelings of dejection and hopelessness, and sometimes suicidal tendencies (3): a re-duction in activity, amount, quality, or force (4): a lower-ing of vitality or functional activity (5): a period of low general economic activity marked esp. by rising levels of unemployment.   *Webster's*

The word 'depressing' or 'depression' is used, of course, in two different emotional senses: one by the unemployed, and the other by psychiatrists or therapists.

The latter mean by it, an emotional illness of uncertain ori-gin and cure. If we are the victims of *this* kind of depression, it usually antedates our period of unemployment, and is some-thing we have wrestled with for years. It may have a virulency like unto pneumonia, or be as low-grade as a cold. When it is as virulent as pneumonia, the emotional illness of depression is a burden that threatens to crush the soul, and many brave souls

have endured this 'dark night of the soul' for years, with as-
tounding courage -- though there are now medicines and treat-
ments that can often hold it completely, or mostly, at bay.
Anyone who is unemployed, and is feeling so depressed as to be
suicidal, needs to get to a psychiatrist, therapist, or doctor, immediately, for help. *This is a medical emergency.*

Depression can be much milder, and in that form it is like a
series of 'blue Mondays,' or it may be a gentle perpetual tinge of
sadness that does not keep us from our feasts, but 'is just enough
to appear as a death's-head at all our feasts.'[2]

In whatever form, it is estimated by experts that some 10
million Americans experience depression sometime during the
year.[3] And sometimes the unemployed are among them.

---

2. The phrase is William Law's, who used it to describe token religion.

3. A patient's guide to Depression is available from Depression, P.O. Box 8547, Silver
Spring, MD 20907, free. You may also call 1-800-358-9295, to ask for it. For further
reading, I refer you to: *The Good News About Depression,* by Mark S. Gold, M.D. Bantam
Books, 666 Fifth Ave., New York, NY 10103. 1987. There is also *Depression, the Mood
Disease (revised edition),* by Francis Mark Mondimore, M.D. Available from the Johns
Hopkins University Press, Hampden Station, Baltimore, MD 21222, 1-800-537-5487.
Let me repeat that depression is not a character failure, but often has a physical basis,
in one's body chemistry (e.g., the brain does not produce enough seratonin, etc.). If
you cannot move yourself out of the depression by exercise, and activity, then you
ought to get yourself to an experienced M.D. or therapist.

So much for the medical approach to depression. Now, when we are unemployed and we say, *"I feel depressed,"* we usually mean it in a somewhat different sense than doctors and psychiatrists do. It is not a medical diagnosis on our part; it is, rather, a metaphor, crying out for translation. When we are unemployed and say, "I'm depressed," we mean: *'I've got the blues.'* We mean: *'I feel sad.'* We mean: *'I'm not my usual self.'* We mean: *'I feel down, because it's hard to stay upbeat or optimistic in this situation.'* We mean: *"I'm depressed."* This feeling of being *depressed* is our emotional response to *that situation*. Once we have found a job, it lifts, and we start feeling happy and upbeat once again. So the question is, when your job-hunt is draggin', how do you avoid feeling blue, or feeling down?

© Copyright 1980, United Feature Syndicate, Inc. Used by special permission.

HOW TO AVOID
FEELING DEPRESSED
WHEN UNEMPLOYMENT DRAGS ON
AND ON

Anyone who has a facile or glib answer to this problem, should be avoided like the plague. There is no universal guaranteed-to-work formula, believe me. Every person in this world is unique, and what works for one person, doesn't work for another. Especially, when we are dealing with the emotions.

But after talking to thousands of job-hunters, I do think there are five approaches you can take, that seem to banish, or at least lift, feelings of being depressed, for *most* job-hunters.

Those five approaches deal, in turn, with the: (1) physical; (2) emotional; (3) mental; (4) spiritual; and, finally, (5) activity

-- during your time of unemployment. And they are not a kind of smorgasbord, from which you choose the one or two that you like best; you need to do all five, because *each* of the five *contributes* toward the feelings of depression. In this sense, depression is like a river, fed by these five tributaries.

THE PHYSICAL REALM

> Problem: you will likely feel depressed if you are short on your sleep, or your body is otherwise run-down.

Let me repeat: you will almost always feel depressed if you are short on your sleep.

The world never looks bright or happy to people who are *very short of sleep.*

The world never looks bright or happy to people who are *feeling depressed.*

It is therefore easy to confuse the two feeling-states. What you may imagine is depression may in fact be simply the feelings that come from sleep-deprivation. So, please don't take this matter lightly. It has been amazing to me, in the past, to see very-depressed job-hunters turn into happier, more upbeat people, just by catching up on their sleep. Turn off the TV by 10 o'clock, and *go to bed!* It may be difficult to do at first, but in time you'll like the new schedule. And, you'll feel better -- sometimes *much* better.

If you are trying to take this seriously, but are having trouble sleeping, the remedies are pretty well-known by now, but -- with my rich skills at overkill -- let me spell them out, anyway:

5 RULES FOR DEALING WITH SLEEP PROBLEMS

1. Try to keep regular hours, going to bed at the same time every night.
2. Go to bed before midnight, preferably by 11 p.m.
3. Avoid things that might keep you awake, such as caffeine, from dinner to bedtime. Reduce drinking to one drink, or none at all.
4. Use the bed only for sleeping or love-making.
5. If you lie awake for more than 30 minutes, get up and read, or meditate, until you get sleepy.

In addition to the sleep thing, there are other things that need to be done to keep yourself physically fit while unemployed.[4] When I was myself out of work I found it important to:

get out in sunlight as much as possible, or sit under bright lights in your apartment or house, especially during the winter (*it is a well-known fact that many people get particularly depressed during winter, because they need light, and especially sunlight; the affliction is called S.A.D.*);

get regular exercise, involving a daily walk;

drink plenty of water each day (*I try for at least eight glasses of water a day -- this seems silly, but it is often very important*);

eat balanced meals, with plenty of fiber (*don't pig out just on junk food in front of the telly; if ever you've thought about cutting down on fats (meats, dairy products), sugar, baked goods, and caffeine, now is an excellent time to do it*);

eliminate sugar as much as possible from the diet;[5]

---

4. Of course, these principles make sense equally when one has found a job.

5. The sugar/depression connection is a matter that has been well-established, and were I feeling depressed the first thing I would eliminate from my diet would be sugar. See *Sugar Blues*, by William Duffy. Warner Books, Inc., 666 Fifth Ave., New York, NY 10103. 1975. (Available in your library or in health-food stores, if not elsewhere.)

take supplementary vitamins daily *(no matter how often doctors and nutritionists may tell you that you already get plenty, just from your daily food);*

and all that other stuff that our mothers always told us to do.

Physical also means *physical space* around you, in your home or apartment -- which is important because it often mirrors how we feel about ourselves. If our physical environment looks like a disaster area, that in itself can make us depressed. If you've always vowed you wanted to learn to live neater, here is a simple way: each time you handle a *thing*, take it all the way to its destination; don't put it down, thinking that you will deal with it later. Do it now.

e.g., when you take clothes off, either put them in the clothes basket or hang them back up; don't just drop them on the floor.

e.g., when you finish eating, put the dishes where they are to be washed, and put the food back in the refrigerator.

e.g., if you get a screwdriver out, to fix a screw that's dropped out of something, when you're done, take the screwdriver all the way back to the tool chest or wherever its final destination is. Etc., etc., etc.

When things are put away in a timely fashion, neatness will start to appear in your physical environment; it will help lift your spirits immensely. Of course, if you were already keeping your place as neat as a pin, you will ignore this whole thing, and forget I ever mentioned a word, won't you?

THE EMOTIONS

Problem: after you are 'let go,' you will likely feel depressed if you are still carrying around a lot of anger, expressed or suppressed, about *what they did to you.*

Our instinctive first reaction to the fact that we were laid-off, fired, terminated, summarily dismissed, or made redundant -- especially *after all these years* -- is usually anger. Sometimes fierce, hot anger. Sometimes just a kind of dull, cold disillusionment about the workplace and how it treats people.

Need I mention that we would probably drop our anger quickly if it were relatively easy to find another job, doing basically the same thing at the same level of responsibility and at the same salary in the same town. But, given our Neanderthal job-hunting system, it is not. It is not easy to find such jobs even when they exist. Hence, much of the blame for our anger should lie at the door of this so-called job-hunting *'system'* -- which leaves us feeling devalued and discarded by our society for weeks, months, and sometimes years. Our anger is justified and understandable, in the beginning.

But if it keeps on and on, then that's another story. And if our anger is directed not against the job-hunting system in this country, but against our ex-employers, that's the beginning of trouble. I see this often, as people who have been let go discuss the place where they used to work: *'I'll never forgive them. They've ruined the rest of my life.'*

Of course, the only way our former employers can actually ruin the rest of our lives is if *we* help them out, by holding on to our anger forever. This *will* wreck the rest of our lives. I have seen it happen many many times in the lives of the unemployed.

We forget an ancient truth: that when anger becomes a burning fire within us, that fire gradually consumes not its object, but its host. Certainly it doesn't achieve its desired effect upon the objects of our anger. They are sleeping soundly, while it is we who are lying awake at night. No, anger consumes its host not its object, and it does this by giving birth within us to irritability, withdrawal, loneliness, broken relationships, divorce (often), and sometimes (rarely) suicide.

During this process, the anger very commonly segues into depression. It has struck me forcibly over the years that these two emotions often seem to be reverse sides of the same coin. It is as though *anger/depression* were an energy, which at first is directed outward toward others, but then like a boomerang eventually turns back against the self. This *feels* like depression, but it is born of the anger.

So, if you feel depressed as unemployment stretches on, it is helpful to consider the possibility that anger that may lie beneath that depression. Dealing with that anger often takes away the depressed feelings. People who have successfully done this, cite the following steps:

5 RULES FOR DEALING WITH ANGER

1. Your basic need is to face forward, toward the future, not backward, toward the past. You only have enough energy for one or the other, not both. Staying rooted in your anger keeps you rooted facing toward the past.

2. The way to get out of your anger is to face it, openly and honestly. Talk it out, with a good friend, or write a letter to yourself about it; but do not act it out in real life. Do not write to, or threaten, the objects of your anger. That way lies trouble of major dimensions.

3. If this doesn't help you let go of your anger, seek out a good family therapist, whom friends recommend.

4. If you have a lot of angry energy, so that you feel you'd like to punch someone, punch a pillow instead. A big pillow. Or a mattress. Get the angry energy out of your system, harmlessly. Daily, if necessary.

5. If you are a woman or man of faith, hand the anger over to God, and ask That Higher Power to help you set your face toward the future.

THE MENTAL

Problem: you will likely feel depressed if you view this
experience of being laid-off, and having to spend a long
time finding a new job, as essentially a random, senseless
and meaningless event in your life.

Let us begin here with a riddle:

This is a glass
containing fruit-
juice. Is it half-
empty, or is it
half-full?

Most people have heard this riddle, but that doesn't mean it
is well-understood. On its surface it seems to say that there are
different ways of looking at a situation.

But that is not its major point. Its major point is that you *can
change* how you view it. You can go from viewing it as *half-empty*
to viewing it as *half-full.*

There is a habit of mind that is deadly, which is to spend
much of our time each day, every day, brooding about what is
wrong. What is wrong with people, what is wrong with our life,
what is wrong with our situation, what is wrong with anything
and everything. In our conversation with friends or family, we

focus our attention on what we didn't like about the conversation . . . or *them*. In a movie or play, we focus on what we
didn't like about it. When we travel, we focus on what we didn't
like about each place we visited. This habit of mind focusses
always on other people's failings, on what is not the way we want
it to be, on what is (from our point of view) missing. It calls
every glass, and every situation, *half-empty* -- focussing on what is
lost, or never was. On the other hand, *half-full* focusses on what
you have, on what still is, and is good. The first habit of mind
leads to complaint and bitterness; the second habit of mind
leads to gratitude and joy. If you would avoid getting depressed,
it is *crucial* to look at how you think, and what you focus your
attention on, all day long. It is crucial to avoid the deadly habit
of mind alluded to, above. As Baltasar Gracián put it,[6] "Get used
to the failings of your friends, family, and acquaintances. . . ."

Depression arises, in part, from a sense of powerlessness.
However, as the riddle reminds us, we *always* have power -- the
power to change how we view a situation, and thus to alter that
situation. Let me give an example.

At a medical symposium which I attended many years ago, a
doctor was reviewing the puzzle of healing. Two patients, he
said, of the same age and with the same medical history, would
undergo the same operation. Yet, one would heal rapidly, while
the other's healing was long delayed. Doctors had no idea why
this was so. They set up a study at a major New York hospital, to
see if they could identify what factors explained this difference.[7]
Using a computer, they decided to compare *everything* about the
patients who healed quickly, with those same factors -- or to be
more exact, the *absence* of those same factors -- in the patients
who healed slowly. And so they began to ask the computer their
questions.

Were those who healed quickly characterized by *optimism,*
while those who healed slowly were not? No, said the computer;
that wasn't the answer.

---

6. Baltasar Gracián, *The Art of Worldly Wisdom: A Pocket Oracle.* Doubleday/Currency,
Publishers. 1992. Baltasar was a Spanish writer who lived in the 1600s.

7. I have, in the intervening years, tried to go back and identify that study, but have
been basically unsuccessful in this search. I am left only with a clear memory of *the
findings,* as they were reported by that doctor at the symposium.

Were those who healed quickly characterized by *some kind of religious faith,* while those who healed slowly were not? No, said the computer; that wasn't the answer.

And so it went.

What the answer finally turned out to be was this: those who healed quickly felt there was some meaning to every event that happened to them in their lives, even if they did not understand what that meaning was, at the present time; while those who healed slowly felt that most events which happened to them had no meaning; they were merely random or senseless. Hence, if both patients were being operated on for cancer, the one who viewed the cancer as having some meaning in the larger scheme of things, for their life, healed quickly; while the one who viewed the cancer as a senseless and meaningless interruption in their life, healed slowly. *Everything depended on how they viewed the situation.*

Surely you see how this applies to such events as being terminated. Being fired or terminated is rarely the outrageous, meaningless event that it at first seems to be. It may begin that way; but it does not end that way. You have the power to shape it, by how you choose to view it.

The last time I was fired, the firing occurred shortly before

noon, and at 3 o'clock that same afternoon I had an appointment with my dentist, to have some drilling done. *'What a wonderful day this is turning out to be!'* I thought, with rich irony. Anyway, he was a wise man, on in years, and when I told him of my plight, he said some words I have never forgotten: "Someday," he said, "you will say this was the best thing that ever happened to you. I don't expect you to believe a word I am saying now, but wait and see. I have seen this happen in so many people's lives, that I know it will come true for you." Strangely enough, he turned out to be absolutely right. And he helped shape how I viewed that event. I now say, that firing was indeed the best thing that ever happened to me, for it caused me to rethink my whole life and what I wanted to contribute to the world. Thus, it proved to be a great blessing, as light was born out of the darkness of unemployment.

I now believe that every event in our lives has meaning, or can be given meaning, even though we don't always know what that meaning is, at the time. If this is how *you* view your life -- including the experience of being laid-off -- then that depression which arises from a sense of meaninglessness will not afflict you.

Spelling out more specifically what this means, we can state it in terms of our usual five rules (in this case, affirmations):[8]

5 RULES FOR DEALING WITH MEANINGLESSNESS

1. Your life is like a tapestry, being woven by God and history on an enchanted loom. Every bobble of the shuttle has meaning, every thread is important.

2. As a thread in that tapestry every event in your life has some meaning and purpose, for the larger pattern, even if you cannot see what this is, at the moment.

3. You will discover that meaning more quickly if you direct what thoughts you focus your mind on, during your time of unemployment.

4. To aid this, make a list of all the things you enjoy about your life, even while unemployed -- the simple pleasures: working with your hands, breathing fresh air, enjoying beautiful music, etc.

---

8. The reference to the *loom,* which follows, comes by analogy to Sir Charles Sherrington's description of the brain: *"It is as if the Milky Way entered upon some cosmic dance. Swiftly the brain becomes an enchanted loom where millions of flashing shuttles weave a dissolving pattern, always a meaningful pattern though never an abiding one; a shifting harmony of subpatterns."*

5. When you are having any dark times, sit down and write out stories. Stories about your life past, when you were most enjoying yourself. Write down what meaning you now see in those stories. This will increase your confidence that there is meaning in your present story, now unfolding.

To rule #4, above, we might add: conversation, cuddling, drives in the country, exercise, praying, helping others, singing, sitting in front of a fireplace, thinking, etc.

Ah, yes, *thinking.* Unemployment is a wonderful time for *thinking.* You've got time to think, contemplate, look at your life, decide on maybe some new directions, etc. In other words, it can be for you a time of philosophical or spiritual renewal.

If you need help there are useful books you can take out of your library, or procure at your bookstore.[9]

THE SPIRITUAL

Problem: you will likely feel depressed if you believe in God, but feel that He[10] has somehow deserted you in this crisis.

---

9. Especially helpful is Barbara Ann Kipfer's *14,000 things to be happy about.* Workman Publishing Company, 708 Broadway, New York, NY 10003. 1990.

10. I know there are those, in our time, who do not like the male pronoun applied to God. I am very sensitive to sexist language, but here we are in a different realm. *All* language about God is metaphor, anyway, and because I grew up on the Old Testament (and the New), I myself prefer *this* metaphor, grounded as it is in some 4,000 years of usage. You can always alter it, in your mind, as you read, if you wish.

There are about 6% of my readers who would probably prefer I omitted all mention of the spiritual, in a book on job-hunting. I am sensitive to those feelings, but if we are going to discuss depression, there is no way to omit it. According to Gallup Polls conducted since 1960, about 94% of the population in this country believe in *some* concept of God.[11] When they find themselves summarily dismissed from a job that they may have held for *years,* many find their faith in God a bulwark of strength that helps them through this very difficult period, daily.

Others, however, are often plunged into a depressing crisis of faith. The common form of the questioning, when it comes, is: *How could God let this happen to me, if He truly loved me?* Many of the unemployed decide from this that there must be no God, or at least not One who cares what happens to them. They conclude then that they must face the future resolutely alone, relying on their own strength, and their own strength alone, to carry them through their period of unemployment.

Needless to say, this period is often far more difficult than they had supposed it would be, and their resolution to bear it all by themselves often flounders. They may find their own strength inadequate for the task. They are left feeling very alone. Naturally, a feeling of despair, or depression follows, like the night the day.

---

11. Reported in George Gallup's *The People's Religion: American Faith in the 90s.* Macmillan & Co. 1989. In addition to reporting that 94% of us believe in God, the Gallup polls also discovered that 90% of us pray, 88% of us believe God loves us, and 33% of us report we have had a life-changing religious experience; and these figures have remained pretty unvarying during the last thirty years of opinion polls conducted by the Gallup Organization.

What are we to say to all this? What is the remedy when our depression has -- even in part -- a spiritual origin? The remedy, apart from discarding our faith, is obviously that we need to put some energy into rethinking that faith on a higher level.

I said earlier that 94% of the people claim they have *some* concept of God. But what unemployment, or any crisis, often reveals is how poor and inadequate that concept is. It is inadequate because it holds God responsible for *everything*, and makes no allowance for the free will and freedom of choice that He has given to His creatures. The wonder is not that it breaks down under the pain of unemployment, but that it didn't break down sooner.

Well, then, to what higher concept might we press? Let's try this: imagine that you have, in your dining room, a fine wooden chair, which one day has its back broken off completely -- I mean, into *smithereens* -- by someone in the house. You run down the street, to call a carpenter who lives nearby. He comes and examines the chair. He pronounces the back *unrepairable.* "But," he says, "I think I could make a fine wooden stool out of the remainder of the chair, for you." And so he spends much time, shaping, polishing and sanding it, and fashioning out of the former chair a fine stool, more resplendent than anything you have ever dreamed. He inlays it with gold, and soon it is the treasure of your house.

Let me underline a couple of key points in this parable. First of all, the carpenter did not break the chair. Someone else did that. But the carpenter came quickly, and with all his art and powers, to see if he could not only repair it, but make of it something even finer than it had been before. And, he labored mightily, to that end.

And so, a higher concept of God holds that God does not create our unemployment or any of the calamities in our life -- *that* responsibility belongs to our fellow human beings. *They* are the ones who create our calamities. *But,* God -- like the carpenter -- comes quickly, with all His art and powers, to see if He can not only repair our life, but make of it something even finer than it had been before: not a physical thing, like the stool inlaid with gold, but a work on the spiritual level that corresponds to the stool, in splendor. And He labors mightily, within our mind and heart and spirit, toward that end.

If unemployment pushes us thus to rethink our faith, we should not only find our depression lifting, but also our self-esteem. Here are some helpful rules -- worth pasting up on your bathroom mirror:

5 RULES FOR DEALING WITH A SENSE OF ABANDONMENT

1. The 94% of us who believe in God usually need a larger conception of God, as we face each new crisis in our life. If you've got an old faith hanging in the closet of your mind, now would be a good time to take it out and dust it off.

2. Hold high the truth that God does not save us from hard times. Hard times come to believer and non-believer, alike.

3. On the other hand, God does not cause us to go into hard times (our fellow human beings do that).

4. But God is always in the middle of those times with us because He has promised to be with us, in all times. His role is that of Sustainer, Strengthener and Rescuer. You should seek that Sustaining, that Strength, daily, even hourly, in prayer, especially when you get to feel that you just can't go on.

5. If you can't feel God's presence during hard times, that does not mean anything. Feelings many times fail to correspond to reality. We can be in a fog, as we say, that obscures our vision. Do not give such feelings more weight than they deserve.

To feel abandoned -- by God or man or woman -- while you are unemployed is *extremely* depressing. Everything you can do to avoid that feeling of being abandoned, will help you greatly in 'chasing away the blues.' You start with your faith in God, you continue on with the people around you: family, relatives, friends and acquaintances. If these last leave you feeling rather alone and unsupported, you should heed the advice in Chapter 4 about seeking, or forming, a support group with others who are unemployed.[12] If you can find no such group, and you feel you possess neither the wit nor the skill to start one yourself, then seek out whichever one of the established Twelve-Step groups there are in your community.[13] While strictly speaking they are designed to help you with personal growth, and job-hunting is never mentioned, they will at least keep you from feeling alone or unsupported in *life*, as you go about that hunt.

12. Such groups as *Experience Unlimited, Forty-Plus,* job-clubs, classes at your local Employment Office, or at your local Chamber of Commerce, etc.

13. AA (Alcoholics Anonymous), OA (Overeaters Anonymous), NA (Narcotics Anonymous), PA (Parents Anonymous -- for people who are having trouble being the kind of parents they want to be), GA (Gamblers Anonymous), and other similar groups are known collectively as 'Twelve-Step Groups.' They are usually wonderful about giving you a feeling of support. If you have trouble finding a particular 'Twelve-Step' Group that interests you, start by looking up Alcoholics Anonymous in the white pages of your telephone book, and ask them where you can find the other groups. They usually will know.

ACTIVITY

Problem: you will likely feel depressed if you only have one goal for your time of unemployment.

Back in the days when you were working, suppose you decided to take a quick vacation with your spouse, or partner, or friend. You weren't quite sure what you wanted the vacation to accomplish for you. You thought that maybe you wanted to get a good rest, and not do a lick of work while you were at your vacation hideaway. On the other hand, you thought that maybe you wanted to catch up on some stuff at work that has been dogging you for weeks. You weren't sure. So, you took the work along, but determined you wouldn't feel guilty if you came back with it absolutely untouched.

Now that was going to be a rewarding vacation for you, as you knew even before you set out. Why? Because you had two alternative goals for the vacation, and *one* of them was bound to be achieved. *Either* you were going to get a good rest, *or* you were going to get some work accomplished. You couldn't lose.

Half of our misery *in our goal-driven lives* arises from our failure to thus have two alternative goals for a particular period. Again and again, we set only one goal. And then, if we fail to achieve it, as is so often the case, given the vagaries of human nature, we get depressed.

It is hardly a wonder, then, that when we get fired, sacked, terminated, or whatever, we approach unemployment in the same manner. We set ourselves only one goal for the period while we are unemployed: to find a *(meaningful)* job.

When we don't find a job -- *right away, at least* -- we get depressed. Real depressed. It is therefore important to face the activity problem here that may be contributing to that depression, and to fix it. How to fix it is obvious:

You need to have more than one goal for your time of unemployment.

You need to define this period of unemployment in some such terms as this: *"My goals during this time of unemployment are: (1) to find a good job; and (2). . . ."* Aye, there's the rub; what should (2) be? (Or, not to be.)

The most important characteristic of this second goal must be that it is *achievable*. It does our self-esteem no good, after all, to have two goals if we then fail to achieve either one of them. The second one *must* be achievable.

Certain goals which might at first suggest themselves to us, are therefore disqualified by this consideration: for example, a goal like determining to use this period of unemployment to lose 40 pounds permanently. That *is* a nice, admirable goal, except we all know by now that diets often have a yo-yo effect --

down, up; off again, on again. Consequently, very iffy goals such as this may only increase your depressed feelings, when you can't find a job *and* you can't lose weight, either.

What kind of goals, then, *are* achievable? Studying successful job-hunters for some twenty or more years, it has become clear to me that there are several, which vary in appropriateness depending on how long you've been out of work. I'll summarize them accordingly.

You should take the time-divisions on the following file cards with a grain of salt. *Obviously,* if your money dictates that your job-hunt *has to* proceed much faster, then you will want to speed up all the time divisions on these cards, accordingly -- like, one month, two months, three months, and four months.

IF YOU'VE BEEN OUT OF WORK TWO MONTHS OR LESS

Your goals for this time of unemployment are that you are going to use this time (1) to find a (meaningful) job; and (2) to work on what kind of person you are, and what kind of person you would like to be.

Take an inventory, first of all, of all that you have already: your skills (see Chapter 9), your knowledge (Chapter 10), your values, your worldly goods, your spiritual blessings, etc.

Then write out the kind of person you would like to be, and what you would like to do with your family, friends, etc. Write out a plan for starting to do this. Do a lot of meditating on what you have written, preferably outdoors amongst nature, or indoors with some of your favorite music playing.

Does *a person who has no job* still matter, in the larger scheme of things? That is the question which plagues many of us, when we have been out of work for anything up to two months. If that's the case with you, doubtless along about now you could stand some reassurance that you still matter as a person. Doing the paper-and-pen exercises mentioned on the file card, can contribute *immensely* toward that end.

> The truth is, who we are is more important than what we do. And who we are is: someone designed to be a blessing to this planet Earth.

IF YOU'VE BEEN OUT OF WORK FOUR MONTHS OR MORE

Your goals for this time of unemployment are to use this time (1) to find a (meaningful) job; and (2) volunteering to help others less fortunate than you are.

It is important to preserve four weekdays (say, Monday, Tuesday, Thursday, Friday) for your job-hunt, but one weekday (say, Wednesday) can be given to the work of helping others who are less fortunate.

You can volunteer your services:
- at places which feed or give shelter to the homeless;
- at places which give help to those afflicted with AIDS;
- at places which help battered women or abused children;
- at places which work with the disabled; and
- at places which work with the elderly or the dying.

If you have been out of work for four months or more, you will likely be hungering for some way in which to reassure yourself that you are still making a meaningful contribution to society. Volunteering one day a week can accomplish this. According to the Bureau of Labor Statistics, at least one person out of five, 16 years or older, does some volunteer work, without pay, during a typical year. It doesn't matter whether you are employed or unemployed. It's a way of occupying your time meaningfully, helping others, and incidentally picking up some new skills.

The crucial aspect of this particular activity is that it be work which puts you *face-to-face* with those who are in need, rather than doing administrative services at a desk or in an office. The latter is important, but it is not the kind of engagement that you most need at this juncture.

Your goal here is to avoid self-pity, and depression, by seeking greater compassion for those who are in need -- and particularly those who *(as the phrase has it)* are less fortunate than you.

Incidentally, if your own particular misfortunes are making you feel there is no one in the whole world who is as bad off as you are, believe me, there are *always* others less fortunate than you are. As the old saying puts it, *"I cried for a lack of shoes, until I saw a man who had no feet. . . ."*[14]

If you need more ideas of places where you might volunteer your services than are listed on the file card above, I refer you to the footnote below.[15] One important word of caution here: do not get so engrossed in this secondary goal for your time of unemployment, that you forget/neglect your primary goal: that of finding a job. The rule is: four days a week on your primary goal -- job-hunting; one day a week on your secondary goal -- volunteering.[16] You should stick like glue to that kind of division of your time. Let nothing tempt you to give four days a week to the volunteering, and only one day a week to your job-hunt,

---

14. If you're *really* feeling sorry for yourself, the best restorative is to turn off the TV, and sit down and read stories of others who have had a lot to deal with on their plate, in life, but refused to be beaten down by adversity. Such books as:

Diane Cole's, *After Great Pain: A New Life Emerges.* Summit Books, 1992.

Arnold R. Beisser's *Flying Without Wings: Personal Reflections on Being Disabled.* Doubleday, 666 Fifth Ave., New York, NY 10103. 1989. As one wise man said about his disability: "Every disabled person has the choice of either 'crying the blues' about their disability every day of their life, or realistically acknowledging what they have to do in order to have a successful, productive life." Beisser has ultimately opted for the latter, though it was not an easy battle, as this book reveals.

John Callahan's *Don't Worry, He Won't Get Far on Foot: The Autobiography of a Dangerous Man.* William Morrow & Co., Inc. 1989. John became a quadriplegic at the age of 21, due to an automobile accident. However, he has a wicked sense of humor, and so has become a famous cartoonist. This book is John's autobiography, and it is graphic, funny, touching, and irreverent. Arnold Beisser (above) wrote a most relevant passage in his book, apropos of such 'disabled humor' as John's: "The able-bodied person is likely to be appalled by 'disabled humor' and find nothing funny at all about it. But . . . tragedy and comedy are but two aspects of what is real, and whether we see the tragic or the humorous is a matter of perspective." John's perspective is clearly that he prefers to see the humorous amid the tragedy.

15. Your first lead is to inquire whether or not there is an 'umbrella' volunteer organization in your community. Ask your county information center or social services department.

Your second resource is/are the Yellow Pages in your local telephone book, to find individual places which may have paid staff, but also welcome volunteers. Look under "Social Service Organizations," "Handicapped & Disabled Services," "Hospitals," etc. for ideas. Also, your local churches or synagogues may know what facilities there are

unless you have enough income to last for a long time, *and* the volunteering turns out to be the work you most love doing, in the whole world.

Otherwise, your *main* goal for this period -- finding meaningful, paid work -- still requires the lion's share of your time, no matter *how long* you've been out of work.

IF YOU'VE BEEN OUT OF WORK SIX MONTHS OR MORE

Your goals for this time of unemployment are to use this time (1) to find a (meaningful) job; and (2) to enroll at your local community college, or the adult education program in your town (if it has one) in order to learn something new.

This something new will be either:
- a subject that intrigues you, from past reading in newspapers or magazines; or
- a subject which upgrades your skills in your present (interrupted) career; or
- a subject which gives you skills or knowledge related to a possible new career that you are thinking about going into.

---

for helping those in need, where you might volunteer.

Your third resource -- useful for ideas of *kinds* of places you might locate in your own community -- is that of books, which you search for in your local library, and if nothing is there, in your local bookstore. You will find such titles as the following (you can order them by mail if they are not in your local library); new titles keep appearing regularly:

Volunteer USA: A comprehensive guide to worthy causes that need you--from AIDS to the environment to illiteracy--where to find them, and how you can help, by Andrew Carroll. Fawcett Columbine Books, Ballantine Books, New York, NY. 1991.

For our Canadian readers there is:

Directory of Volunteer Opportunities, edited by Ellen Shenk, Career Information Centre, University of Waterloo, Waterloo, Ontario, N2L 3G1 Canada. 1986.

In a poll reported in *USA Today*,[17] where people were asked what they would do if they won one million dollars, 20% of them said they would go back to school. So, apparently this is a very common wish. It often gets lost, however, in the time-pressures we are under, when holding down a full-time job.

But, during this current period of unemployment, you are not holding down a full-time job, so now is a wonderful time to go back to school, and fulfill that longtime wish. Attending school is also a great way to keep your mind occupied with something other than your current misfortune.

One important word of caution here, as earlier: do not get so engrossed in this secondary goal for your time of unemployment, that you forget/neglect your primary goal, that of finding a job. The rule is the same as earlier: four days a week on goal #1 -- job-hunting; one day a week on goal #2 -- attending a class or two. Let nothing tempt you to give four days a week to school, and only one day a week to your job-hunt, unless you have enough income to last for the duration *and* you have decided this would be a good time to go back to school and get retrained for a new career. If that is the case, first read Chapters 9 and 10 very carefully, *please.*

Otherwise, your *main* goal for this period -- finding meaningful, paid work -- still requires the lion's share of your time, no matter *how long* you've been out of work. As far as your second goal is concerned, here, it should be a class, or two at the most, that you are dealing with, at this juncture. Agreed? Okay. If there is a nearby campus, go visit it, get their catalog, and see

---

For our older readers there is:

Volunteerism and Older Adults, by Mary K. Kouri, ABC-CLIO, Inc., 130 Cremona Dr., P.O. Box 1911, Santa Barbara CA 93116-1911. 1990.

You may also want to look at books about social service careers -- *if* they list places where you would be working directly with those in need, rather than doing administrative, legislative, or managerial work. Such books include:

Good Works: A Guide to Careers in Social Change, 4th ed., edited by Jessica Cowan, Preface by Ralph Nader. Barricade Books Inc., Publisher, 61 Fourth Ave., New York, NY 10003; distributed by Publishers Group West, 4065 Hollis, Emeryville, CA 94608. 1991. It has a topical index, a geographical index, and an alphabetical index.

16. The weekend is for leisure, re-creation, sleep catchup, time with your family, friends, doing job-hunting homework, etc.

17. 7/25/89.

what they offer. If you can't afford the big college or university, look at a community college or local adult education program in your community.

If money is a problem, you should *always* talk to the Financial Aid office on the campus that interests you, to see what accommodations they can make to the fact that you are unemployed.[18]

If you are living out in the middle of *nowhere,* and there isn't any kind of adult education facility for a hundred miles around, you may want to consider a correspondence course *(now frequently called 'off-campus study program')* from some college that offers one.[19] (Even if you live in a metropolis, you may like this idea, though since the job-hunt is so often a lonely enterprise, I myself would elect to go sit in a classroom with other people. *Anything* you can do to make the job-hunt period of your life less lonely, is to be prized.)

18. Also see *(Bear's Guide to) Finding Money for College: The not-well-understood sources of unconventional and ordinary financial help and how to pursue them,* by John B. Bear and Mariah P. Bear. Ten Speed Press, Box 7123, Berkeley, CA 94707. 1993, revised ed.

19. The best books, by a long shot, about how to find a good correspondence course, are John Bear's. There is *Bear's Guide to Earning College Degrees Non-Traditionally,* available directly from the author, John Bear, P.O. Box 826, Benicia, CA 94510, 1-800-835-8535. 1992. Cost: $23. There is also a shorter version of it, John Bear's *College Degrees by Mail.* Ten Speed Press, Box 7123, Berkeley, CA 94707. 1991. $12.95. John's books deal with taking courses, as well as getting degrees. He covers *everything,* including schools overseas that offer correspondence degrees to Americans and Canadians, how to get a degree while in prison, and other subjects nobody but John would think of.

> ## IF YOU'VE BEEN OUT OF WORK EIGHT MONTHS OR MORE
>
> Okay, this is beginning to drag on forever. You still want two goals for this period of unemployment, but now after eight months you're thinking they should be equal goals, rather than a primary and a secondary one.
>
> The first remains the same as always, to find meaningful work, doing what you've done before. But the second goal is now equal: to consider some things you've never tried before: moving, starting your own business, etc. And that's what the next chapter is all about.

SUMMARY

When it looks like your job-hunt is going to stretch on for quite some time, you need to figure out how to avoid getting depressed. 'The blues,' sadness, discouragement, dejection, apathy, or feelings of being 'down,' all add up to the same thing: "I'm depressed."

Unemployment depression (*or, as some have called it, 'recession depression'*) is like a kind of phantom octopus, which has five tentacles: physical, emotional, mental, spiritual, and activity. If you would ward off feelings of depression, you must tackle all five, rather than just hacking away at one or two causes of it. As we know from studying thousands of job-hunters, the physical contribution toward depression, is the state of being very tired, and out of shape. The emotional source of depression is stored-up anger. The mental source is the idea of meaninglessness. The spiritual source of depression resides in feelings of abandonment. And the activity side of our being contributes to our depression when we have only one goal, and that one goal is getting completely frustrated.

You tackle depression while you are out of work by staying physically fit, and rested, by getting the anger out of your system, by believing in the meaning of every event, by strengthening whatever relationship you have with God, and by setting at least two goals for your period of unemployment, only one of which should be that of finding meaningful work.

I do want to reiterate, however, that if you attack depression on all five fronts and it doesn't yield, you should immediately get yourself to a doctor or therapist, for further help. There are drugs and medicines, much as you may hate the idea, and there is also psychotherapy. The major point I'm making is that you should fight against accepting depression as though it were an inevitable and permanent part of your life. It isn't.

On the other hand, it will not do to view depression simply as a dark intruder into your life. When it arises in response to a crisis, like finding yourself unemployed, *and only then,* it often is a messenger bearing a gift. The gift is the announcement that the old center, around which your life used to revolve, is no longer sufficient. The depression is often a feeling of having abandoned the old center, but not yet finding the new. It's like an astronaut's journey from circling one planet to another. It's while you're *out there,* in between, that you feel depressed.

Hence, the depression is a wake-up call to your soul, telling you not just to stay out there, in the ozone. It is time to move on, time to look for a new destination, and find a new center, time to rethink your lifestyle, the way you typically do things, the goals you want to achieve, and the values (like honesty) that you want your life to enshrine.

You can use unemployment well, face the future rather than the past, and so, rebuild your life -- *if* you reject any picture you may have of yourself as passive, pitiable martyr, and opt instead for a picture of yourself as one who is actively at work, rebuilding your life, on new and stronger foundations.

Every human drama -- even *unemployment* -- is ultimately a drama about the survival of the spirit. Even in an unpredictable world. Even in a life that you wish were otherwise. You can be

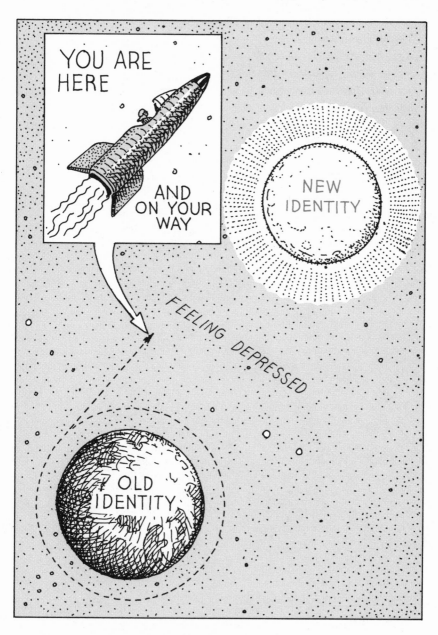

joyful in your daily living, even after considering all the facts. Your spirit *will* survive, and life can be even more triumphant than before.

Why should we be
in such desperate haste to succeed,
and in such desperate enterprise?
If a man does not keep pace
with his companions,
perhaps it is because he hears
a different drummer.
Let him step to the music
which he hears,
however measured
or far away.[1]

Henry David Thoreau
Walden, Chapter XVII, conclusion

1. I hope our readers will forgive Henry for using the masculine pronoun throughout. He wrote in terms of the sensitivities of *his* day, not *ours.*

CHAPTER SIX

Trying Something New: Working at Home, Starting Your Own Business, etc.

Chapter 6

THE WORLD'S
FASTEST COMMUTE

Sure, you've thought about it, a million times. Hasn't everyone? Everytime you're tied up in traffic going to or from

work. You've toyed with the idea of not having to go to an office or other place of business, but of running your own business, out of your own home, making your own product or selling your own services, being your own boss, and keeping all the profits for yourself. It's called 'the world's fastest commute,' or 'going downstairs, instead of downtown.'[2]

Great idea! *But,* nothing's ever come of it. Until now. Now, you're at a crossroads. You're out of work, or you're fed up with your job, and you're thinking to yourself: *Maybe it's now, or never. Maybe I ought to just* do *it.*

Three hundred years ago, of course, nearly everybody did it. They worked at home or on their farm. But then the industrial revolution came; and the idea of working *away from* home became normal. In recent times, however, the idea of working at home has been finding new life, due to congestion on the highways, and the development of new technologies, such as fax machines, modems, etc.

U.S. Statistics

Surveys indicate that currently 39 million people (nearly a third of the U.S. work force) do at least some work out of their homes. Advancing technology, such as fax machines, computer notebooks, modems, software that effortlessly connects home computers to office networks, have caused their numbers to increase dramatically -- sometimes on the order of 20% per year, in the U.S. Currently these 39 million are divided as follows:

23.8 million work at home running their own business. 12.1 million of these are *full-time;* 11.7 million are *part-time.*

8.6 million work outside the home during office hours, but take work home for their employers, *after* office hours.

And, 6.6 million[3] work at home for their employers (businesses or government agencies) *during* office hours; these are the ones officially called *'telecommuters.'* 3.5 million of these are men, 3.1 million, women.[4] Telecommuters usually put in at least *some* time at the office or place of work each week; typically they work at home between 2 to 4½ days a week.[5]

---

2. Coined by Robert E. Calem in *The New York Times,* 4/18/93.

3. Link Resources, reported in *The New York Times,* Section 3, 4/18/93. The statistic is for the most recent year available (1992), as I write.

4. *The New York Times,* Section 3, 4/18/93.

5. Note well, if you are thinking about telecommuting, that it is definitely a mixed bag -- depending a great deal on the disposition, self-discipline, and home conditions of the individual concerned. Some telecommuters boost their output and productivity by 3–5%, due to lack of interruption from co-workers, and the consequent ability to concentrate on the task at hand -- *not to mention their desire to prove that they aren't goofing*

You will note that not everyone who works at home is necessarily in business for themselves. Some people have been able to talk their boss into letting them do at least *some* of their work at home; in other cases their boss has *asked* them to work at home, connected to their offices by computer-network telephone lines. These people, as noted, are called *'telecommuters'*-- a term coined by Jack Nilles in 1973.

GOING INTO BUSINESS FOR YOURSELF

If you are thinking about working at home *for yourself,* you would be joining the more than 23.8 million in the U.S. who already do that, plus the estimated 25 million additional workers who are *thinking* about doing it.

When people do decide to work out of their own home, they sometimes haven't the foggiest notion of what *kind* of home business to start, as we shall see. However, often they already know what they want to do. They've been doing it for years, full-time, for someone else. Now they want to do it on their own. We call this *free-lancing* or *contracting out your services.*[6] It is *relatively* easy if you have been a business expert, lawyer, consultant, childcare worker, writer, craftsperson, or the like, where your interaction with others could just as easily be done by telephone,[7] modem, fax machine, catalog or mail -- as from an

---

off. A few telecommuters, however, experience a fall-off in productivity, due to childcare demands, and other interruptions. Other downsides are: sometimes having uneven work flow, or when the work flow is heavy, working nonstop at all hours, your mate's feeling that they need their own space, a lack of social contact and interaction with other workers, resentment from colleagues at the office who feel you're just taking days off, and the feeling that you are often passed over when it comes time for promotion. Therefore, if telecommuting is of any interest to you, be sure that before you talk to your boss about the possibility, you talk to some experienced telecommuters -- at your place or elsewhere -- to find out what telecommuting is *really* like. If you want to *read* further about this idea, see Brad Schepp, *THE TELECOMMUTER'S HAND-BOOK: How to Work for a Salary – Without Ever Leaving the House.* Pharos Books: A Scripps Howard Company, 200 Park Ave., New York, NY 10166. 1990. It describes the jobs best suited for telecommuting, names and addresses of more than 100 companies that allow employees to work at home, pros and cons of telecommuting for both employee and employer. In order for this to work, you will need a sympathetic, supportive boss or supervisor, and you will need a reputation as a mature and responsible individual. In the end, you will probably have to be *more* productive than those who work in the office full-time, to continue to justify their faith in you, if they give you a trial *go-ahead.*

office downtown somewhere.

In fact, if your business could be done in this fashion, then you could *literally* work wherever your preferred environment in the whole world is -- whether that be out in nature, or at your favorite vacation spot,[8] or skiing chalet, or in some other country altogether. Think about it. And if the idea grows on you, set about exploring it.

6. If you decide to launch yourself on this path, be sure to talk to people who have been free-lancers, until you know the name of every pitfall and obstacle in *free-lancing*. Where do you find such people? Well, free-lancers are *everywhere*. Independent screenwriters, copy writers, artists, songwriters, photographers, illustrators, interior designers, video people, film people, consultants, and therapists, are only *some* examples of the type of people who must free-lance, in the very nature of their job. Talk with enough of them, even if they're not free-lancing in the same business you have in mind, until you learn all the pitfalls of free-lancing. For further exploration of your chosen specialty, see such catalogs as that of Writer's Digest Books/North Light Books, 1507 Dana Ave., Cincinnati, OH 45207.

7. This family includes cellular telephones, 'call-forwarding' -- the technology where people call your one fixed telephone number, and then get automatically forwarded to wherever you have told the phone company you currently are -- and voice/electronic mail.

8. Jeffrey Maltzman, *Jobs in Paradise: The Definitive Guide to Exotic Jobs Everywhere*. Perennial Library, HarperCollins, 10 East 53rd St., New York, NY 10022. 1990. Describes jobs at lakes, rivers, coasts and beaches, snow and skiing, tropical islands, mountains, deserts, and so forth. You will probably not want to look so much at the *jobs* described here, as at the *categories*, to help you think out just what *kind* of place you might like to be a telecommuter from. As a place to *start* some informational interviewing, this is a great book -- *if* you're interested in working exactly where you'd also like to spend your leisure time.

THE THREE MAJOR PROBLEMS
OF HOME BUSINESSES

(1) The first major problem of home businesses, according to experts, is that on average home-based workers in the U.S. only earn 70% of what their full-time office-based equals do. Think carefully whether you could make enough money to survive -- *or prosper.*

(2) The second major problem of home businesses is that it's often difficult to maintain the balance between business and family time. Sometimes the *family* time gets short-changed, while in other cases the demands of family (particularly with small children) may become so interruptive, that the *business* gets short-changed. So, do investigate thoroughly, ahead of time, *how* you would go about doing this *well.* There are books that can help.[9]

(3) Lastly, a home business puts you into a perpetual job-hunt.

Some of those of us who are unemployed *hate* job-hunting, and are attracted to the idea of a home business because this seems like an ideal way to cut short their job-hunt. The irony is, that a home business makes you in a very real sense a *perpetual* job-hunter -- because you have to be *always* seeking new clients or customers -- which is to say, new *employers.* (I call them *employers,* because they *pay* you for the work you are doing. The only difference between this and a full-time job is that here *the contract is limited.* But if you are running your own business, you will have to *continually* beat the bushes for new clients or customers -- who are in fact short-term employers.)

Of course, the dream of most home business people is to become so well known, and so in demand, that clients or customers will be literally beating down your doors, and you will be

9. Books to help you do this, include:

Barbara Brabec, *Homemade Money: The Definitive Guide to Success in a Home Business.* 3rd ed. Betterway Publications, Inc., White Hall, VA 22987. 1989, 1986, 1984. A very fine book, with an A to Z business section, and a most helpful summary of which states have laws regulating (or prohibiting) certain home-based businesses; it is updated regularly. Barbara also publishes a newsletter, *National Home Business Report.* If you wish more information, you can ask for her catalog, by writing to National Home Business Network, P.O. Box 2137, Naperville, IL 60567.

Lynie Arden, *The Work-at-Home Sourcebook.* 3rd ed. Live Oak Publications, P.O. Box

able to stop this endless job-hunt. But that only happens to a relative minority, and your realistic self must know that.

The greater likelihood is that you will *always* have to beat the bushes for employer/clients. It may get easier as you get better at it, or it may get harder, if economic conditions take a severe downturn. In any event, it will probably be the one aspect of your work that you will *always* cordially dislike. If you're going to go this route, you must learn to make your peace with it -- however grudgingly.

If you can't manage that, if you avoid that task like the plague until there's literally no bread on the table, you're probably going to find *a home business* is just a glamorous synonym for *'starving.'* I know *many* home business people to whom this has happened, and it happened precisely because they couldn't

---

2193, Boulder, CO 80306. 1990.

Paul and Sarah Edwards, *Working from Home: Everything You Need to Know about Living and Working under the Same Roof.* J. P. Tarcher, Inc., 5858 Wilshire Blvd., Los Angeles, CA 90036. 1985. Now revised and expanded. 436 pages. Has a long section on computerizing your home business, and on telecommunicating.

Homeworking Mothers, a quarterly newsletter for women who want to start their own businesses and work from their homes. Mother's Home Business Network, Box 423, East Meadow, NY 11554.

Frank and Sharon Barnett, *Working Together: Entrepreneurial Couples.* Ten Speed Press, P.O. Box 7123, Berkeley, CA 94707. 1989.

stomach going out to beat the bushes for clients or customers. If that's true for you, you should plan to start out by *hiring, co-opting, volunteering* somebody part-time, who is willing to do this for you -- one who, in fact, 'eats it up.'

TRYING SOMETHING
BRAND NEW

If you've decided, in spite of these downsides, that you'd like to think seriously about a home business, *but* you haven't a clue as to what *kind* of business you'd like to run, there are four steps you can take.

First, read. There are oodles of books out there that are *filled* with ideas for home businesses.[10] Browse your local library, or bookstore.

Secondly, dream. In evaluating any ideas you pick up from books, the first thing you ought to look at are your dreams. What have you always dreamed about doing? Since childhood? Since last week? Now is the time to dust off those dreams.

And please don't pay any attention, for now, to whether those dreams represent *a step up* for you in life, or not. Who cares? Your dreams are yours. You may have been dreaming of earning *more* money. But then again, you may have been dreaming of

---

10. Jay Conrad Levinson, *555 Ways to Earn Extra Money: The ultimate idea book for supplementing your income.* Revised for the '90s. Henry Holt and Company, Inc., 115 W. 18th St., New York, NY 10011. 1991. Ideas for people who are artistic, or oriented toward people, or things, or ideas.

Entrepreneur Magazine's *184 Businesses Anyone Can Start and Make a Lot of Money.* 2nd ed., Bantam Books, 666 Fifth Ave., New York, NY 10103. 1990. Ideas related to Personal Services, Business Services, Food, Retail, Sports and Entertainment, Automotive Businesses, Publishing, and miscellaneous.

Entrepreneur Magazine's *168 More Businesses Anyone Can Start and Make a Lot of Money.* 2nd ed., Bantam Books, 666 Fifth Ave., New York, NY 10103. 1991. Same categories as above, plus Computer Businesses.

Sharon Kahn and The Philip Lief Group, *101 Best Businesses to Start.* Doubleday, a division of Bantam Doubleday Dell Publishing Group, Inc., 666 Fifth Ave., New York, NY 10103. 1988. The categories here are the same as above, plus Healthcare and Fitness, Household Services, Real Estate, Sales and Marketing, and Travel.

Paul and Sarah Edwards, *The Best Home Businesses for the 90s: The Inside Information You Need to Know to Select A Home-based Business That's Right For You.* Jeremy P. Tarcher, Inc., 5858 Wilshire Blvd., Suite 200, Los Angeles, CA 90036. 1991. The book profiles 70 top businesses (in their view).

doing work that you really love, even if it means a lesser salary or income than you have been accustomed to. Don't *judge* your dreams, and don't let anyone else judge them either.

Thirdly, look around your own community, and ask yourself what services or products people seem to need the most. Or what service or product already offered in the community could stand a lot of *improving?* There may be something there that *grabs* you.

The underlying theme to 90% of the businesses that are *out there* these days is *things that save time.* It's what single parents, families where both parents work, and singles who have over-crowded lives, most want.

If none of the books you look at have any ideas that grab you, here are some other ideas that you might consider: Offering home deliveries of local restaurants' dinners, or home delivery of grocery orders from any downtown supermarket. Evening delivery services of laundry, etc. Daytime or evening office clean-ing services and/or home cleaning services. Home repairs, es-pecially in the evening or on weekends, of TVs, radios, audio systems, laundries, dishwashers, etc. Lawn care. Care for the elderly in their own homes. Childcare in their own homes. Pick up and delivery of things (even personal stuff, like cleaning) at the office. Automobile care or repair services, with pickup and delivery. Offering short-term business consultancy in various fields. Other successful businesses these days deal with leisure activities.

Fourth, consider mail order. If you find no needs within your own community, you may want to broaden your search, to ask what is needed in the country as a whole -- or the world. After all, mail order businesses can be started *small* at home, and catalogs can be sent *anywhere.* If this interests you, read up on the subject.[11] Also, for heaven's sakes, go talk to other mail order people (for names, just look at the catalogs you're already likely receiving).

---

11. Cecil C. Hoge, Sr., *Mail Order Moonlighting.* Ten Speed Press, Box 7123, Berkeley, CA 94707. 1988.

WHAT ARE YOUR CHANCES
OF 'MAKING A GO' OF IT?

If you investigate the odds of succeeding at your own business, the first thing you will come across are some *intimidating* statistics. Hidden in them is not just bad news, but also some good news.

U.S. Statistics

Currently, 10,200,000 people -- or one out of every twelve people in the work force -- have started their own business. *But,* at least 65% of all new businesses fail within their first five years of operation -- that's more than one out of every two. A well-known statistic, and the only debate you'll get on it from experts is whether or not the figure is *too low.* 96,100 businesses went bankrupt in 1992.[12] So, if you want to go into business for yourself, there's a great risk that it's going to go belly-up[13] *early on.* That is, as they say, the bad news.

The good news is that *if* you survive this early-on period, things start to look up. The risk decreases. There are two evidences for saying this.

First, only about 25% of new businesses fail *in any given year;* so, taking it on just a year to year basis, you have a 75% chance of *not* going belly-up *that* year.[14] Secondly, there are about 28 *old* businesses in the U.S. for every new business that starts up. So, the national bankruptcy/failure rate -- taking *all* businesses into account -- is *much* lower than most people think. In one year recently, out of each 10,000 businesses in this country, only 120 failed.[15] That means that 9,880 out of each 10,000 businesses survived.

What these statistics add up to, is that *if* you can make it through the first few years in your home business, you'll probably survive thereafter. That leaves the BIG question: how do you survive those first few difficult years? The answer is: *Research. Homework. Interviewing people.* You're trying to find out some-

---

12. *San Francisco Chronicle,* Thursday, 1/21/93, p. C1.

13. If any of my readers outside the U.S. do not understand the slang phrase "belly-up," other more familiar synonyms would be: bankrupt, out of business, kaput.

14. These figures are from David Birch's *Job Creation In America.* The Free Press, 866 Third Ave., New York, NY 10022. 1987. David is an excellent researcher, and knows more about small businesses than anyone else in the country that I know of; I recommend this book, highly. It describes at length where the new jobs are coming from, and how our smallest companies put the most people to work.

15. 1986, the most recent year for which I have statistics.

thing. That *something* can be summarized in the following formula:

A, MINUS B,
EQUALS C

It is *mindboggling* to discover how many people start a new business, at home or elsewhere, without ever going to talk to other people, who have started up the same kind of business. One job-hunter told me she started a homemade candle business, without ever talking to anyone else who had tried a similar endeavor. Her business went belly-up within a year and a half.

She concluded: no one should go into such a business.

I concluded: she hadn't done her homework, before she started.

Here, then, are the rules for the homework you *must* do, before starting your own home business -- or any kind of new venture. Please *memorize* them:

A – B = C

1. You write out exactly what kind of business you are thinking about starting.

2. You identify towns or cities that are at least twenty-five miles away, and you try to get their phone books, addresses of their Chambers of Commerce, etc.

3. By using the phone book and the Chambers, you try to identify names of three businesses in those towns, that are identical or similar to the business you are thinking of starting. You journey to that town or city, and talk to the founder/owner of same.

4. When you talk to them, you ask them what pitfalls or obstacles they ran into. You ask them how they overcame them. You ask them what skills or

knowledges do they think are necessary to running this kind of business successfully. You make a list of the latter. When you've finished talking to all three owners, you put together a list of the skills and knowledges they agreed on, as necessary to running the business. We'll call this list "A."

5. Back home you sit down and inventory your own skills and knowledges, perhaps using Chapters 9 and 10 in this book. We'll call this list "B."

6. Finally, you subtract "B" from "A," and this results in a list we will call "C." That's the list of the skills or knowledges you don't have, but must find -- either by taking courses, or by getting volunteers with those skills, or by hiring someone with those skills.

Why twenty-five miles away? Well, actually, that's a minimum. You want to interview businesses which, *if they were in the same town* with you, would be your rival. And if they were in the same town with you, wouldn't likely tell you how to get started. After all, they're not going to train you just so you can then take business away from them.

But, when a guy, a gal, or a business is twenty-five miles away -- even better, fifty miles away -- you're not as likely to be perceived as a rival, and therefore they're much more likely to tell you what you want to know about their own experience, and how *they* got started, and where the landmines are hidden.

Doubtless at this point you would like an example of this whole process. Okay. Our job-hunter is a woman who has been making harps for some employer, but now is thinking about going into business for herself, not only *making* harps at home, but also *designing* harps, with the aid of a computer. After interviewing several homebased harpmakers and harp designers, and finishing her own self-assessment, her chart of A – B = C came out looking like this:

A − B = C

Skills and Knowledges Needed to Run This Kind of Business Successfully	Skills and Knowledges Which I Have	Skills and Knowledges Needed, Which I Do Not Have, and Which I Will Therefore Have to Get Someone to Volunteer, or I Will Have to Go Out and Hire
Precision-working with tools and instruments	Precision-working with tools and instruments	
Planning and directing an entire project	Planning and directing an entire project	
Programming computers, inventing programs that solve physical problems		Programming computers, inventing programs that solve physical problems
Problem solving: evaluating why a particular design or process isn't working.	Problem solving: evaluating why a particular design or process isn't working.	
Being self-motivated, resourceful, patient, and persevering, accurate, methodical, and thorough	Being self-motivated, resourceful, patient, and persevering, accurate, methodical and thorough	
Thorough knowledge of: Principles of electronics	*Thorough knowledge of:*	*Thorough knowledge of:* Principles of electronics
Physics of strings	Physics of strings	
Principles of vibration	Principles of vibration	
Properties of woods	Properties of woods	
Computer programming		Computer programming
Accounting		Accounting

If she decides to try her hand at becoming an independent harpmaker and harp designer, she now knows what she needs but lacks: *computer programming, knowledge of the principles of electronics, and accounting.* Column C. These she must either go to school to acquire for herself, OR enlist from some friends of hers in those fields, on a volunteer basis, OR go out and hire, part-time.

That's how you do this *essential* research. Now, let's look at some special problems you may encounter, when trying to apply *A minus B equals C.*

WHEN YOU WANT TO HAVE TWO OR MORE DIFFERENT BUSINESSES AT THE SAME TIME

Research
Problem

#1

> ### U.S. Statistics
>
> Currently, the number of people having two careers, businesses, or jobs *(one or both of them part-time)* is at least 50% higher than it was ten years ago. This year one out of every 16 workers, will be holding down two or more jobs. That comes to 7,500,000 people.

Surveys reveal that half of these 7,500,000 people are *not* holding down two jobs because they love to work. They are holding down two jobs because they can't make ends meet, otherwise. It is the hard '90s, an era of decreased standards of living, decreased expectations, decreased income, and lower salaries. Twenty years ago, when things got tight, the solution was to have your spouse go to work. Now, in the '90s, when most spouses are *already* working, the only solution left, is for you to take on a second, part-time, job -- preferably at home.[16]

---

16. You may decide, in such a case, that your best shot at a second job does not consist in a home business, but in working at night or on weekends for someone else. If so, call up your brother, or your uncle, or your best friend, and see if they have any suggestions, or know of any part-time vacancies. If they don't, then you'll probably want to go to Chapter 4 -- which applies to finding a part-time job, as much as it does to finding a full-time job -- and follow its advice. Sad to say, many of the part-time jobs that pay really well *are* boring beyond belief. Nobody wants such jobs. That's *why* employers pay such big bucks -- to get someone to take the job. Bridge toll-takers (in some States) are an example of this. Your refuge: do Chapters 9–11, to help you identify even this second job.

You may, of course, already have a home business -- one you started *ages* ago; and now you need to start up a second one, as well, if you're going to survive, financially.

Perhaps you have a different reason for considering two home businesses. Perhaps *variety* is your middle name. You were born to be a *two-career-at-the-same-time* person.

In any event, the advice is the same as it is for one business. For *each* of the businesses you propose, you need to go interview people who have already done this -- to find out A – B = C.

You may also want to talk to people who have juggled two (or more) careers, at the same time. Since it may be difficult for you to find the names of such people, you should know about Jay Conrad Levinson. He was in just such a situation, and has written a book about his choices -- and his philosophy -- called *Earning Money Without A Job*. If you can't find people in your town or city who have gone this route, then you will profit by reading his experience.[17]

---

17. Jay Conrad Levinson, *Earning Money Without A Job*. Revised for the '90s. Henry Holt and Company, Inc., 115 W. 18th St., New York, NY 10011. 1991. One of my favorite books. The first part of this excellent book is devoted to his story, and his idea of "modular economics" -- putting together several small jobs, rather than one big one. The second part of the book is devoted to actual businesses that can thus be put together. Also by the same author: *Guerrilla Marketing Excellence: The Fifty Golden Rules for Small Business Success*. Houghton Mifflin Company, 215 Park Ave. South, New York, NY 10003. 1993. Very useful little book.

WHEN YOU'VE THOUGHT OF
A BUSINESS OR CAREER
THAT NO ONE'S EVER HEARD OF
BEFORE

No matter how inventive you are, you're probably *not* going to invent a job that *no one* has ever heard of, before. You're only going to invent a job that *most* people have never heard of, before. But the likelihood is *great* that someone, somewhere, in this world of endless creativity, has already put together the kind of job you're dreaming about. Your task: to find her, or him, and interview them thoroughly. And then . . . well, you know the drill: A – B = C.

If there isn't someone doing *exactly* what you are dreaming of, there is at least someone who is *close*. This is how you find them:

WHEN NO ONE HAS DONE WHAT YOU WANT TO DO

You can always find someone who has done something that at least approximates what you want to do. The rules are:

1. Break down your projected business or career into its parts.

2. Then take any two of those parts at a time. See what kind of person that describes.

3. Find out the names of such persons, preferably two or more.

4. Go see, phone, write, him or her; you will learn a great deal, that is relevant to your dream.

5. They, in turn, may be able to give you a lead to someone whose business is even closer to what it is you want to do. And then you can go interview them. And so on, and so forth.

For example, let's suppose your dream is -- here we take a ridiculous case -- to use computers to monitor the growth of plants at the South Pole. And suppose you can't find anybody who's ever done such a thing. The way to tackle this seemingly insurmountable problem, is to break the proposed business down into its parts, which -- in this case -- are: *computers, plants,* and *the Antarctic.*

Then you try combining any two parts, together, to define the person or persons you need to talk to. In this case, that would mean finding someone who's *used computers with plants here in the States,* or someone who's *used computers at the Antarctic,* or someone who has *worked with plants at the Antarctic,* etc. You go talk to them, and along the way you may discover there *is* someone who has used computers to monitor the growth of plants at the South Pole. Then again, you may not. In any event, you will learn most of the pitfalls that wait for you, by hearing the experience of those who are in *parallel* businesses or careers.

Thus, it is *always* possible -- with a little blood, sweat and imagination -- to find out what A − B = C is, for the business you're trying to invent.

"... and give me good abstract-reasoning ability,
interpersonal skills, cultural perspective, linguistic comprehension,
and a high sociodynamic potential."

WHEN YOU'VE INVENTED SOMETHING --
OR WOULD LIKE TO

Research
Problem

#3

If you are inclined toward invention or tinkering, you might want to start by improving on an idea that's already *out there.* Start with something you like, such as bicycles. You might experiment with making -- let us say -- a folding-bicycle. Or, if you like to go to the beach, and your skills run to sewing, you might think about making and selling beach towels with weights sewn in the corners, against windy days.

If you've already invented something, and it's been sitting in your drawer, or the garage, but you've never attempted to duplicate or manufacture it before, now might be a good time to try. Think out very carefully just how you are going to get it manufactured, advertised, and marketed, etc. There are firms out there which claim to specialize in promoting inventions such as yours, for a fee. However, according to the Federal Trade Commission, in a study of 30,000 people who paid such promoters, not a single inventor ever made a profit after giving their invention to such firms.[18] If you want to gamble some of your hard-earned money on such firms, consider whether you might better drop it at the tables in Las Vegas. I think the odds are *better* there.

You're much better off, *of course,* doing your own research as to how one gets an invention marketed. Through the copyright office, and your library, locate other inventors, and ask if they were successful in marketing their own invention. When you find those who were, pick their brains for everything they're worth. Of course one of the first things they're going to tell you is to go get your invention copyrighted or trademarked or patented.[19]

---

18. *San Francisco Chronicle,* 1/26/91.

19. Richard C. Levy, *The Inventor's Desktop Companion: A Guide to Successfully Marketing and Protecting Your Ideas.* Visible Ink Press, a division of Gale Research Inc., 835 Penobscot Bldg., Detroit, MI 48226-4094. 1991. From securing a patent for it, to selling it, a very complete compendium.

Fred Grisson and David Pressman, *The Inventor's Notebook.* Nolo Press, 950 Parker St., Berkeley, CA 94710. 1989. A manual to help you keep records about your invention.

WHEN THE BUSINESS
IS TOO LARGE FOR THE HOUSE:
DREAMS AND FRANCHISES

Your dream may be to do something that's too big for the house. You *know* you're gonna have to go rent a place, or sell your home and buy some acreage. For example, *I want a horse ranch, where I can raise and sell horses.* Or *I want to run a bed-and-breakfast place.*[20] Stuff like that. If so, you'd better go talk to other people who have already done that. Pick their brains for everything they're worth.

Research
Problem

#4

If you don't have a dream, but you still want your own business -- and you don't *mind* if it's too big for the house -- then you may want to think about a franchise. Though some of them can be done from your home,[21] the majority require an outside site.

Franchises exist because some people want to have their own

20. Barbara Notarius and Gail Sforza Brewer, *Open Your Own Bed & Breakfast.* John Wiley & Sons, Inc., Business/Law/General Books Division, 605 Third Ave., New York, NY 10158-0012. 1987.

21. Lynie Arden, *Franchises You Can Run From Home,* John Wiley & Sons, Professional and Trade Division, 605 Third Ave., New York, NY 10158-0012. 1990.

business, but don't want to go through the agony of starting it up. They want to *buy in* on an already established business, and they have the money in their savings with which to do that (or they know where they can get a bank loan). Fortunately for them, there are more than 2,100 franchised businesses operating in this country, with more than 478,000 outlets, employing more than 6 million people. Your library or bookstore will have books that list many of these.[22]

Overall, the failure rate for franchises is less than 4%.[23] You want to keep in mind that some *types* of franchises have a failure rate *far* greater than that. The ten *riskiest* small businesses, according to experts, are local laundries and dry cleaners, used-car dealerships, gas stations, local trucking firms, restaurants, infant clothing stores, bakeries, machine shops, grocery or meat stores, and car washes -- though I'm sure there will be some new nominees for this list, by the time you read this. *Risky* doesn't mean you can't make them succeed. It only means the odds are greater than they would be with other small businesses.

You want to keep in mind also that some individual franchises are *terrible* -- and that includes well-known names. They charge too much for you to *get on board,* and often they don't do

---

22. *Franchise Opportunities,* 22nd ed., Sterling Publishing Co., Inc., 387 Park Ave. S., New York, NY 10016. 1991. This is a reprint of the 22nd edition of *Franchise Opportunities Handbook,* issued by the U.S. Government Printing Office. An immensely thorough book, together with a good introductory section about how to investigate a franchise.

Erwin J. Keup, *Franchise Bible: A Comprehensive Guide.* The Oasis Press®/PSI Research, 300 N. Valley Dr., Grants Pass, OR 97526. 1990. Mr. Keup is a lawyer who has specialized in franchise law and franchise consulting for the past 32 years. He covers 'buying an existing business,' as well as franchises. Also, if you have a successful business already, he discusses the pros and cons of turning it into a franchise.

Ray Bard and Sheila Henderson, *Own Your Own Franchise: Everything You Need to Know about the Best Opportunities in America.* A Stonesong Press Book, Addison-Wesley Publishing Co., Inc., Route 128, Reading, MA 01876. 1987.

Robert Laurance Perry, *The 50 Best Low-Investment, High-Profit Franchises.* Prentice-Hall, Business & Professional Division, A division of Simon & Schuster, Englewood Cliffs, NJ 07632. 1990. Since there is a disturbing trend in franchises these days toward higher and higher start-up fees, up in the $150,000 category or higher, Perry attempts to list ones which people can afford; most of them are less than $20,000, some less than $5,000.

Constance Jones, *The 220 Best Franchises to Buy.* Philip Lief Group, 319 E. 52nd St., New York, NY 10022. 1987. A sourcebook for evaluating the best franchise opportunities.

23. Ray Bard and Sheila Henderson, *Own Your Own Franchise,* page 1.

the advertising or other commitments that they promised they would.

There isn't a franchising book that doesn't warn you eighteen times to go talk to people who have *already* bought that same franchise, before you ever decide to go with them. And I mean *several* people, not just one. Most experts also warn you to go talk to *other* franchises in the same field, not just the kind you're thinking about signing up with. Maybe there's something better, that such research will uncover.

If you are drawn to the idea of a franchise, because you are in a hurry, and you don't want to do any homework first, *'cause it's just too much trouble,* you will deserve what you get, believe me. That way lies madness.

CONCLUSION

There are three rules about trying something new that you should forever keep in mind:

---

1. There is always some risk, in trying something new. Your job is not to avoid risk -- there is no way to do that -- but to make sure ahead of time that the risks are *manageable.*

2. You find this out before you start, by first talking to others who have already done what you are thinking of doing; then you evaluate whether or not you still want to go ahead and try it.

3. Have a Plan B, already laid out, *before you start,* as to what you will do if it doesn't work out; i.e., know where you are going to go, next. Don't wait, *puh-leaze!* Write it out, now. *This is what I'm going to do, if this doesn't work out:*

These rules always apply, no matter where you are in your life: just starting out, already employed, unemployed, in mid-life, recovering after a crisis or accident, facing retirement, or whatever. Do take them very seriously.

If you're sharing your life with someone, sit down with that partner or spouse and ask what the implications are *for them* if you try this new thing. Will it require all your joint savings? Will they have to give up things? If so, what? Are they willing to make those sacrifices? And so on.

If you aren't out of work, you will need to debate the wisdom of quitting your job before you start up the new company, or business. And what do the experts say, here? In a word, they say, if you have a job, *don't* quit it. Better by far to move *gradually* into self-employment, doing it as a moonlighting activity first of all, while you are still holding down that regular job somewhere else. That way, you can test out your new enterprise, as you would test a floorboard in an old run-down house, stepping on it cautiously without at first putting your full weight on it, to see whether or not it will support you.[24]

If your investigation revealed that it takes good accounting practices in order to turn a profit, and you don't know a thing about accounting, you go out and hire a (part-time) accountant *immediately* -- or, if you absolutely have no money, you talk an accountant friend of yours into giving you some volunteer time, for a while.[25]

It is up to you to do your research thoroughly, weigh the risks, count the cost, get counsel from those intimately involved with you, and then if you decide you want to do it (whatever *it* is), go ahead and try -- no matter what your well-meaning but pessimistic acquaintances may say.

You only have one life here on this earth, and that life (under God) is *yours* to say how it will be spent, or not spent.

---

24. See Philip Holland, *How To Start A Business Without Quitting Your Job: The Moonlight Entrepreneur's Guide.* Ten Speed Press, P.O. Box 7123, Berkeley, CA 94707. 1992.

25. There are also books that may help you out of the financial thicket, such as James D. Schwartz's *"ENOUGH" A Guide to Reclaiming Your American Dream.* Labrador Press, distributed by RE/MAX International, Inc., 5445 DTC Pkwy., Suite 1200, Englewood, CO 80111. 1992.

"Same career, change of career, same career…change of…"

Two roads diverged in a yellow wood,
And sorry I could not travel both
And be one traveler, long I stood
And looked down one as far as I could
To where it bent in the undergrowth;

Then took the other, as just as fair,
And having perhaps the better claim,
Because it was grassy and wanted wear;
Though as for that the passing there
Had worn them really about the same,

And both that morning equally lay
In leaves no step had trodden black.
Oh, I kept the first for another day!
Yet knowing how way leads on to way,
I doubted if I should ever come back.

I shall be telling this with a sigh
Somewhere ages and ages hence:
Two roads diverged in a wood, and I–
I took the one less traveled by,
And that has made all the difference.

Robert Frost (1874–1963)[1]

---

1. The title of this poem is "The Road Not Taken," from THE POETRY OF ROBERT FROST edited by Edward Connery Lathem. Copyright 1916, © 1969 by Holt, Rinehart & Winston. Copyright 1944 by Robert Frost. Henry Holt and Company, Publisher. Used with permission. Incidentally, Scotty Peck's modern classic, *The Road Less Traveled,* takes its title from this poem.

CHAPTER SEVEN

Retiring
Or Moving
To A New Place

Chapter 7

WHEN YOU WANT
TO PULL UP STAKES,
MOVE, AND RELOCATE

Surveys reveal that the average American moves eleven times between birth and death. Sometimes that's within the same town.[2] Other times it's to a faraway place. Similar patterns of mobility often occur in other countries, as well.

There are two reasons, above all else, why people relocate:

(1) You may have reached the point where you decide that where you live is more important to you than any other consideration. Maybe you're living in some city, town, or rural area that you detest more, every day you are there. Finally you decide you can't stand it any longer. You've only one life to live, on this earth, and you want to spend the rest of it in a place you really enjoy. This crisis can occur when you're twenty, forty, or sixty. Or, perhaps you're retiring, and you want a place where it's always warm, or a place where you can always ski, or whatever.

(2) You like where you're living, but you just can't find any work -- decent–paying work, anyway -- there. It seems as though every job there is filled, numbered, and has a waiting list besides. You've decided you've *got* to move.

HOW TO CHOOSE
A NEW PLACE

When facing a move, some people already know *where to:*

You may choose a town or city where you already have friends, or family. You decide to move *there,* because you will have their support and help. Or you may choose a town or city where

2. While I was growing up in Teaneck, New Jersey, my parents could only afford to rent, and when rents changed, we moved. Between the time I was five and eighteen years old, we moved seven times, within the same town. This is a typical experience for many urban dwellers who rent.

you've always *dreamed* of living. You're confident you'll be able to find a job there, somehow, somewhere, once you get there. You'll *make it work*, some way, somehow.

In such a case, where you *know* where you're going (and you know who's going with you), you need no advice from me.

But there are those other times, when you need or want to move, but you have no idea where to move to.

At such a time, you have one of two choices:

a) Your first consideration is that it be a place you could love. And you want some help in figuring *that* out. You're pretty confident you'll be able to find a job there, some way, somehow.

b) Your first consideration is that it be a place where it is easy to find the kind of work you do, or want to do. And you want some help in figuring *that* out. You're pretty sure that you'll get used to living there, once you settle in.

Let's look at these two scenarios, taking the second first:

CHOOSING A PLACE BY
WHETHER OR NOT IT HAS JOBS

If jobs are the first thing on your mind, you have two ways to go. One is to move where the unemployment rate is low for *all* jobs. Your local Federal/State employment office can usually give you the current statistics about all 50 States. You look for the States with the lowest unemployment rate. Within the U.S., currently, as I write, these are Nebraska, Hawaii, North and South Dakota, Arizona, and Utah. They are followed by Iowa, Colorado, Kansas, Minnesota, Wisconsin, and Nevada. Then you pick one or more metropolitan areas in those States, and write to their Chambers of Commerce (pick up your phone and ask *Information* for their phone numbers, in each city). You ask those Chambers for all the information they have in writing about businesses which deal with your trade or specialty, and you ask that these lists be sent to you.

Send them a thank-you note *the day* the stuff arrives, *please.* You may need to contact them again later, perhaps when you're actually in the area, and it will help you a lot if they can say, *"Oh yes, you're that nice person who sent us a thank you note when we sent you our materials. First thank-you note we've gotten in three years."* Chances are, they will bend over *backwards* to help you.

Your other strategy for choosing a place by whether or not it has jobs, is to find out what places in the country (if any) have a particular need for your kind of skills. This is hard to do in the case of some kinds of jobs -- like that of a writer, say, but easier to do if you are a craftsperson or practice a particular trade. In the latter case, you would go to your local library, and ask the librarian to help you find a trade association directory, or directories. (See Appendix B.) You would then look up the association that deals with your occupation, and jot down the address of their national headquarters. Then write or phone them and ask if they know where the demand is greatest, in that industry, nationwide. If their answer turns out to be 'several places,' then you can fall back on such books as Richard Boyer's and David Savageau's *Places Rated Almanac,* to decide which of those is your first choice, which is your second, etc.

JOBS HEAD AWAY FROM BOTH COASTS

Measured by percentage change in non-agricultural jobs from September 1991 through September 1992

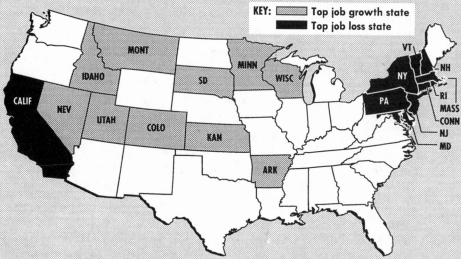

KEY: ▬ Top job growth state
▬ Top job loss state

■ **Top 10 States in Job Growth**

Rank/State	Percent change	Net gain
1 Utah	3.02%	22,800
2 Arkansas	2.88	27,500
3 Idaho	2.84	11,600
4 Montana	2.35	7,300
5 Colorado	2.02	31,300
6 Nevada	1.74	11,200
7 Minnesota	1.74	37,600
8 Kansas	1.72	19,000
9 South Dakota	1.53	4,600
10 Wisconsin	1.50	34,800
UNITED STATES	0.11	119,000

■ **Worst 10 States in Job Losses**

Rank/State	Percent change	Net loss
41 Vermont	-1.24	-3,100
42 New Hampshire	-1.31	-6,400
43 Pennsylvania	-1.46	-74,000
44 Rhode Island	-1.82	-7,700
45 California	-1.97	-246,100
46 Massachusetts	-2.07	-58,100
47 New York	-2.09	-164,600
48 Maryland	-2.18	-45,800
49 New Jersey	-2.55	-88,600
50 Connecticut	-3.15	-49,000

Source: Economic Outlook Center, Arizona State University

Note: Nevada's percentage gain was fractionally higher than Minnesota's

CHRONICLE GRAPHIC

*From the San Francisco Chronicle.
Used with permission.*

CHOOSING A PLACE
BY WHETHER OR NOT
YOU LOVE IT THERE

It is relatively easy to figure out a place you could love. First of all, you can interview all your friends and acquaintances, to ask them what places *they* have loved the most, in the U.S. or in whatever country you live. And *why*. This task can be a lot of fun. And then, out of all the *candidates* they propose, you can choose two or three places for further investigation.

Secondly, you can turn to books. These days, there are quite a number of them that rate various cities and towns according to *factors* that may be important to you, such as *weather, crime, educational system, recreational opportunities,* etc.[3] The best of these, by a long shot, is Richard Boyer's and David Savageau's *Places Rated Almanac.* One word of caution: do remember, in all these books, that a computer was usually used to sum up, and rate, all the factors. You may find that *the whole* is less than the sum of its *parts*.

Lastly, you can do a thorough-going analysis of all the places you have ever lived, to come up with *descriptors* -- and then *names* -- of places that combine all the factors that were ever important to you in any town or city from your past.[4]

---

3. Richard Boyer and David Savageau, *Places Rated Almanac: Your Guide to Finding the Best Places to Live in America.* Rand McNally & Co., Box 7600, Chicago, IL 60680. 1989. A marvelous book. Immensely helpful for anyone weighing where to move next. All 333 metropolitan areas are ranked and compared for living costs, job outlook, crime, health, transportation, education, the arts, recreation, and climate. Has numerous helpful diagrams, charts and maps, showing (for example) earthquake risk areas, tornado and hurricane risk areas, the snowiest areas, the stormiest areas, the driest areas, and so on. Don't leave home without it.

David Savageau, *Retirement Places Rated.* Prentice-Hall Press, a division of Simon & Schuster, Inc., 15 Columbus Circle, New York, NY 10023. 1990. Although purportedly about retirement, it is useful information for anyone. Compares 151 top geographical areas in the U.S.

G. Scott Thomas, *The Rating Guide to Life in America's Small Cities.* Prometheus Books, 700 E. Amherst St., Buffalo, NY 14215. 1990. Compares 219 small cities in areas of climate, economics, education, health care, housing, public safety, transportation, proximity to urban centers, sophistication, and diversions.

Jill Andresky Fraser, *The Best U.S. Cities for Working Women.* Plume Books, New American Library, 1633 Broadway, New York, NY 10019. 1986.

In the end, you want to try to come up with three names, because if your first choice doesn't pan out for some reason, you will have a backup, and also a backup to that backup.

WHEN YOU WANT TO 'GO RURAL'

It may be you will discover, as you go about this task, that your idea of *paradise* is to 'go rural' -- to move, at last, to the country. If so, take this vision seriously. You only have one life. Just be sure to investigate it *thoroughly*. Fortunately, if this idea interests you, there are a number of resources to help you move to the country.[5]

"Look before you leap" is always a splendid caution, and it means -- in this particular case -- that if there's a place that sounds good to you, *be sure* to go visit it as a tourist before you up and move there. I mean, go there, and talk to *everyone*. Get the good side, and the bad. Then weigh what you learn.

You will find that one of the side benefits from such a proposed move is that rural life is cheaper than in metropolitan areas -- which you probably already know.

---

4. Detailed instructions on how to do this are to be found in my workbook entitled *How To Create A Picture of Your Ideal Job.* You can order it from the publisher, Ten Speed Press, Box 7123, Berkeley CA 94707. It costs $5.95.

5. They include:

William L. Seavey, ed., *The Eden Seeker's Guide.* 1989. Loompanics Unlimited, PO Box 1197, Port Townsend, WA 98368, or from the author (see below). What kinds of places offer optimum quality of life. The author also has a business called *Greener Pastures Institute,* which publishes a newsletter entitled *Greener Pastures Gazette* (Sample back issue: $3). They also have a pamphlet which tells you the basic resources for moving to the country or a small town. Greener Pastures Institute, P.O. Box 2190, Henderson, NV 89009-7009, 800-688-9017, or 818-355-1670.

John F. Edwards, *Starting Fresh: How to Plan for a Simpler, Happier, and More Fulfilling New Life in the Country.* Prima Publishing & Communications, P.O. Box 1260SF, Rocklin, CA 95677.

Frank Levering and Wanda Urbanska, *Simple Living.* Viking Penguin, 375 Hudson St., New York, NY 10014. 1992.

Frank Kirkpatrick, *How to Find and Buy Your Business in the Country.* Storey Communications, Inc., Pownal, VT 05261. 1985. How to find a simpler life-style, away from the hustle and bustle of the city.

Marilyn and Tom Ross, *Country Bound!™ Trade Your Business Suit Blues For Blue Jean Dreams™.* Communication Creativity, P.O. Box 909, 425 Cedar St., Buena Vista, CO 81211. 1992.

WHEN YOU WANT TO
WORK OVERSEAS

On the other hand, if you've always wanted to live and work overseas, then that too is a dream you should explore. I will assume here that we are talking about job-hunters in the U.S. who want to move to Europe, Africa, Asia, Canada, or South America. However, there are readers of this book who live in those places and want to move to the U.S. Much of what I have to say here will apply, as general principles, also to them.[6]

First of all, be sure you're not going overseas in order to find Utopia. Utopia rarely lives up to expectations. Even if (big *if*) you do not find the same things that irritate you about your present country, I guarantee you that you will find some brand new things to irritate you.

---

6. Allan Wernick's *The International Student Handbook: A Legal Guide to Studying, Working, and Living in the United States,* published by the American Immigration Law Foundation, 1400 Eye St. NW, Suite 1200, Washington, D.C. 20005. 1992. May also give you some helpful pointers about a move to the U.S. They may be able to recommend other resources, as well. Their telephone, if you need it, is 202-371-9377.

Regarding the mechanics of going overseas: many people assume you find an overseas job by packing a bag, buying a ticket and passing out resumes once you reach your foreign destination. No, no, no. Work-permit requirements and high unemployment make finding jobs at foreign destinations often difficult, and sometimes impossible.

For example, if you were to study employment classifieds in, say, a newspaper from London, England, you would at first sight think you had found some grand opportunities for yourself. *Unfortunately,* these are in most cases job opportunities open only to British nationals or citizens of EEC nations. What is true in England is true elsewhere. Your U.S. citizenship will actually preclude you from working in a foreign country -- even Canada -- unless your employer can prove that a local national is unavailable to take the job, and thus secure a work permit for *you.*

Your wisest approach to overseas employment is to conduct your job-hunt for an overseas job while you are still here in the U.S. How do you go about it? Well, first of all, research the country or countries that interest you, as to living conditions, conditions of employment, et cetera. Talk to everyone you possibly can who has in fact been overseas, most especially to those country or countries. A nearby large university will probably have such faculty or students *(ask)*. Companies in your city which have overseas branches *(your library should be able to tell you which they are)* should be able to lead you to people also -- possibly to the names and addresses of personnel who are still "over there" to whom you can write for the information you are seeking. Alternatively, try asking every single person you meet for the next week (at the supermarket checkout, at your work, at home, at church or synagogue, etc.) if they know someone who used to live overseas and now lives here in your city or town. You may be amazed at how many normal looking people are actually world travelers. By doing research with such people, you will learn a great deal. Find out what they liked and didn't like, about the country which interests you. Find out what they know about the conditions for working over there.

Next, you need to research what kinds of job possibilities exist in that country. Every *successful* overseas search starts with *some* sources of information on "who's hiring now." *Which* sources you access, and how you make use of them, will greatly affect your chances of landing an overseas assignment.[7]

What do I mean? Well, for openers, beware of such sources as employment agencies that promise to find you an overseas job for an advance fee. This is always a scam. This fleecing industry has flourished for years, with a few individuals often running scores of companies under an assortment of names. Such companies regularly go out of business or file for bankruptcy *once they've fleeced enough suckers.* Beware. If you patronize them, you will be out your fee, and have nothing to show for it.

---

7. As for the general facts about living overseas, books get outdated very fast; but currently the live ones are:

Robert Sanborn, Ed.D., *How To Get A Job in Europe: The Insider's Guide.* Surrey Books, 230 E. Ohio St., Suite 120, Chicago, IL 60611. 1991. Includes tips on how to find a job in the New Europe.

Dale Chambers, *Passport to Overseas Employment: 100,000 Job Opportunities Abroad.* Arco Books, Simon & Schuster, Inc., 200 Old Tappan Rd., Old Tappan, NJ 07675. 1990. Deals with overseas study programs, international careers, temporary employment, airlines and cruises, embassies and consulates, United Nations, and volunteer programs.

Howard Schuman, *Making It Abroad–The International Job Hunting Guide.* John Wiley & Sons, 605 Third Ave., New York, NY 10158-0012. 1988.

Joy Mullett and Lois Darley, *Careers for People Who Love to Travel.* Arco Books, 200 Old Tappan Rd., Old Tappan, NJ 07675. 1986.

Curtis W. Casewit, *How to Get a Job Overseas.* Arco Publishing, Inc., 200 Old Tappan Rd., Old Tappan, NJ 07675. 1984.

Susan Griffith, *Work Your Way Around the World.* Writer's Digest Books/North Light Books, 1507 Dana Ave., Cincinnati, OH 45207. 1989.

Susan Griffith and Sharon Legg, *The Au Pair & Nanny's Guide to Working Abroad.* Writer's Digest Books/North Light Books, 1507 Dana Ave., Cincinnati, OH 45207. 1989.

Mary Green and Stanley Gillmar, *How to Be an Importer and Pay for Your World Travel.* Ten Speed Press, Box 7123, Berkeley, CA 94707.

For teachers wishing to work overseas, the Department of Defense publishes a pamphlet, with application, entitled *Overseas Employment Opportunities for Educators.* Write to U.S. Department of Defense Dependent Schools, Recruitment and Assignments Section, Hoffman Bldg. I, 2461 Eisenhower Ave., Alexandria, VA 22331-1100, for the pamphlet/application.

Your library should also have books such as Angel, Juvenal, *Dictionary of American Firms Operating in Foreign Countries* (World Trade Academy Press).

And to research overseas public companies which sell stock in this country, the Securities Exchange Commission will have their Form 6-K, which they filed in order to be able to sell that stock.

If you want more books about overseas work (or study), write to WorldWise Books, P.O. Box 3030, Oakton, VA 22124, and/or Writer's Digest Books, 1507 Dana Ave., Cincinnati, OH 45207, and ask for their catalogs.

Beware also of directories advertised in newspapers, etc. as *listing overseas employers*. Many, though not all, of these job listings are out of date and tend to report on "who *was* hiring" rather than "who is hiring *now*."

You can still make effective use of any such directory by taking care that *if* you contact an organization listed therein, you include a cover letter which requests that your resume be kept on file 'for further consideration *if there are no current openings*.' As I have emphasized elsewhere in this book, pure dumb luck -- which means, having your name in 'the right place at the right time' -- plays a crucial role in finding most jobs. Since you can't get *over there*, at the moment, you will have to rely more heavily on resumes here than I would normally advise, to keep your name in the right place. In the case of overseas employment, the more employers who have your resume, the better.

Rather than the kind of resources mentioned above, I think your best bet for job leads are authoritative directories such as

those listed below.[8] Also, in your job-search do not forget that
the U.S. Government is a heavy overseas employer. Understand-
ably, in the post-USSR world, with the end of the cold war, there
are numerous cutbacks going on overseas. Nonetheless, this
possibility is still well worth exploring. *How* you explore it, is
described in the book listed below.[9]

If you run into an absolute stonewall in your search for an
overseas job, there are two backup strategies for you to consider.
The first is to seek an international internship. How you do this
is described below.[10] The second strategy begins with the fact
that many companies operating in this country, both domestic

---

8. *International Employment Hotline,* Box 3030, Oakton, VA 22124. Published monthly
since 1980, this newsletter provides job-search advice and names and addresses of
employers currently hiring for international work in government, nonprofit organizations, and private companies. They also have other titles on overseas work, which you
can ask them about. Incidentally, do *not* confuse this reputable firm with International
Employment Hotline in Amsterdam, Holland, or London; there is *no* connection
whatsoever.

The Fischer Report and *Manlink,* Group Fischer, 110 Newport Center Dr., Suite 150,
Newport Beach, CA 92660. You can write to them and ask for their pamphlet "Group
Fischer Information Services," which describes their programs and package, whose
cost is expensive, from the point of view of a *poor* job-hunter. The *best* sentences in their
pamphlet: "If you are looking for a job, you should understand that no one can get you
a job except you. You will be hired because you are in the right place, at the right time,
with the right skills. . . . The ONLY services that anyone can render you in your job
search are: 1) Information, 2) Introduction, 3) Advice. No employment agency, employment service, job listing service, membership organization (excluding unions),
recruiting or executive search firms, or any publication can do more. How this is done
is what makes the difference." Amen, brother.

9. Will Cantrell and Francine Modderno, *How To Find an Overseas Job with the U.S.
Government.* Worldwise Books, P.O. Box 3030, Oakton, VA 22124. 1992. Comprehensive
guide to finding work with the organization that hires the greatest number of Americans abroad. In-depth job descriptions and application procedures are provided for
over 17 individual government agencies, along with information on how to complete
the government's standard application for employment (SF-171), and how to prepare
for and pass the Foreign Service exam. Highly recommended.

10. Will Cantrell and Francine Modderno, *International Internships and Volunteer Programs.* Worldwise Books, P.O. Box 3030, Oakton, VA 22124. 1992. Up-to-date information on programs serving as 'stepping-stones' to international careers, for both students
and professionals. Positions include salaried and volunteer opportunities, both abroad
and also here in the U.S.

Arthur Frommer, *New World of Travel 1992: A Guide to Alternative Vacations in America
and Throughout the World.* 5th ed. A Frommer Book, published by Prentice-Hall Trade
Division, One Gulf+Western Plaza, New York, NY 10023. 1991. Revised annually. A
wonderful book by a great guy, on opportunities for travel here and abroad.

and foreign-owned, *have branches overseas.* Thus, *sometimes* your ticket to getting overseas may be to start working here in the U.S. for such a company, hoping they will eventually send you overseas. It *does* happen. And if it happens, they will likely take care of the visa and work permit red tape, pick up your travel bill, and provide other helpful benefits. Unfortunately, however, you can't *count* on their ever sending you overseas. In other words, it's a big fat gamble. *You* have to decide whether you're willing to take it, or not.

If you decide it is worth it, you'll find the names of such organizations by going to your local library and asking the reference librarian to help you find such directories as these: *Principal International Businesses,* published by Dun's Marketing Service; *International Directory of Corporate Affiliations,* published by Corporate Affiliations Information Services, of the National Register Publishing Company; and *International Organizations, revised annually,* published by Gale Research, Inc.

Lastly, contact every friend you have who already lives overseas -- even if it's not in the country that is your target. Ask for their counsel, advice, help, and prayers. They went before you; hopefully they can now be your guide, and door-opener.

One final word about hunting for an overseas job: above all, be patient. The search for an overseas job takes *more* time than looking for a job in this country. Don't expect to be in an exotic foreign capital within 90 days. Perseverance is the key.

EXPLORING THE FARAWAY
PLACE OF YOUR CHOICE

And now, whether your choice is overseas or here in your own country, whether your choice is urban or rural, there is the $64,000 question: how do you go about finding out about *jobs* in your chosen city/town? Naturally, there are *ways.*

If it has a local newspaper, *subscribe,* even while you are still living *here.* Read the whole paper, when it comes, however long delayed. Look particularly for: news of companies that are *expanding,* news of *promotions* or *transfers* (that creates vacancies *down below* in 'the company store'), and the like.

If you can get the Chamber of Commerce there, or someone

you know there, to send you their phone book, particularly the Yellow Pages, by all means do so.

And finally, when you're ready to go visit that town or city *in*

person (on your summer vacation, perhaps) try to line up contacts and interviews *ahead of time,* before you go there. If you have trouble connecting with someone, see if that town has any church, synagogue, or national organization that you belong to here. Write, tell them of your local affiliation, and ask for their help in finding the person you're trying to connect with.

If you have a spouse or partner, who works, they should be doing the same kind of research, and setting up the same kinds of interviews, as you are.

When you get there, in addition to interviewing about jobs, you will want to explore (of course) the issues of apartment vs. house, of rental vs. buying, and the like. Back home again, you will want to weigh what you have learned, and weigh whether or not it will be easy to sell your present home, if you own one -- or are on your way toward owning one.

WHAT TO DO
WHEN YOU CAN'T GET THERE,
TO VISIT OR INTERVIEW

If your finances are tight, it may not be possible for you to go there, at least in the forseeable future. In which case, you do your best to research the place from a distance, as described above. And when that research seems complete, and you have discovered some organizations that, at a distance, look like *possibles,* you then contact them by mail or through whatever contacts you have developed in that city or town, as I am about to describe.

You will first want to research each organization that you are planning to approach by mail, so that you know *who* to address the letter to, *by name.* And then you want to keep in mind that that letter will carry a lot more weight if you can mention, in it, the name of *a mutual friend.*

Toward that end, it is important that you have previously discovered people in that city or town who can be your *contacts.* For example, if you went to college, find out if any graduates of that college live in this new city or town. (Contact the alumni office of your college, and ask.) Also any church, synagogue, or national organization you belong to, that has a presence there -- as mentioned above. Also ask your friends locally, if they know of anyone who lives in that city or town.

Use these names *if* they know the employer to whom you are writing, because *generally speaking* your letter to employers in that faraway city will will receive much more favorable attention *if* you mention some mutual friend, than would be the case if you merely wrote as a total stranger.[11]

Should you also enclose a resume? Professional opinions vary widely. *Everything* depends on the nature of the resume, and the nature of the person you are sending it to. With some employers I know, a resume is *death.* It will *ensure* that your letter is merely tossed aside. Other employers like to see one. Just to

---

11. Unless -- the job-hunter's nightmare -- your mutual "friend"/contact has *misrepresented* how close he or she is to your target employer, and as a matter of fact said employer can't stand the sight of this "mutual friend." *It has happened.* It is to die. Asking a question beforehand, of the "mutual friend," like "How *well* do you know him -- or her?" may help avoid this.

play it safe, I think a well-composed letter summarizing all you would say in a resume, may be your best bet.

CONCLUSION

There is a great joy in moving to a new place, particularly if it is to a place that you love. One job-hunter described this joy to me, in words which many other job-hunters could echo:

"In 1990, my wife and I took a trip out to the Southwest from our home in Annapolis, Maryland, to see the Grand Canyon and sights like that. We both fell in love with the Southwest, and said, 'Wouldn't it be great if I could get a job out here as a highway engineer, and maybe we could work with the Native Americans.' Back in Annapolis, I purchased Parachute and read it with extreme interest. So I started some network planning, and scheduled another upcoming trip to Arizona in February of 1992, planning to visit various engineering offices and check out living conditions.

"Meanwhile, I visited the U.S.G.S. Headquarters in Reston, Virginia. On the way out, I noticed an ad on the bulletin board for 'Highway Engineer–Bureau of Indian Affairs, Gallup, New Mexico.' Naturally, I applied for the job but received notice that the position had been cancelled. Disappointed, my wife and I decided to each spend a day in prayer. On the following day I received a call from that office in Gallup informing me there was another position for Highway Planner now open; was I still interested? Still interested?!

"Using your advice, I called the Bureau in Gallup and got the names of the bosses of the various divisions or sections that would impinge upon my application. I sent in the application to the person by name who was the chief decision-maker. In February of 1992 we carried out the trip I had been planning, now including a visit to Gallup. We visited headquarters there, though they weren't yet ready to formally interview, since not all applicants had yet been screened. However, it was a useful visit, and on returning, I wrote Thank You notes to all the people I had met, and hoped for the best.

"In March I received another phone call, asking for further information; I used this to invite myself out for an actual interview, at my expense. My offer was accepted, I was out there in two days, the interview went well, and I received official notice to report for work in May. We were ecstatic! And we found a house in Gallup, through a friend in

Annapolis who had a friend in Gallup, who knew of a co-worker who was moving out.

"In short, ours is a wonderful story. Who would think a 66 year old man could leave one job and move into another full-time job, at a salary almost equal to his present one, in a place 2600 miles away, that he and his wife truly love! What a blessing! And what you said has stuck with me all this time: I've remembered to write my Thank You notes."

This is the true joy in life –
That being used for a purpose recognized
By myself as a mighty one . . .
I am of the opinion that my life belongs
To the whole community,
And as long as I live
It is my privilege to do for it
Whatever I can . . .
Life is no brief candle to me.
It's a sort of splendid torch
Which I've got to hold up
For the moment
And I want to make it burn
As brightly as possible
Before handing it on
To future generations.

George Bernard Shaw

CHAPTER EIGHT

How to Choose
Or Change
A Career

Chapter 8

Whether you're employed or unemployed, the basic question you always have to ask yourself about your current (or most recent) job is: "Is this *really* what I want to do for the rest of my life?"

By permission of Johnny Hart and Creators Syndicate, Inc.

The answer often is "No," -- for millions and millions of workers. And maybe for you. This doesn't necessarily mean that you made a big fat mistake in ever taking your current job (though that happens often enough, Heaven knows).

But even if it *was* a good choice, it is a law of the '90s that jobs can alter profoundly in a day and a night. You are given new additional responsibilities, without any raise in salary. Or your much-beloved supervisor moves on, leaving you working for a jerk. Or, your workplace comes under stringent budget cuts. Or your funding is lost, entirely. Whatever. The job which was a perfect match for you just a year ago, is now *'the job from hell.'*

You may want to change careers for other reasons, too. When we are very young, work is largely a matter of how to find bread to eat, and clothes to wear, and how to put a roof over our head. But as we move through the various stages of our life, our work becomes increasingly a matter *also* of how our soul lives out its dreams. For example, if we have been working too hard, we want to figure out how we can take more time 'to smell the roses.'

And, through each of our *work* choices during our lifetime, we increasingly find ourselves looking for the work we feel we were *born* to do. This is what we mean when we speak of looking for **our vocation,** or **calling.** By *vocation* we mean work which is the deepest fulfillment of our being, reflecting who we most truly are. By *calling* we mean *from God* -- in whom over 94% of us believe (see the Epilogue).

Most of us are engaged in a life-long search for, and journey toward, *meaning* -- a process in which career-change plays an important part.

IS THIS THE RIGHT TIME
TO CHANGE CAREERS?

Whenever we are unhappy in our present job or career, we usually can hear two voices raging back and forth within our mind:

Is this what you want to do for the rest of your life?

"No."

Then what are you going to do about it?

"I don't know. Perhaps this just isn't the right time."

And so the dialogue goes -- while in our inmost spirit we know that waiting for 'the right time' is *often* just another name for *procrastination.*

Friend, there will probably never be *a right time.* Conditions will always be *difficult.* Obstacles will always be *in your way,* which you must overcome. It will always be a challenge, if you decide to launch out into the deep and mysterious destiny to which you feel called, by the dreams of your soul.

Yet a time comes in each of our lives when we *know* we simply *must* accept that challenge. When we know we must go do what we really want to do with our life -- no matter how hard the times, and no matter how difficult the struggle may be. We know that there is always a chance that we may not succeed at it. But we know we will never feel we have really lived our life, until we at least *try.*

U.S. Statistics

The average person currently can expect to have three different careers during their lifetime.

In the most recent year surveyed, 1986, it was discovered that 10 million workers changed careers[1] that year.

5.3 million of them changed careers *voluntarily*, and in 7 out of 10 cases their income went up;

1.3 million of them changed careers *involuntarily*, because of what happened to them in the economy, and in 7 out of 10 cases, their income went down;

3.4 million of them changed careers for a *mixture* of voluntary and involuntary reasons (such as needing to go from part-time to full-time work, etc.).

Despite the *myth* that people only contemplate career-change in mid-life, in point of fact *only one million* out of the ten were in mid-life. People can and do change careers at *all* ages.

Many experts think, however, that the remainder of the '90s will see a lot more 'mid-life career-change,' since this is the decade when a whopping number -- the U.S.'s 76 million 'baby boomers' -- are entering mid-life.[2]

---

1. The word **career** remains a very fuzzy word in the English language, but there are three principal senses in which it is used. It is used, first of all, to mean *work* in contrast to *learning* or *leisure*. Thus when clothing ads speak of "a career outfit," they are referring to clothes which are worn primarily at work, rather than during learning-activities or leisure-activities. It is used, secondly, to sum up *a person's whole life in the world of work.* Thus when people say of someone at the end of their life, "He or she had a brilliant career," they are not referring to a particular occupation, but to *all* the occupations this person ever held, and all the work this person ever did. Thirdly, in its most common sense, as I indicated above, it is used as a synonym for the word *occupation* or *job* -- particularly where that occupation or job offers opportunity for promotion and advancement, toward the top. (This *movement toward a goal* is its most primitive meaning, as it dates from the origin of the word. *Career* comes from the Latin *carrus*, referring to a race-track where horses compete in an effort to win a race.) *From the article on "Careers" in* Collier's Encyclopedia, *written by the author. Copyright © 1991 by Macmillan Educational Company.*

2. The following resources deal with career-change at mid-life:

Paula I. Robbins, *Successful Midlife Career Change: Self-Understanding and Strategies for Action.* AMACOM, 135 W. 50th St., New York, NY 10020. Very thorough, very helpful. The best book dealing with this problem.

Betsy Jaffe, Ed.D., *Altered Ambitions: What's Next in Your Life? Winning Strategies To Reshape Your Career.* Donald I. Fine, Inc., 19 W. 21st St., New York, NY 10010. 1991.

Godfrey Golzen and Philip Plumbley, *Changing Your Job After 35.* Kogan Page Ltd., 120 Pentonville Rd., London N1 9JN. 1988.

Jack Falvey, *What's Next? Career Strategies After 35.* Williamson Publishing, Charlotte, VT 05445. 1987.

And, in some ways, it is a journey in which we cannot fail. Even if we are not able to *pull it off*, in any way that the world calls 'successful,' we know we will at the very least be a better man or woman, for having tried. There is something about *adversity* and *challenge* that tests and refines *character*, even as the fire tempers steel. A challenge toward growth and change -- willingly accepted -- can often bring out the very best in us.

If nothing else, it brings *clarity of vision*. As the late Sylvia Sims,[3] the legendary singer, once said about adversity, "I'm down to the bottom of my sound, but I'm up to the clearest understanding of my life."

THE EIGHT PARTS OF A JOB OR CAREER

There are eight parts to a career (or job), and career-change involves changing one or more of those eight parts.

We can illustrate those eight parts with an occupation most people are familiar with, namely that of a waiter or waitress at a restaurant: (1) *the workplace:* here it is the restaurant, an indoor place (usually) with lots of supervision; (2) *the stated goal:* here it is to wait on customers, keep them happy, and make a profit for the restaurant owners; (3) *the tasks assigned:* here they may include: to clean and set tables, to bring the customers a menu, water and bread; to take their orders; to hand the orders in to the kitchen; to serve the orders, when ready; to stay alert to any additional service the customers may require; to bring them their check when done; and to clear off and set the table again; (4) *the tools:* here they are the uniform (if there is one), cleaning-rags, silverware, napkins, plates, menus, food, checks, pen or pencil, and perhaps a calculator; (5) *the salary:* here it is whatever the boss and waiter/waitress agree upon, plus tips, of course; (6) *the time involved:* here it is whatever number of hours there are on the worker's shift; (7) *the talents or skills needed:* here they are: *punctuality* -- being able to get to work on time; *taking instructions* from both boss and customer; *advising* (customers on what is good on the menu, if they ask); *empathy* (conveying

---

3. Born in *1918*, died in *1992*.

warmth); *memory* (remembering who ordered what); *finger-dexterity* (being skillful at handling dishes); *copying* (prices on to the check); *computing* (the total on the check); and *problem-solving* (when problems arise, with the customer); (8) *the fields of knowledge needed:* here they include: *food* (what the items on the menu mean); *mathematics* (addition, and subtraction, at least); *machine operation* (knowing how to operate a cash register and/or calculator).

If you're contemplating a new career because you've been unhappy in your previous job or career, it is useful to sit down and figure out *which* of these eight areas you were *most* unhappy with.

'THE ESSENCE'
OF CAREER-CHANGE

As I said, career-change can involve changing any, or all, of these eight parts.

But *in its essence* it is a change in *two* of these areas, above all. Those are: the skills you want to use, and the fields of knowledge you want to use them with.

It will help you to understand this, if you memorize two simple equations:

1. Skills ≈ general job-titles.[4]   Job-titles ≈ skills. *and*
2. Knowledges ≈ field.[5]   Field ≈ knowledges.

Note that in the equations above we use the sign for *correspond to* (≈) instead of the *equals* (=) sign. The equation is *approximate*, not *exact*.

The *essence* of a career-change is that you change one or both of these: your general job-title, *and* the field you operate in. You do this by *redefining* what skills you most want to use, and/or by *redefining* what knowledges you most want to use them with.

You may change just the field, but not your general job-title (**A** to **B** in the diagram on the next page). Or you may change just your general job-title, but not your field (**A** to **C** in the diagram). Or, for the completest and most *dramatic* career-change you may change *both* (**A** to **D** in the diagram).

Types of Career Change Visualized

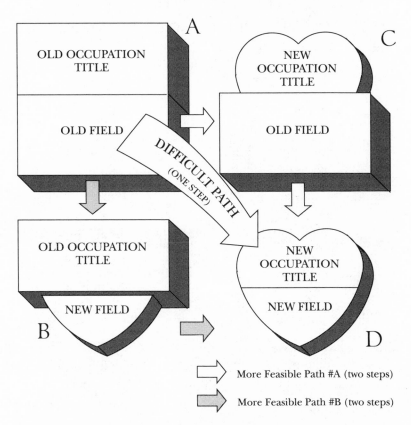

More Feasible Path #A (two steps)

More Feasible Path #B (two steps)

To illustrate, let's say you're an accountant, and you work for a television station. If you move to a new field, but keep the same general job-title (**A** to **B**), then you might, let us say, become an accountant with a medical firm. If you keep the same field, but move to a new general job-title (**A** to **C**), you might become an reporter at that television station. And if you

---

4. A general job-title is *not* the same thing as an organizational title. A general job-title refers to *skills* -- such as *teacher, mechanic, accountant,* etc. Whereas an organizational title would be something like *assistant bookkeeper, comptroller,* etc. Okay, now: if you start with a general job-title that you like, then *that* title determines what skills you will get a chance to use. On the other hand, if you reverse that process, and begin by determining what skills you would like to use, then they will *point to* a general job-title.

5. If you choose your field first, then that field determines what knowledges you need to use or acquire. On the other hand, if you reverse that process, and begin by determining what fields of knowledge you are most at home in, and enjoy -- e.g., *gardening, airplanes, antiques, travel, religion, psychology, etc.* -- they then *point to* a field.

Types of Career Change Visualized

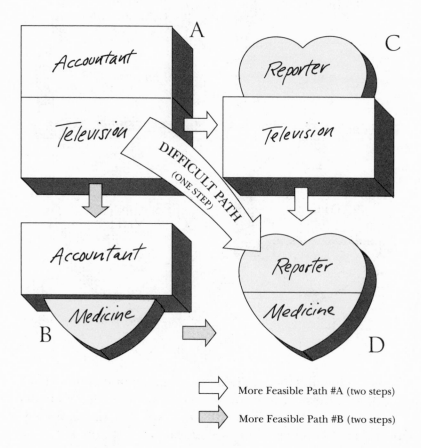

Accountant / Television — A

Reporter / Television — C

DIFFICULT PATH (ONE STEP)

Accountant / Medicine — B

Reporter / Medicine — D

⇨ More Feasible Path #A (two steps)

⇨ More Feasible Path #B (two steps)

change both title and field (**A** to **D**), you might become a reporter for a medical journal. So, the completest and most dramatic career-change would, in this case, be that of moving from being an accountant at a television station, to a reporter for a medical journal. New general job-title, new field.

Note, in the diagram above, that were you to pursue this profoundest career-change (**A** to **D**), there are three ways you can move into your new career -- gradually or abruptly, in steps or all at once -- as shown by the arrows.

MUST I GO BACK TO SCHOOL?

When people change careers, voluntarily or involuntarily, it is widely assumed that there is only *one* way to go about it: *go back to school, for retraining*. With this approach, you look at the diagram above, and you see that career-change involves a field and a general job-title -- so you *choose* a field or general job-title -- often on the basis of very little knowledge -- and then go major in that field at some nearby college or university.

This is the way that 98% of all career-choice or career-change is done. But there are four problems with this approach to career-change.

Problem #1: There's a bewildering menu of choices out there. In the U.S., for example, experts can *name* at least 12,860 different occupations or careers that you might choose between, and these have 8,000 alternative job-titles, for a total of approximately 20,000. A description of all these 20,000 occupations or careers is to be found in the *Dictionary of Occupational Titles*, familiarly known as the *D.O.T.*, published by the U.S. Department of Labor's Bureau of Labor Statistics.[6] Similar volumes exist in a number of other countries.

---

6. The D.O.T. is updated periodically -- most recently in 1991, with the previous revision 1977, supplemented in 1982, 1986, and 1987.

Most people, however, find that trying to choose between 20,000 of anything, is almost humanly impossible. That's why, as it's turned out, ninety per cent of the workforce of 119 million workers in the U.S. are employed in 300 job-titles, and fifty per cent are employed in just 50 job-titles.[7] A lot of these careers don't require you to go back to school for retraining. On the other hand, even for those that do, if none of them really interest you, then what's the point?

Problem #2: Many times, if you enroll in a particular degree program, you spend *a lot of time* learning knowledges and skills you really already have. I once spent a weekend with a group of graduate students in Spokane, Washington, who asked me to help them identify the skills and fields of knowledge which they already possessed; when they saw that they already had the skills they were allegedly trying to pick up in their graduate school program, they were more than just a little *mad.* And who can blame them? Why work so hard to acquire what you already possess?

Problem #3: You *think* that *if* you get this degree, you will be much more *marketable* and able to command a higher salary -- but unfortunately there is no guarantee, *whatsoever,* that this is true. Every year thousands and thousands of people finish a degree program, and then find out they *still* cannot find a job. The degree does *not* come with a job automatically attached. If you could see my mail, from dejected adult-graduates, 22 years of age, 30 years of age, 40 years of age, 50 years of age, who

---

7. These 50 job-titles are: automobile mechanics, carpenters, electricians, light- or heavy-truck drivers, construction laborers, welders & cutters, groundskeepers & gardeners, electrical and electronic engineers, freight, stock, and material movers or handlers, guards and police, production occupations supervisors, farmers, commodities sales representatives, laborers, lawyers, farm workers, stockhandlers & baggers, insurance sales, janitors & cleaners, managers & administrators, supervisors & proprietors, machine operators, teachers -- university, college, secondary and elementary school, stock & inventory clerks, accountants & auditors, underwriters and other financial officers, secretaries, receptionists, childcare workers, registered nurses, typists, bookkeepers, textile sewing machine operators, nursing aides, orderlies & attendants, hairdressers & cosmetologists, waiters & waitresses, maids and housemen, cashiers, general office clerks, administrative support occupations, sales workers, computer operators, miscellaneous food preparation occupations, production inspectors, checkers & examiners, cooks, real estate sales, and assemblers.

lament that their new degree *(bought with blood, sweat and tears)* hasn't improved their chances of finding a job in their new career *one bit,* you would cry. In their letters, they are still unemployed, a year or two after graduation, or hired only for a pittance, often in occupations totally unrelated to their hard-won degree. They feel our culture lied to them, and they are depressed, and often very bitter. Thus they illustrate the unwitting irony in the phrase, "*Getting a job by degrees.*"

Problem #4: Even if you do find a job, there's often a dramatic chasm (the size of the Grand Canyon) between the skills and fields of knowledge that you *thought* you were going to get a chance to use in this career, vs. the reality. *Oops!* Incidentally, this happens to many first-time college graduates, as well as to those who go back later in life. And so it is, that your new career may turn out to be just as unfulfilling as your old career. You will be just as miserable, only in a different environment. (This will remind some people of jumping into a second marriage without having first taken time to learn the lessons from the first).

The moral here is: don't assume that the only way to make a career-change is by going back to school. That takes a lot of your time, a lot of your money, and doesn't do *a thing* to guarantee you a job in your new career. It *can't* be the only way.

OKAY, WHAT'S 'THE OTHER WAY'? (THERE MUST BE ONE)

The other way -- the creative way -- involves forgetting about going back to school, at least for the time being, and forget about *starting with* a field and a general job-title.

You start instead by doing some hard homework on yourself, first doing a thorough inventory of *What* skills you most enjoy using; and then doing a thorough inventory of *Where* you want to use those skills, in terms of your favorite knowledges which you already have or want to acquire. Then you let those *point to* a new career, whose name you discover through some investigation, interviews, and research.

This alternative approach looks like this, and will be the subject of our next three chapters:

The Creative Process of Career Change

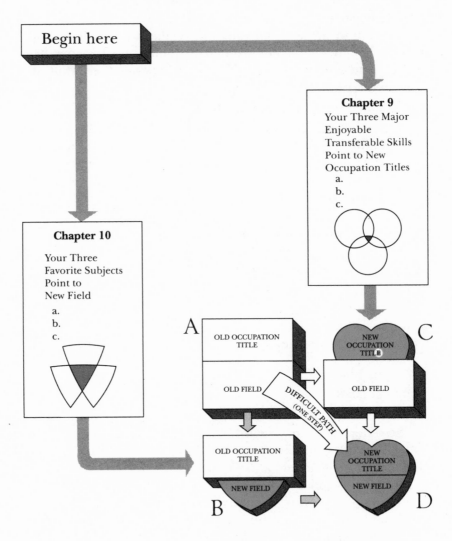

Begin here

Chapter 9
Your Three Major Enjoyable Transferable Skills Point to New Occupation Titles
a.
b.
c.

Chapter 10

Your Three Favorite Subjects Point to New Field
a.
b.
c.

A

OLD OCCUPATION TITLE

OLD FIELD

NEW OCCUPATION TITLE

C

OLD FIELD

DIFFICULT PATH (ONE STEP)

OLD OCCUPATION TITLE

NEW FIELD

B

NEW OCCUPATION TITLE

NEW FIELD

D

Then, you do interviewing and some library research to discover what title, and what field, your skills and knowledge point to. (**Chapter 11**)

LET'S NOT BE SILLY:
SOMETIMES SCHOOL
WILL TURN OUT
TO BE NECESSARY

When you finish the process illustrated above -- that is, when you have finished doing the work in Chapters 9, 10, and 11 -- it may turn out that you *do* need some further schooling, for the career you eventually decide upon. But then again, it may not.

It is claimed by experts that one-third of all careers require less than twelve years of schooling;[8] one-third of all careers require at least a high school degree; and one-third of all careers require a college degree, or beyond. So, two-thirds of all careers *don't* require you to go back to school. *But,* one-third do.

Example: if after inventorying your skills and knowledges, and doing your own research, you discover that you want to move from being a typist to being a surgeon, this *will* require going back to school.

Example: if after inventorying your skills and knowledges, and doing your own research, you discover that you want to move from being a sales manager to being an author, this may *not* require going back to school at all.

The point is, with the creative approach to career-change, you make this decision *after* some thoughtful homework on yourself, and after some careful investigation -- and not on whim or impulse. What do I mean by *whim and impulse?* Once, I overheard two college students talking, in Central Park in New York City. We'll call them Jim and Fred. In half a minute of conversation they perfectly illustrated *whim and impulse:*

Jim: Hey, what are you majoring in?
Fred: Physics.
Jim: Physics? Man, you shouldn't major in physics.
Computer science is the thing these days.
Fred: Naw, I like physics.

---

8. *The Guide to Basic Skills Jobs, Vol. 1.* RPM Press, Inc., Verndale, MN 56481. 1986. A catalog of viable jobs for individuals with only basic work skills. This volume identifies 5,000 major occupations within the U.S. economy which require no more than an eighth grade level of education, and no more than one year of specific vocational preparation. Immensely useful book.

Jim: Man, physics doesn't pay much.
Fred: Really? What does?
Jim: Computer science. You should switch to computer science.
Fred: Okay, I'll look into it tomorrow.

You see my point. Huge life-decisions often are made in the whim of a moment. This is, indeed, the way most career choices (and career-changes) are made. No wonder surveys of worker dissatisfaction find that up to 80%, or four out of every five workers, are dissatisfied with some important aspects of their jobs or careers. *It's not a pretty picture.*

The alternative to *whim and impulse* is *planning,* and *hard thinking* and *work.* For the lazy, this is not good news. But as we grow older, and hopefully wiser, most of us begin to see the merit of this kind of homework.

TRAVELS WITH FARLEY by Phil Frank © 1982 Field Enterprises, Inc. Courtesy of Field Newspaper Syndicate

Choices made intelligently, based on the sure knowledge of who we are, almost always turn out to be far superior to choices made by a roll of the dice.

This is why it is so important for you to do your homework, identifying your favorite and strongest skills, and your favorite fields of knowledge, before you choose a career, change a career, or go out to pound the pavement.

Herein lies your safety, for as Jim and Fred made clear:

You have got to know what it is you want, or else someone is going to sell you a bill of goods somewhere along the line that can do irreparable damage to your self-esteem, your sense of worth, and your stewardship of the talents that God gave you.

Work is Love made visible.
And if you can't work with love but only with distaste,
It is better that you should leave your work
and sit at the gate of the temple and
take alms of the people who work with joy.

Kahlil Gibran, *The Prophet*

CHAPTER NINE

The Systematic Approach To The Job-Hunt and Career-Change:

PART I

What
Skills Do You Most Enjoy Using?

Chapter 9

SHOULD I DO THIS HOMEWORK EVEN IF I'M NOT THINKING ABOUT CHANGING CAREERS?

Oh yes. You want to remember, as we go through these next three chapters, that this process of creative career-change is *also* the process one must use for ***creative job-hunting,*** when times are difficult, you are unemployed, and you just can't find your old kind of work, *or even a new kind of work,* no matter how hard you've tried, following all the tips in our earlier chapters.

Even if you're happily employed, many *do* these chapters in order to get a fresh view of what their skills and talents are. As one worker wrote, "I like my present job a lot. Still, the skills inventory you have people do in your book is something I do every two or three years. Each time I do it, I find out more specific things about what I do well. This information tells me what to watch for in the world -- what kind of tasks I can volunteer for and do very well at. I know more about the *kind* of thing I want to be, do, be surrounded by. I am now sensitized and ready to recognize them when they swim by." And so say many others.

So, let us turn now to that process.

AN OUTLINE OF THE CREATIVE APPROACH TO CAREER-CHANGE

The creative approach to career-change[1] always has three parts to it. We can best state these parts in the form of three questions: *What, Where* and *How.*

1. **WHAT?** This has to do with your **skills or talents.** You need to inventory and identify what skills you have that you

---

1. It was the late John Crystal who first formulated this creative approach to career-change and job-hunting, in the form which I explain here.

most enjoy using. The experts call these transferable skills, because they are transferable to any field/career that you choose,
regardless of where you first picked them up, or even if you've
had them since you were born. The full question here is *what are
the skills you most enjoy using?*

2. **WHERE?** This has to do with the **fields of knowledge** you
have already acquired, and most enjoy using. Think of yourself
as a flower. You know that a flower which blooms in the desert
will not do well at 10,000 feet up -- and vice versa. Every flower
has an environment where it does best. So do you. Your favorite
knowledges help create the environment in which you thrive
the most, and do your most effective work. The full question
here is *where do you most want to use those skills?*

3. **HOW?** This has to do with then putting a name to the
skills and the knowledges, by finding out what job-titles and
fields they point to. *And,* the names of organizations (in your
preferred geographical area) which have such jobs to offer. *And,*
the names of the people or person there who actually has the
power to hire you. The full question here is *how do you find such
jobs, that use your favorite skills and your favorite fields of knowledge?*

This chapter will be devoted to **What**. Chapter 10 will be
devoted to **Where**. And Chapter 11 will be devoted to **How**.

So, let us begin.

THE MOST MISUNDERSTOOD
WORD IN THE WORLD OF WORK:
SKILLS

You begin career-change (or a thorough job-hunt) by first identifying your transferable, functional, skills. Here you are looking for the basic building-blocks of your work.

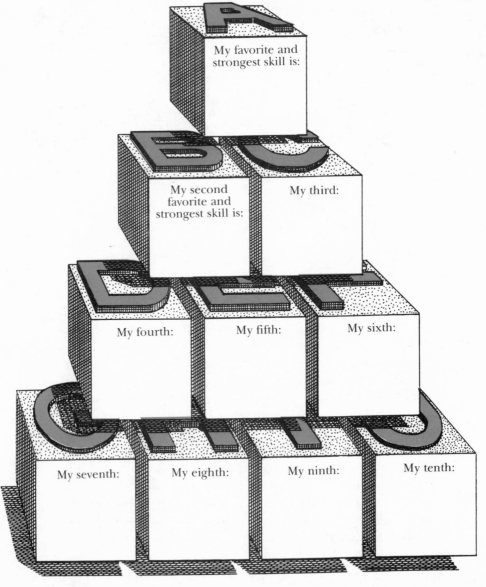

My favorite and strongest skill is:

My second favorite and strongest skill is:

My third:

My fourth:

My fifth:

My sixth:

My seventh:

My eighth:

My ninth:

My tenth:

Change this arrangement, and you change your career.

Unfortunately, many people totally misunderstand this word *'skills,'* and consequently are always putting themselves *down,* by their use of it. This habit begins early: "I haven't really got any skills," high school graduates will say. It continues with college students: "I've spent four years in college, studying my (head) off; I haven't had time to pick up any skills." And it lasts through the middle years, especially when a person is thinking of changing his or her career: "I want to change careers, but all my skills are in my old career." This misunderstanding is shared, we might add, by altogether too many employers, human resource departments, personnel people, and other so-called 'vocational experts.'

The most common misunderstanding about skills is the one which defines them as: *having lots of energy, gives attention to details, gets along well with people, shows determination, works well under pressure, is sympathetic, intuitive, persistent, dynamic, dependable,* etc. Popular tests, such as the *Myers-Briggs,* measure this sort of thing.

However, these are not skills, they are **traits** or **temperaments.** They are the *style* with which you do your skills. *Style* is important, as we will see later; *but,* **traits** are not the basic building blocks of your work.

So, let's see what *are* the basic building blocks of your job, work, or career:

Your Talents
or Transferable Skills

A CRASH COURSE ON
TRANSFERABLE SKILLS

Here are the eight most important truths you need to keep in mind about transferable, functional, skills:

1. Transferable (functional) skills are the most basic unit -- the atoms -- of whatever career you may choose.

When you ask yourself what you have to offer to an employer, the most basic answer is: **my transferable skills.** You can see this from this diagram:

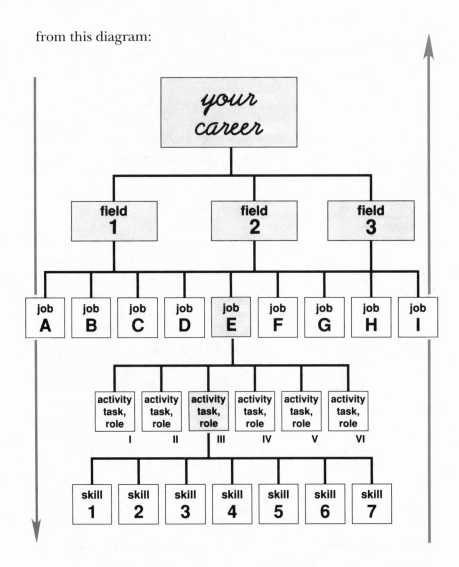

2. As their name implies, these skills are transferable from one job to another, from one field to another, from one career to another.

Skills are the one thing that all jobs, and all careers, have in common. Thus skills serve as a bridge from one job to another, or one career to another. Once you have demonstrated or mastered a skill in one career, you can easily *transfer* it to another career, and use it there.

3. The essence of career-choice or career-change is not so much the mastering of *new* skills, as it is the rearrangement of your *old* transferable skills into new *priorities*, and hence new *patterns*.

It is most akin to the rearranging of *building blocks* that we used to do, as a child (see page 172). Change the order of these building blocks *(which skills you now decide are most important to you)*, and you have defined a new career.

4. There are many transferable skills, but basically they break down into three *families*, according to the object upon which the skill *acts*.

The three families are defined by whether or not the skills are being used with **Data (Information),** or **People** or **Things**. Within each family, there are *simple* skills, and there are higher, or *more complex* skills. If these are listed as vertical pyramids, in rising order of complexity, with the simpler skills at the bottom, the diagram will come out looking like this:[2]

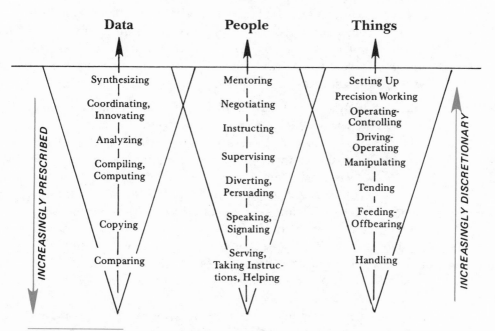

---

2. If you desire more explanation of what these skills are, I refer you to the *Dictionary of Occupational Titles,* the 1991 revised fourth edition, pp. 1005–1006 in vol. II. It should be available in any public library.

5. You should always claim the *highest* transferable skills you legitimately and honestly can, on the basis of your past performance.

Each higher skill generally *includes* all those skills listed below it (on the pyramid diagram) -- so of course you can do *those,* as well.

6. The higher your transferable skills, the more freedom you will have on the job.

Simpler skills can be, and usually are, heavily *prescribed* (by the employer), so if you claim only the simpler skills you will have to *'fit in'* -- following the instructions of your supervisor and doing exactly what you are told. The *higher* the skills you have, the more you will be given discretion to carve out the job the way you want to -- so that it truly fits you.

7. The higher your transferable skills, the less likely it is that the jobs which use such skills will be advertised through normal channels.

Not for you the way of classified ads, resumes, and agencies. No, you *must* follow the more creative job-hunting methods described in Chapters 11 and 12, if you are going to uncover the jobs and careers where you will be allowed and encouraged to use your highest transferable skills.

8. The higher your transferable skills, the less competition you will face for whatever job you are seeking.

The essence of the creative approach to job-hunting or career-change is that you will be approaching *any organization that interests you, whether they have a known vacancy or not.* So of course, at whatever place you visit -- and particularly at those which have not advertised any vacancy -- you will find fewer job-hunters that you have to compete with. In fact, if those employers whom you visit happen to like you well enough, they may be willing to create for you a job that does not presently exist. *In which case, you will be competing with no one, since you will be the sole applicant for that newly created job.*

It is amazing how many times this happens in the world of work. *The reason* it does is that these employers may have been *thinking* about creating such a job within their organization, for quite some time -- but with this and that, they just never got around to *doing* it. Until they saw you. Then they decided they didn't want to let you get away, since *good employees are as hard to find as are good employers.* Voila! It is now time to create that job they have been thinking about for many weeks or months. That new job which is not only what they need, but is exactly what you were looking for. Match-match. Win-win.

Note well: you have not only gotten a job, but by this job-hunting initiative of yours, have helped *accelerate* the creation of more jobs in your country, which is so much on everybody's mind here in the '90s.

How nice to help your country, as well as yourself.

And so, the paradoxical moral of all this: The less you 'stay loose,' the higher you can legitimately define your skill level with *Data/Information* and/or *People* and/or *Things*, **the more likely you are to find a job.**

Just the opposite of what the typical career-changer starts out believing.

"I WOULDN'T RECOGNIZE MY SKILLS IF THEY CAME UP AND SHOOK HANDS WITH ME"

Well, now that you know what skills *are*, the problem is figuring out your own. You would think this would be easy; but most people wouldn't know their skills even if they came up and shook hands with them. What we therefore need, if we're going to successfully choose or change a career, is some *process* by which we can figure out what our skills are.

The best process, the most thorough and helpful process, follows. It consists of asking yourself, "When I was most enjoying myself in my life, *what was I doing?*" And then, once you know what you were doing, to figure out what transferable skills it took to do *that*. The underlying theory, here, is that **we most enjoy life when we are using our best, and most enjoyable, skills.**

So, this process requires us to tell stories to ourselves, about ourselves. How nice! For, the human being is by nature a story-teller. So, we are blessed that our skills are hidden in our stories.

GATHER YOUR STORIES

You are going to need seven of them.

Generally speaking, they should not be stories about your **feelings** (ecstasy or sorrow), or stories about things that happened **to** you.

Rather, they should be stories about your own **actions** or achievements. You want times of action, when you were most enjoying yourself **accomplishing** something. The most useful stories will be those that include, in one order or another, these five parts:

Column I Your Goal: What You Wanted To Accomplish	II Some Kind of Hurdle or Restraint You Faced	III What You Did Step by Step *(Use your verb, plus other verbs)*	IV Description of the Result *(What you accomplished)*	V Any Measure or Quantities To Prove Your Achievement

Start with just one story. It can be from any time in your life. It can be something you accomplished at work, or something you accomplished in your leisure. If, initially, you jot down just a sentence or two, try then to *flesh out* the story, so that it follows the outline above, in one order or another.

The total story should be about a paragraph long, two paragraphs at the most.

Here is a specific example, so you can see how it is to be done:

"I wanted to be able to take a summer trip with my wife and four children. I had a very limited budget, and could not afford to put my family up, in motels. I decided to rig our station wagon as a camper. First I went to the library to get some books on campers. I read those books. Next I designed a plan of what I had to build, so that I could outfit the inside of the station wagon, as well as topside. Then I went and purchased the necessary wood. On weekends, over a period of six weeks, I first constructed, in my driveway, the shell for the 'second story'

on my station wagon. Then I cut doors, windows, and placed a six-drawer bureau within that shell. I mounted it on top of the wagon, and pinioned it in place by driving two-by-fours under the station wagon's rack on top. I then outfitted the inside of the station wagon, back in the wheelwell, with a table and a bench on either side, that I made. The result was a complete homemade camper, which I put together as we started our trip, and disassembled after we got home. When we went on our summer trip, we were able to be on the road for four weeks, and we stayed within our budget, since we didn't have to stay at motels. In fact, I estimate I saved $1900 on motel bills, during that summer's vacation."

You will notice this sample story has all the parts in the outline above:

I.) **Your goal: what you wanted to accomplish:** *"I wanted to be able to take a summer trip with my marriage partner and four children."*

II.) **Some kind of hurdle, obstacle, or constraint that you faced** (self-imposed or otherwise): *"I had a very limited budget, and could not afford to put my family up, in motels."*

III.) **A description of what you did, step by step** (how you set about to ultimately achieve your goal, above, in spite of this hurdle or constraint): *"I decided to rig our station wagon as a camper. First I went to the library to get some books on campers. I read those books. Next I designed a plan of what I had to build, so that I could outfit the inside of the station wagon, as well as topside. Then I went and purchased the necessary wood. On weekends, over a period of six weeks, I . . ." etc., etc.*

IV.) **A description of the outcome or result:** *"When we went on our summer trip, we were able to be on the road for four weeks, and we stayed within our budget, since we didn't have to stay at motels."*

V.) **Any measurable/quantifiable statement of that outcome, that you can think of:** *"In fact, I estimate I saved $1900 on motel bills, during that summer's vacation."*

My transferable skills dealing with

THINGS

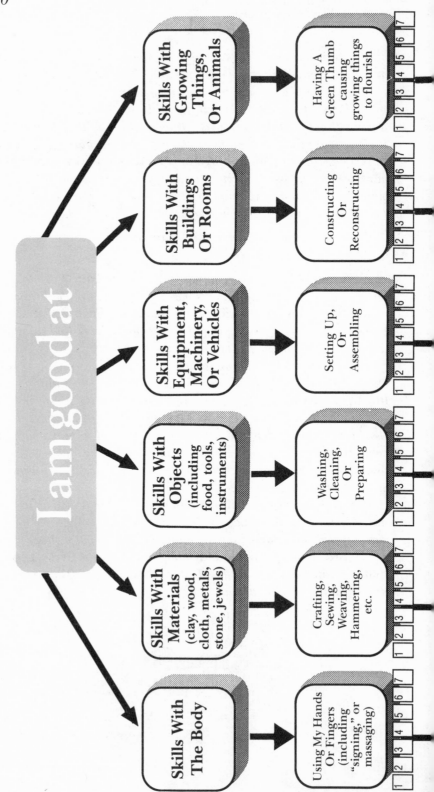

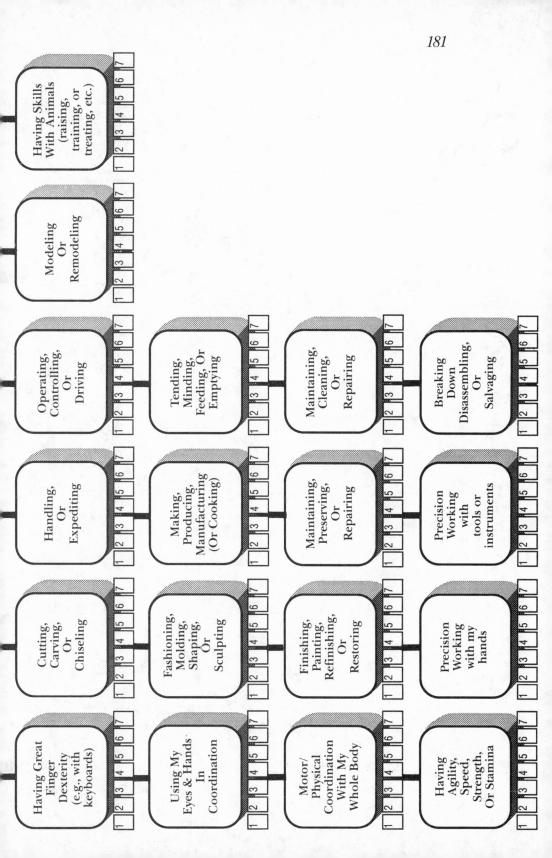

My transferable skills dealing with

PEOPLE

I am good at

With Individuals one at a time

- Taking Instructions, Serving, Or Helping
  1 2 3 4 5 6 7
- Diagnosing, Treating, Or Healing
  1 2 3 4 5 6 7

With Groups, Organizations, or the masses

- Communicating Effectively to a group or a multitude
  1 2 3 4 5 6 7
- Playing Games, or a particular game, Leading Others in recreation or exercise
  1 2 3 4 5 6 7
- Managing, Supervising, Or Running (a business, fund drive, etc.)
  1 2 3 4 5 6 7

Following Through, Getting Things Done, Producing
1 2 3 4 5 6 7

Leading, Taking The Lead, Being A Pioneer
1 2 3 4 5 6 7

Initiating, Starting Up, Founding, Or Establishing
1 2 3 4 5 6 7

Negotiating between two parties, or Resolving Conflicts
1 2 3 4 5 6 7

Teaching, Training, or designing educational events
1 2 3 4 5 6 7

Guiding A Group Discussion, conveying warmth
1 2 3 4 5 6 7

Persuading A Group, Debating, Motivating, Or Selling
1 2 3 4 5 6 7

Consulting, Giving Advice to groups in your area of expertise
1 2 3 4 5 6 7

By Using Words Expressively in speaking or writing
1 2 3 4 5 6 7

By Making Presentations in person, or on TV or film
1 2 3 4 5 6 7

By Performing, Entertaining, Amusing, or Inspiring
1 2 3 4 5 6 7

"Signing," Miming, Acting, Singing, Or Playing an Instrument
1 2 3 4 5 6 7

Referring People, or helping two people to link up
1 2 3 4 5 6 7

Assessing, Evaluating, Screening, Or Selecting Individuals
1 2 3 4 5 6 7

Persuading, Motivating, Recruiting, Or Selling To Individuals
1 2 3 4 5 6 7

Representing Others, Interpreting Others' Ideas or Language
1 2 3 4 5 6 7

Communicating Well in conversation, in person, or on the phone
1 2 3 4 5 6 7

Communicating Well in writing (e.g., excellent letters)
1 2 3 4 5 6 7

Instructing, Teaching, Tutoring, Or Training Individuals
1 2 3 4 5 6 7

Advising, Coaching, Counseling, Mentoring, Empowering
1 2 3 4 5 6 7

My transferable skills dealing with

INFORMATION, DATA, AND IDEAS

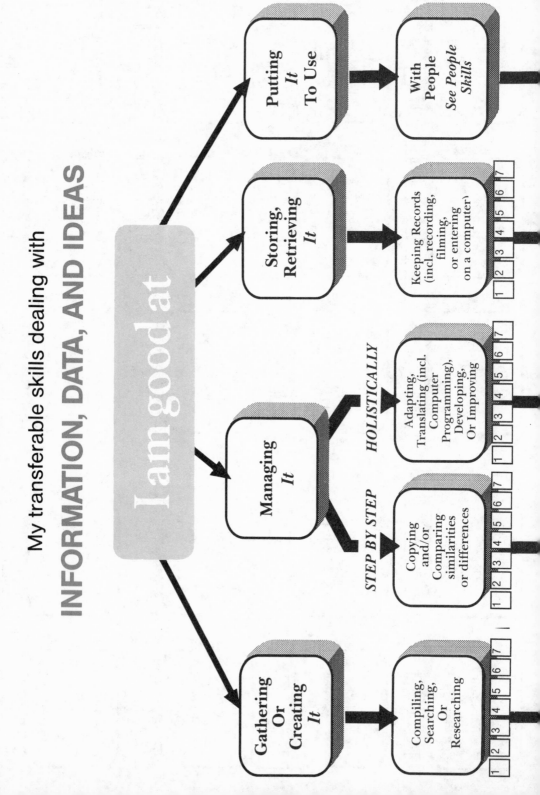

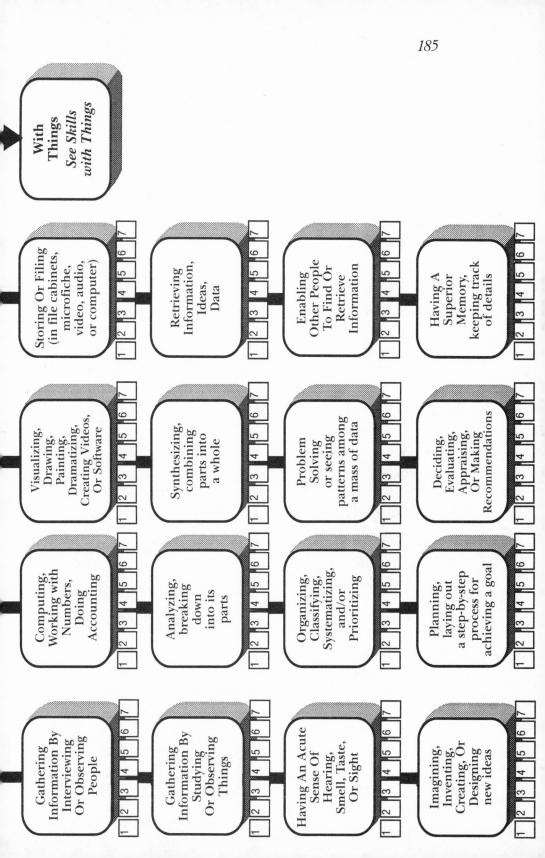

ANALYZE THE STORY
USING THE 'SKILLS KEYS'
DIAGRAMS

Once you have your first story thus written, put a title at the top. In this case, "Story/Achievement #1."

Then, go to the *skills* diagrams, found on pages 180–185. These diagrams are a kind of *rhapsody* upon the *Data, People,* and *Things* skills that we saw earlier, on page 175. And they are here laid out as *mock typewriter keys* (hence we call them *skills keys*).

On each page of those diagrams, work down each vertical column of the *skills keys*. Ask yourself, as you look at each *key*, "Did I use this transferable skill *in this story?*"

If you decide you probably did, color in the *little box* that is right under that key. Since this is your Story/Achievement #1, it is the #1 *little box* under that key, that you color in. I suggest you use a **red** pen, pencil, or crayon, to do this coloring.

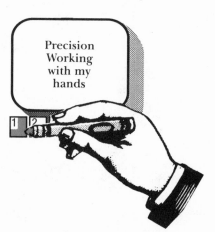

Keep going down each vertical column, in turn, on each of the *skills keys* pages. Under each key, color in box #1 *only if* you feel you used that skill *in this story*.

When you have gone over all the *skills keys*, for Things, People, and Information, once, you will have identified your transferable skills. Or, at least, *those* transferable skills which you used in story #1.

Now, you only have six more stories to go, and you will know your transferable skills.

HELP ME MAKE IT
THROUGH MY LIFE

Many people run into trouble at just this point, when they try to think of six more stories to tell about their actions and accomplishments. It is therefore necessary, for most of us, that we sit down and take some kind of overview of our life, before we continue further.

This should not be seen as a digression from this task of identifying your transferable skills, or talents. First of all, this step only takes about three hours, and you have lots of time; if you're unemployed, that means 16 weeks on average.

Secondly, choosing or changing a career is a time in your life to think out where you want your life to go. And having an overview of your life to date, is a wonderful aid to your doing this, well.

So, how to go about constructing an overview of your life to date? There are two alternative ways open to you. We'll call them: Plan A, and Plan B.

Plan A

The preferred way of doing this, by far, is to write an *outline* of your life, which we call *A Memory Net*. It is faster than writing the autobiography suggested in Plan B, below. The Memory Net usually takes three hours at most -- even allowing for heavy thinking, and a couple of long walks.

The Net is on the next two pages. The first three columns are alternative ways of establishing *pegs* on which to hang your memories. You can use five-year periods of your life (Column 1), *or* jobs you have held (Column 2), *or* places you have lived (Column 3). *Naturally,* you can use alternative *pegs* if you wish: people who were influential in your life at various times, schools you attended, etc., etc.

As you continue across the Memory Net, after Column 3, you should fill out Columns 4, 6, and 8 first *(Activities)*. Then go back and fill in Columns 5, 7, and 9 *(Accomplishments)*. The Activities are more general, and easier to recall. The Accomplishments are more specific, and can use some memory-jogging -- which

Memory

| Column 1 | Column 2 | Column 3 | Column 4 | Column 5 |

Jogging Your Memory
Leisure

In Terms of Five-Year Periods	In Terms of Jobs You Have Held	In Terms of Places You Have Lived	Activities	Accomplishments
e.g. 1990–1994				
1985–1989				
1980–1984				
1975–1979				
1970–1974				
1965–1969				
1960–1964				
1955–1959				
1950–1954				
1945–1949				
1940–1944				
1935–1939				

Net

	Learning			Labor	
Column 6	Column 7		Column 8	Column 9	
Activities	Accomplishments		Activities	Accomplishments	

the *Activities* furnish. In all the columns, put down just a few words, to jog your memory, rather than attempting a more detailed description, *at this time.*

Plan B

If you just draw a blank when trying to construct an *outline* of your life, then you will probably have to take the longer way, and write out a detailed mini-autobiography of your entire life. An informal summary for your eyes only -- *who cares about your spelling or grammar?* -- of

where you've ever been, and

what you've ever done,

where you were ever working, and

what you did there (not in terms of job titles -- *forget them* -- but **in terms of what you feel you accomplished** there).

As you write this, take the time to describe **your spare time,** in each place where you lived. What did you do? What did you most enjoy doing? Any hobbies? Avocations? Great. Were there any activities in your work that paralleled the kinds of things you enjoyed doing in your leisure?

Concentrate both on the things you have done, and also on the particular characteristics of your surroundings that were important to you, and that you really enjoyed: green grass, the theater, tennis, warm climate, skiing, or whatever.

Keep yourself open and sensitive to whatever insights may pop up, about your life outside the workplace. Notice particularly as you go, what values keep surfacing. Truth, beauty, color, light, nature, justice, spirituality, righteousness, ambition, compassion, security, service, popularity, status, power, friends, achievement, love, authority, freedom, glamor, giving, integrity, honesty, loyalty, sensitivity, caring -- which of these holds the most meaning and importance for you? Stay alert and sensitive to questions such as this. You will get much clearer about who you are willing to work with and for, and who you are not.

Sift later. For now, put down anything that helped you to enjoy a particular moment or period of your life. Keep your eye constantly on: *enjoyable.* It's not *always* a guide to what you should be putting down, but it sure is more reliable than any other key that people have come up with.

Don't be afraid if at times it sounds, to your modest ears, like boasting. Who's going to see this document besides you, God, and any loved one that you choose to show it to? So, let it rip. Just be *sure* to back up your elation and sense of pride with concrete examples, and figures.

Don't try to make this mini-autobiography very structured. You can bounce back and forth in time, if that's more congruent with *your* way of doing things.

When your mini-autobiography is all done, you may have a small book -- it can run 30 pages or more. *(My, you've done a lot of living, haven't you?)* Now, you have something to search, looking for evidences of your skills.

Once you have finished this overview of your life, whether through the mini-autobiography, or the Memory Net, you are ready to choose your next story.

SELECTING STORY #2

Look over the overview you have constructed, and select *another* story -- describing some experience when you were achieving something, and truly enjoying yourself. If you are using the Memory Net, study particularly columns 5, 7, and 9.

Choose, if possible, an entirely different kind of story/ achievement than story #1 -- perhaps from another time in your life, or in another arena *(work/leisure/learning)*.

Once you have selected this story, write it out in detail, following the same procedures as you did with Story/Achievement #1.

Back to the *skills keys,* back to the same question -- different box -- for each *skill key:* "Did I use this skill *in this story* (#2)?" If the answer is "Yes," or even "I think so," color in the little box right under that *key,* that has the number 2 in it.

You're beginning to get the hang of it. Continue through all the *keys* in the same fashion as before.

AND ANOTHER, AND ANOTHER

Repeat the same process five more times, choosing a new story each time -- until you have been through Story/Achievement #7, and the little boxes under each *skill key* that are numbered 7.

LOOK BACK,
FOR PATTERNS

You will now want to ask yourself these questions, as you study the completed *skills keys* pages, with their filled-in little red boxes:

1) Which transferable skills are *most* colored-in -- those on the Things page, or those on the People page, or those on the Data/Information page? Which of the three families are my personal favorites -- regardless of whether the little boxes are colored-in under them, or not? Is my strong-suit with Things, or People, or Data? And if the answer is *More than one,* in what order of priority?

2) Looking at all the *skills keys* pages, which are my ten favorite skills, regardless of which *family* they belong to? Are they the *skills keys* that got the most little boxes colored-in under them, or does my intuition tell me I chose bad stories, and my really favorite skills include some that are not well colored-in? (If so, write some new stories, that demonstrate you have those skills that are your favorites.)

3) Do I see any *patterns* -- where the same transferable skills *popped up* again and again, in most of my stories? (Experts call this *the irresistibility* of skills -- some skills, in each of us, *insist* on getting used.)

PRIORITIZE,
PRIORITIZE

As I mentioned previously, every full-fledged career-change requires that you *rearrange* the 'building blocks' of your skills, into a new order of priority. The priority is *everything.* It will ultimately help determine *what* career you choose.

Also, in the best of all possible worlds, it is not always possible to get a job that uses *all* your transferable skills. But you want to take care that you are pursuing a job which at least allows you to use *the most important of your skills.*

Furthermore, down the line this prioritizing will help you to better describe yourself during a job-interview. Instead of saying, in effect, "I have some skills," you will be prepared to say, "This is my greatest strength or talent, this is my next greatest, etc."

Hence the absolute importance, once you have fleshed out your skills, of putting them in order of importance or priority to you. If you skip over this step, you are essentially committing job-hunting suicide.

Take your ten favorite skills, and put them in absolute order of importance to you. You can do this prioritizing either by guess and by gosh, *or* you can use the prioritizing grids on the following pages.

How to Prioritize Your Lists of Anything ●●●●●●

On the next page is a method for taking ten items, of any kind, and figuring out which one is the most important to you, which one is next most important, and so forth.

• Insert the items to be prioritized, in any order, in Section A, on the following page. Then, in Section B, compare just the *two* items that are in each small box. For example, the first little box has a *1 and a 2 in it,* standing for whatever you listed as item #1 and item #2 in Section A. Which one of these is more important to you? You might ask it in some such form as this: "If I were offered two jobs, and the first job gave me a chance to use the skill in item #1, but *not* the skill listed in item #2 -- while the second job gave me just the opposite: a chance to use the skill listed in item #2, but *not* the skill listed in item #1 -- which job (other things being equal) would I take?" You then circle, in that first box in Section B, whichever skill you preferred *in that pair.* Then go on to the next pair in the next little box of Section B, which has *1 and 3 in it,* and ask the same *kind* of question.

• When you have finished circling one number in each small little box, turn to Section C. The first question there is: "How many times circled?" -- referring to the Items, by number, immediately above. So, count how many times Item #1 got circled, and enter that total immediately under the "1" in Section C. Then count how many times Item #2 got circled, etc., through all ten items. The next question in Section C is: "Final rank?" The one with the most circles is counted as first (copy it down as *new* number 1 in Section D). The one next most circled is counted as second (*new* number 2 in Section D). And so forth.

A similar prioritizing grid for a larger number of items (twenty-four) appears on the page following the ten-item prioritizing grid.

> *Each time you use a grid, make a photocopy of it,*
> *and fill in the photocopy rather than the original.*

194

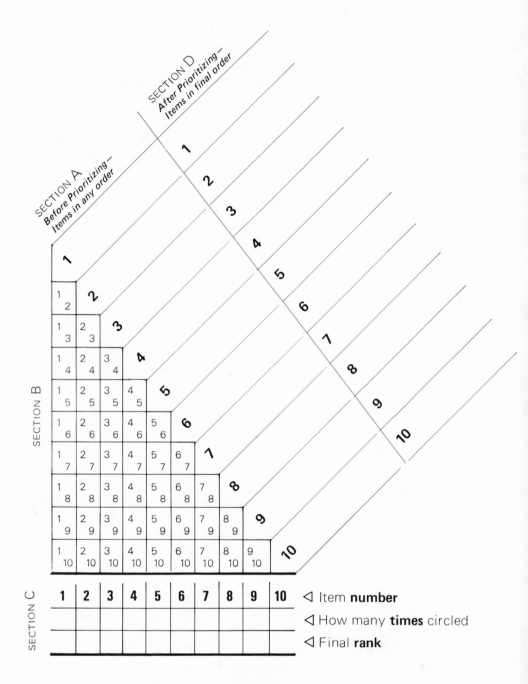

Prioritizing Grid
for 10 Items

```
1  1  1  1  1  1  1  1  1  1  1  1  1  1  1  1  1  1  1  1  1  1  1
2  3  4  5  6  7  8  9  10 11 12 13 14 15 16 17 18 19 20 21 22 23 24

2  2  2  2  2  2  2  2  2  2  2  2  2  2  2  2  2  2  2  2  2  2
3  4  5  6  7  8  9  10 11 12 13 14 15 16 17 18 19 20 21 22 23 24

3  3  3  3  3  3  3  3  3  3  3  3  3  3  3  3  3  3  3  3  3
4  5  6  7  8  9  10 11 12 13 14 15 16 17 18 19 20 21 22 23 24

4  4  4  4  4  4  4  4  4  4  4  4  4  4  4  4  4  4  4  4
5  6  7  8  9  10 11 12 13 14 15 16 17 18 19 20 21 22 23 24

5  5  5  5  5  5  5  5  5  5  5  5  5  5  5  5  5  5  5
6  7  8  9  10 11 12 13 14 15 16 17 18 19 20 21 22 23 24

6  6  6  6  6  6  6  6  6  6  6  6  6  6  6  6  6  6
7  8  9  10 11 12 13 14 15 16 17 18 19 20 21 22 23 24

7  7  7  7  7  7  7  7  7  7  7  7  7  7  7  7  7
8  9  10 11 12 13 14 15 16 17 18 19 20 21 22 23 24

8  8  8  8  8  8  8  8  8  8  8  8  8  8  8  8
9  10 11 12 13 14 15 16 17 18 19 20 21 22 23 24

9  9  9  9  9  9  9  9  9  9  9  9  9  9  9
10 11 12 13 14 15 16 17 18 19 20 21 22 23 24

10 10 10 10 10 10 10 10 10 10 10 10 10 10
11 12 13 14 15 16 17 18 19 20 21 22 23 24

11 11 11 11 11 11 11 11 11 11 11 11 11
12 13 14 15 16 17 18 19 20 21 22 23 24

12 12 12 12 12 12 12 12 12 12 12 12
13 14 15 16 17 18 19 20 21 22 23 24

13 13 13 13 13 13 13 13 13 13 13
14 15 16 17 18 19 20 21 22 23 24

14 14 14 14 14 14 14 14 14 14
15 16 17 18 19 20 21 22 23 24

15 15 15 15 15 15 15 15 15
16 17 18 19 20 21 22 23 24

16 16 16 16 16 16 16 16
17 18 19 20 21 22 23 24

17 17 17 17 17 17 17
18 19 20 21 22 23 24

18 18 18 18 18 18
19 20 21 22 23 24

19 19 19 19 19
20 21 22 23 24

20 20 20 20
21 22 23 24

21 21 21
22 23 24

22 22
23 24

23
24
```

Total times each number got circled

1	2	3	4	5	6
7	8	9	10	11	12
13	14	15	16	17	18
19	20	21	22	23	24

Prioritizing Grid
for 24 Items

Each time you use this grid, make a photocopy of it, and fill in the photocopy rather than the original. (You will need to photocopy this grid many times as you go through this process.)

'FLESH OUT'
YOUR TOP TEN

Once you have identified your ten favorite transferable skills *(or however many you wish)*, you need to *flesh out* your skill-description for each of those ten. Currently, each one is basically only *one word*. One word is a good place to begin, but a poor place to end. In the end, you want to be able to describe each of your talents or skills in more than just one word.

"I'm good at *organizing*" doesn't tell us much. Organizing what? People, as at a party? Nuts and bolts, as on a workbench? Or lots of information, on a computer? Those are three entirely different skills. The one word *"organizing"* doesn't tell us which one is *yours*.

So, *please* go back over the transferable skills you identified as your ten favorites, and make sure that each one-word definition gets *fleshed out* with an object -- some kind of Data/Information, or some kind of People, or some kind of Thing. Add an adverb or adjective, too.

Why adjectives? Well, "I'm good at analyzing (people with marital problems) *painstakingly, by asking them a lot of questions*," and "I'm good at analyzing (people with marital problems) *in a flash, by intuition*," are two *entirely different* skills. The difference between them is spelled out not in the verb, nor in the object, but in the adjectival or adverbial phrase there at the end. When you are face-to-face with an employer, and you are trying to explain what makes you different from nineteen other people who can basically do the same thing that you can do, it is often the adjective or adverb that will save your life. So, expand each definition of your ten favorite skills as much as you can, in the fashion I have just described.

When you are done, turn to the *Flower Diagram* on pages 228-229, and on the *petal* called **My Favorite Skills,** copy the list of your ten favorite skills, *fleshed out.* There is, on that diagram, room for only your top *three* favorite skills, but if you copy the whole diagram on a larger piece of paper (and I encourage you to), you will have room to list all ten -- *in the manner of this diagram:*

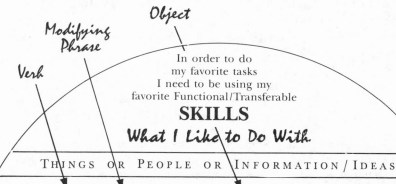

Object

Modifying Phrase

Verb

In order to do
my favorite tasks
I need to be using my
favorite Functional/Transferable

SKILLS

What I Like to Do With.

THINGS OR PEOPLE OR INFORMATION / IDEAS

1. Writing, particularly with humor, for people who need to know more information about one of my favorite fields of interest/knowledge   INFORMATION
2. Crafting, with precision, wooden objects of my own design   THINGS
3. Precision working with my own tools and instruments to do woodcrafting THINGS
4. Planning and directing an entire activity (physical project), bringing it to completion, with great attention to the last detail   INFORMATION
5. Inventing solutions to problems in the physical world, by creating new technologies   IDEAS
6. Programming computers, particularly with programs that solve particular problems in the physical world   IDEAS
7. Laying out a step-by-step process for achieving the implementation of a design of my own devising   IDEAS
8. Evaluating why a particular design or process in the physical world isn't working   INFORMATION
9. Teaching a group of people who need to know more information about one of my favorite fields of interest/knowledge   INFORMATION
10. Starting, initiating new physical projects involved with design, problem-solving, and the employment of electronics   IDEAS

My Style of Doing Them:

I am a person who is self-motivated, takes lots of initiative, is resourceful and creative, patient and persevering despite obstacles. I enjoy a challenge, maintain neatness and order in my workplace, am accurate, methodical, thorough, particularly with details, and achievement oriented.

THE 'STYLE' WITH WHICH
YOU USE YOUR SKILLS

There is one final task, left, in your skill-identification. You will notice on the diagram above, that there is a space at the bottom called 'My Style of Doing Them.' This serves as a kind of *catch-basin* for what people traditionally call *Traits,* as I mentioned earlier in this chapter. When you are face-to-face with an employer, they will be useful, as you try to describe what makes you different from nineteen other people who can do the same thing that you do.

Voila! You now know your talents, or -- as we prefer to call them -- your transferable skills.

SOME PROBLEMS YOU MAY RUN INTO,
WHILE DOING YOUR SKILL-IDENTIFICATION

In doing the aforementioned skill-identification, it will not be surprising if you run into some problems. Let us look at the more common ones that have arisen for career-changers, in the past:

1. *"I don't know exactly what is an achievement."*

When you're looking for a story/achievement to illustrate one of your skills, you're *not* looking for something that only you have done, in the history of the world. What you're looking for is a lot simpler than that. You're looking for *any* time in your life when you did something that was, at that time of your life, a source of pride and accomplishment *for you.* It might have been learning to ride a bike. It might be achieving your first quota, at work. It might be a particularly significant project that you designed, in mid-life. It doesn't matter whether or not it pleased anybody else; it only matters that it pleased you.

I like Bernard Haldane's definition of an achievement. He says it is: something you yourself feel you have done well, that you also enjoyed doing and felt proud of. That's the kind of thing you are looking for: an accomplishment which gave you two pleasures: enjoyment while doing it, and satisfaction from the outcome. It doesn't mean you may not have sweated as you did it, or hated *some parts* of the process, but it does mean that basically you enjoyed *most of* the process. The pleasure was not simply in getting it done.

Generally speaking, an achievement will have all the parts outlined on page 178.

2. "I don't see why I should look for skills I enjoy; it seems to me that employers will only want to know what skills I do well. They will not care whether I enjoy using the skill or not."

Well, sure, it is important for you to find the skills you do well, above all else. But, generally speaking, that is hard for you to evaluate about yourself. *Do I do this well, or not?* Compared to whom? Even aptitude tests can't resolve this dilemma for you. So it's better to take the following reverse equations, which experience has shown to be true:

If it is a skill you do well, you will generally enjoy it.

If it is a skill you enjoy, it is generally because you do it well.

Experience has shown that people *rarely* enjoy something they do very badly. There are, however, occasional exceptions, usually when you are engaged in amateur athletics or leisure.

With these equations in hand, you will see that -- since they are equal anyway -- it is much more useful to ask yourself, "Do I enjoy doing it?" instead of hunting for the elusive "Do I do it well?" I repeat: listing the skills you most enjoy is -- in most cases -- just another way of listing the skills you do best.

The reason why this idea -- of making *enjoyment* the key -- causes such feelings of uncomfortableness in so many of us is that we have an old historical tradition in this country which insinuates you shouldn't really *enjoy* yourself in life. To suffer is virtuous.

Sample: Two girls do babysitting. One hates it. One enjoys it thoroughly. Which is more virtuous in God's sight? According to that old tradition, the one who hates it is more virtuous. Some of us feel this instinctively, even if more logical thought says, *Whoa!*

We have this subconscious fear that if we are caught enjoying life, punishment looms. Thus, the story of two Scotchmen who met on the street one day: "Isn't this a beautiful day?" said one. "Aye," said the other, "but we'll pay for it."

We feel it is okay to talk about our failures, but not about our successes. To talk about our successes appears to be boasting, and *that* is manifestly a sin. Or so we think. We shouldn't be enjoying so much about ourselves.

But look at the birds of the air, or watch your pets at play. You will notice one distinctive fact about that part of God's creation: when a bird or a pet does what it is meant to do, by God and nature, it manifests true joy.

Joy is so clearly a part of God's plan for us. God wants us to eat; therefore He made eating enjoyable. God wants us to sleep; therefore He made sleeping enjoyable. God wants us to procreate, love, and make love; therefore He made sex enjoyable, and love even more so.

Likewise, God gives to each of us unique *combinations of* skills and talents which He wants us to contribute to His general plan -- to the symphony of the world, and the music of the spheres. Therefore, **when we use the talents He most wants each of us to use, He attends it with a feeling of great joy.** Everywhere in God's plan for His creation, joy rewards right action.

You need to identify the skills you *enjoy* using -- not only now, as you are in the process of choosing a new career, but also later when you are face-to-face with an employer. True, *bad* employers will not care whether you enjoy a particular task, or not. But *good* employers will care greatly. They know that unless a would-be employee has **enthusiasm** for his or her work, the quality of that work will *always* suffer.

3. *"I've never had any experience in the world of work. I've been a home-maker all my life. I can think of stories of enjoyable achievements* within *the home, but I'm not sure I could ever sell an employer on that."*

If this is proving to be a hurdle for you, then you will want to write to the Educational Testing Service, Publication Order Services, CN 6736, Princeton, NJ 08541-6736, and ask for their I CAN lists, which are contained in the following inexpensive books, all of which are authored by Ruth B. Ekstrom: *HAVE SKILLS Women's Workbook -- Finding Jobs Using Your Homemaking and Volunteer Work Experience; How to Get College Credit for What You Have Learned As a Homemaker and Volunteer; HAVE SKILLS Employer's Guide -- Matching Women and Jobs; HAVE SKILLS Counselor's Guide -- Helping Women Find Jobs Using Their Homemaking and Volunteer Work Experience.* The I CAN lists classify all the skills of the homemaker under various roles and job titles in business, such as: administrator/manager, financial manager, personnel manager, trainer, advocate/change agent, public relations/communicator, problem surveyor, researcher, fund raiser, counselor, youth group leader, group leader for a serving organization, museum staff assistant, nutritionist, child caretaker, designer, clothing and textile specialist, and so forth. *Very* helpful to *anyone* who has never had any work experience outside the home, *not just women or homemakers.* It's helpful to teenagers, persons who happen to have disabilities and have not yet worked out there in the world, and so forth.

4. *"I have no difficulty finding stories to write up, from my life, that I consider to be enjoyable achievements; but once these are written, I have great difficulty in seeing what the skills are -- even if I stare at the skills keys diagram for hours. I need somebody else's insight."*

You will want to consider getting two friends or two other members of your family to sit down with you, and do skill identification through the practice of 'Trioing' which I invented some twenty years ago to help with this very problem. This practice is fully described in my book, *Where Do I Go From Here With My Life?* But to save you the trouble of reading it, here is -- in general -- how it goes:

a. Each of the three of you quietly writes up some story of an accomplishment in their life that was enjoyable.

b. Each of the three of you quietly analyzes just your own story to see what skills you see there; you jot these down.

c. One of you then volunteers to go first. You read your story aloud. The other two jot down on a piece of paper whatever skills they hear you using. They ask you to pause if they're having trouble keeping up. You finish your story. You read aloud the skills *you* picked out in that story.

d. Then the second person tells you what's on their list: what skills *they* heard you use in your story. You copy them down, below your own list, even if you don't agree with every one of them.

e. Then the third person tells you what's on their list; what skills *they* heard you use in your story. You copy them down, below your own list, even if you don't agree with every one of them.

f. When they're both done, you ask them any questions for further elaboration that you may have. *"What did you mean by this skill? Where did you think you heard me using it?"*

g. Now it is the next person's turn, and you repeat steps 'c' through 'f' with them. Then it is the third person's turn, and you repeat steps 'c' through 'f' with them.

h. Now it is time to move on to a second story for each of you, so you begin with steps 'a' through 'g' all over again, except that each of you writes a new story. And so on, through seven stories.

5. *"How do I know if I've done this all correctly? What if I just think I understood what I was supposed to do, but I really didn't? I want to be sure the stuff I've identified is really going to help me in my job-hunt."*

It will, if you've followed *all* the directions above *(no shortcuts)* and *if* you avoided stating your skills in the jargon or language of your past career. This is a point on which some professions fall down: people who formerly were in professions filled with a lot of jargon. Let us take clergy as an example. It is not useful to conclude, from your skill-identification, *"I am good at preaching."* If you are going to choose a new career, out there in what you call the secular world, you must not use language that locks you into the past. Or suggests that you can do one field and one field only. So, in the case of preaching, for example, ask yourself, what is its larger form? *"Teaching?"* Perhaps. *"Motivating people?"* Perhaps. *"Inspiring people to the depths of their being?"* Perhaps. *Only you can say what is true, for you.* But in one way or another be sure to get your skills out of *any jargon that locks you into your past career.*

Let's look at a few other questions, to be sure you've done the job of skill-identification *well*. Have you thus far steered clear of putting a job title on what you're aiming toward? Skills can point to many different jobs, which have a multitude of titles, as we shall see in Chapter 11. Don't lock yourself in, prematurely. "I'm looking for a job where I can **use** the following skills," is fine. But, "I'm looking for a job where I can **be** a (job title)" is a no-no, at this point in the process of career-change.

Are you willing to look at a number of alternatives, as you move through Chapters 10 and 11? Or is your desire to finish this off *fast* leading you to push prematurely for just one way to go? *Stay loose.* Keep *all* your options open.

6. *"As this chapter began, you indicated we would be taking our top* three *skills, not* ten, *to point to a general job-title. When do we do that?"*

Later.

7. *"I don't want to do the lengthy process you described, writing out seven stories, and working through the skills keys, etc. Is there any shortcut to the process of identifying your skills?"*

Sure. Following is a sampler of *skill-verbs.* The way in which this list is typically used by career-changers or job-hunters is to put a check-mark in front of each skill that: a) you believe you possess; b) you enjoy doing; and c) you believe you do well:

Once you have checked these off, choose your ten *favorites.* You will need, then, to *flesh these out,* with at least one story for each verb. This is necessary because when you are in an actual job-interview, you do not want to just *claim* you have a skill. You want to *prove* you have the skill you are claiming. What your story says, for each skill, is that you *can* do it, because you *did* do it.

A List of 250 Skills as Verbs

achieving	detailing	handling	meeting	raising	studying
acting	detecting	having	memorizing	reading	summarizing
adapting	determining	responsibility	mentoring	realizing	supervising
addressing	developing	heading	modeling	reasoning	supplying
administering	devising	helping	monitoring	receiving	symbolizing
advising	diagnosing	hypothesizing	motivating	recommending	synergizing
analyzing	digging	identifying	navigating	reconciling	synthesizing
anticipating	directing	illustrating	negotiating	recording	systematizing
arbitrating	discovering	imagining	observing	recruiting	taking
arranging	dispensing	implementing	obtaining	reducing	taking
ascertaining	displaying	improving	offering	referring	instructions
assembling	disproving	improvising	operating	rehabilitating	talking
assessing	dissecting	increasing	ordering	relating	teaching
attaining	distributing	influencing	organizing	remembering	team-building
auditing	diverting	informing	originating	rendering	telling
budgeting	dramatizing	initiating	overseeing	repairing	tending
building	drawing	innovating	painting	reporting	testing and
calculating	driving	inspecting	perceiving	representing	proving
charting	editing	inspiring	performing	researching	training
checking	eliminating	installing	persuading	resolving	transcribing
classifying	empathizing	instituting	photographing	responding	translating
coaching	enforcing	instructing	piloting	restoring	traveling
collecting	establishing	integrating	planning	retrieving	treating
communicating	estimating	interpreting	playing	reviewing	trouble-
compiling	evaluating	interviewing	predicting	risking	shooting
completing	examining	intuiting	preparing	scheduling	tutoring
composing	expanding	inventing	prescribing	selecting	typing
computing	experimenting	inventorying	presenting	selling	umpiring
conceptualizing	explaining	investigating	printing	sensing	understanding
conducting	expressing	judging	problem	separating	understudying
conserving	extracting	keeping	solving	serving	undertaking
consolidating	filing	leading	processing	setting	unifying
constructing	financing	learning	producing	setting-up	uniting
controlling	fixing	lecturing	programming	sewing	upgrading
coordinating	following	lifting	projecting	shaping	using
coping	formulating	listening	promoting	sharing	utilizing
counseling	founding	logging	proof-reading	showing	verbalizing
creating	gathering	maintaining	protecting	singing	washing
deciding	generating	making	providing	sketching	weighing
defining	getting	managing	publicizing	solving	winning
delivering	giving	manipulating	purchasing	sorting	working
designing	guiding	mediating	questioning	speaking	writing

A Friendly Word to Procrastinators

If two weeks have gone by, and you haven't even *started* doing the inventory in this chapter, then -- I hate to tell you this -- you're going to have to get someone to help you. Choose a helper for your job-hunt -- a friend rather than family, if possible. A *tough* friend. You know, *taskmaster.* Ask them if they're willing to help you. Assuming they say yes, put down in *both* your appointment books a regular *weekly* date when you will guarantee to meet with them, and they will guarantee to meet with you, check you out on what you've done already, and be very stern with you if you've done little or nothing since last week's meeting. Tell them that it is at least a 20,000-hour, $200,000 project. It's also responsible, concerned, committed Stewardship of the talents God gave you.

Where did we get 20,000 hours? Well, a forty-hour-a-week job, done for fifty weeks a year, adds up to 2,000 hours annually. So, how long are you going to be doing this new career that you are looking for? How many years do you plan to stay in the world of work? Ten years? That means 20,000 hours. Twenty years? That's 40,000 hours. So, it's at least a 20,000-hour project.

Why $200,000? Well, figure it out for yourself. If you earned, let us say, at least $10 an hour in your new career, that *times* 20,000 hours adds up to $200,000. If by chance you were to earn $20 an hour, that would be $400,000.

So, in working through this chapter and the two following ones, you're working on a 20,000 hour, $200,000 project, at least. It's *worth* giving the time to, believe me.

And if you don't have the self-discipline to stick at it, it's worth enlisting a friend to help you.

If you have no friend who will help you, then you're probably going to want to think about professional help. Read, study, memorize, Appendix A in the back of this book. Go talk to several career-counselors. Choose the one you like best, and *get on with it.*

You've only one life to live, my friend. And every day is precious.

"WHILE YOU'RE WAITING FOR YOUR SHIP TO COME IN, WHY DON'T YOU DO SOME MAINTENANCE WORK ON THE PIER?"

How far you go in life
Depends on your being
Tender with the young,
Compassionate with the aged,
Sympathetic with the striving, and
Tolerant of the weak & strong;
Because someday in your life,
You will have been all of these.

George Washington Carver

CHAPTER TEN

The Systematic Approach To
The Job-Hunt and Career-Change:

PART II

Where

Do You Want To
Use Your Skills?

Chapter 10

INTRODUCTION

We saw in the last chapter that you need to know **What** your favorite skills are, for they will ultimately define your job *title*. But now you must press on to this next question in systematic career-change: **Where** do you want to use these skills? And the **Where** is defined -- above all else -- by the field/subjects/language you choose to work with.

Suppose you had a dream, one night, where you found your-self working at a fast-food place which had twelve other employ-ees -- none of whom spoke any language except Portuguese. All the customers, also, spoke nothing but Portuguese. And, in this dream, you spoke nothing but English. You can imagine how difficult it would be, in the dream, for you to enjoy that job.

The *language* spoken at your workplace is crucial. Except that in real life, *language* is not merely a question of whether a place's employees speak English or Portuguese. There are other languages *at work*. I myself once worked as *a secretary,* so let us take that job-title as an example, and see how this truth works out.

If you work as a legal secretary, there's a lot of talk there, all day long, about legal procedures. Therefore, Law is the *language* you have to live with, all day, at that workplace.

If you work as a secretary at a gardening store, there's a lot of talk there, all day long, about gardens and such. Therefore, Gardening is the *language* you have to live with, all day, at that workplace.

If you work as a secretary at an airline, there's a lot of talk there, all day long, about airlines procedures. Therefore, Air-lines is the *language* you have to live with, all day, at that work-place.

If you work as a secretary at a church, there's a lot of talk there, all day long, about church procedures and matters of faith. Therefore, Religion is the *language* you have to live with, all day, at that workplace.

If you work as a secretary in a photographic laboratory, there's a lot of talk there, all day long, about photographic procedures. Therefore, Photography is the *language* you have to live with, all day, at that workplace.

If you work as a secretary at a bank, there's a lot of talk there, all day long, about banking procedures. Therefore, Banking is the *language* you have to live with, all day, at that workplace.

If you work as a secretary at a chemical plant, there's a lot of talk there, all day long, about chemicals manufacturing. There-fore, Chemistry is the *language* you have to live with, all day, at that workplace.

If you work as a secretary for the Federal government, there's a lot of talk there, all day long, about government procedures. Therefore, Government is the *language* you have to live with, all day, at that workplace.

You may object that what I am here calling *languages* are, in reality, **Fields of knowledge,** or **Subjects** -- and so they are.

But the significance of the *field* you choose for your next vocation or career is precisely this: it determines the *language* which you have to listen to, speak, and work in, all day long. If you enjoy the *field,* you will enjoy the language you are dealing with all day long, and therefore you will be happy in that career. However, if you don't enjoy the *field* -- if, say, *gardening* is one of your favorite subjects, but you work at a place where *law* is the language you have to listen to, and work in, all day long, and you *hate* that field and language -- then you are not going to be happy in that career.

So, we begin this step in career-change (or creative job-hunting) by making a list of your **Favorite Subjects,** about which you already know something.

"THIS MUCH I DO KNOW"

As this old expression implies, there are a lot of things that you know *something* about. This is where you begin, in identifying your favorite subjects.

What you need is a list of the subjects that:

a) You *already* know quite a bit about[1] -- though it is *not* necessary that you have a *mastery* of them; *and* that

b) You love.

It can be subjects that you studied in school -- *e.g.,* psychology, electronics, business science, law, theology -- but it doesn't have to be. It could be *interior decorating,* or *movies,* or *psychology,* or *the kind of subjects that come up on television 'game shows.'* It is sufficient that you picked up a working knowledge of the subject, and who cares where or how? As the late John Crystal used to

---

1. You could identify as one of your favorites a subject that, at present, you like the sound of, but know *absolutely nothing about.* And then go learn about that subject at a nearby adult education center, or community college, or college. *But,* it is much better to start by asking what subjects you already know something about. The reasoning here: if it is truly a *favorite* subject of yours, it is very unlikely that you have gotten this far in life without delving into it, at least somewhat.

say, it doesn't matter whether you learned it in college, or sitting at the end of a log. If it's one of your favorite subjects, that's sufficient.

For example, *antiques* could be one of your favorite subjects. Yet, you never studied it in school. You picked up a knowledge of antiques by going around to antique stores, and asking lots of questions. And you supplemented this by reading a few books on the subject, and you subscribe to an antiques magazine. That's enough, for you to put *antiques,* on your list of fields/ subjects/languages.

Keep clearly before you that the issue you are working on here, is **Where** do you want to be using your skills? And, that this is best identified by asking what *language* you want to be speaking, and listening to, and working with, all day long? *How* you picked up that language, or your degree of *mastery* of that language, are irrelevant -- *unless you want to work at a level in that field that demands and requires mastery.*

FIRST, REMEMBER;
THEN, EVALUATE

One way to approach this issue of *what are your favorite subjects?* is to use the table on the next page, and simply make a list of all the things you've ever studied or learned or learned about, in *each* of the places mentioned there.

Do not list just your favorites, in the beginning. Trying to cast too narrow a net too early in the game is usually self-defeating.

We have found, over the years, that career-changers first need to cast a wider net than just *their favorites.* The reason for this, is that if all you're looking for are your *favorites,* from the get-go, you will essentially be trying to do two things at once -- *remember* and *evaluate.* And if you try to do two things at once, you are like a bareback rider trying to stand on two different horses that are starting to go in different directions. Separating the two tasks is necessary. First, *remember.* Then, later, *evaluate.*

We'll pause here, while you take time to remember -- and fill out the table. Copy it on to a larger piece of paper, if you need to.

212

Subjects I Learned About in High School or College	Subjects I Learned About on the Job (Apprenticeship, Internship, Training, etc.)	Subjects I Learned About by Self-Study (Reading at Home, Correspondence Course, Video, TV, Audiotapes, Computer Programs)	Subjects I Learned About in a Workshop, Conference, Continuing Education, or Training Event	Subjects I Learned About on Vacation, or During Hobby Time

During this *remembering* phase, you may want to look back at your Memory Net, pages 188–189, and see what subjects come to mind as you look over all the notes you jotted down, there. Anything helpful, there?

Then, when you are all done, go back over the list for a second time, and cross off all the subjects you checked, that are *not* one of your favorites.

IF YOU JUST CAN'T REMEMBER, TO SAVE YOUR LIFE

If, in general, you're not having much luck coming up with the names of the subjects you picked up some knowledge about, in these various arenas, then you will of course want a list. *Unfortunately,* there is no list in the world that could possibly cover all the subjects that *you* might know something about. We will have to settle for **A Sampler** only.

> # A Sampler of Subjects
> ## You May Know Something About

In using this list, the same admonition as set forth with the table above, applies here: "First, *remember.* Then, *evaluate.*" Go through the list a first time, and check off any subject that you know *anything* about. Do remember that the list is A Sampler. It's just a bunch of pegs on which to hang your memories. Be *sure* and jot down any other subjects you know something about, as they occur to you, which are not on this list.

Again, when you are all done, go back over the list for a second time, and cross off all the subjects you checked, that are *not* one of your favorites.

General Fields[2]

☐ History
☐ Biology
☐ Physics
☐ Chemistry
☐ Geometry
☐ Astronomy
☐ Geography
☐ Knowledge of foreign countries
   (which one/s?)
☐ Spanish or some other language
   (which one/s?)
☐ Psychology
   ☐ The way the brain works
The Arts
   ☐ Principles of art
   ☐ Cinema
   ☐ Musical knowledge and taste
   ☐ Drawing
   ☐ Graphic arts
   ☐ Art materials
   ☐ Music appreciation
   ☐ Photography
   ☐ Broadcasting
   ☐ Woodcuts, engravings, lithographs
   ☐ Paintings, drawings, silk screens
   ☐ How to make videos

---

2. If you want a much more detailed list of general fields, I refer you to pages 130–136 in another one of my books, entitled, *The Three Boxes of Life, and How To Get Out of Them: An introduction to life/work planning* (Ten Speed Press, 1981) -- available in your library, bookstore, or possibly on your own shelf (if you already own a copy).

☐ Music (what kinds?)
☐ Principles of recording
☐ Sociology
☐ Linguistics or languages
☐ Communication
    ☐ Human nature's need for symbols
    ☐ The use and meaning of words
    ☐ Numbers or statistics
    ☐ Instructional principles and techniques
    ☐ Speed reading
How to Create Visuals
    ☐ Designs
    ☐ Blueprints
    ☐ Wall-charts
    ☐ Schematics
How To Produce
    ☐ Procedures
    ☐ Guidebooks
    ☐ Manuals
    ☐ Newsletters

Particular How-To's

☐ How to run a particular
    machine (which one/s?)
☐ How to drive an automobile
☐ How to sew
☐ Carpentry
☐ Plumbing
☐ Painting
☐ Electrical work
☐ Household repairs
☐ Typing or 'keyboarding'
☐ How to operate a computer
☐ How computers work
☐ Computer programming
☐ Knowledge of a particular program
☐ Design engineering
☐ Interior decorating
☐ Knowledge of antiques
☐ Knowledge of gardening
☐ Horticulture
☐ Car repairs
☐ How to play a musical instrument
    (which one/s?)
☐ Principles of comparison shopping

**Kinds of Personal Problems People Have
That I Know Something About, and
Know How To Deal With**

Economic/Planning Problems for Individuals
- ☐ Identifying and finding meaningful work
- ☐ Job-hunting, career-change, unemployment, being fired or laid off
- ☐ Work satisfaction
- ☐ Life/work planning
- ☐ Personal economics
  - ☐ Financial planning
  - ☐ Budgeting
- ☐ Financial planning and management
- ☐ How to do taxes

Educational Problems
- ☐ Illiteracy, educational needs
- ☐ Performance problems, appraisal

Health Problems
- ☐ Physical fitness
- ☐ Physical handicaps
- ☐ Principles of outdoor survival
- ☐ Weight control
- ☐ Low energy
- ☐ Sleep disorders
- ☐ Principles of behavioral modification
- ☐ Mental/emotional/psychosomatic illness
  - ☐ Depression
  - ☐ Psychiatric hospitalization
  - ☐ Stress
  - ☐ Various kinds of mental/emotional problems
- ☐ Holistic health
- ☐ Self-healing, psychic healing
- ☐ Nutritional problems
- ☐ Addictions
  - ☐ Drug problems
  - ☐ Alcoholism
  - ☐ Smoking
- ☐ Principles of preventative health care
- ☐ Dealing with hypertension
- ☐ Allergies
- ☐ Pain control
- ☐ Dealing with people in terminal illness

Relationship Problems
- ☐ Relationships
- ☐ Personal insight, therapy
- ☐ Sexual education, sexual problems
- ☐ Sexual dysfunction

- ☐ Marriage problems
- ☐ Pregnancy and childbirth
- ☐ Parenting
- ☐ Discipline problems, self-discipline
- ☐ Physical abuse, rape, sexual harassment
- ☐ Divorce
- ☐ Death and grief

Religious/Value Problems

- ☐ Spiritual principles
- ☐ Values identification
- ☐ The nature of religion or religions (which ones?)
- ☐ Philosophy of religion
- ☐ Philosophical problems
- ☐ Ethics
- ☐ Life after death
- ☐ Psychic phenomena

Kinds of Organizational Problems
I Know Quite a Bit About and
Know How to Deal With

With People

- ☐ Manpower requirements analysis and planning
- ☐ Personnel administration
- ☐ Recruiting
- ☐ Industry in-house training
- ☐ Principles of group dynamics
- ☐ The how-to of customer relations and service
- ☐ Performance specifications

With Finances

- ☐ Accounting
- ☐ Bookkeeping
- ☐ Financial records
- ☐ Fiscal analysis, controls, reductions, and programming
- ☐ Statistical analyses

With Organization Planning

- ☐ Principles of planning and management
- ☐ Systems analysis
- ☐ Data analysis studies
- ☐ Industrial applications
- ☐ Government contracts
- ☐ Merchandising
- ☐ Marketing/sales
- ☐ Packaging
- ☐ Distribution
- ☐ Policy development
- ☐ R & D program and project management
- ☐ How a volunteer organization works

When you are done checking off subjects on this list, *well --
you know the drill.* Look only at the subjects you checked, and
now cross out *any* which are not your favorites (clue: you
couldn't stand working at a place where *this* was the language
you had to listen to, all day long). Study what's left -- that you
checked but *didn't* cross out.

A LIST OF
YOUR TOP TEN
FAVORITE SUBJECTS

No, no, you don't need to run through another list. You
already have this information. Your favorite subjects are, quite
simply, all the subjects on the table and/or on the long list you
have just covered that you:

a) Checked off, *but*

b) Didn't later cross out

You *may* want to put the two lists together by copying all 'the
survivors' on a separate piece of paper, so you can see them
clearly. Then, what you need to do next is to look at all these
'survivors' and, by guess and by gosh, circle your ten favorites.[3]
Don't sit and agonize about this. Just quickly circle the ten that
your instincts tell you are your favorites -- never mind in what
order (for the moment). Later, review, meditate, ponder, and
agonize, if you wish.

When you are pretty well satisfied that you've got your top ten
favorites, you will then need to prioritize them in *exact* order,
using the Ten Item prioritizing grid on page 194, so that you
end up with a list of your absolutely favorite subject in the
number one position, your next favorite in the number two, etc.

It is always wise, when you are done, to review your list, and
ask yourself, "Do I *really* want this subject to be one of the
languages of my new career, or not?" Example: you may know
how to play the trumpet, and this may have come up as number
two or three on your prioritized list of favorite subjects. *But,* you
know in your heart you don't *really* want to talk about, or deal
with, trumpets all day. Or do you? Only you can say.

---

3. If you just *can't* get it down to 10, then remember there *is* a prioritizing grid that
deals with as many as 24 items, on page 195.

PUTTING THEM ON
THE FLOWER DIAGRAM

Now, turn to the *Flower Diagram* on page 228, and on the *petal* called **My Favorite Subjects** copy the list you just prioritized. There is, on page 228, room for only your top *three* favorite subjects, but if you copy the whole diagram on a larger piece of paper (and I encourage you to), you will have room to list all ten.[4]

Now you know the languages you would most like to listen to, speak, and deal with, at your workplace, in your next career or job. Put them all together (Chapter 11), and you have your field.

WHAT ELSE
DETERMINES *WHERE?*

You noticed, of course, that there were other *petals* on the *Flower,* that you haven't filled in, yet. They are there because there are other factors -- besides your *favorite subjects* -- which will determine **Where** you want to use your skills. The following lists correspond, each in turn, to those *petals.*

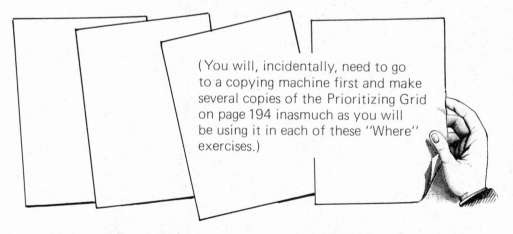

(You will, incidentally, need to go to a copying machine first and make several copies of the Prioritizing Grid on page 194 inasmuch as you will be using it in each of these "Where" exercises.)

---

4. A more elaborate process than the one discussed here in Chapters 9, 10, and 11, is available from Ten Speed Press, Box 7123, Berkeley, CA 94707, as a workbook -- with the Flower Diagram and the other exercises appearing on larger, 8½ x 11" sheets. It is called "How to Create A Picture of Your Ideal Job," and you can order it directly from them ($5.95). If all you want is just a larger size picture of the Flower diagram, that is available from them, also, as a poster you can write on. The *skills keys*, enlarged, appear on the reverse side ($4.95).

*Title
of the Petal:*

**The Kind of Place
I'd Like to
Work:**

Please check off one or more of your preferences in the following categories. *"I would prefer to work for an organization that . . .*

- ☐ Produces information
- ☐ Invents/produces/sells a product
- ☐ Serves people

And one which is

- ☐ Outdoors
- ☐ Indoors
- ☐ A place with 5 or less employees
- ☐ A place with 20 or less employees
- ☐ A place with 100 or less employees
- ☐ A large corporation
- ☐ A place in a large city
- ☐ A place in the suburbs
- ☐ A place in the country
- ☐ In a particular part of this country (see Chapter 7)
- ☐ A profit-making firm
- ☐ A nonprofit firm or organization
- ☐ A service organization
- ☐ An old organization
- ☐ A new organization
- ☐ A place which is 'going and growing'
- ☐ An organization with lots of problems
- ☐ My own business (see Chapter 6)

Add any other items that may occur to you; then take the items you have checked and prioritize them -- put them in their order of importance to you -- and enroll at least the top three on the appropriate *petal* on *The Flower Diagram*, page 228.

*Title
of the Petal:*

**At a Place That
Deals With,
or Has:**

Please check off one or more of your preferences in the following categories. *"I would prefer to work for an organization that deals with, or has, . . .*

Growing Things
- ☐ Trees, bushes, landscaping stuff
- ☐ Flowers, plants
- ☐ Garden tools
- ☐ Crops
- ☐ Ploughs
- ☐ Threshing machines, reapers, harvesters

Materials
- ☐ Paper
- ☐ Woods, plywood, etc.
- ☐ Pottery, pewter
- ☐ Bronze, brass, or aluminum
- ☐ Textiles, cloth, felt, hides, synthetics

Clothing
- ☐ Sewing machines
- ☐ Patterns, safety pins, buttons, zippers
- ☐ Dyes
- ☐ Shoes
- ☐ Ski clothes, swimming suits

Shelter
- ☐ Tents
- ☐ Trailers
- ☐ Apartments, condos, houses
- ☐ Carpenter's tools
- ☐ Paints, wall coverings, carpeting
- ☐ Heating elements, furnaces, air-conditioners, fans
- ☐ Security devices, alarm systems, fire extinguishers, fire alarms
- ☐ Furniture
- ☐ Household items, furniture, kitchen items
- ☐ Washing machines, dryers

- [ ] Kitchen appliances, refrigerators, microwaves, ovens, dishwashers, compactors
- [ ] Cosmetics
- [ ] Tools, power tools

Food

- [ ] Meats
- [ ] Breads and other baked goods
- [ ] Health foods
- [ ] Vitamins
- [ ] Dairy equipment
- [ ] Winemaking equipment

Health Equipment or Materials

- [ ] Medicines, vaccines, thermometers
- [ ] Anesthetics
- [ ] Dental equipment
- [ ] X-ray machines
- [ ] False parts of the human body, hearing aids
- [ ] Spectacles, glasses, contact lenses
- [ ] Gym Equipment

Transportation

Land
- [ ] Roads
- [ ] Bicycles, motorcycles, mopeds
- [ ] Automobiles
- [ ] Trains

Air
- [ ] Gliders
- [ ] Balloons
- [ ] Airplanes
- [ ] Parachutes

Water
- [ ] Rivers, streams, canals
- [ ] Lakes, oceans
- [ ] Boats, steamships, sailboats, canoes, kayaks

Amusement

- [ ] Amusement parks, game parks, aquatic parks
- [ ] Toys
- [ ] Cards, board games, checkers, chess, Monopoly, etc.
- [ ] Kites
- [ ] Musical instruments
    Specify:

Sports equipment
- [ ] Fishing rods, fishhooks, bait
- [ ] Skis, lodges

Manufactured Stuff

- ☐ Office supplies: pens, pencils, desks, tables
- ☐ Computers, typewriters
- ☐ Copying machines, fax machines, printers, printing presses
- ☐ Walkie-talkies, telephones, cellular phones, voice mail, answering machines
- ☐ Tools
- ☐ Clocks
- ☐ Telescopes
- ☐ Microscopes
- ☐ Electrical and electronics equipment
- ☐ Calculators
- ☐ Adding machines
- ☐ Cash registers
- ☐ Money
- ☐ Laser beams
- ☐ Educational materials: easels, projectors, flipcharts, etc.

**If I Have To Find Information Someone Else Has
Already Gathered, I Prefer to Read or Gather It From:**

- ☐ Newspapers
- ☐ Magazines
- ☐ Computers
- ☐ Computer printouts
- ☐ Books
- ☐ Catalogs
- ☐ Handbooks
- ☐ Records, files
- ☐ Trade or professional literature
- ☐ Videotapes
- ☐ Audiotapes
- ☐ Interviewing others, in person or by phone
- ☐ Seminars, learning from trainers
- ☐ Courses, learning from teachers

**If It Is My Job to Go Gather the Information, Which
Nobody Else Has, I Would Like to Participate In**

- ☐ Investigations
- ☐ Surveys or polls
- ☐ Research projects, research and development projects, project reports
- ☐ Data analysis studies
- ☐ Add your own:

Add any other items that may occur to you; then take the items
you have checked and prioritize them -- put them in their order
of importance to you -- and enroll at least the top three on the
appropriate *petal* on *The Flower Diagram,* page 228.

*Title
of the Petal:*

**Kinds of
Co-workers
I'd Like**

Please check off one or more of your preferences in the following categories. *"I would prefer to work for an organization that has the following kinds of co-workers, colleagues, bosses, or subordinates within that organization . . .*

☐ Men primarily
☐ Women primarily
☐ Both sexes
☐ Heterosexuals
☐ Homosexuals
☐ All people regardless of sexual orientation
☐ People of all ages
☐ Adolescents or young people
☐ College students
☐ Young adults
☐ People in their thirties
☐ The middle-aged
☐ The elderly
☐ The retired
☐ People of a particular cultural background:
☐ People of a particular economic background:
☐ People of a particular social background:
☐ People of a particular educational background:
☐ People of a particular philosophy or religious belief:
☐ Certain kinds of workers (blue-collar, white-collar, executives, or whatever):
☐ People in a particular place (the Armed Forces, prison, etc.):
☐ All people regardless of background
☐ People who are easy to work with:
☐ People who are difficult to work with
☐ Any other kind you can think of:

Add any other items that may occur to you; then take the items you have checked and prioritize them -- put them in their order of importance to you -- and enroll at least the top three on the appropriate *petal* on *The Flower Diagram,* page 228.

*Title
of the Petal:*

**Kinds of People
I'd Like to
Help:**

Please check off one or more of your preferences in the following categories. *"I would prefer to work for an organization that allows me to help or serve the following kinds of customers, clients, or people . . .*

☐ Men
☐ Women
☐ Individuals
☐ Groups of eight or less
☐ Groups larger than eight
☐ Babies
☐ School-age children
☐ Adolescents or young people
☐ College students
☐ Young adults
☐ People in their thirties
☐ The middle-aged
☐ The elderly
☐ The retired
☐ All people regardless of age
☐ Heterosexuals
☐ Homosexuals
☐ All people regardless of sex
☐ People of a particular social background:
☐ People of a particular educational background:
☐ People of a particular philosophy or religious belief:
☐ Certain kinds of workers (blue-collar, white-collar, executives, or whatever):
☐ People who are poor:
☐ People who are easy to work with:
☐ People who are difficult to work with:
☐ People in a particular place (the Armed Forces, prison, etc.)
☐ Any other kind of customers or clients that you can think of:

Add any other items that may occur to you; then take the items you have checked and prioritize them -- put them in their order of importance to you -- and enroll at least the top three on the appropriate *petal* on *The Flower Diagram,* page 228.

*Title
of the Petal:*

**My Primary Goals
In My New
Career:**

Please check off one or more of your preferences in the following categories. *"I would prefer to work for an organization that has, or allows me to have, one or more of the following goals in all I do there . . .*

☐ To do work which brings more information/truth into the world.
☐ To do work which brings more beauty into the world.
☐ To do work which brings more justice, truth, and ethical behavior into the world.
☐ To serve or help those who are in need.
☐ To have an impact, to cause change.
☐ To influence people and gain a response.
☐ To impress people with my going the second mile, in meeting their needs.
☐ To begin a new business, or do some project from start to finish.
☐ To be in charge of whatever it is that I am doing, so that I get to be the decision-maker.
☐ To develop or build something, where there was nothing.
☐ To have a vision of what something could be, and help that vision to come true.
☐ To fix something that is broken,
☐ To improve something or make it better.
☐ To do something that no one has done before.
☐ To do something that everyone says couldn't be done.
☐ To combat some force/influence/pervasive trend, persevere and prevail.
☐ To master some technique, or field.
☐ To excel and be the best at whatever it is I do.
☐ To be in the spotlight, gain recognition, and be known.
☐ To make it into a higher echelon than I currently am, in terms of reputation, and/or prestige, and/or membership, and/or salary.[5]

Add any other items that may occur to you; then take the items you have checked and prioritize them -- put them in their order of importance to you -- and enroll at least the top three on the appropriate *petal* on *The Flower Diagram,* page 228.

Title
of the Petal:

Salary
or Level
I'd Like

Please check off one or more of your preferences in the following categories. *"I would prefer to work for an organization that gives me the following . . .*

☐ Salary and level I would like to have, at a minimum:
☐ Salary and level I would like eventually to reach, if I can:

Then take these items as you have described them, and enroll them on the appropriate *petal* on *The Flower Diagram*, on the following page:

---

5. I am indebted to my friend, Arthur Miller, for suggesting many of these goals. His pioneering work with respect to goals is enshrined in his book, *The Truth About You*, by Arthur F. Miller & Ralph T. Mattson; available from Ten Speed Press, Box 7123, Berkeley, CA 94707.

The Flower Diagram

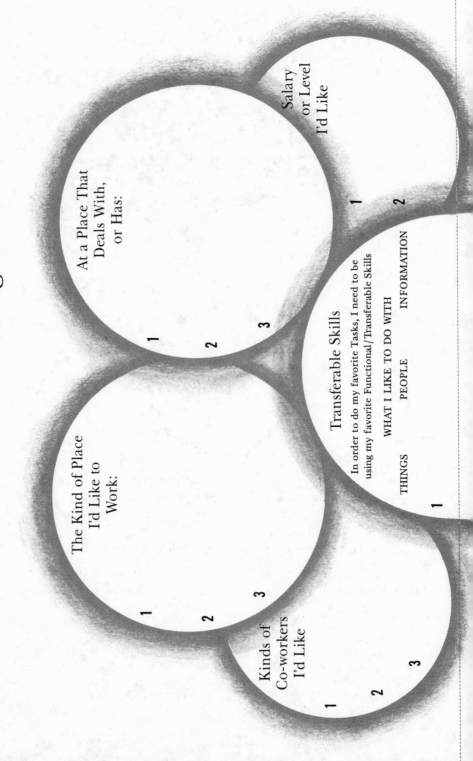

At a Place That Deals With, or Has:

1
2
3

Salary or Level I'd Like

1
2

The Kind of Place I'd Like to Work:

1
2
3

Transferable Skills

In order to do my favorite Tasks, I need to be using my favorite Functional/Transferable Skills

WHAT I LIKE TO DO WITH

PEOPLE   INFORMATION

THINGS

1

Kinds of Co-workers I'd Like

1
2
3

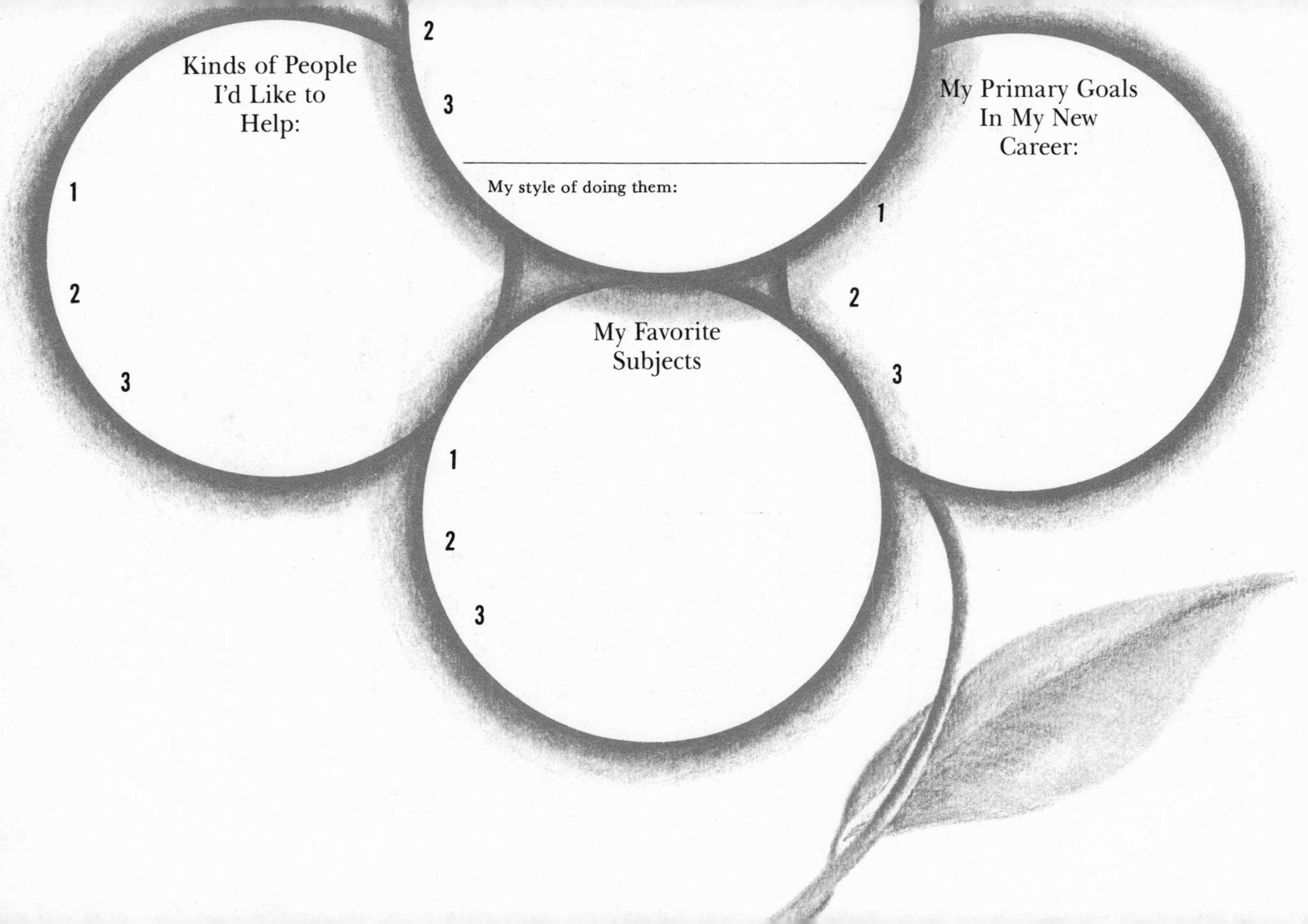

My Primary Goals
In My New
Career:

1

2

3

Kinds of People
I'd Like to
Help:

1

2

3

My style of doing them:

My Favorite
Subjects

1

2

3

YOUR OBITUARY
AS YOU WOULD LIKE IT
WRITTEN

Well, you are done with the **Where.** At this point, you may be troubled by the thought: *What if I've missed something; something important?* Well, in case the preceding lists or *exercises* didn't capture all your dreams, we've found there's an effective *catch-basin,* to check things out. It consists of what your obituary would say, were you able to have from now on the life you really want. It goes like this:

ON THE LAST DAY
OF MY LIFE

Spend as much time as necessary writing an article entitled "Before I die, I want to..." (And then list all the things you would like to do, before you die.) Confess them on a piece of paper now, and maybe you can begin to make them happen.

As you get involved with this exercise, you may notice that it is impossible to keep your focus only on your proposed new career. You will find some dreams creeping in concerning your leisure or your lifelong learning, of places you want to visit, and experiences you want to have that are not on-the-job. Don't omit these. Be just as detailed as you can be.

IN CONCLUSION

As you look over your completed *flower* picture, the beginnings of an idea may be forming in your head, as to what your new career might be. Fine. Just two warnings: first, don't prematurely close out *other* possibilities. Wait until you've done the work described in the next chapter.

And secondly, please *don't* say to yourself, at this point: "Well, I now see what it is that I would die to be able to do, but I *know* there is no job in the world like that, that *I* would be able to get."

You don't know any such thing. You need to do your (re)search first *(next chapter)*. Of course, it's possible that at the end of that search, you still may not be able to find *all* that you want, down to the last detail. But why not aim for it, and then settle for less *if and when* you find that you simply have to? Until then, you may be surprised at what you are able to turn up.

Of course, the *implementation* of your fondest vocational dream *may* have to be taken in stages. One man we know of, who had been a senior executive with a publishing company, found himself not enjoying retirement, after age 65. In fact, he was bored to death. He contacted a business acquaintance, who said apologetically, "We just don't have anything open that matches or requires your abilities; right now all we need is someone in our mail room." The 65-year-old executive said, "I'll take that job!" He did, and over the ensuing years steadily advanced once again, to just the job he wanted: as a senior executive, where he utilized all his prized skills, for some time. He retired as senior executive for the second time, at the age of 85.

It is amazing how often people do get their dreams, whether in stages or directly. The more you don't *cut* the dream down, because of what you *think* you know about *the real world,* the more likely you are to find what you are looking for.

Most people don't find their heart's desire, because they decide to pursue just half their dream -- and consequently they hunt for it with only *half a heart.*

If you decide to pursue all of your dream, you will hunt for it *with all your heart.* And therein lies the difference between finding it, or missing it.

Students spend four or more years
learning how to dig data out of the library
and other sources, but it rarely occurs
to them that they should also apply some of
the same new-found research skill to their
own benefit – to looking up information
on companies, types of professions, sections
of the country that might interest them.

Professor Albert Shapero
The late William H. Davis Professor
of The American Free Enterprise System
at Ohio State University

CHAPTER ELEVEN

The Systematic Approach To
The Job-Hunt and Career-Change:

PART III

How

Do You Go About
Finding Such A Job?

Chapter 11

What Career?

This is where you take the information you gathered about your favorite skills, and your favorite fields/subjects/*languages* in Chapters 9 and 10, and make some sense out of it all. Look at those two *petals* on your flower diagram (page 228 or the larger sheet you may have copied it on to) and study them for a while. Then take a sheet of blank notebook paper, and write out your hunches about the following questions:

1. Thus far, what type of job or career interests you the most, in terms of your favorite subjects? As I pointed out at length in Chapter 10, every job or career requires you to know a bit -- sometimes *quite* a bit -- about *something*. Various jobs or careers require you to know something about: health, or construction, or law, or computers, or buildings, or art, or the Japanese, or oceanography, or physics, or psychology, or the human body, or religion, or building materials, or cars, or gardening, or sports, or drama, or almost any subject you can name. It is, therefore, important for you to look over the *prioritized* list of your favorite subjects, at this point, to see which subjects/fields/languages you would *like* to be working *in*, and *with*, all day, at work. Jot the top three down, on your *hunch* paper.

Now, you don't want to find a field that uses just *one* of these. No, believe me, you want to combine *your top three* favorite subjects/*languages*, if you possibly can. That way lies job happiness. So, look them over, now. Any idea of how to put these all together? Jot down all hunches.

If hunches aren't coming, here's how to go at it a little more systematically. Suppose you discovered from your exercises in Chapters 9 and 10 that the three fields/subjects/*languages* you are trying to combine are: carpentry, plants, and psychiatry.

How do you go about finding what career will unify and combine all three of these -- carpentry, plants, and psychiatry? Well, first of all, you draw your friends and family into the game. Show them the three, and ask them for any ideas they may have. But if your family draws a blank, you're obviously then going to have to go talk to some strangers. The question is: *which* strangers?

To figure that out, you mentally translate each of the three into a corresponding person. In this particular case, Carpentry = a carpenter, plants = a gardener, and psychiatry = a psychiatrist. Next, you ask yourself which of these persons is most likely to have the largest *overview*. (This is often, but not always, the same as asking: who took the longest to get their training?) The particular answer here: the psychiatrist. You would then go see a psychiatrist -- say, the head of the psychiatry department at the nearest college or university,[1] and ask them: *Do you have any idea how to put these three subjects -- carpentry, plants, and psychiatry --*

---

1. If there is no psychiatrist at any academic institution near you, then pick the name of a psychiatrist out of the phone book, and ask to come see them. Pay them for their time, if there is no other way.

together in one job or career? And if you don't know, who do you think might? Keep going until you find someone who has a bright idea.

In this particular case (this is from an actual career-changer's experience), you will eventually be told: "Yes, it can all be put together. There is a branch of psychiatry that uses plants to help heal people. That takes care of your interest in plants and psychiatry. And then you can use your carpentry to build the planters for those plants."

When you have this much of a *lead,* you can flesh it out a little more, by going to some reference books to see what additional stuff they can tell you.[2]

That's how this process works.

That's how you go about putting three or four of *anything* together into one unified job or career.

*2. Starting at the other end, thus far what type of job or career interests you the most, in terms of **career families?** You can state this, first of all, in terms of three overarching career families: is it something*

---

2. For further information in the library about careers which may interest you, see:

Dictionary of Occupational Titles (DOT), 4th ed., revised 1991. *In two volumes.* Supt. of Documents, U.S. Govt. Printing Office, Washington, DC 20402. A catalog of the 12,860 occupations known to exist in the U.S. at present. It has an alphabetical index, by occupations. It is also available in an exact reprint from JIST Works, Inc., 720 North Park Ave., Indianapolis, IN 46202-3431. This is a very useful, though difficult, book. If you want to plumb its depths, I would recommend **strongly** that you *first* use Holland's Self-Directed Search, and thence *his* Dictionary *(both are explained more fully on pages 240ff.)* to tell you which occupations to go seeking in the DOT.

Occupational Outlook Handbook, 90–91. Bureau of Labor Statistics, available from Supt. of Documents, U.S. Govt. Printing Office, Washington, DC 20402. 225 occupations organized by interest and job title. This has also been published commercially under the title, *America's Top 300 Jobs,* by JIST Works, Inc., 720 N. Park Ave., Indianapolis, IN 46202-3431. 1990. The latter has some helpful indices and supplemental material.

Selected Characteristics of Occupations Defined in the Dictionary of Occupational Titles. U.S. Dept. of Labor, Employment and Training Admin., available from Supt. of Documents, U.S. Govt. Printing Office, Washington, DC 20402.

Job Selection Workbook, for use with Guide for Occupational Exploration. U.S. Employment Service, Employment and Training Admin., available from Supt. of Documents, U.S. Govt. Printing Office, Washington, DC 20402. 1979.

William E. Hopke, ed., *Encyclopedia of Careers and Vocational Guidance, 8th ed. 4 volumes.* Garrett Park Press, Box 190, Garrett Park, MD 20896. 1990.

There are also *numerous* books in most libraries, and certainly in most bookstores, on various groups of careers. You will find titles like Ten Speed Press's *Offbeat Careers: The Directory of Unusual Work,* career books on the health fields, etc., etc.

in AGRICULTURE, or something in MANUFACTURING, or something in INFORMATION/SERVICES?[3] Look over your list of favorite subjects and jot down your hunch.

Then you can narrow it a bit further. Not to *job-titles,* just yet -- there are 20,000 of them, in this and many other countries. But they have been reduced to 19 'families' or 'clusters,' by the U.S. federal government,[4] and these are relatively easy to make some choices between. So, read over your three favorite subjects/

languages, from question #1 above, and then look at the list below to see if any of these look as though they might combine your three. If so, copy them down on your *hunch* paper. (If not, don't be discouraged; later research, in this chapter, will help you uncover ones which do.)

---

3. It is of historical interest to note that these large fields have changed dramatically in their dominance of the workplace, during this century, here in the U.S. and elsewhere. There was a time, around the turn of the century, when the majority of the work force -- that is, over 50% of all workers -- were employed in agriculture. Then, by mid-century, that had changed, and the majority of workers were employed in manufacturing. Today, that has changed again, and the majority of workers in this country are employed in careers which deal with information, and/or render services to people. Consequently, though many individuals still choose a career in manufacturing or even in agriculture, it is the services/information sector that is growing the most rapidly today, and therefore creating the most job opportunities. Hence, the common statement that the U.S. has become "The Information Society." From the point of view of the job-hunter, however, what the dominant economy is in this country at any one time, should never be the determining factor in choosing your career. If you want to be a blacksmith, you should be one, even if there *were* only three left in the country. (There's a blacksmith shop right in the heart of San Francisco, for example.)

4. Through the U.S. Department of Labor, Bureau of Labor Statistics, (published in the *Occupational Outlook Handbook,* available in any library).

**CAREER OR OCCUPATIONAL
FAMILIES**[5]

1. Executive, Administrative, and Managerial Occupations
2. Engineers, Surveyors, and Architects
3. Natural Scientists and Mathematicians
4. Social Scientists, Social Workers, Religious Workers, and Lawyers
5. Teachers, Counselors, Librarians, and Archivists
6. Health Diagnosing and Treating Practitioners
7. Registered Nurses, Pharmacists, Dieticians, Therapists, and Physician Assistants
8. Health Technologists and Technicians
9. Writers, Artists, and Entertainers
10. Technologists and Technicians, Except Health
11. Marketing and Sales Occupations
12. Administrative Support Occupations, Including Clerical
13. Service Occupations
14. Agricultural, Forestry, and Fishing Occupations
15. Mechanics and Repairers
16. Construction and Extractive Occupations
17. Production Occupations
18. Transportation and Material Moving Occupations
19. Handlers, Equipment Cleaners, Helpers, and Laborers

---

*3. Looking now at your **favorite skills,** what interests you the most: a job where you would work primarily with **Things,** or one where you would work primarily with **Information/Data/Ideas,** or one where you would work primarily with **People?***

This *sounds* as though it were almost identical with #2, above; but it isn't. That was about broad *career families.* However, within almost any career family there are a wide variety of jobs open to you, and the question above is a good way to classify those jobs.

---

5. If you wish a more detailed explanation of these families, you can order *Matching Yourself With the World of Work, 1986 edition, reprinted from the Occupational Outlook Quarterly, Fall 1986,* from the Superintendent of Documents, U.S. Government Printing Office, Washington, DC 20402. It describes types of job characteristics for each family, in the form of an extended table, that you can compare to your skills and interests.

Let's take agriculture as an example. Within agriculture, you could be driving tractors and other farm machinery -- and thus working primarily with *things;* or you could be gathering statistics about crop growth for some state agency -- and thus working primarily with *information/data;* or you could be teaching agri-

YOU'LL LIKE THIS JOB, EXCEPT EVERY NOW AND THEN, WHEN THEY DUMP A LOT OF PAPER WORK ON YOU.

culture in a college classroom, and thus working primarily with *people* and *ideas.*

Almost all careers as well as career families offer you these three kinds of choices, though *of course* many jobs combine two or more of the three. Still, you do have to tell yourself what your *preference* is, and what you *primarily* want to be working with.

It is your favorite skills that will give you the clue. Look them over now, and see what you think. You can always refine your choice, or even change it, later. For now, jot down those hunches.

Well, that does it. Your *hunch* sheet is all assembled, in what we may think of as *its first draft.* It is, at this moment, only a 'working platform' for you to begin your information-gathering.

But now that you have finished assembling it, are you: a) inspired? b) puzzled? or c) depressed? If the latter, *don't give up hope.* We have some other cards up our sleeve.

A SHORTCUT

Bet you perked up, when you saw *that* heading!

The task of doing all the work suggested above can seem daunting. So, *naturally,* you want to know if there are any short-cuts. And, of course there are. Let's look at the most popular one.

It's called the RIASEC theory, and was invented by John L. Holland.[6]

In John's system, all jobs, careers, skills, and personality types are first reduced to just six clusters or families, rather than the nineteen we saw above. Then, those six families are later corre-lated with a whole list of possible careers, from the U.S. Dictio-nary of Occupational Titles, so you end up with many more choices than just Six.

Here's how it works:

First of all, you need to figure out your 'Holland Code.' The most thorough way to do this is to get your hands on a copy of John L. Holland's instrument called **'The Self-Directed**

---

6. John Holland developed this more than twenty years ago, and has continually updated it since then. It has been used by more than 12 million people, thus far.

Search (SDS).'[7] You can order an SDS Specimen Set from the publisher, Psychological Assessment Resources, Inc., Box 998, Odessa, FL 33556, (1-800-331-8378, or in Florida 1-813-968-3003). The cost is $10.45 *(at this writing)* -- which includes handling and shipping by UPS. This set contains not only the SDS, but also a Form R,[8] a brief *Occupations Finder* and a booklet 'You and Your Career.' The SDS is a self-marking test, which takes about 30–40 minutes. You score it yourself, and it will tell you *exactly* what your 'Holland code' is.[9]

A shorter, faster, not quite so accurate, way of going about identifying your 'Holland Code' is to do this 'Party Exercise' which follows:[10]

---

7. If you want a different approach to Holland's 'codes,' there is also *Your Career: Choices, Chances, Changes* by David C. Borchard, John J. Kelly, and Nancy-Pat K. Weaver. Kendall/Hunt Publishing Company, Dubuque, Iowa. 1992. Fifth Edition. Pages 64–104 deal with Holland exercises.

8. There is a Form E, for those with limited reading skills or for young people; there are also Canadian editions, in either English or French.

9. Holland codes are useful for other purposes than identifying interesting jobs or careers. They can also be used for choosing one's major in college, and for choosing one's leisure activities.

If you are just starting college, and are puzzled about what to major in, you may want to get your hands on the *College Majors Finder.* It helps identify the college majors that match your Holland 'code.' Over 900 college majors are listed. Psychological Assessment Resources, Inc., P.O. Box 998, Odessa, FL 33556.

If you want to choose leisure activities that are the *opposite* of the skills you use all week long at work, see: *The Leisure Activities Finder: For Use with the Self-Directed Search and the Vocational Preference Inventory.* 1990. Psychological Assessment Resources, Inc., P.O. Box 998, Odessa, FL 33556. This takes your Holland Code and relates it to leisure activities. We recommend, however, that instead of taking your *favorite* corner, e.g., 'S,' you go *across the hexagon* (as in The Party exercise, page 242) -- which in this example, would be 'R,' and look up *those* leisure activities. The reason for this advice, is that leisure is best when it is an *alternating rhythm* to the stuff you do, and the skills you use, when you are at work.

The background theory for Holland's 'codes' is carefully explained in:

John L. Holland, *Making Vocational Choices. A Theory of Vocational Personalities and Work Environments,* 2nd ed., Prentice-Hall, Inc., Sylvan Ave., Englewood Cliffs, NJ 07632. 1985. You can order it from Psychological Assessment Resources, Inc., Box 998, Odessa, FL 33556, (1-800-331-TEST, or in Florida 1-813-968-3003). $19.95.

10. I am the inventor of this exercise. I mention this because we receive *many* inquiries each year as to who invented it, and how can one get permission to buy or make multiple copies of it -- particularly from career counselors. The answer is, that in order to avoid competing with John Holland's SDS, which I don't want to do, the Party Exercise is not available separately, nor can it be reproduced by itself.

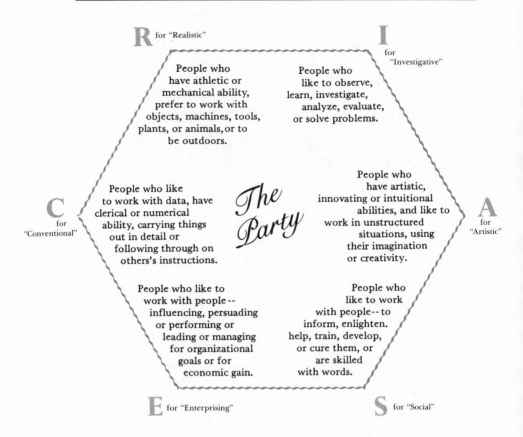

People who have athletic or mechanical ability, prefer to work with objects, machines, tools, plants, or animals, or to be outdoors.

People who like to observe, learn, investigate, analyze, evaluate, or solve problems.

People who like to work with data, have clerical or numerical ability, carrying things out in detail or following through on others's instructions.

The Party

People who have artistic, innovating or intuitional abilities, and like to work in unstructured situations, using their imagination or creativity.

People who like to work with people -- influencing, persuading or performing or leading or managing for organizational goals or for economic gain.

People who like to work with people -- to inform, enlighten. help, train, develop, or cure them, or are skilled with words.

Above is an aerial view of a room in which a *two-day* party is taking place. At this party, people with the same or similar interests have (for some reason) all gathered in the same corner of the room. It is a six-sided room, and all six corners are filled with babbling people. What they are babbling about, I have made clear by each corner. Now, the questions:

• Which corner of the room would you instinctively be drawn to, as the group of people you would most *enjoy* being with for the longest time? (Leave aside any question of shyness, or whether you would have to talk with them.)

Write the *letter* for that corner here:

• After fifteen minutes, everyone in the corner you have chosen leaves for another party crosstown, except you. Of the groups *that still remain* now, which corner or group would you be drawn to the most, as the people you would most *enjoy* being with for the longest time?

        Write the letter for that corner here:

• After fifteen minutes, this group too leaves for another party, except you. Of the corners, and groups, which remain now, which one would you most enjoy being with for the longest time?

        Write the letter for that corner here:

These three letters, in the order in which you wrote them -- such as 'S I A' -- are known as your 'Holland code.'

Once you know your 'Holland code,' you then want to look up *what* jobs or careers match that 'code.' The brief *Occupations Finder,* that is included in the Specimen Set, will *not* do.

Instead, buy, borrow, or go to your local library to consult a

copy of the *Dictionary of Holland Occupational Codes: A Comprehensive Cross-Index of Holland's RIASEC Codes with 12,000 DOT Occupations,* by John L. Holland and Gary D. Gottfredson. 1989. 2nd ed., revised and expanded. If you can't find it *anywhere,* it is available from the same publisher listed above for the SDS; be aware that it costs $33.

Still, it is an immensely helpful book, if you are working with Holland's system, for it gives a comprehensive list of occupations which your 'code' suggests, plus the DOT number for each of 12,860 occupations. So, look up your 'code' here in the *Dictionary of Holland Occupational Codes,* and from among all the occupations you find there, with that 'code,' jot down on a piece of paper ten or fifteen that look *really* interesting, to you. Ones that you want to explore further.

Then go to the U.S. Government's *Dictionary of Occupational Titles (DOT)* -- it is to that mammoth volume (actually two volumes) you should turn, which you can find at your local public or college library. From Holland's *Dictionary* you will have picked up the DOT number for each interesting occupation, so look up those numbers in the DOT. The DOT will then tell you, *in detail,* about those ten or fifteen careers you're trying to find out more about. On your list of those ten or fifteen, *cross out* any that no longer interest you, after you look them up in the DOT. This ultimately will leave you with less than fifteen[11] to go investigate with personal interviews, as I will shortly describe.

HOW TO FIND
THE MOST DEPENDABLE
INFORMATION

Having completed *Holland* or the *hunch* sheet, you will need some additional information, *of course.* And how do you find it? Well, the most dependable and up-to-date information will usually be found from talking to *people,* rather than trying to find the stuff you want to know, in *books.*

The reason for this is that *things are just moving too fast.* Yesterday's absolutely true certifiably guaranteed 100% accurate information is, tomorrow, completely outdated. Books just can't

---

11. If, by chance, none of the fifteen still interest you after those interviews, then go back to Holland's dictionary and choose fifteen new ones.

keep up. So, it's mostly people you must go see -- with *some* reading on the side, as we shall see.

This idea -- that during this information-gathering part of your job-hunt or career-change you're going to have to actually go *talk to people* -- is very terrifying to some job-hunters. But remember, you're going to have to do that *anyway* at some point during your job-hunt or career-change. You simply can't get a job without talking to people -- in what is called, as you know, 'the job-interview,' or *employment-interview*.

This earlier task which is before us now -- of talking to people *in order to get information* -- is not all that different. Talking to people is talking to people. We can, however, make a distinction between these two kinds of talking. Let's call the job-interview **E** for *employment*. Then we can call this talking with people just to get *information*, **I.**

These, then, are the two types of *talking to people*, or 'interviewing,' that you have to do during your job-hunt or career-change: **I** and **E.**

Since we have two different times when we need to *talk to people*, anyway, during the job-hunt, the late John Crystal[12] suggested that you throw in a third: a kind of warm-up for the other two types of 'interviewing.' Here you go out and talk to people about *anything* just to get good at *talking to people*. He thought shy people particularly needed this. And so they do. We'll call this third type of 'interviewing' -- this just for *practice,* just for *pleasure* -- **P.**

There are, then, *three* times when you need to *talk to people* during your job-hunt. And there is an order in which you do the three. First, **P.** Then, **I.** And, finally, **E.**

People who have followed John's advice, in this regard, have had a success rate of 86% in finding a job -- not just any job, but *the* job they were looking for.

Daniel Porot, the job-hunting expert in Europe, has put these three types of *talking to people* all together in a chart for the job-hunter or career-changer, called *'The PIE Method,'* which has helped thousands of job-hunters and career-changers in Europe. I reproduce it here, with his kind permission:

---

12. John also was the inventor of WHAT, WHERE and HOW -- which I have used as the basic framework for Chapters 9, 10, and 11, here.

Initial:	Pleasure **P**	Information **I**	Employment **E**
Kind of Interview	Practice Field Survey	Informational Interviewing or Researching	Employment Interview or Hiring Interview
Purpose	To Get Used to Talking with People to Enjoy It; To "Penetrate" Networks	To Find Out If You'd Like a Job, Before You Go Trying to Get It	To Get Hired for the Work You Have Decided You Would Most Like to Do
How You Go to the Interview	You Can Take Somebody with You	By Yourself or You Can Take Somebody with You	By Yourself
Who You Talk To	Anyone Who Shares Your Enthusiasm About a (for You) Non-Job-Related Subject	A Worker Who Is Doing the Actual Work You Are Thinking About Doing	An Employer Who Has the Power to Hire You for the Job You Have Decided You Would Most Like to Do
How Long a Time You Ask For	10 Minutes (and DON'T run over -- asking to see them at 11:50 may help keep you honest, since most employers have lunch appoint-ments at noon)	Ditto	
What You Ask Them	Any Curiosity You Have About Your Shared Interest or Enthusiasm	Any Questions You Have About This Job or This Kind of Work	You Tell Them What It Is You Like About Their Organization and What Kind of Work You Are Looking For.

Initial:	Pleasure **P**	Information **I**	Employment **E**
What You Ask Them *(continued)*	If Nothing Occurs to You, Ask: 1. How did you start, with this hobby, interest, etc.? 2. What excites or interests you the most about it? 3. What do you find is the thing you like the least about it? 4. Who else do you know of who shares this interest, hobby or enthusiasm, or could tell me more about my curiosity? a. Can I go and see them? b. May I mention that it was you who suggested I see them? c. May I say that you recommended them? ***Get their name and address***	If Nothing Occurs to You, Ask: 1. How did you get interested in this work and how did you get hired? 2. What excites or interests you the most about it? 3. What do you find is the thing you like the least about it? 4. Who else do you know of who does this kind of work, or similar work but with this difference: _____? 5. What kinds of challenges or problems do you have to deal with in this job? 6. What skills do you need in order to meet those challenges or problems? ***Get their name and address***	You tell them the kinds of challenges you like to deal with. What skills you have to deal with those challenges. What experience you have had in dealing with those challenges in the past.
AFTERWARD: That Same Night	SEND A THANK YOU NOTE	SEND A THANK YOU NOTE	SEND A THANK YOU NOTE

Let's see how all this applies to the *How* phase of your career-change or creative job-hunt, which you are now in. I will expand upon **P** and **I** in this chapter, and **E** in the next.

ooooooooooooooooooooooooooooooooooooooooo

THE   IN PIE

ooooooooooooooooooooooooooooooooooooooooo

WARMING UP, TO GET OVER ANY SHYNESS

Effective 'interviewing' for your job-search *always* involves some kind of warmup, first -- just as physical exercise does. John Crystal named this warmup "The Practice Field Survey." Daniel Porot calls it **P** for *pleasure* -- that is, 'interviewing' for pleasure. Of course, it could equally well be **P** for *practice*.

Whatever its name, the purpose of this first kind of 'interviewing' is simply to get you comfortable about going out and talking to people *one-on-one*. This is achieved by having you choose a topic -- *any* topic -- that is a pleasure for you to talk about with other people. And by encouraging you to make it a topic that *isn't* connected to your job-hunt (thus to reduce anxiety). That is to say, it should be a topic that has *nothing* to do with any present or future career of yours you are considering. Kinds of topics that work best, for the purposes of this exercise, are:

• **a hobby** you *love,* such as skiing, bridge playing, exercise, computers, etc.

• **any leisure-time enthusiasm** of yours, such as a movie you just saw, that you liked a lot

• **a long-time curiosity,** such as how do they predict the weather, or what do policemen do

• **an aspect of the town or city you live in,** such as a new shopping mall that just opened

• **an issue** you feel strongly about, such as the homeless, AIDS sufferers, ecology, peace, health, etc. [13]

WHO TO GO VISIT
(or Whom to go Visit)

As you can see from the first part of Daniel's diagram, you want to go talk to someone who is as enthusiastic about the thing you love to talk about. It should be someone you don't already know, but otherwise, there are no rules. Use the Yellow Pages, ask around among your friends, *who do you know that* loves *to talk about this topic?* It's relatively easy to find the kind of person you're looking for.

You love to talk about skiing? *Try a ski-clothes store, or a skiing instructor.* You love to talk about writing? *Try a professor on a nearby college campus, who teaches English.* You love to talk about physical exercise? *Try a trainer, or someone who teaches physical therapy.*

The wonderful aspect of this **P**ractice kind of 'interviewing' is that it helps those of us who are shy, even *terminally* shy, to get over it.[14] What this exercise teaches us is that shyness always loses its power and its painful self-consciousness -- *if* and *when* you are talking about something *you love.*

---

13. If you want further instructions about this whole process, I refer you to "The Practice Field Survey," pp. 187–196 in *Where Do I Go From Here With My Life?* by John Crystal and friend. Ten Speed Press, Box 7123, Berkeley, CA 94707.

14. Job-hunters often imagine that books like this are written by very aggressive, *take charge* kind of people. Not true. I, for example, am painfully shy; always have been. Unless, of course, I'm talking about a subject *I love.* The same will be true for you.

If you want to do further reading about shyness, its nature and causes, the classic text is: Phillip G. Zimbardo, *Shyness, What It Is, What to Do About It.* Jove Publications, 757 Third Ave., New York, NY 10017. 1977.

For example, if you love gardens you will forget all about your shyness when you're talking to someone else about gardens and flowers. *"You ever been to Butchart Gardens?"*

If you love movies, you'll forget all about your shyness when you're talking to someone else about movies. *"I just hated that scene where they. . . ."*

If you love computers, then you will forget all about your shyness when you're talking to someone else about computers. *"Do you work on a Mac or an MS-DOS machine?"*

Once you've defined your enthusiasm, and identified some-one you think shares that enthusiasm, you then go talk with

them. You can do this with or without an appointment. It is often better with this **P**ractice kind of 'interviewing' if the visit is spontaneous, rather than planned. But you have to use your own intuition about each particular case.

When you meet them, you ask for *ten minutes of their time, only.* Period. Stop. Exclamation point. And you watch your wrist-watch *like a hawk,* to be sure you stay no longer. You *never* stay longer, unless they *beg* you to. And I mean, *beg.*[15]

Once they've agreed to give you ten minutes, you ask them whatever questions are on your mind about the topic you have chosen. It is crucial that this topic, as described above, be one which you *love* to talk with other people, about. Absent that kind of enthusiasm, this exercise will be *a bomb.*

---

15. A polite, "Oh do you have to go?" should be understood for what it is: politeness. Your response should be, "Yes, I promised to only take ten minutes of your time, and I want to keep to my word." This will almost always leave a *very* favorable impression behind you.

> **Enthusiasm**
>
> Throughout the job-hunt (and career-change) the key to 'interviewing' is not found in memorizing a dozen rules about what you're *supposed* to say.
>
> No, the key is just this one thing: now and always, be *sure* you are talking about something you feel *passionate about.*[16]
>
> **Enthusiasm** is the key -- to *enjoying* 'interviewing,' and conducting *effective* interviews, at any level.
>
> That's why it is important that it be your enthusiasms -- here, your hobbies; later, your *favorite* skills and your *favorite* subjects -- that you are exploring and pursuing in conversations with others.

WHAT IF I'M TOO SHY TO DO THIS STUFF?

Well, you can't stay shy (down the line). At some point, if you want a job, you're going to have to *talk to people,* in what is called the job-interview. Since job-hunting means you *have* to talk to people, it might as well be *now.* Practice makes perfect.

But because you're *not* interviewing for a job at this point, it's perfectly okay for you to take someone with you during *this* **P** stage of the job-hunt: your best friend, a fellow career-changer, your mother, whoever.

And if you're absolutely tongue-tied when you go to see people, this *someone* can be someone who is more outgoing than you feel you are. And on the first few interviews, you can let them take the lead in the conversation, while you watch to see how they do it.

Once it is *your turn* to conduct the interview, it will by that time usually be easy for you to figure out what to talk about. You may discuss anything and ask any questions which come to your mind, just as long as you're having *fun* talking to this person about the *enthusiasm* you have chosen.

16. This is what the late Joseph Campbell used to call 'your bliss.'

WHAT IF I CAN'T THINK OF
A THING TO SAY?

But if no questions come to mind, the following ones have proved to be good conversation starters for thousands of job-hunters and career-changers before you. So, look these over, memorize them *(or copy them on a little card that fits in the palm of your hand)*, and give them a try:

Addressed to the person you're doing the practice field survey with:

- How did you get involved with/become interested in this? (*"This"* is the hobby, curiosity, aspect, issue, or enthusiasm, that you are so interested in.)
- What do you like the most about it?
- What do you like the least about it?
- Who else would you suggest I go talk to that shares the same interest?
- Can I use your name?
- May I tell them it was you who recommended that I talk with them?
- *Then, choosing one person off the list of several names they may have given you, you say,* Well, I think I will begin by going to talk to this person. Would you be willing to call ahead, so they will know who I am when I go over there?

Anyway, alone or with someone, keep at this **P** phase of 'interviewing,' until you feel very much at ease in talking with people and asking them questions about things you are curious about. In all of this, *fun* is the key. If you're having fun, you're doing it right. If you're not having fun, you need to keep at it, until you are. It may take your seeing four people. It may take ten. Or twenty. You'll know.

When you feel comfortable doing this, and it's easy to talk to people about topics in which you take great pleasure -- in other words, when you're having fun -- then you are ready for the second phase of *talking with people*, or 'interviewing':

○○○

THE IN PIE

○○○

THE REAL THING: RESEARCHING OR 'INFORMATIONAL INTERVIEWING'

Having gotten the **P** *for Practice and Pleasure* under your belt, you are now ready for this **I** phase: *'Interviewing' for Information* -- or, as it is often called, 'Informational interviewing.' All the confidence you picked up during the **P** phase of interviewing, will stand you in good stead, as you now go into Informational interviewing.

And why do you need this phase? Because, to complete this **How** phase of your career-change, or creative job-hunt, you need some more information than you've already got.

The information you badly need breaks down into four separate questions -- which you need to approach separately, solving each one in turn before you move on to the next. Here are the four:

• QUESTION #1

What are the names of jobs or careers that would give me a chance to use my most enjoyable skills, in a field that is based on my favorite subjects?

• QUESTION #2

What kinds of organizations would and/or do employ people in these careers?

• QUESTION #3

Among the kinds of organizations uncovered in the previous question, what are the names of the organizations that I particularly like?

• QUESTION #4

Among the organizations that I particularly like, what needs do they have or what outcomes are they trying to produce, that my skills and knowledge could help with?

We will tackle this last question in the next chapter. So that leaves us Questions #1, 2, and 3 to deal with here.

We begin then with #1. You've already done quite a bit of work on that one, back at the beginning of this chapter, when you wrote down all your hunches, and tried to figure out how to put three of your favorite subjects together, as one field or career. Or when you went through your Holland 'code,' until you came up with the names of ten or fifteen careers or occupations -- maybe less -- that look *real interesting*, on paper.

The question now is: are these careers really *that* interesting *in actual fact?* The only way you're going to be able to figure that out, is to go see **the workers** who actually do that kind of work. *They'll* be able to tell you. You'll find out 'from the horse's mouth' whether these jobs are as attractive to you, as they look on paper.

Not Employers

It is not *employers* you want to see *at this point* in your research -- unless they are the ones who are doing the work that interests you. It is *workers* you want to see, at this point. Go back and look at Daniel Porot's chart, and you will see who it is you go see at each step along the way: **P** = fun people; **I** = workers; and **E** = employers.

I have to underline this, because some job-hunters and career-changers *have* mixed them up in the past, often deliberately, and gone to visit employers at this stage. Informational interviewers shouldn't be visiting employers -- just, *workers,* at this point.

But there is no honest, open-hearted *technique* that cannot be twisted by those with clever, devious hearts, into some kind of *trick.* This has happened with Informational interviewing. *Some* job-hunters have thought, "Wouldn't this be a great *trick* to use so as to get in to see employers -- asking them for some of their time, claiming you need *information,* and then hitting them up for a job?"

In case *you,* even for a moment, are tempted to follow in their footsteps, let me gently inform you that employers universally detest such deception, and have in the past usually thrown the liar/trickster out of their offices. One New York employer said to such a trickster: "You came to see me to ask for some information. And I gladly gave you my time. But now, it is apparent you really want a job here, and think you found a 'trick' that would open the door. Let me tell you something: on the basis of what I have just seen of your style of doing things, I wouldn't hire you if you were the last person on earth. I know this Informational interviewing process well -- I've read *Parachute* -- but

---

> by turning it into a *trick,* you give the whole process a bad name, and make life difficult for every job-hunter who comes after you." *Ouch!*
>
> In this Age of Rudeness, Lies, and Manipulation, **you** will want, above all else, to be a beacon of integrity, truth, and kindness throughout your job-hunt or career-change. *That's* the kind of employee employers are *dying* to find. On the other hand, the quota for those who practice deception is already *more than* filled, in this fractured world.

WHAT DO YOU WANT TO LEARN FROM THE WORKERS?

When you go to meet workers who are doing work you think you might really like, you ask them *the same* four things we saw earlier, during our Practice Field Survey:

- How did you get into this work?
- What do you like the most about it?
- What do you like the least about it?
- And, where else could I find people who do this kind of work? *(You should always ask them for more than one name, so that if you run into a dead end at any point, you can easily go back and visit the other people they suggested.)*

In effect, what you are doing here is trying on jobs to see if they fit you. It is exactly analogous to your going to a clothing store and trying on different suits (or dresses) that you see in their window. Except instead of suits, it is jobs you are trying on. And why? Well, the suits that look terrific in the window don't always look so terrific when you see them on you. They don't hang quite right, etc., etc. Likewise, the jobs that look so terrific in the books or in your imagination don't always look so terrific when you see them up close, in all their true reality. You're looking for a job that looks terrific in the window, *and* on you.

If it becomes apparent to you, during any informational interview, that this kind of career, occupation, or job definitely *doesn't* fit you, then the last question (above) is turned into a different kind of inquiry: "Do you have any ideas as to who I could go talk to about these *other* kinds of work" -- here mentioning one of the unexplored careers you listed on your *hunch* paper).

Then you go visit the people they suggest.

"FRANKLY, IT'S NOT EASY BEING A PURITAN IN THIS HEDONISTIC SOCIETY!"

"I LIKE THE WORK THEY DESCRIBE, BUT NOT HOW LONG THE PREPARATION TAKES"

In trying to find out more about a new field, or career, look for the exceptions to the rules about what it takes to get into that field. People might *tell* you the rule is:

> *"In order to do this work, you have to have a master's degree and ten years' experience at it."*

But, if you aren't willing to go that long route, you will want to search for the exception:

"Yes, but do you know of anyone in the field who got into it
without that master's degree, and ten years' experience?
And where might I find him or her?
And if you don't know of any such person, who might know?"

Throughout your informational interviewing, don't assume anything ("But I just assumed that . . ."). Question *all* assumptions, no matter how many people tell you that 'this is the way things are.'

There are people out there who will tell you something that absolutely *isn't* so, with every conviction in their being -- because they *think* it's true. Sincerity they have, one hundred percent. Accuracy is something else again. You will need to check and cross-check any information that people tell you or that you read in books (even this one). One person's word should rarely be taken as *gospel*. Believe me, there are exceptions to almost *every* rule, except where there are rigid examinations one must take, as in medicine or law. Yet, even here, you can get *close* to the profession *without* such exams, as in para-medical, or para-legal, work.

Be careful. Be thorough. Be persistent. This is your life you're working on, and your future. Make it glorious. Whatever it takes, find out the name of your ideal career, your ideal occupation, your ideal job -- *or jobs.*

PEANUTS reprinted by permission of UFS, Inc.

THE OTHER QUESTIONS

> • QUESTION #2
>
> What **kinds of organizations** would and/or do
> employ people in these careers or occupations?

Once you've identified a career you *really* like, you are ready
to tackle *this* question.

Kinds of organizations is an important issue. Don't try to leap
over it. Jobs are hard to find, these days. You need to be sure
you have identified *every kind of organization* that might employ
you, before you get down to actual names and places. If you
don't discover *kinds* of organizations, first, before you get down
to actual names, you will automatically be missing many names
of organizations that would have been useful to know about.
Casting too narrow a net will doom your job-hunt before it has
even begun.

Let's take an example. Suppose you want to be a teacher, in your new career. And we ask you: *what kinds of organizations have such jobs?* You might answer, *"just schools,"* -- and finding that schools have no openings in your geographical area, you might say, *"Well, I can't find a job doing that."*

But no, my friend, the answer is not *'just schools.'* There are countless other *kinds* of organizations and agencies out there which have a teaching arm, and therefore employ teachers. For example, corporate training and educational departments, workshop sponsors, foundations, private research firms, educational consultants, teachers' associations, professional and trade societies, military bases, state and local councils on higher education, fire and police training academies, and so on, and so forth.

'Kinds of organizations' also means places with different *hiring modes,* such as:

• places that would employ you full-time;

• places that would employ you part-time (maybe you'll end up deciding to hold down two or even three part-time jobs, which altogether would add up to one full-time job, in order to give yourself more variety);

• places which you yourself would start up, if you want to be your own boss;

• places that are for profit;

• places that are nonprofit;

• places that take temporary workers, on assignment for one project at a time;

• places that take consultants, one project at a time;

• places that operate with volunteers, etc.

You want to discover all such *kinds* of places. And how do you do that? Well, your local town or city librarian can be a great help. So can people at universities or at businesses, who have an overview of the field or career that interests you. Contrary to your fears, people you seek information from will *usually* welcome you warmly, *provided . . .* (and you must take these provisos very seriously)

a. *provided* that you know what questions you are trying to find answers to; *and*

b. *provided* the answers can't easily be found in printed materials (reference books, magazines, journals), microfiche, or whatever;[17] or in any printed materials that *this place* may have, for distribution. *Be sure to go pick those up first there, before you take up someone's valuable time unnecessarily.* The reason you read these printed materials, *first,* comes from courtesy, kindness, thoughtfulness, consideration, and all those other qualities so difficult to find these days. But which *you* want to be known for, throughout your job-search, believe me; *and*

c. *provided* that when it is time for you to approach people, you approach first of all those people *whose business it is to give out information to the public.* I am thinking of such people as librarians, receptionists, public relations officers, the front desk in personnel offices, and the like; *and*

d. *provided* that if you approach some organization, you approach those in lesser authority first, to find out everything that *they* know, *before* you approach anyone higher up in the same organization.

---

17. Most of the reference books you will want, may be found in your local libraries *(that's plural):* the public library, your local community college library, university library, business library, and so forth. Before browsing, you need to be clear about what you are looking for.

If you *are* clear about what information you're looking for, there are then three ways to proceed:

a) Look at the list of books at the beginning of Appendix B in the back of this book, and see if you can guess which ones may tell you what you are trying to find out. Then go to the library, and look those books up in the card catalog or reference section, and see if you can put your hands on them.

b) If you don't know what books might be helpful, walk right up to the helpful librarian, and tell him or her what you're trying to find out. Ask them what directories, or other reference book(s), they think would help. If necessary, ask them to help you find them.

c) If there's no librarian available, or at least no *helpful* librarian, there are *(mercifully)* indexes (indices) to all the directories likely to have the stuff you're trying to find out. Names of those directories to directories are:

• Klein's *Guide to American Directories;* and

• *Directories in Print, 1994,* 10th ed. Gale Research, Inc., P.O. Box 33477, Detroit, MI 48232-5477, which contains over 15,000 current listings of directories, indexed by title or key word or subject (over 3,500 subject headings).

Ask Me Only
What I Alone Know

The principle here is that you approach people for the information *they alone* know.

If some of their subordinates know this information, don't waste the time of the senior person. Get it from their subordinates.[18]

If the information you are seeking exists in print, and is easily found, don't bother the subordinates, either.

People with jobs are busy people. When you, in effect, expect them to do your research for you, they will be *very* turned off to you.

Many times, of course, you will not have to go seeking this kind of help. While you were interviewing workers for question #1, you will often practically *stumble* over the answers to these other questions. When workers tell you about their jobs or careers, *of course* they will accidentally volunteer information about

---

18. Incidentally, visiting a senior person in an organization unannounced ("I just happened to be in the neighborhood") is universally perceived as the mark of an idiot. If you would like to be taken seriously, ALWAYS:

    a) make an appointment; *and*

    b) state at that time what amount of time you will need (eighteen minutes, *max*); *and*

    c) state at that time what it is that you are trying to find out. (Someone other than the person you are trying to see may actually be the one who has the information you are looking for. Often the aide/assistant/secretary/receptionist can tell you over the phone who that is, thus saving you from a fool's chase.)

kinds of organizations, and actual names of organizations, that have such jobs -- including what's good or bad about the place where *they* work. Jot it all down. Study it later.

CUT DOWN THE TERRITORY WITH A 'SEARCH STATEMENT'

The end result of looking at different *kinds* of organizations in your chosen field or career, is that you should be able to summarize all this research as a sort of *search statement,* describing what you are looking for. The *fodder* or *raw material* for putting together this *search statement* is the research you have just concluded, plus things you wrote back in Chapter 7 or on the *petals* on your Flower Diagram, page 228.

The function of this *search statement* is that it should **cut the territory down,** for the remainder of your job-hunt.[19] Since you are going to be approaching *any* organization that interests you, whether or not they have an advertised vacancy, you *have* to find some way to narrow down the list of organizations that you will need to weigh, consider, research, and then go visit. A successful job-hunt and career-change must look essentially like the diagram on the following two pages.

19. If you resist this idea, if you feel you could be happy *anywhere* just as long as you were using your favorite skills, then almost no organization in the country would be ruled out. Well, in the U.S. currently there are 5,708,000 organizations, hence 5,708,000 job-markets, out there for you to go look at. (And similar statistics for other countries.) You'll have to visit them all. We'll see you again in about 43 years.

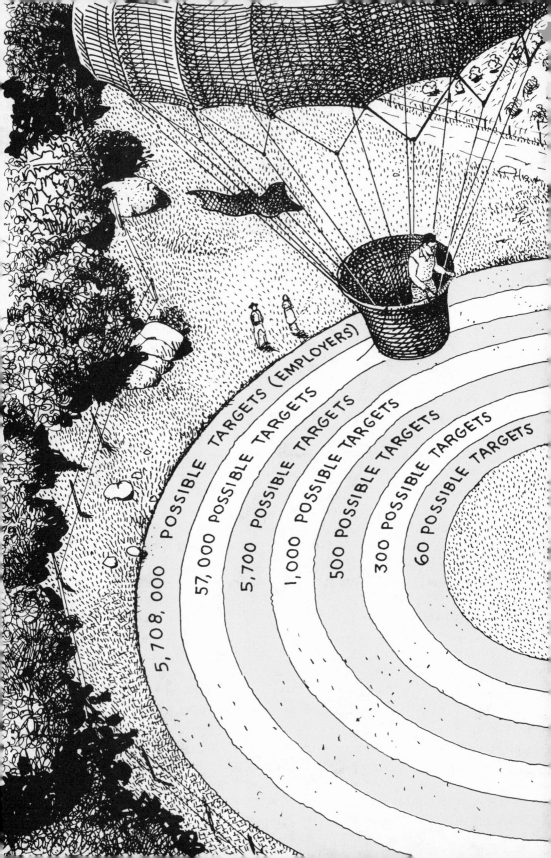

5,708,000 POSSIBLE TARGETS (EMPLOYERS)

57,000 POSSIBLE TARGETS

5,700 POSSIBLE TARGETS

1,000 POSSIBLE TARGETS

500 POSSIBLE TARGETS

300 POSSIBLE TARGETS

60 POSSIBLE TARGETS

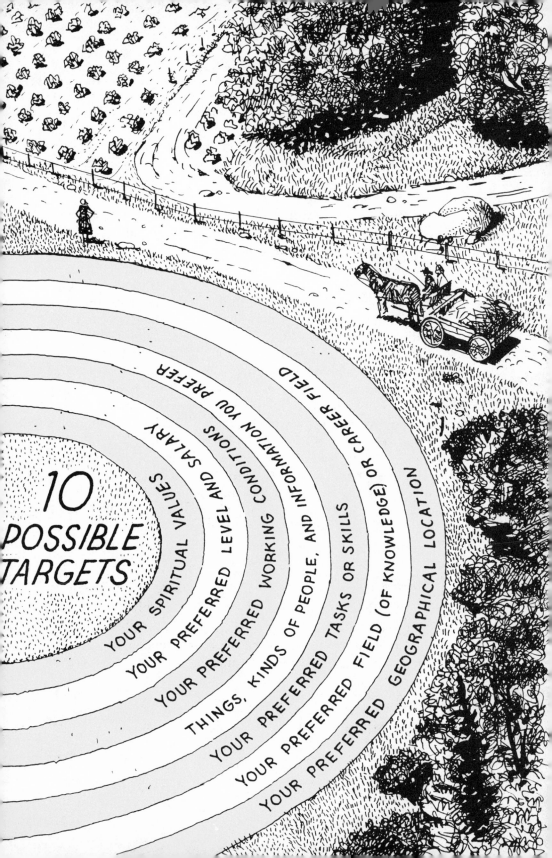

Now, let's see how it works. Suppose that in answer to question #1, you discovered that the career which interests you the most is *welding*.

Your search statement would then *begin* with the phrase: *"I'm looking for the names of organizations that hire welders."* Well, that's a beginning. You've cut the 5,708,000 job-markets in your country, say, down to just those that hire welders.

But the territory is still too large. There might be thousands of places that use welders. You can't go visit them all. So, you've got to cut the territory down, further.

So, let's see how you do that. Look at whatever you wrote about geography in Chapter 7. Suppose you decided there that you really want to live and work in, let us say, the San Jose area of California. You modify your search statement accordingly, so that it now reads: *"I'm looking for the names of organizations in the San Jose area which hire welders."*

It's still too large. That could be 100, 200, 300. So you look at the Flower Diagram, on page 228, and study the *petal* on "Kind of Place I'd Like to Work." Suppose you decided there that you really want to work for an organization with fifty or less employees. You add *this* to your search statement, so that it now reads: *"I'm looking for the names of organizations having fifty or less employees which hire welders, in the San Jose area."*

It still may be too large. So you look again at the Flower Diagram, and study the *petal* on "At A Place That Deals With, or Has." Suppose you decided there that you really want to work for an organization which works with, or produces, *wheels*. You add *this* to your search statement, so that it now reads:

"I'm looking for the names of organizations in the San Jose area, which hire welders to work on wheels, and have fifty or less employees."

And so it goes. You can keep refining the *search statement* until there are no more than 10 places -- perhaps less -- that would fit it. That's a manageable area on which to perform the next task in your job-search:

THE THIRD QUESTION

> **• QUESTION #3**
>
> Among the kinds of organizations uncovered in the previous question, what are the **names of particular places** that I especially like?

If you didn't already *stumble* over names during previous phases of your Informational interviewing, then you're going to have to consult some directories. If it's the name of large organizations that you're looking for, see the list at the beginning of Appendix B, in the back of this book. There are *many* directories of such large organizations. Also consult special guides, such as guides to 'socially-responsible companies.'[20]

If it's the name of smaller organizations that you're looking for, consult the yellow pages of your phone book, under every related heading that you can think of. You won't likely lack for names, believe me -- unless it's a very small town you live in, in which case you'll need to cast your net a little wider, to include other places that are within commuting distance.

---

20. Careers in this arena are often called "public service careers." Public service careers include such varied occupations as:
- city planner,
- community services officer at a community college,
- gerontology specialist,
- officials dealing with foster parent programs for mentally retarded persons,
- public health officials,
- recreation education,
- social service technician,
- welfare administration,
- workers in the child welfare program,
- workers with the handicapped.

Potential employers for social or public service occupations include government (Federal, State, or Local), nonprofit organizations, agencies (independent of state or local government, but often cooperating with them), colleges (particularly community colleges), associations, social welfare agencies, public health departments, correctional institutions, government offices, Job Partnership Training offices, hospitals, rest homes, elementary and secondary schools, parks and recreation agencies, etc.

If you are interested in this general field of social service, you ought to do extensive research, with a heavy emphasis on talking with people actually doing the work you

If, from your contacts and from all this research, you can't turn up *any* names, then you need to consider a career counselor (see Appendix A). Or you need to consider *moving* (see Chapter 7).

OKAY, I HAVE THEIR NAME, BUT WILL I LIKE IT THERE?

But we'll assume you do turn up some names. Almost all job-hunters or career-changers do, who take the previous steps in this chapter seriously. What next?

Well, once you've identified organizations *(plural, not singular)* by name, that fit your *search statement* above, you then try to think of every way in the world that you could find out more about those places, to see if you like them. There are several ways you can do this.

• **Friends and Neighbors.** Once you have the name of a place you ask *everybody* you know, if they know anyone who works there. And, if they do, you ask them if they could arrange for you and that person to get together, for coffee or tea. At that time, you tell them the place interests you, and you'd like to

---

think you would like to do; you will find their names through the national associations in the fields that interest you, also in State departments, and County and City governments (your local reference librarian in your local library can help you locate these associations -- also see the list on page 389).

If you know exactly what it is you want to do, but funding is the problem, thorough research on your part will often reveal ways in which funding can be found for positions not yet created; it all depends on your finding a person who knows something about that.

As for what career to choose within this broad category, there are these helps:

Alternative America. 1991 ed. Alternative America, Resources, 40 Welles Ave., Boston, MA 02124. 1991. A directory of 12,000+ alternative, progressive, innovative, experimental groups and organizations, with a geographical index, name index, and subject index. Lists such groups as bookstores, communes, ecology groups, film/video groups, human potential movement, alternative radio stations, women's groups, etc. Includes about 1,000 foreign places.

Devon Smith, ed., and James LaVeck, asst. ed., *Great Careers: The Fourth of July Guide to Careers, Internships, and Volunteer Opportunities in the Nonprofit Sector.* 2nd ed. Garrett Park Press, Box 190, Garrett Park, MD 20896. 1990. Very useful book with essays and lists of places; includes arts-related careers, and careers dealing with such issues as hunger, animal rights, the environment, homelessness, international jobs, working with people who are disabled, social action, and peace.

Community Jobs: The Employment Newspaper for the Non-Profit Sector, published by ACCESS: Networking in the Public Interest, 1601 Connecticut Ave., NW, Room 600F,

know more about it. (It helps if your mutual friend is sitting there with the two of you, so the purpose of this little chat won't be misconstrued.) This is the vastly preferred way to find out about a place. However, obviously you need a couple of alternatives up your sleeve, in case you run into a dead end here. The first alternative is *volunteer work,* and the second is *temporary agencies.*

• **Volunteer Work.** This is a useful way to explore a place, if you have a long period of unemployment staring you in the face. You offer to do volunteer work at a place you're trying to find out more about. Because you offer your services *without pay* for a brief, limited period of time, it's relatively easy to talk them into letting you work there for a while. Thus you get a chance to know them from the inside. Not so coincidentally, if you decide you would really like to work there permanently, they've had a chance to see you in action, and when you are about to end your volunteer time there, *may* want to hire you permanently. I say *may.* Don't be mad if they simply say, "Thanks very much for helping us out." (That's what *normally* happens.) You've still learned a lot, that will stand you in good stead, in the future -- even with other organizations.

Washington, DC 20009. Lists jobs and internships in nonprofit community organizations. Write directly to them for subscription information.

Lilly Cohen and Dennis R. Young, *Careers for Dreamers and Doers: A Guide to Management Careers in the Nonprofit Sector.* The Foundation Center, 79 Fifth Ave., New York, NY 10003. 1989. The authors say that this sector has 900,000 organizations and employs over 8 million people.

Peter F. Drucker, *Managing The Non-Profit Organization: Practices and Principles.* HarperCollins Publishers, 10 E. 53rd St., New York, NY 10022. 1990. Very helpful, as is anything from Peter Drucker's pen.

Paul Schmolling, Jr., with William R. Burger and Merrill Youkeles, *Careers in Mental Health: A Guide to Helping Occupations.* Garrett Park Press, Box 190, Garrett Park, MD 20896.

The CEIP Fund, *The Complete Guide to Environmental Careers: Forestry, Parks & Recreation, Environmental Planning, Air & Water Quality Control, Hazardous Waste Mangement, Land & Water Conservation, Fishery & Wildlife Management, Solid Waste Management.* Island Press, Washington, DC. 1989. Order from: The CEIP Fund, Dept. BKS, 68 Harrison Ave., Fifth Fl., Boston, MA 02111-1907. Also available from Garrett Park Press, Box 190, Garrett Park, MD 20896.

Mary Scott, *Companies With a Conscience: Intimate Portraits of Twelve Firms That Make a Difference* (Birch Lane Press, New York), 1992.

TEMPORARY AGENCIES:
A SPECIAL WAY OF
EXPLORING

• **Temporary Agencies.** Many job-hunters and career-changers have found that a useful way to explore organizations, alternatively, is to sign up with some temporary agency. Temporary agencies, in the old days, were solely for clerical workers and secretarial help. But the field has seen an explosion of services in recent years -- according to the Bureau of Labor Statistics, temporary or part-time workers now number over 35 million, and represent 29% of the total civilian labor force.

The Going Rate

Estimated hourly wages for temporary workers in 1991.

Computer analyst	$23.40
Registered nurse	23.15
Computer programmer	20.40
Manager	15.70
Licensed practical nurse	14.85
Word processor	10.55
Secretary	9.85
Machinist	9.45
Bookkeeper	7.05
Typist	7.00
Data entry keyer	6.95
Telemarketer	6.85
Receptionist	6.80
General office clerk	6.35
Guard/hospital orderly janitor/kitchen worker	6.05
Laborer	5.15

Source: National Association of Temporary Services

Now there are temporary agencies *(at least in the larger cities)* for many different occupations. In your city you may find temporary agencies for: accountants, industrial workers, assemblers, drivers, mechanics, construction people, engineering people, management/executives, nannies (for young and old), health care/dental/medical people, legal specialists, insurance specialists, sales/marketing people, underwriting professionals, financial services, and the like, as well as for the more obvious specialties: data processing, secretarial, and office services.[21] See your local phone book, under 'Temporary Agencies.'

The advantage to you of temporary work is that if there is an agency which loans out people with your particular skills and expertise, you get a chance to visit a number of different employers over a period of several weeks, and see each one from the inside. Employers turn to these agencies in order to find: a) job-hunters who can work part-time for a limited number of days; and b) job-hunters who can work full-time for a limited number of days.

Incidentally, it is perfectly okay for you to provide the temporary agency with names of organizations and places that interest you, since many if not most agencies try to secure *a job order* by calling companies up, cold, anyway. Many spend half a day, or more, on the phone, doing just that. They are grateful for *names of places*. It does them good, as well as you.

It is possible that the agency won't ever send you out, of course. Some agencies have many more *candidates* than they do job-orders, these days. In which case you may want to sign up with several temporary agencies. But mostly likely one or the other will eventually send you out. And once you're inside an organization, even temporarily, you can learn a great deal about it.

Do keep firmly in mind, however, the fact that you are still in the **I** or Informational interviewing part of your job-hunt. Don't, I repeat *don't*, try to *leap* over to **E** and the question of, "Can I get employed here?"

---

21. Donald Mayall and Kristin Nelson, *The Temporary Help Supply Service and the Temporary Labor Market*. Olympus Research Corp., 1670 E. 13th South, Salt Lake City, UT 84105. 1992.

You do still want time to check out other places. Trust me. And, besides that, employers hire temporaries today because they want to avoid the *benefits package* they would have to pay were this to turn into a *permanent* hire. *Sometimes* an employer may invite a temporary worker to stay on, as a permanent employee -- *if the employer likes their work, and if the employer's business picks up permanently.* But you should not set much store on this hope.

WHY ALL THIS WORK?

Mostly, these are simply a way for you to *scout out* organizations and find out which ones you like, and which ones you don't like, *and why.* Better to learn these lessons *before* you seek employment there, rather than *after.*

A survey of the Federal/State employment service, for example, found that 57% of those who found jobs there were not working at that job just 30 days later. They were not working at that job just 30 days later, *because* they used the first ten or twenty days *on the job* to screen out the job. By doing the exercises in this chapter, you are choosing a better way, by far. Essentially, you are *screening out* careers, jobs, places *before* you commit to them. How sensible! How smart!

WHAT IF I GET OFFERED A JOB ALONG THE WAY, WHILE I'M STILL ONLY GATHERING INFORMATION

You probably won't. Let me remind you that during this information gathering, you are *not* talking primarily to employers. You're talking to workers.

Nonetheless, an occasional employer *may* stray across your path during all this Informational interviewing. And that employer *may* be so impressed with the carefulness you're showing, in going about your career-change and job-search, that they want to hire you, on the spot. So, it's *possible* that you might get offered a job while you're still doing your information gathering. Not *likely*, but *possible.* And if that happens, what should you say?

Well, if you're desperate, you will of course say *yes.* I remember one wintertime when I had just gone through the knee of

my last pair of pants, we were burning old pieces of furniture in our fireplace to stay warm, the legs on our bed had just broken, and we were eating spaghetti until it was coming out our ears. In such a situation, *of course* you say yes.

But if you're not *desperate*, if you have a little time to be more careful, then you respond to the job-offer in a way that will buy you some time. You tell them what you're doing: that the average job-hunter tries to screen a job *after* they take it. But you are doing what you are *sure* this employer would do if they were in your shoes: you are examining careers, fields, industries, jobs, organizations *before* you decide where you can do your best and most effective work.

And you tell them that since your Informational interviewing isn't finished yet, it would be premature for you to accept their job offer, until you're *sure* that this is the place where you could be most effective, and do your best work.

But, you add: "Of course, I'm tickled pink that you would want me to be working here. And when I've finished my personal survey, I'll be glad to get back to you about this, as my preliminary impression is that this is the kind of place I'd like to work in, and the kind of people I'd like to work for, and the kind of people I'd like to work with."

In other words, *if you're not desperate yet,* you don't walk immediately through any opened doors; but neither do you allow them to shut.

A SUMMARY FOR THOSE
WHO LIKE SUMMARIES

This has been a chapter filled with many ideas. Your head is swimming. You want to recall the central underlying theme in all of this. Okay, here it is:

Job-hunting is a two-way street. For the time being, whether the places you are interested in, happen to have a vacancy, or happen to *want* you, is irrelevant.
In this dance of life, called the job-hunt, you get first choice: you get to decide first of all whether or not *you* want *them.*
Only after you have decided that, is it appropriate to ask if they also want you.

You're a bunch of jackasses. You work your rear ends off in a trivial course that no one will ever care about again. You're not willing to spend time researching a company that you're interested in working for. Why don't you decide who you want to work for and go after them?

Professor Albert Shapero
The late William H. Davis Professor of The American Free Enterprise System at Ohio State University

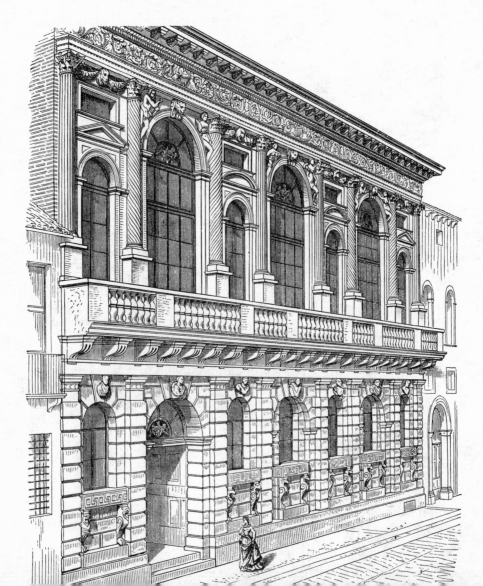

CHAPTER TWELVE

Securing the Interview

How

Do You Find The Person Who Has The Power To Hire You For The Job That You Want?

Chapter 12

Okay, so you've found a place -- better yet, *places* -- where you'd *love* to work. But the person you'd have to see, in order to get hired there, is in an office with a ring of fire around it, three knights in full-armor guarding it, in a castle with fifty-foot walls, surrounded by a wide moat whose deep waters are filled with hungry alligators. And you want to know how to get in there for a job-interview. Right?

Well, it isn't as difficult as it might at first seem. There is a way:

ooooooooooooooooooooooooooooooooooooooooooooooooooooooooooooooooooooo

THE  IN PIE

ooooooooooooooooooooooooooooooooooooooooooooooooooooooooooooooooooooo

E, as you recall if you read the previous chapter, stands for Interviewing for **Employment**. Job-interviews are terrifying to a lot of people -- turning the knees to jelly, and causing the palms to sweat. There are two problems: one is even getting in to *see* the person--who--has--the--power--to--hire--you. That's a biggie. The other is persuading them to hire you, once they do agree to see you. That's even more difficult.

Interviewing. *Yuk!*

HOW TO BE
AN INTERVIEWING VETERAN

However, most of us make it more difficult for ourselves than it needs to be, because we wait until it's time for the job-interview, before we even think about *how do you do interviewing?* We're rusty. Out of practice. Out of shape. And so, we crash and burn right in front of the prospective employer we care the most about.

But -- as we saw in the previous chapter -- successful job-hunters and career-changers avoid this humiliation by only facing employers after they have been doing interviews *throughout their whole job-hunt*. They realize there are actually three types of *interviews* one must do, in the job-hunt. Early on, in your job-hunt, you tackle interviewing whose purpose is merely that of **P**ractice and pleasure; in the middle of your job-hunt, you tackle interviewing whose purpose is to dig up **I**nformation you need about careers, organizations, and employers; and then toward the end of your job-hunt, you approach *employers* for the first time, to see about **E**mployment, or getting hired there -- but by then you're *an interviewing veteran*. Voila! **P--I--E is the key.**

That's the way to tackle it. Most job-hunters, of course, don't.

If you would be wise beyond your years, my friend, go back and read *and do* Chapter 11. That's how you defang interviewing of all its terrors.

Then you are fully ready to tackle the two problems we are about to discuss: getting in to *see* the person--who--has--the--power--to--hire--you (which is the subject of *this* chapter). And persuading them to hire you, once they do agree to see you (which we deal with in the next).

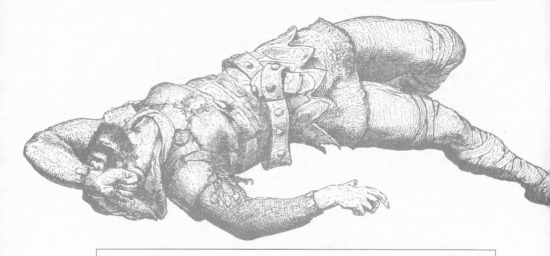

Half Our 'Ills' In Life Are Self-Inflicted

This is a hard truth for me to write about, and hard for each of us to take to heart in our own lives.

However, here it is: when we have a problem, life often shows us the solution, but we duck it because it involves work, and we wait instead for magic -- which never comes. And so, the problem remains.

We like then to pretend to ourselves that some mysterious outside influence -- life, the labor market, the government, an uncaring society -- is doing this to us. But by refusing to adopt the solution life has shown us, it is actually we who are doing it to ourselves.

We are like prisoners in a cell where the jailor is gone and the door is open. But we still just sit there, claiming we are a prisoner still.

To apply this to our present problem: the P–I–E method will solve the terror of interviewing, on which our job-hunt depends. But most of us duck doing the P–I–E method because it involves work, and we hope instead for magic -- which never comes. And so, interviewing continues to terrify us.

THE FIRST CRUCIAL QUESTION: HOW LARGE IS THE ORGANIZATION?

All techniques or strategies for securing an interview fall into two groups, *depending* on whether the organization you are trying to approach is a relatively large organization, *or* is what we call 'a small organization' -- one which has twenty-five or less employees.

Most discussions of job-interviewing *assume* you are approaching a large organization -- you know, the ones where you need a floor-plan of the building, and an alphabetical directory of the staff. There *are* huge problems in approaching such giants for a job-interview, not the least of which is that in the U.S. -- and throughout much of the rest of the world -- they are doing more layoffs than hiring, here in the '90s.

Two-thirds of all the new jobs that are being created, are being created by small organizations, and they are *much* easier to get into.

Aim At Small Organizations *Exclusively*

After you've figured out, as in the previous chapter, what your ideal job looks like, and you have collected a list of those workplaces that have such jobs, in your chosen geographical area, then you circle only the names and addresses of those which have 25 or less employees -- and go after them, in the manner I will describe later in this chapter. Look particularly for small organizations that are ***established*** or ***growing***. And if *'organizations with 25 or less employees'* eventually doesn't turn up enough *leads* for you, then broaden your search to *'organizations with 50 or less employees,'* and finally to *'organizations with 100 or less employees.'* But start *small*.

With a small organization, there is no Personnel or Human Resources Department to screen you out.

With a small organization, you don't need to wait until there's a *known* vacancy, because they rarely advertise vacancies even when there is one. You just go there and ask if they need someone.

With a small organization, if it's growing, there is a greater likelihood that they will be willing to create a new position for you, *if they think you are too good to let you slip out of their grasp.*

With a small organization, there's no problem in identifying the person–who–has–the–power–to–hire–you. It's *the boss.* Everyone there knows who it is. They can point to their office door, easily.

With a small organization, you do not need to approach them through the mail; you can go in to see the boss. And if, by chance, he or she is well-protected from intruders, it is relatively easy to figure out how to get around *that*. Contacts are the answer, as we shall see.

THE FOUR WAYS TO APPROACH LARGE ORGANIZATIONS FOR AN INTERVIEW

In securing job-interviews, it's the large organizations that are the problem -- the ones, as I mentioned above, where you need a floor-plan of the building, and an alphabetical directory of the staff. The ones where you can't even figure out *who* is the person–who–has–the–power–to–hire–you, much less get in to see them.

There is a way, as I will make clear.

It is the person–who–has–the–power–to–hire–you that you want to get in to see. But most job-hunters *don't* even *try* to find out *who* that person is.

Rather, they approach each large organization in what can only be described as a haphazard, scatter-shot fashion -- through one of four avenues. I will list these methods in order of *increasing* effectiveness, starting with the least effective method.[1]

1. *The **Most Ineffective** Way to Approach Large Organizations:* Going to some centralized place (such as a Job Fair) where employers come to hire people -- and getting an interview with the representative there. If you are a senior in college, the analog of this is a getting in to see a recruiter when -- and increasingly *if* -- they come to your campus.

This method *looks as though* it should have a 100% effectiveness rate in *getting a job-interview.* This is however an illusion, for two reasons.

First of all, there's no assurance that the large organization *you are particularly interested in* will even be there. If it's not there, the effectiveness of this particular approach to getting an interview with them is zero.

Secondly, even assuming it is there, your concern is not merely to get an interview with just *anyone* in that organization. *That's* easy. You could swing by their personnel department and get *that.*

No, your concern as a job-hunter is to get an interview with one particular person: namely *(all together now)* the actual **person–who–has–the–power–to–hire–you,** for the job you want. In the case of centralized Job Fairs or recruiter visits to campuses, you will be talking (in most cases) only to a *representative* of the company -- who, if they like you, have no power except to *pass you on* to the **person–who–has–the–power–to–hire–you.** And if they don't like you, to turn you down. Flat.

In other words, that representative or recruiter has a function similar if not identical to that of the personnel department, and

---

1. You will notice, of course, that some job-hunters use these approaches with small organizations, as well -- sad to say. It's so unnecessary.

in many if not most cases they *are* from the personnel department.

Because of this, the effectiveness of this approach in getting you an interview with the actual **person–who–has–the–power–to–hire–you** at the organization of your choice is -- as I said -- *somewhere* between 8% and zero.

2. *The* **Next Most Ineffective** *Way to Approach Large Organizations* (Yes, that means 'next to the worst.'): Contacting the organization first of all through the mail, by sending them your resume or some covering letter, and hoping *they* will invite *you* in. This is based on the theory that your resume or covering letter will serve as a kind of job application, or function as a kind of extended calling-card -- that you *hope* will pique the employer's interest.

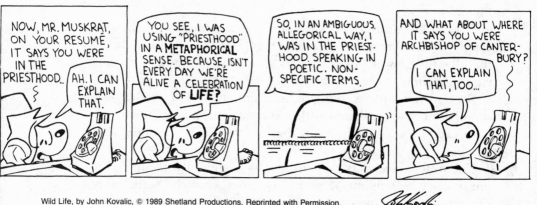

Wild Life, by John Kovalic, © 1989 Shetland Productions. Reprinted with Permission.

This is job-hunters' favorite way of approaching an organization for a job-interview. Never was faith so misplaced. True, when it works, it works well enough, but you *can* approach eight hundred organizations by mail (as millions of job-hunters have) and get not even one invitation to come in for an interview. Effectiveness rate in that case: zero.

Taken overall, when used with a number of organizations, this approach turns out to have an effectiveness rate of 8% in getting an interview and subsequently a job.

I covered the reason for this in Chapter 3, but if you skipped it or read it three months ago -- it is this: this 'mail approach' enables employers to screen you out *fast* without ever 'wasting their time' on an interview.

How fast? *Most* employers, or their subordinates, can *screen you out* in approximately thirty seconds, if your resume is sitting in a stack of, say, fifty, on their desk. And if it's in a stack of several hundred, the screening person picks up speed and -- we know by actual count -- can screen you out in as little as eight seconds. So, in eight to thirty seconds, *you're gone.* And, with it, any chance for an interview with the actual **person–who–has–the–power–to–hire–you** at that organization of your choice.

Organizations which have the time and the budget for it will subsequently send you a nice polite acknowledgement and turn-down. (Job-hunters seem to place an inordinate amount of hope upon the fact that they got a letter -- any letter -- from an organization they've applied to. Believe me, even when they say, *"However, we will keep your resume on file and should anything . . ."* it's still a turndown). They mean *the round file* (on the floor).

Those organizations which have neither the time nor the budget will not even send you a letter. You'll have to guess whether they ever even saw your resume, or whether they 'deep-sixed' it, unopened and unread.

The next method I shall tell you about is six times as effective as this approaching an organization by mail.

3. *The **Next to Most Effective** Way to Approach Large Organizations:* Going *face-to-face* at that organization, to seek a job -- though without any introductions or use of 'third-parties.' 47.7% of those job-hunters who use this approach, get an interview and job thereby.

This doesn't necessarily mean presenting yourself at an organization's personnel department. 85% of all organizations these days don't even have personnel departments (*or, as they prefer to be called now, Human Resources Departments*), so when you go face-to-face to 85% of all places, you simply talk to the receptionist in the front office.

But in the case of those 15% which *do* have personnel offices or departments -- and that includes *all* really large organizations -- when you go face-to-face it is with the personnel office that you will be speaking, if you have no 'third-party' introduction.

Coming in 'cold' this way, the receptionist or personnel department will probably ask you to fill out a job application. Job applications are application forms which have such simple questions as: Name, Address, Age, Places of Previous Employment, etc. Such applications vary greatly in their complexity, from ones used by fast-food chains, to those used by, say, engineering firms. If you've never seen one in your life, and you plan to approach organizations this way, you should familiarize yourself with an application form ahead of time. One way to do this without jeopardizing your job chances, is to go to visit some fast-food place or any large organization that has a personnel department, and simply *ask* for a job application, then immediately go back out the front door. Take the form home with you, where you can study it, and take a stab at filling it out, just for practice. Then throw it in the waste basket, after you've learned what you need to know. Now you know what an application form looks like, and how to fill it out. I hope you never need to.

Why is the effectiveness rate of this approach only 47.7%? The reason is that receptionists' or personnel departments' primary function, vis-a-vis job-hunters, is either to screen you *out,* or -- if they like you -- to pass you on to some person 'upstairs' -- namely, the **person–who–has–the–power–to–hire–you.** In over half the cases, you *do* get screened out. No personnel employee wants some *upstairs* executive screaming, "You're sending me too many people." Therefore, Personnel tends to live by the motto: *"When in doubt, screen them out."*

The last method of approach I am about to describe has almost *twice* the effectiveness rate of this method. *However,* it should be noted that in their pioneering study of the job-hunt some years ago, *The Job Hunt: Job-Seeking Behavior of Unemployed Workers in a Local Economy,* Harvey Belitsky and Harold A. Sheppard discovered that going face-to-face at a workplace, without introduction or *leads,* was *the* most effective job-hunting method if you were a blue-collar worker. Blue-collar workers take note.

4. *The **Most Effective** Way to Approach Large Organizations:* Going face-to-face at that organization, to seek a job -- after you *first* use your personal acquaintances or contacts to find out *who* at that organization has the power to hire you for the position you have in mind, and after you use your contacts to help you secure an appointment there, with that **person–who–has–the– power–to–hire–you.** When used with a number of organizations, and not just one, this method has an 86% effectiveness rate, for getting an interview and, subsequently, a job. (I shall say more about this, in a minute.)

Okay, now you've seen the four ways to approach the large organization of your choice for a job-interview.

You get to choose: which approach do you want to use: one that gets you a job-interview with the organization of your choice:

☐ Zero percent of the time
☐ 8% of the time
☐ 47.7% of the time
☐ 86% of the time

It's your *call.* Personally, I vote for the 86% approach. So, let's examine it in more detail.

It begins of course with the assumption that you are going to approach directly the **person–who–has–the–power–to–hire–you.** Small problem:

HOW DO I FIND OUT WHO HAS THE POWER TO HIRE ME?

Hey, in a small organization with 25 or less employees, as I said earlier, this is an easy problem. Calling the place and asking for the name of the boss, should do it. It's what we call *The One Minute Research Project.*

But if the place where you are dying to work is a much larger organization, then the answer is: "Through the research you already learned how to do (in Chapter 11), and by asking every *contact* you have."

Since this subject of *contacts* is widely misunderstood by job-hunters, let's be very specific, here.

Every person you know, is a contact.

Every member of your family.

Every friend of yours.

Every person in your address book.

Every person on your Christmas-card list.

Every merchant or salesperson you ever deal with.

Every person who comes to your apartment or house to do any kind of repairs or maintenance work.

Every check-out clerk you know.

Every gas station attendant you know.

Every leisure partner you have, as for walking, exercising, swimming, or whatever.

Every doctor, or medical professional you know.

Every professor, teacher, etc. you once knew or maybe still know how to get a hold of.

Every clergyperson, rabbi, or religious leader you know.

Every person in your church, synagogue, mosque, or religious assembly.

Everyone you know in Rotary, Kiwanis, Lions, or other service organizations.

Every person you are newly introduced to.

Every person you meet, stumble across, or blunder into, during your job-hunt, whose name, address, and phone number you have the grace to ask for. (*Always* have the grace to ask for it.)

Got the picture?

CULTIVATING NEW CONTACTS

Some job-hunters cultivate new contacts wherever they go, during their time of unemployment. For example, if they go to hear a speaker on some subject that interests them, they make it a point to join the crowd that gathers 'round the speaker at the end of the talk, and -- with notepad poised -- ask such questions as: "Is there anything special that people with my expertise can do?" And here they mention their *generalized* job-title: computer scientist, health professional, chemist, writer, or whatever. Very useful information has thus been turned up. You can also ask if you can contact the speaker for further information -- "and at what address?"

Conventions, likewise, afford rich opportunities to make contacts. Says one college graduate: "I snuck into the Cable Advertisers Convention at the Waldorf in N.Y.C. That's how I got my job."

Another way people have cultivated contacts, is to leave a message on their telephone answering machine which tells everyone who calls, what information they are looking for. One job-hunter used the following message: "This is the recently laid off John Smith. I'm not home right now because I'm out looking for a good job as a computer trouble-shooter in the telecommunications field; if you have any leads or just want to leave a message, please leave it after the tone."

You may also cultivate contacts by studying the *things* that you like to work with, and then writing to the manufacturer of that *thing* to ask them for a list of organizations in your geographical area which use that *thing*. For example, if you like to work on a particular machine, you would write to the manufacturer of that machine, and ask for names of organizations in your geographical area which use that machine. Some manufacturers will not be at all responsive to such an inquiry; but others graciously will, and and thus you may gain some very helpful leads.

GET OUT THE FILE CARDS

Because your memory is going to be overloaded during your job-hunt or career-change, it is useful, as you begin this process, to put each of the above names on a 3×5 card, with addresses, phone numbers, and anything about where they work or who they know that may be of use at a later date. Go back over those cards frequently.

Yes, that does add up to *a lot* of file cards. You've got *a lot* of contacts. But that's the whole point.

You may need *every one* of them.

Whenever a job-hunter writes me and tells me they've run into a brick wall, as far as finding out names of organizations or names of the **person–who–has–the–power–to–hire** is concerned, the problem *always* turns out to be: they aren't making sufficient use of their contacts.

The more people you know, the more people you meet, the more people you talk to, the more people you enlist as part of your own personal job-hunting network, the better your job-finding success is likely to be.

It takes about eighty pairs of eyes, and ears, to help find the career, the workplace, the job that you are looking for.

Your contacts are those eyes and ears.

They are what will help you get the ideal job you are looking for.

HOW DO YOU USE
YOUR CONTACTS?

Well, let's say it is a mythical organization called *Mythical Corporation* that interests you.

You know the kind of job you'd like to get there, but first you want to find out the name of the **person–who–has–the–power–to–hire–you** there. What do you do?

If it's a large organization, you go to your local public library, and search the directories there that I listed at the beginning of Appendix B *("Sampler of Information Sources")*. Hopefully that search will yield the name of the person you want.

If it doesn't, which will particularly be the case with smaller organizations, *then you turn to your contacts.*

You approach as many people as necessary, among all those you know, and you ask each of them, "Do you know anyone who works, or used to work, at *Mythical Corporation?*"

You ask that question again and again of *everyone* who is on your file cards, until you find someone who says, *"Yes, I do."*

Then you ask them:[2]

• "What is the name of the person you know who works, or used to work, at *Mythical Corporation?* Do you have their phone number and/or address?"

• "Do you think it would be worth my while to go see them?"

• "May I tell them it was you who recommended that I talk with them?"

• "Would you be willing to call ahead, to set up an appointment for me, and tell them who I am?"

---

2. I am indebted to my friend Daniel Porot for these suggestions.

You may then want to conduct the appointment over the phone, at an agreed-upon time, or you may want to go see them face-to-face, away from their worksite.

If you do go see them, try *never* to travel across town so as to arrive there just on time. This makes no allowance for the normal unpredictable things that happen to delay us all, when we least expect it.

No, you always leave for the appointment with about *double the time* you think it will take to get there, which means you will usually arrive at the site ahead of time. Then you go get a cup of coffee nearby, or you park down the block if you need to, until it's actually time for the appointment. Then you go in the front door right on time.

(When a reporter arrived late, once, for an appointment with a very famous person, that person replied, "How dare you keep me waiting? Are you that stupid?" You may wince at the put-down, *but* that's how a lot of people *feel* about people who are late for appointments, even if they would *never* say it, or at any rate not so strongly. You *don't* want anyone thinking that about *you* -- and especially not, when you are coming to them to ask for their help.)

After the usual polite chit-chat, you ask them the question you are dying to know. Because they are *inside* the organization that interests you, they are usually able to give you the exact answer to your question: "Who would have the power to hire me here, for this kind of position *(which you then describe)*?"

Then you further ask them what they can tell you about that person's job, that person's interests, and anything about their style of interviewing.

You also ask them about the organization, in general, for any information that they might think useful for you to know.

Finally, you ask them if they could help you get an appointment with that person.

Then you thank them, and leave; and you *never never* let the day end, without sitting down to write them a thank-you note. *Always* do it. *Never* forget to.

GETTING IN

If the contact you talked to, doesn't know the **person–who–has–the–power–to–hire** well enough to get you an interview, then you go back to your other contacts -- now armed with the name of the person you are trying to get in to see -- and pose a new question. Approaching as many of your contacts as necessary, you ask each of them, "Do you know Ms. or Mr. See, at *Mythical Corporation* or do you know someone who does?"

You ask that question again and again of *everyone* who is on your file cards, until you find someone who says, "*Yes, I do.*"

Then of course, over the phone or -- better -- in person, you ask them the same familiar questions:

- "What can you tell me about him -- or her?"
- "Given the kind of job I am looking for *(which you here describe),* do you think it would be worth my while to go see them?"
- "May I tell them it was you who recommended that I talk with them?"
- "Do you have their phone number and/or address?"
- "Would you be willing to call ahead, to set up an appointment for me, and tell them who I am?"

Getting in to see someone, even for the purpose of a job-interview, is not that difficult. Everyone has friends, including this **person–who–has–the–power–to–hire–you.** You are simply approaching them through their friends. And you are doing this, not as one who is coming to ask a favor. You are doing it as one who is coming to offer a gift.

A gift? Yes, because while *you* are bemoaning the difficulty of getting in to see an employer of your choice -- for a job-interview -- employers are having an equally difficult time getting interviews with the person *they* are looking for: namely, you.

I cannot tell you the number of employers I know who can't figure out how to find the right employee. It is absolutely mind-boggling, particularly in these hard times when job-hunters would seem to be gathered on every street corner.

You're having trouble finding the employer. The employer is having trouble finding you. *What a great country!*

However, if you now present yourself directly to the **person–who–has–the–power–to–hire–you,** you are not only answering your own prayers. You are hopefully answering the employer's, as well. You are *just* what the employer is looking for, but didn't know how to find, if . . .

if you took the trouble to do Chapters 9, 10, and 11, and

if you took the trouble to figure out what your favorite and best skills are, and

if you took the trouble to figure out what your favorite and best subjects or *languages* are, and

if you took the trouble to figure out what places *might* need such skills and such *languages,* and

if you took the trouble to figure out who there has the power to hire you.

Of course, you don't for sure *know* they need you; that remains for the job-interview to uncover. But at least, by this thorough preparation, you have *increased* the chances that you are at the right place -- whether they have an announced vacancy or not. And, if you are, you are not imposing on this employer. You are coming not as 'job-beggar,' but as 'resource person.' You are rescuing him or her, believe me.

CONCLUSION

I close this chapter with my favorite (true) story about approaching an organization. This concerns a job-hunter in Virginia. He decided he wanted to work for a particular health-care organization in that State, and not knowing any better, he approached them by visiting their Personnel department. After dutifully filling out a job application, and talking to someone there in that department, he was told there were no jobs available. Stop. Period. End of story.

Approximately three months later he learned about this technique of approaching your favorite organization by using contacts. He did the kind of work described above, and succeeded in getting an interview with the person–who–had–the–power–to–hire–him for the position he was interested in. The two of them hit it off, immediately. The appointment went swimmingly. "You're hired," said the person–who–had–the–power–to–hire–him. "I'll call Personnel and tell them you're hired, and that you'll be down to fill out the necessary stuff."

Our job-hunter never once mentioned that he had previously approached that same organization through that same Personnel department, and been turned down.

*Well, yes, you do have
great big teeth; but, never mind
that. You were great to at
least grant me this interview.*
                    Little Red Riding Hood

CHAPTER THIRTEEN

Conducting The Interview

Chapter 13

IS THIS ANY WAY
TO RUN A BUSINESS?

To begin with, the job-interview is not a very reliable way of choosing an employee. In a survey conducted among a dozen top United Kingdom employers, and reported in the *Financial Times Career Guide 1989* there, it was discovered that the chances of an employer finding a good employee through the hiring interview was only *3% better* than if they had picked a name out of a hat. In a further ironic finding, it was discovered that if the interview were conducted by someone who would be working directly with the candidate, the success rate dropped to *2% below* that of picking a name out of a hat. And if the interview were conducted by a personnel expert, the success rate dropped to *10% below* that of picking a name out of a hat.

FRANKLY, THE FACT THAT YOU WANT TO WORK HERE IS A STRIKE AGAINST YOU RIGHT OFF.

No, I don't know how they came up with these figures. But they strike me as totally consistent with what I know of the world of work. I have watched so-called personnel experts make wretchedly bad choices about hiring for their own office, and when they would morosely confess this some months later, over lunch, I would puzzle out loud, "If you don't even know how to hire well, yourselves, how do you keep a straight face when you're called in as consultant to another organization?" And they would ruefully reply, "We treat it *as though it were* a science."

Let me tell you, folks, the job-interview is *not* a science. It is a very very hazy art, and done badly by most of its employer-practitioners, in spite of their best intentions and goodwill.

Moreover, it requires you as job-hunter to do something that runs against the grain, for many people. You are required to *compete* with others, and show the employer why you are *better* than the other people competing for the same job. Many job-hunters *hate* this aspect of job-interviewing.

I once met an eighty-year-old woman who was telling me about a different culture altogether. Back in the early '30s, she said, there was a small mine up in the hills above the town where she lived. One day, the news in the town was that the mine was hiring, at a little shack up in the hills. The men in the town, many of whom were out of work, lined up early outside the hiring shack, to try to get those jobs. The men were called in, one at a time. Her father was in the line, she said, and while waiting, he struck up a conversation with the man in the line behind him. That conversation was interrupted when it was her father's turn to go into the shack. The man who was hiring there, said to him, "Man, you're lucky. This is the last job I have to give out, today." "Well, in that case," replied her father, "give it to the next man out there. He has five children depending on him to feed them, while I have only three. I'll find another job, I'm sure."

I'm sure this nobility of spirit was not *universal* in that Age. But that it existed at all, compared to the current popular *rule* of life -- *every man for himself,* or *every woman for herself* -- seems stirring and inspiring. This cut-throat competition of our Day is *extremely* depressing, and even obscene.

And, the job-interview process in our country, and elsewhere in the world, *contributes* mightily to this continuing fragmentation of the human family. Nonetheless, if you would work for another, this job-interview process -- competitive and unscientific though it may be -- is the *only* doorway to getting a job in today's world of work. So, you're going to have to participate in the whole dumb and Neanderthal ritual, no matter how much it offends your simple common sense.

If you simply can't stand the idea, and would pay *millions* to avoid it, the only way to avoid it is to go into business for yourself (see Chapter 6). Even then, if you are successful you will eventually will have to hire someone else, in which case you'll be back into this whole job-interview process -- only, on the other side of the table. *(Remember to bring the hat, to put the names in!)*

THE ELEVEN MOST IMPORTANT TRUTHS ABOUT A JOB-INTERVIEW

You want to prepare, of course, for the interview -- do a little planning ahead of time, don't you? *How much time do you have?* I ask, because whole books have been written about the job-interview, so obviously there's a lot that can be said.[1]

If you don't have the time, or inclination, to do all that reading, perhaps I can condense it for you. Over the years it has seemed to me that there are eleven really important, basic truths about interviewing, which stand out above all the rest. I list those eleven -- with titles -- on the file cards which follow, along with some brief commentary of mine:

1. Martin John Yate, *Knock 'Em Dead with Great Answers to Tough Interview Questions.* Bob Adams, Inc., 260 Center St., Holbrook, MA 02343. 1992.

H. Anthony Medley, *Sweaty Palms: The Neglected Art of Being Interviewed.* Ten Speed Press, Box 7123, Berkeley, CA 94707. 1992, revised.

David Krause, *Get The Best Jobs in DP: The Computer Professional's Technical Interview Guide.* Mind Management, 24304 100th Ave. West, Edmonds, WA 98020. 1989. How to survive interviews that are essentially tests of your technical expertise.

Phillip G. Zimbardo, *Shyness, What It Is, What to Do About It.* Jove Publications, 757 Third Ave., New York, NY 10017. 1977.

David Bowman and Ronald Kweskin, *Q: How Do I Find The Right Job? A: Ask The Experts.* John Wiley & Sons, Inc., Professional and Trade Division, 605 Third Ave., New York, NY 10158-0012. 1990.

John Caple, *The Ultimate Interview.* Doubleday, 666 Fifth Ave., New York, NY 10103. 1991.

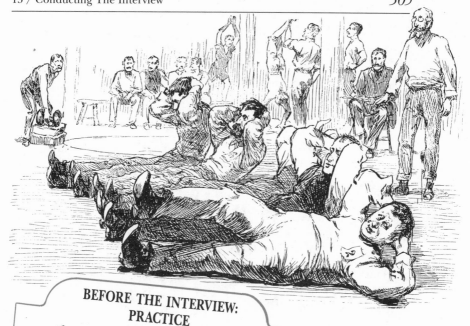

BEFORE THE INTERVIEW: PRACTICE

1. Before you go on job-interviews, be sure to practice the PIE process first (see page 246ff) until you are so used to talking with people about mutual interests, that interviewing has lost all of its terrors for you.

If you have several organizations to interview at, you should probably save the interview you care the most about until last, so you can make all your mistakes at the interviews you don't care about as much.

The manner in which you do your interviews -- and the manner in which you would do the job you are seeking -- are not assumed by most employers to be two unrelated subjects, but one and the same. A

slipshod half-hearted interview is taken as a warning that you might do a slipshod half-hearted job, were they foolish enough to hire you. Therefore, prepare thoroughly for each interview; know a lot about the place, before you walk in.

INTERVIEWING IS A TWO-WAY STREET

2. Your natural question to yourself, as you approach any job-interview, will be, "How do I convince this employer to hire me?" Wrong question. It implies that you have already made up your mind that this would be a grand person to work for, so all that remains is for you to sell yourself. That is rarely the case. In most cases, you don't know enough yet, to say that -- despite all your research. You have to use the job-interview as a chance to gather further information about this organization, and this boss, before you can decide, "Do I really want to work here?" That's the nature of the job-interview: each of you has to gather information, and if you both like what you see, then each has to 'sell' the other on the idea of working there.

If you understand *this* about an interview, you will be ahead of 98% of all other job-hunters -- who all too often go to the job-interview as a lamb goes to the slaughter, or as a criminal goes on trial before a judge.

You *are* on trial, of course, in the employer's eyes. *But,* so is that employer and that organization, in *your* eyes. This is what makes the job interview tolerable or sometimes *borderline* enjoyable: you are studying everything about this employer, at the same time that they are studying everything about you.

Two people, both sizing each other up. You know what that reminds you of. Dating. Well, the job interview is every bit like 'the dating game.' Both of you have to like each other, before you can even discuss the question of *'going steady,'* i.e., a job.

The importance of your actively weighing this organization and this job, *during* the job-interview, cannot be overstated. As we discussed in Chapter 11, the tradition in the U.S., and throughout the world for that matter, is to find a job, take it, and *then* try to figure out after you're in it whether it is a good job or not.

You're going against that tradition, as any sensible job-hunter or career-changer should, by using the job-interview to screen the organization *before you go to work there.*

The employer will thank you, you will thank you, your Mother will thank you.

WHAT THE EMPLOYER IS TRYING TO FIND OUT

3. Beneath the dozens of Possible Questions that employers may ask in a job-interview, there are really only five basic ones:

1. "Why are you here?" They mean by this, why did you pick out our organization to seek a job at?

2. "What can you do for us?" They mean by this, what are your skills and your fields of knowledge?

3. "What kind of person are you?" They mean by this, do you have a personality that they will enjoy working with, or not? Do you get along with people? What are your values?

4. Assuming you can do the job, "what distinguishes you from nineteen other people who can do the same thing?"

5. "Can we afford you?" They mean by that, if they decide they want you, what will it take to get you, and are they willing and able to pay that amount?

Books on interviewing, of which there are many, often publish lists of up to eighty-nine questions that an employer may ask you. They list things like:

- Tell me about yourself.
- Why are you applying for this job?
- What do you know about this job or company?
- How would you describe yourself?
- What are your major strengths?
- What is your greatest weakness?
- What type of work do you like to do best?
- What are your interests outside of work?
- What accomplishment gave you the greatest satisfaction?
- What was your worst mistake?
- Why did you leave your last job?
- Why were you fired (if you were)?
- How does your education or experience relate to this job?
- Where do you see yourself five years from now?
- What are your goals in life?
- How much did you make at your last job?

But they all boil down, in essence, to the five basic questions on the file card above. And this is the case, even if the interview begins and ends with these five questions never once being uttered aloud. They're still there, beneath the surface of the conversation, all the time.

The good news is that since there are really only five questions, there are really only five answers you need to know. But, you had *better* know those five answers. Of course, if you did your homework (Chapters 9, 10, and 11) you will. If you didn't, you won't, sad to say. Period. End of story.

**WHAT YOU ARE
TRYING TO FIND OUT**

4. The most basic thing you are trying to figure
out, as described above, is do you want to work there?
(The answer is not necessarily Yes.)

If you have any kind of a real or imagined handicap --
age, inexperience, physical or mental disability, ethnic
background, etc. -- you are also trying to find out
which kind of employer you are talking to:

a) Those who are bothered by your handicap
b) Those who are not bothered by your handicap

If you discover you are talking to one who is
bothered, you want to thank them for their time and
quickly excuse yourself. If you discover this employer
isn't bothered by your handicap, then you want to
continue the discussion.

Every job-hunter or career-changer in the world is handicapped -- so far as the job-hunt is concerned. If you doubt this,
sit down and think a minute. There are, let us say, 13,000 truly
different skills that human beings possess. We have discovered
over the years that the average job-hunter has 700 skills. That's a
lot, but it still means that there are 12,300 things each of us *can't*
do. Believe me, we're *all* handicapped. The only question is:
what is your handicap, and how much does it show?[2]

Typical job-hunting handicaps are: I have held too many jobs
before; I am overqualified; I am too inexperienced; I am too
old; I am too shy; I've only worked for large organizations; I've
only worked for small organizations; I've only worked for volunteer organizations; I've only worked at home; I'm a woman; I
am gay; I belong to an ethnic minority; I'm a recent immigrant;
I am too much of a generalist; I am too much of a specialist; I

2. For those with evident disabilities, I refer you to a companion booklet to *Parachute*
entitled, *Job-Hunting Tips For The So-Called Handicapped or People Who Have Disabilities*,
Ten Speed Press, Box 7123, Berkeley CA 94707. 1991. To save yourself some money, see
if your library has it, first.

have a police or prison record; I have a psychiatric history; I didn't get good enough grades in school; I have a physical or mental disability; I have a chronic illness; I have AIDS, etc.

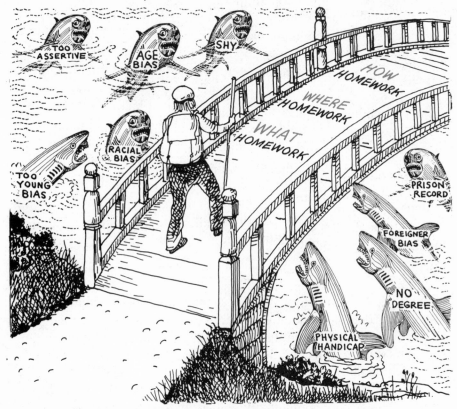

Our job-hunting handicaps always lead us to say something like *'Employers' won't hire me.* However, there's no such thing as just *'Employers,'* because (all together, now):

> There are two kinds of employers *out there:*
> • those who *will* be put off by your job-hunting handicaps, and therefore *won't* hire you;
> AND
> • those who will *not* be put off by your job-hunting handicaps, and therefore *will* hire you, if you are qualified for the job.

You are only looking for the second kind of employer, who is *not* put off by your job-hunting handicap, and therefore will hire you if you can do the job. The first kind of employer is of no interest to you, *except as they may give you leads to the second* -- and you must not allow yourself to become discouraged because you are running into a lot of *them,* and they are all rejecting you.

To take a 'worst case' scenario, if out of 100 employers, 90 would be bothered by your job-hunting handicap or history, but 10 wouldn't care about it in the slightest -- so long as you can do the work well -- your task is to make your way as quickly as you can through the 90, and find those other 10. They are the only ones you want to work for, anyway. You wouldn't *really* want to work for those who are prejudiced against you, now would you? We all want to work for an employer who's rootin' for us to succeed, not one who's just waiting for us to fall flat on our face.

In reading all this, I'm sure you think *you've* got the one handicap that *all* employers would find bothersome. For example, that you're over 60 years old, and 'employers' wouldn't want someone that old. Okay, let's all repeat it anew:

"All employers divide into two groups:
• those who would be put off by your age,
AND
• those who would not be put off by your age, so long as you are qualified for the job.
Your job is to find the second kind of employer, and not pay any attention to the first, except as they may give you *leads* to the second."

And so it goes. So, it always goes.[3]

---

3. Remember the story of one 66-year-old man, at the end of Chapter 7.

WHAT THE EMPLOYER DOES DURING THE INTERVIEW

5. The employer observes everything about you and also asks questions. Most of those questions are about your past. But their intent is to find something in your past, that will predict the future -- because, in the end, all any employer can really be interested in is the future. You need to pay attention to the time frame of the employer's questions. For example, "Where did you go to high school?" is in the past. If the questions' time frame stays stuck in the past, you are not likely to be hired. As the employer's questions move, in their time frame, from being preoccupied with the distant past, to the near past, to the present, and then to the future, this is very favorable for you. It means they're thinking seriously about hiring you.

Distant past: *"Where did you grow up?"*
Near past: *"Tell me about your last job."*
Present: *"What kind of a job are you looking for?"*
Future: *"If you were offered this job, where would you see yourself five years from now?"*
I will have more to say about the employer's questions, at the end of this chapter.

Now -- just as you are studying the employer during the job-interview, so the employer is studying you. It is likely that *nothing* will escape the scrutiny of that person on the other side of the desk. And I mean: your haircut or hairdo; your manner of dress; your posture; your use of your hands; your body odor or perfume; your breath (good or bad); your fingernails (dirty or clean, clipped or not); the sound of your voice; the way in which you do or don't interrupt; the hesitant or assured manner in which you ask your questions or give your answers; your values as evidenced by the things which impress you or don't impress you in the office, in your history, and so on; the carefulness with

which you did or didn't research this company before you came in; the thoroughness with which you know your own skills and strengths; your awareness of what you are willing to sacrifice in order to get this job *and* what you are *not* willing to sacrifice in order to get this job; your enthusiasm for your work; and blah, blah, blah. We can also throw in whether or not you smoke *(in a race between two equally qualified people, the nonsmoker will win out over the smoker 94% of the time, according to a study done by a professor of business at Seattle University);* whether, if at lunch, you order a drink or not (don't); whether you show courtesy to the receptionist, secretary, waiter or waitress, or not (do); and so forth. *Everything* is grist for the mill, as the employer tries to divine "what kind of person is this?"

What the employer will typically use to screen you *out,* are:

- any signs of dishonesty or lying;
- any signs of irresponsibility or tendency to goof off;
- any sign of arrogance or excessive aggressiveness;
- any sign of tardiness or failure to keep appointments and commitments on time, including the job-interview;

- any sign of not following instructions or obeying rules;
- any sign of constant complaining or blaming things on others;
- any sign of laziness or lack of motivation;
- any sign of a lack of enthusiasm for this organization and what it is trying to do;
- any sign of instability, inappropriate response, and the like.

Since the employer would probably end up having to fire anyone with these personality traits, the employer would like to find these things out *now*.

Beyond these tangibles, there are the intangibles of *making a good impression*. Study after study has confirmed that if you are a male, you will make a better impression if:

- your hair or beard are neatly trimmed;
- you have obviously freshly bathed, used a deodorant and mouthwash, and have clean fingernails;
- you have freshly laundered clothes on, and a suit rather than a sports outfit, and sit without slouching;
- your breath does not dispense gallons of garlic, onion, stale tobacco, or strong drink, into the enclosed office air;

- your shoes are neatly polished, and your pants have a sharp crease;
- you are not wafting tons of after-shave cologne fifteen feet ahead of you.

And, if you are a female, you will make a better impression if:

- your hair is newly 'permed' or 'coiffed';
- you have obviously freshly bathed, used a deodorant and mouthwash, and have clean or nicely manicured finger-nails;
- you wear a bra, freshly cleaned clothes, a suit or sophisti-cated-looking dress, and sit without slouching;
- your breath does not dispense gallons of garlic, onion, stale tobacco, or strong drink, into the enclosed office air;
- you wear shoes rather than sandals;
- you are not wafting tons of perfume fifteen feet ahead of you.

Now please, dear friend, do not send me mail telling me how asinine you think some of these 'requirements' are. I already *know* that. I'm only reporting what study after study has revealed about why you get hired -- or *don't* get hired. There are of course employers who care about none of these things, and will hire you if you can do the job. Period. Do remember, however, that where you have to work with other people, these things will often be given a lot of weight. This employer already has other employees; you must, at least generally, 'fit in.'

If you don't want to 'fit in,' then you might want to consider forming your own (one-person) business (see Chapter 6). Then -- particularly if it is a mail-order business -- you can dress or conduct yourself as you please, and no one will notice.

If, however, you want to work for someone else, all the above factors are likely to count.

WHAT YOU MUST DO DURING THE INTERVIEW

6. You are trying to find out the answers to five questions. Though they will rarely ever be said out loud, you must keep them in your head throughout the interview:

1. What does this job involve?
2. Do my skills truly match this job?
3. Are you the kind of people I would like to work with?
4. If we do match, can I persuade you that there is something unique about me, that makes me different from nineteen other people who can do the same thing I can do?
5. Can I persuade you to hire me, and at the salary I need or want?

If you did the homework in Chapters 9, 10, 11, and 12 in this book, you might begin your part of the job-interview by reporting to them just exactly how you've been conducting your job-hunt, and what impressed you so much about *their* organization during your research, that you decided to come in and talk to them about a job. Then you can devote your attention, during the remainder of the interview, to exploring the five questions on the file card above.

"*I'll tell you why I want this job. I thrive on challenges. I like being stretched to my full capacity. I like solving problems. Also, my car is about to be repossessed.*"

If you're not there about a job that already exists, but rather, you want them to *create* a job for you, then your five questions get changed into four statements:

1. What you like about this organization.

2. What sorts of **needs** you find intriguing in this field and in this organization (don't ever use the word *"problems,"* as most employers prefer synonyms, such as *'needs'*-- unless you hear the word *'problems'* coming out of their mouth, first).

3. What skills seem to you to be needed in order to meet such needs.

4. Evidence from your past experience that demonstrates you have the very skills in question, and that you perform them in the manner or style you claim.

5. What is unique about the way *you* perform those skills. This is something you must devote some thought to, ahead of time. For example, if you analyze problems, how do you do that? *Painstakingly? Intuitively, in a flash? By consulting with greater authorities in the field?* You see the point. You are trying to put your finger on the 'style' or 'manner' in which you do your work, that is distinctive and hopefully appealing, to this employer.

As for what else makes you different from nineteen other people who can do the same kind of work as you do, our remaining five cards, or points, may be basically thought of as ways in which you *want* to be different from other job-hunters.

And how do you demonstrate that you are? Well, of course: by the way you conduct yourself in the interview.

THE FIRST THING THAT MAKES YOU DIFFERENT FROM 'THE OTHERS' WHO ARE APPLYING FOR THE SAME JOB

YOU AS TIMEKEEPER

7. You want to come across as someone who knows the value of Time. For example, when you ask for an appointment with an employer, ask for twenty minutes only, of their time, and don't stay one minute longer, unless the employer begs you to. Watch your watch like a hawk. Tell them you like to honor agreements. That will almost always make a big impression.

You want to come across as someone who doesn't hog the Time. Whenever you are interviewing with an employer, talk one-half the time only, and let the employer talk the other half of the time. When the employer asks you a question, don't 'hold forth' for longer than two minutes, at any one time.

You want to come across as someone who values Timing, also. For example, the timing of salary negotiation should be the very last thing you two ever discuss, and only after they have definitely said they want you. Observe that timing, rigorously.

There are reasons for the above advice. For example, studies[4] have revealed that generally speaking the people who get hired are those who mix speaking and listening fifty-fifty in the interview. That is, half the time they spend letting the employer do the talking, half the time in the interview the job-hunter does the talking. People who didn't follow that mix, were the ones who didn't get hired, according to the study. I think the *reason* why this is so, is that if you talk too much about yourself, you come across as one who would ignore the needs of the organization; while if you talk too little, you come across as trying to hide something about your background.

Again, studies[5] have revealed that when it is your turn to speak, you should not speak any longer than two minutes at a time, if you want to make the best impression. In fact, a good answer to an employer's question sometimes only takes twenty seconds to give. This is useful information for you to know, in conducting a successful interview -- as you certainly want to do.

With regard to *Timing,* observe it rigorously, even if the employer doesn't. He or she may ask you *early on,* "What kind of a salary are you looking for?" You need to resist the question *at that time,* and gently insist that until *they* have said "We want you," and you have decided, "I want them," all discussion of salary is highly inappropriate. This is explained further, in the next chapter.

4. This one done by a researcher at Massachusetts Institute of Technology.
5. This one conducted by my colleague, Daniel Porot, in Geneva, Switzerland.

THE SECOND THING THAT MAKES YOU DIFFERENT FROM 'THE OTHERS' WHO ARE APPLYING FOR THE SAME JOB

YOU AS PROBLEM-SOLVER

8. You want to come across as focussed on what you can do for the employer, rather than on what the employer can do for you. You want the employer to see you as a Resource Person, rather than as a 'job-beggar,' to quote Daniel Porot. The major issue is not merely what skills you have, but also how you use them. You want to come across as a Problem-Solver there at work, rather than as one who simply 'keeps busy.' If you don't know what kind of problems, think of what a bad employee would do, in your position (come in late, take too much time off, not care about what the employer wants, etc.). Emphasize how much you do the opposite. You want them to know you will increase the organization's effectiveness, and (where applicable) their profits.

Every organization has two main topics for its continuing day-by-day preoccupation: the problems they are facing, and what the solutions might be.

The main thing the employer is trying to figure out during the job-interview, is -- if they hire you -- will you be part of the solution there, or just another part of their problems.

You will be part of the solution if you come to them as A Resource Person. And the secret of coming to them as A Resource Person is that you have previously tackled Chapters 9, 10, and 11 in this book, systematically and methodically, prior to the job-interview. The three questions there -- WHAT, WHERE, and HOW -- when thoughtfully and diligently answered, will identify you immediately as more than just a job-beggar.

During the course of the interview, you need to make it clear that you are there to see this employer, in order to make an oral proposal, followed hopefully by a written proposal, of what *you can do for them*. You will see immediately what a switch this is from the way most job-hunters approach an employer! (*"How much do you pay, and how much time off will I have?"*) Will he or she be glad to see you, with this different emphasis? In most cases, you bet they will. They *want* a resource person, and a problem-solver.

Toward this end, you need to find out as much about that organization as you possibly can, before you ever go in for an interview. Lay your hands on everything you can, that is in print about them. If this is a large organization, read as many of their brochures, annual reports, addresses of the chairman or boss -- whatever -- as you can. If they have a personnel or human relations department, or a public relations department, that's where you'll find that stuff. Also, go to your local library and ask the librarian or reference librarian to see every clipping they may have about that organization.

If it is a small organization, you can still find out if there is anything in print about their work or what they do. (*Even places that only have two employees often have something in print about what the organization is trying to achieve. Also, some local daily or weekly paper may have run an article about them.*) Be sure and talk to everybody you know, to find out anything they may know, about this organization.

This is not a matter of prying into their private life. It is a matter of knowing their history, so that you can understand their purposes and goals. Moreover, all organizations, be they large or small, profit or nonprofit, love to be loved. If you have gone to all this trouble, to learn so much about them -- before you ever walk in their doors, they will be impressed, believe me.

Most job-hunters never go to this trouble. They walk in knowing little or nothing about the organization. This drives employers *nuts*. One time, the first question an IBM college recruiter asked a graduating senior was, "What do the initials IBM stand for?" The senior didn't know, and the interview was over. Another time, an employer said to me, "I'm so tired of job-hunters who come in, and ask, "Uh, what do you do here?" that the next time someone walks in who already knows something about us, I'm going to hire him or her, on the spot."

Thus, if *you* come in, and have done your homework on the organization, this immediately makes you stand out from other job-hunters, and dramatically increases your chances of getting a job there. How much information should you gather? Well, in a nutshell, more than you are going to need -- at least during the hiring interview. The depth of your research will pay off in the quiet sense of knowledgeability that you exude.

THE THIRD THING THAT MAKES YOU DIFFERENT FROM 'THE OTHERS' WHO ARE APPLYING FOR THE SAME JOB

YOU AS PROOF-GIVER

9. The most important thing during the interview, regarding your skills, is that you not merely claim you have certain skills, but prove you have them. You must set yourself apart from other job-hunters by being a Proof-giver, not merely a Claimer. Often you do this by the way in which you conduct the interview.

If, for example, you say you are very thorough in all you do, but you haven't researched the organization you are presently interviewing at, your actions will contradict your claims.

If you are an artist, craftsperson, or other person who produces something, try to think of some way to show the employer what you are capable of doing -- through pictures, samples of things you have made or produced, videotape, or whatever -- during the interview.

THE FOURTH THING THAT MAKES YOU DIFFERENT FROM 'THE OTHERS' WHO ARE APPLYING FOR THE SAME JOB

YOU AS COURTEOUS AND KIND

10. Be courteous at all times. Employers are a fraternity. Or a sorority. The task of hiring makes them feel like they are members of the same tribe. During the interview, you want to be observed as one who has courtesy toward all members of that tribe, i.e., all employers. Don't ever bad-mouth a previous employer. Say something nice, or else keep quiet about them. You will immediately stand out from other job-hunters, because of your graciousness.

And, be courteous to this employer, even if they are obviously not going to hire you. During the following week, or two, they may be having lunch with another

employer, who says, "I'm looking for someone. Do you know of anybody?" If you were well-remembered for your courtesy, the employer who turned you down, may submit your name to this new employer.

THE LAST THING THAT MAKES YOU DIFFERENT FROM 'THE OTHERS' WHO ARE APPLYING FOR THE SAME JOB

YOU AS THANKS-GIVER

11. Every evening, after a job-interview, you must take time to sit down and write (with pen or type-writer) a brief thank-you note to each person you saw that day. That means, not only employers, but also their secretaries, receptionists, or anyone else who gave you a friendly welcome or a helping hand. (Be sure and ask for their names, or cards, while you are still there visiting that organization.) Don't make the note just a perfunctory 'Thanks very much for your time.' Add something individual about the way they treated you. Use the note to mention anything you forgot to mention while there, and -- with employers -- to under-line the main points you want them to remember about you. Mail the note promptly the very next morning, or even that night.

A job-hunter presented herself for a job-interview as public relations officer for a major-league baseball team. That evening, she wrote and mailed a thank-you note. She was eventually hired for the job, and when she asked why, they told her that they had decided to hire her because, out of thirty-five applicants, she was the only one who had written a thank-you note.

That's why every expert on interviewing will tell you two things: (1) thank-you notes are *crucial*, because they may be the one factor that gets you the job; and (2) most job-hunters ignore this advice. Indeed, it is safe to say that it is the most overlooked step in the entire job-hunting process.

If you want to stand out from the others applying for the same job, send thank-you notes -- to *everyone* you meet there, that day. If you need any additional encouragements *(besides the fact that it may get you the job),* here are six additional reasons for sending a thank-you note -- particularly to the employer who interviewed you:

First, you are presenting yourself as one who has good skills with people. Your actions with respect to the job-interview must back this claim up. Sending a thank-you note does that. You *are* good with people; you remember to thank them.

Secondly, it helps the employer to remember you.

Thirdly, if a committee is involved in the hiring process, the one man or woman who interviewed you has something to show the committee.

Fourth, if the interview went rather well, and you are hopeful of being invited back, the thank-you letter can reiterate your interest in further talks.

Fifth, the thank-you note gives you an opportunity to correct any wrong impression you left behind you. You can add anything you forgot to tell them, that you want them to know. And from among all the things you two discussed, you can underline the main two or three points that you want to stand out in their minds.

Lastly, if the interview did not go well, and you lost all interest in working there, they may still hear of other openings, elsewhere, that might be of interest to you. In the thank-you note, you can mention this, and ask them to keep you in mind. Thus you may gain additional leads.

Should you include a resume with your thank-you note to the employer who interviewed you? Some experts will advise you to.

Under the third canon above, it gives your interviewer something additional to show the other members of the hiring committee, if there is such.

However, infinitely preferred to a resume is a piece of paper that is, in essence, a *brief* written proposal *(one or two pages at most)* as to what it is you would like to be able to do at that organization, and what you hope you could accomplish for them.

As evidence of your ability to do that, you should cite relevant past accomplishments of yours, taking care in each case to cite:

a) what the problem was

b) what especial obstacle (timewise, or otherwise) you had to overcome

c) what means you used to overcome the obstacle, and solve the problem

d) what the results were, of your actions, stated as concretely as possible in terms of things accomplished, money saved, money earned, etc.

The virtue of such a written proposal is that it looks forward rather than (as the resume does) backward. And it puts into writing the essence of the hiring interview: you are not asking them merely to do something for you. More importantly, you are offering to do something for them.

CONCLUSION:
FEAR AND THE INTERVIEW

If the employment interview were simply two people, job-hunter and employer, trying to get answers to natural questions, the interview would be a snap. Unfortunately, this simple exchange is corrupted by the fact that both individuals sitting there are filled with a number of fears and anxieties, which they don't feel free to discuss openly. Yes, I said, *both of you.* You know *you* are sitting there with sweaty palms, but you will probably assume that the employer is sitting there enjoying this whole masochistic process. That is sometimes, but rarely, true.

The employer is a human being just like you are. He or she may *never* have been hired to do *this. This* just got thrown in with all their other duties. And they may *know* they're not very good at it.

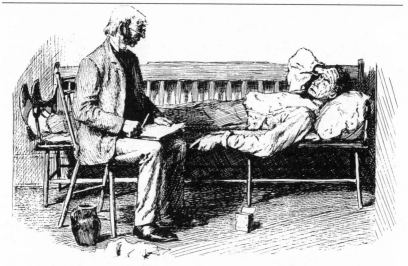

So, let's briefly catalog some of the employer's typical fears. You are sitting there. The employer is sitting there. This is what they are afraid of, as the job-interview begins:

a. That You Won't Be Able to Do the Job: That You Lack the Necessary Skills or Experience

b. That If Hired, You Won't Put In a Full Working Day

c. That If Hired, You'll Be Frequently "Out Sick," or Otherwise Absent Whole Days

d. That If Hired, You'll Only Stay Around for a Few Weeks or At Most a Few Months

e. That It Will Take You Too Long to Master the Job, and Thus Too Long Before You're Profitable to That Organization

f. That You Won't Get Along with the Other Workers There, or That You Will Develop a Personality Conflict with the Boss Himself (or Herself)

g. That You Will Do Only the Minimum That You Can Get Away With, Rather Than the Maximum That You Are Capable Of

h. That You Will Always Have to Be Told What to Do Next, Rather Than Displaying Initiative; That You Will Always Be in a Responding Rather Than an Initiating Mode (and Mood)

i. That You Will Have a Work-Disrupting Character Flaw, and Turn Out to Be: Dishonest, Totally Irresponsible, a Spreader of Dissention at Work, Lazy, an Embezzler, a Gossip, a Sexual Harasser, a Drug-User or Substance Abuser, a Drunk, a Liar, Incompetent -- In a Word: Bad News

j. *(If This Is a Large Organization, and Your Would-Be Boss Is Not the Top Person)* That You Will Bring Discredit upon Them, and upon His or Her Department/Section/Division, etc., for Ever Hiring You in the First Place -- Making Them Lose Face, and Possibly Costing Your Would-Be Boss a Raise or Promotion

k. That You Will Cost A Lot of Money, if They Make A Mistake in Hiring

Incidentally, the cost of the interviewing time, plus the cost of relocation, moving, etc., added up *(as recently as 1988)* to an average cost of $6,076 for each new professional or managerial employee hired, according to the Employment Management Association. Therefore, that is also the minimum cost of a mistake. No wonder the employer is sweating.

Now, how are they going to find out the answers to these fears? Well, in the old days, an employer might have gotten useful information *outside* the job-interview, by obtaining references from your previous employers. No more. In the past decade, as job-hunters have started filing lawsuits left and right, alleging 'unlawful discharge,' or 'being deprived of an ability to make a living,' about half of all Previous Employers have adopted the policy of refusing to volunteer any information about Past Employees, except name, rank and serial number -- i.e., the person's job-title and dates of employment.

The interviewer is therefore completely on his own -- or her own -- in trying to figure out whether or not to hire you. The hiring interview is *everything*.

The most important thing for you to keep in mind during the interview, as I mentioned on an earlier file card, is that no employer cares about your past. The only thing any employer can possibly care about is your future. Therefore, the more a question *appears* to be about your past, the more certain you may be that some Fear is behind it. And that Fear is about your future -- i.e., what will you be like, *after* the employer decides to hire you, *if* they decide to hire you.

It will help you greatly in the interview if you simply remind yourself, "This guy is afraid," or "This woman is afraid." It will also help you if you can sense *what* fear lies beneath each question that employer asks you -- so that you can tacitly answer the fear, and not just the surface question.

Here are some *examples:*

Employer's Question	The Fear Behind The Question	The Point You Try to Get Across	Phrases You Might Use To Get This Across
"Tell me about yourself"	The employer is afraid he/she isn't going to conduct a very good interview, by failing to ask the right questions. Or is afraid there is something wrong with you, and is hoping you will blurt it out.	You are a good employee, as you have proved in the past at your other jobs. (Give the briefest history of who you are, where born, raised, interests, hobbies, and kind of work you have enjoyed the most to date.) *Keep it to two minutes, max.*	In describing your past work history, use any *honest* phrases you can about your work history, that are self-complimentary: "Hard worker" "Came in early, left late" "Always did more than was expected of me" etc.
"What kind of work are you looking for?"	The employer is afraid that you are looking for a different job than that which the employer is trying to fill. e.g., he/she wants a secretary, but you want to be an office manager, etc.	You are looking for precisely the kind of work the employer is offering (but don't say that, if it isn't true). Repeat back to the employer, in your own words, what he/she has said about the job, and emphasize the skills you have to do *that*.	If the employer hasn't described the job at all, say, "I'd be happy to answer that, but first I need to understand exactly what kind of work this job involves." *Then* answer, as at left.
"Have you ever done this kind of work before?"	The employer is afraid you don't possess the necessary skills and experience to do this job.	You have skills that are transferable, from whatever you used to do; and you did it well.	"I pick up stuff very quickly." "I have quickly mastered any job I have ever done."

Employer's Question	The Fear Behind The Question	The Point You Try to Get Across	Phrases You Might Use To Get This Across
"Why did you leave your last job?" *-- or* **"How did you get along with your former boss and co-workers?"**	The employer is afraid you don't get along well with people, especially bosses, and is just waiting for you to 'bad-mouth' your previous boss or co-workers, as proof of that.	Say whatever positive things you possibly can about your former boss and co-workers *(without telling lies)*. Emphasize you usually get along very well with people -- and then let your gracious attitude toward your previous boss(es) and co-workers prove it, right before this employer's very eyes (and ears).	If you left voluntarily: *"My boss and I both felt I would be happier and more effective in a job where (here describe your strong points, such as) I would have more room to use my initiative and creativity."* If you alone were fired: "Usually, I get along well with everyone, but in this particular case the boss and I just didn't get along with each other. Difficult to say why." *You don't need to say any more than that.* If you were laid off and your job wasn't filled after you left: "My *job* was terminated."
"How is your health?" *-- or* **"How much were you absent from work during your last job?"**	The employer is afraid you will be absent from work a lot, if they hire you.	You will not be absent. If you have a health problem, you want to emphasize that it is one which will not keep you from being at work, daily. Your productivity, compared to other workers', is excellent.	If you were *not* absent a lot at your last job: "I believe it's an employee's job to show up every work day. Period." If you *were* absent a lot, say why, and stress that it was due to a difficulty that is now *past*.

Employer's Question	The Fear Behind The Question	The Point You Try to Get Across	Phrases You Might Use To Get This Across
"Can you explain why you've been out of work so long?" -- *or* **"Can you tell me why there are these gaps in your work history?"** *(usually said after studying your resume)*	The employer is afraid that you are the kind of person who quits a job the minute he/she doesn't like something at it; in other words, that you have no 'stick-to-it-iveness.'	You love to work, and you regard times when things aren't going well as challenges, which you enjoy learning how to conquer.	"During the gaps in my work record, I was studying/doing volunteer work/doing some hard thinking about my mission in life/finding redirection." (Choose one)
"Wouldn't this job represent a step down for you?" -- *or* **"I think this job would be way beneath your talents and experience."** -- *or* **"Don't you think you would be underemployed if you took this job?"**	The employer is afraid you could command a bigger salary, somewhere else, and will therefore leave him/her as soon as something better turns up.	You will stick with this job so long as you and the employer agree this is where you should be.	"This job isn't a step down for me. It's a step up -- from welfare." "We have mutual fears: every employer is afraid a good employee will leave too soon, and every employee is afraid the employer might fire him/her, for no good reason." "I like to work, and I give my best to every job I've ever had."
And, lastly **"Tell me, what is your greatest weakness?"**	The employer is afraid you have some character flaw, and hopes you will now rashly blurt it out, or confess it.	You have limitations just like anyone else, but you work constantly to improve yourself and be a more and more effective worker.	Mention a weakness and then stress its positive aspect. e.g., "I don't like to be oversupervised, because I have a great deal of initiative, and I like to anticipate problems before they even arise."

THE TEN GREATEST MISTAKES MADE IN JOB INTERVIEWS

Whereby Your Chances of Finding a Job Are Greatly Decreased

I. Going after large organizations only (such as the Fortune 500).

II. Hunting all by yourself for places to visit, using ads and resumes.

III. Doing no homework on an organization before going there.

IV. Allowing the Personnel Department (or Human Resources) to interview you -- *their primary function is to screen you OUT.*

V. Setting no time limit when you make the appointment with an organization.

VI. Letting your resume be used as the agenda for the job interview.

VII. Talking primarily about yourself, and what benefit the job will be for you.

VIII. When answering a question of theirs, talking anywhere from 2 to 15 minutes, at a time.

IX. Basically approaching them as if you were a job-beggar, hoping they will offer you a job, however humble.

X. Not sending a thank-you note right after the interview.

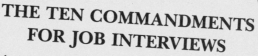

THE TEN COMMANDMENTS
FOR JOB INTERVIEWS

Whereby Your Chances of Finding a Job Are Vastly Increased

I. Go after small organizations, with twenty or less employees, since they create 2/3 of all new jobs.

II. Hunt for interviews using the aid of friends and acquaintances, because a job-hunt requires fifty eyes and ears.

III. Do thorough homework on an organization before going there, using Informational Interviews plus the library.

IV. At any organization, identify who has the power to hire you there, for the position you want, and use your friends and acquaintances' contacts, to get in to see that person.

V. Ask for just 20 minutes of their time, when asking for the appointment; and keep to your word.

VI. Go to the interview with your own agenda, your own questions and curiosities about whether or not this job fits you.

VII. Talk about yourself only if what you say offers some benefit to that organization, and their 'problems.'

VIII. When answering a question of theirs, talk only between 20 seconds and 2 minutes, at any one time.

IX. Basically approach them as if you were a resource person, able to produce better work for that organization than any predecessor.

X. Always write a thank-you note the same evening of the interview, and mail it at the latest by the next morning.

*It has long been an axiom of mine
that the little things
are infinitely the most important.*
Sir Arthur Conan Doyle

God is in the details.
Mies van der Rohe

CHAPTER FOURTEEN

Salary
Negotiation

Chapter 14

The New Poverty

Because of the new 'belt-tightening' that is going on at workplaces throughout the U.S. during the '90s, it is becoming harder and harder to find a salary which will pay you what you got *in the old days* -- five years ago. Consequently, more and more people are being forced to live minimally, and do their own belt-tightening.

There are now 33.6 million people in the U.S. below the poverty line. Two million of these joined the rest just during the year 1990, due to their declining income. (In the U.S. currently, you are considered to be below the poverty line if you are a family of four and are making less than $13,921 annually.) Support for those living below the poverty line is decreasing, from both the Federal and State governments, due to the fact that these governments themselves are in dire financial straits. By 1991, 40 States had cut or frozen benefits to families with children.

Nearly one out of every five workers in the U.S. is currently working part-time, many of them involuntarily -- they'd like to find full-time work, if they could. (The average work-week in the U.S. is now only 34.7 hours.)

Part-timers, on average, earn only 60% as much, per hour, as full-time workers, and are also less likely to have medical or pension benefits.

MEANWHILE, BACK AT THE RANCH

While you are writing out your thank-you note, the employer you saw that day is very likely reflecting on the whole day's interviews -- mentally sifting through all the candidates they saw, trying to decide who stands out, so far. And -- if that includes you -- weighing whether to invite you back, for a second round of interviews. There usually *is* a second round. And, often, a third, and fourth. You, of course, want to be in that second round, and you are wondering how many days you should give them, before you contact them again.

It helps a lot if you established some kind of understanding about all of this, at the end of your *first* interview, by asking three questions: "When may I expect to hear from you?" (Wait for their answer.) "What would be the latest I can expect to hear from you?" (Wait for their answer.) "May I contact you after that date, if for any reason you haven't gotten back to me?" (Wait for their answer.) Then, after you leave, keep this covenant, and don't contact them (except with a thank-you note) until after the deadline agreed upon.

If they forget about you, and you do have to contact them after the agreed-upon date, and if they tell you things are still up in the air, you ask the same three questions all over again. And so on, and so forth.

Incidentally, it is entirely appropriate for you to insert a thank-you note into the running stream, after *each* interview or telephone contact. That will help them remember you.

WHEN EMPLOYERS NEVER INVITE YOU BACK

"I'm hoping to find something in a meaningful, humanist, outreach kind of bag, with flexible hours, non-sexist bosses, and fabulous fringes."

There are many job-hunters who have no difficulty in getting a first interview at various places, but they *never* get invited back for a second interview, and hence never get a job. If this is happening to you, there may be something wrong with the way you are coming across during interviews. Unfortunately, employers will hardly ever tell you this. You will never hear them say something like, "You're too cocky and arrogant during the interview." You will always be left completely in the dark as to what it is you're doing wrong.

One way around this deadly silence, is to ask for *generalized* feedback, from some friendly employer you saw back a while ago. You can try phoning them, reminding them of who you are, and then asking the following question -- deliberately kept generalized, vague, unrelated just to *that* place, and above all, *future-directed:* "You know, I've been on several interviews at several different places now, where I've gotten turned down. From what you've seen, is there something about me in an interview, that is causing me not to get hired at those places? If so, I'd really appreciate your giving me some pointers so I can do better in my future job-interviews."

Most of the time they'll *still* duck saying anything hurtful or helpful. (Said an old veteran to me once, "I used to think it was my duty to hit everyone with the truth. Now I only give it to those who can use it.") *Occasionally* you will run into an employer who is willing to risk giving you the truth, because they think you know how to use it.

In the absence of any help from employers, you might want to get a good business friend of yours to role-play a mock job-interview with you, in case they see something glaringly wrong with how you're 'coming across.' If from either friend or employer-on-the-phone, you do get feedback, no matter how painful it is, thank them from the bottom of your heart. Their advice, seriously heeded, can bring about just the changes in your interviewing strategy that you most need.

WHEN EMPLOYERS DO
INVITE YOU BACK

But, assuming things went favorably in the first interview, you *will* be invited back for another interview, *or interviews* at that place -- either with the person you saw before, and/or with a committee. Eventually, after the second, third, or fourth interview, if *you* like them and *they* increasingly like you, a job offer *will* be made.

Then, and only then, it is time to deal with the question that is inevitably on any employer's mind, as we saw in Chapter 13: *how much is this person going to cost me?* And the question that is on *your* mind: *how much does this job pay?*

It's time for salary negotiation.

FRANK & ERNEST reprinted by permission of NEA, Inc.

Salary negotiation would never happen if *every* employer in *every* job-interview were to mention, right from the start, the top figure they are willing to pay for that position. *Some* employers do. And that's the end of any salary negotiation. But, of course, most of them don't. Hoping they'll be able to get you for less, they start *lower* than they're ultimately willing to go. This creates *a range*. And that range is what salary negotiation is all about.

For example, if the employer wants to hire somebody for no more than $12 an hour, they may start *the bidding* at $8 an hour. In which case, the range runs from $8 to $12 an hour. Or if they want to pay no more than $14 an hour, they may start the bidding at $11 an hour. In which case the range runs from $11 to $14 an hour.

If a range *is* involved, then you have every right to try to negotiate a higher salary *within that range*. The employer's goal, is to save money, if possible. Your goal is to bring home to your family, partner, or your own household, the best salary that you can, for the work you will be doing. Nothing's wrong with the goals of either of you. But it does mean that, where the employer starts lower, salary negotiation is proper, and expected.

Statistics about U.S. Salaries

Of the 12 million new jobs created in the last decade, more than half pay less than $7,000 a year.[1]

The average hourly wage in the U.S. in 1992 was $10.50 per hour.[2] High school graduates earn, on average, $10.72 per hour. College graduates earned, on average, $16.69 an hour. These figures did not include 'perks,' such as health-care, retirement funds, etc., which often add about 28% to the total wage.

The average *individual* income for all full-time workers in the U.S. in 1992 was $22,672. (*Average* means as many were above that figure as below it.) The average individual income for production or non-supervisory workers was $18,946.

The average *family* income was $35,225.[3] (Again, *average* means as many families earned above that figure as below it.)

People making $18,500–$74,000 per year currently are defined as middle-income families.

Pay raises in 1992 were running around 3.2%, on average.

THE FIVE KEYS TO SALARY NEGOTIATION

There are five basic keys to successful salary negotiation during a job-interview. They are:

1. *Never* discuss salary until the end of the interviewing process, when they have definitely said they want you.

2. *Never* be the first one to mention a salary figure.

3. Before you go to the interview, do homework on how much you need.

---

1. Time, 12/17/90.

2. This figure is as of May, 1992, and it is for production or nonsupervisory workers on non-farm payrolls.

3. *The (Bend, Oregon) Bulletin,* p. B-1. This figure was for the most recent year available (1990).

4. During the interview, try to determine whether the salary being offered is fixed or contains room for negotiation.

5. Before you go in, do research on salaries for your field and that organization.

The rest of this chapter is devoted to a discussion of these five keys.

Never discuss salary until the end of the interviewing process, and they have definitely said they want you.

Every expert on salary negotiation will tell you this, but let's really press the point home:

When To Discuss Salary

Not until all of the following conditions have been fulfilled --

- Not until they've gotten to know you, at your best, so they can see how you stand out above the other applicants.
- Not until you've gotten to know them, as completely as you can, so you can tell when they're being firm, or when they're flexible.
- Not until you've found out exactly what the job entails.
- Not until they've had a chance to find out how well you match the job-requirements.
- Not until you're in the final interview at that place, for that job.
- Ni until you've decided, "I'd really like to work here."
- Not until they've said, "We want you."
- Not until they've said, "We've *got* to have you."

-- do you even *mention* salary -- nor do you let *them* mention salary. Period. Exclamation point. End of story.

Until all the above has happened, any salary they mention will be too low. They don't yet understand what you're really worth.

If you'd prefer this to be put in the form of a diagram, here it is:[4]

---

4. Reprinted, by permission of the publisher, from *Ready, Aim, You're Hired,* by Paul Hellman, © 1986 Paul Hellman. Published by AMACOM, a division of American Management Association, New York. All rights reserved.

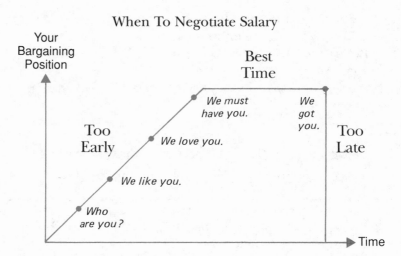

When To Negotiate Salary

Your Bargaining Position

Best Time

Too Early

We must have you.

We got you.

We love you.

Too Late

We like you.

Who are you?

Time

You may think to yourself, "But if they have a certain salary in mind for this position, what's the difference whether I find it out early or late?"

The difference is that if you really *shine* during the job-interview, they may -- at the end -- mention a higher salary than they originally had in mind, just because you stand out above all the other candidates -- and they're determined to have you.

Therefore, until they have made you a firm offer, try to postpone all discussion of salary. You have *nothing* to lose, and *everything* to gain.

If it is the employer who brings up the subject -- early in the job-interview -- with some question like "How much are you expecting to make?" you should simply, kindly, and firmly reply, "Until you've decided you definitely want me, and I've decided I want to work here, I feel any discussion of salary is premature."

Never be the first one to mention a salary figure.

Salary negotiation *is* a kind of contest. As I indicated earlier, the employer wants to pay the least they can. You want them to pay the most they can, *within their range*. And what the experts have learned over the years, just from observing countless job-interviews, is that in this contest *whoever mentions a salary figure first, generally loses at the last.*

That's why experienced employers will *always* toss the ball to you, with the following innocent-sounding question, "What kind of salary are you looking for?" *Well, how kind of them to ask what you want* -- you may be thinking. No, no, no. Kindness isn't the point. They are hoping *you* will be the first to mention a figure, because they know this rule well, that *whoever mentions a salary figure first, generally loses.*

So of course, you will *never* want to respond with a dollar and cents figure. Instead, your response should always be: "Well, you created this position, so you must have some figure in mind, and I'd be interested in knowing what that is."

Before you go to the interview, do homework on how much you need.

You cannot possibly do salary negotiation unless you know what is *the floor,* below which you simply cannot afford to go. And this is particularly important in these troubled '90s, since many employers have *a fixed ceiling* above which they simply cannot afford to go. When you're in the middle of salary negotiation, you've *got* to know instantly if *their* ceiling turns out to be beneath *your* floor.

That means knowing, beforehand, just how much it is you need to make, at a minimum. You can determine this in one of two ways: a) take a wild guess -- and risk finding out after you take the job that it's simply impossible for you to live on that salary *(the favorite strategy in this country, and most others);* or, b) make out a detailed outline of your estimated expenses *now*, listing what you need *monthly* in the following categories:[5]

Housing
    Rent or mortgage payments ....$_____
    Electricity/gas ....$_____
    Water ....$_____
    Telephone ....$_____
    Garbage removal ....$_____
    Cleaning, maintenance, repairs[6] ....$_____

Food
    What you spend at the supermarket
    and/or meat market, etc. ....$_____
    Eating out ....$_____

Clothing
    Purchase of new or used clothing ....$_____
    Cleaning, drycleaning, laundry ....$_____

Automobile/transportation[7]
    Car payments ....$_____
    Gas ....$_____
    Repairs ....$_____
    Public transportation *(bus, train, plane)* ....$_____

Insurance
    Car ....$_____
    Medical or health-care ....$_____
    House and personal possessions ....$_____
    Life ....$_____

Medical expenses
    Doctors' visits ....$_____
    Prescriptions ....$_____
    Fitness costs ....$_____

Support for other family members
    Child-care costs *(if you have children)* ....$_____
    Child-support *(if you're paying that)* ....$_____
    Support for your parents *(if you're helping out)* $_____
Charity giving/tithe *(to help others)* ....$_____
School/learning
    Children's costs *(if you have children in school)* ..$_____
    Your learning costs *(adult education, job-*
    hunting classes, etc.) ....$_____
Pet care *(if you have pets)* ....$_____

Bills and debts *(Usual monthly payments)*
    Credit cards ....$_____
    Local stores ....$_____
    Other obligations you pay off monthly ....$_____
Taxes
    Federal[8] *(next April's due, divided by months*
    remaining until then) ....$_____
    State *(likewise)* ....$_____
    Local/property *(next amount due, divided by*
    months remaining until then) ....$_____
    Tax-help *(if you ever use an accountant, pay*
    a friend to help you with taxes, etc.) ....$_____
Amusement/discretionary spending
    Movies, video rentals, etc................................$_____
    Other kinds of entertainment........................$_____
    Reading, newspapers, magazines, books ....$_____
    Gifts *(birthday, Christmas, etc.)* ....$_____

Total Amount You Need Each Month ....$_____

---

5. If this kind of financial figuring is not your cup of tea, find a buddy, friend, relative, family member, or *anyone,* who can help you do this. If you don't know anyone who could do this, go to your local church, synagogue, religious center, social club, gym, or wherever you hang out, and ask the leader or manager there, to help you find someone. If there's a bulletin board, put up a notice on the bulletin board.

6. If you have extra household expenses, such as a security system for example, be sure and include the quarterly (or whatever) expenses here, divided by three.

7. Your checkbook stubs will tell you a lot of this stuff. But you may be vague about your cash or credit card expenditures. For example, you may not know how much you spend at the supermarket, or how much you spend on gas, etc. But there is a simple way to find out. Just carry a little notepad and pen around with you for two weeks or more, and jot down *everything* you pay cash *(or use credit cards)* for -- on the spot, right after you pay it. At the end of those two weeks, you'll be able to take that notepad and make a realistic guess of what should be put down in these categories that now puzzle you. *(Multiply the two-weeks figure by two, and you'll have the monthly figure.)*

8. Incidentally, looking ahead to next April 15th, be sure and check with your local IRS office or a reputable accountant to find out if you can deduct the expenses of your job-hunt on your Federal (and State) income tax returns. At this writing, some job-hunters can, if -- big IF -- this is not your first job that you're looking for, if you haven't been unemployed too long, and if you aren't making a career-change. Do go find out what the latest "if"s are. If IRS tells you you are eligible, keep careful receipts of everything related to your job-hunt, as you go along: telephone calls, stationery, printing, postage, travel, etc.

Parenthetically, you may want to prepare two different versions of the above budget: one with the expenses you'd ideally like to make, and the other a minimum budget, which will give you what you are looking for, here: the floor, below which you simply cannot afford to go.

> # Try to determine whether the salary being offered is fixed or contains room for negotiation.

Salary negotiation has become infinitely more complicated in the '90s. Many employers have fired or laid off experienced workers who have given years to the company, and they have done so for one reason and one reason only: those experienced, dedicated employees now cost too much. They can be replaced by new workers who may not have the experience, and may make a lot of mistakes. But these new employees have one sterling virtue: they cost *half* of what the previous employees cost.

Even among the new candidates, cost is often *key*.

> It's an old game, played with new determination by employers in the '90s, called "*among a bunch of equally qualified candidates, the one who is willing to work for the lowest salary wins.*"

This is particularly true if applicants for this position are 'a dime a dozen,' and you are viewed by the employer as *only one among many*.

If you want to ask for a higher salary, be prepared to show in what ways you will *make money* or in what ways you will *save money* for that organization, such as will justify your higher salary. What you have to labor to do during the job-interview, of course, is to make clear that you stand out -- way out -- above all the rest. The key to doing this, is to do the careful homework and preparation of Chapter 9 in this book. That's in a section labeled *Career Change,* but it's actually essential homework for any job-hunter who wants to stand out.

As I said earlier, salary negotiation is still possible even in the belt-tightening '90s, anytime the employer does not open the discussion of salary by naming the top figure they have in mind, but starts instead at a lower figure.

Okay, so here is our $64,000 question: how can you tell whether the figure the employer first offers you is only their *starting bid*, or is their *final final offer?* The answer is: by doing some research first.

> ### Before you go in, do research on salaries for your field and that organization.

You, of course, want to know if it's *really necessary* to do this kind of research. Trust me, salary research pays off *handsomely.*

Let's say it takes you from one to three days to run down this sort of information on the three or four organizations that interest you the most. And let us say that because you've done this research, when you finally go in for the job-interview you are able to ask for and obtain a salary that is $4,000 a year higher in range, than you would otherwise have gotten. In just the next three years, you will be earning $12,000 extra, because of your salary research. *Not bad pay, for one to three days' work!* And it can be even more.

If it is true that *information* is the key to a successful job-hunt and to successful salary-negotiation, it is equally true that there is a financial penalty exacted from those who are too lazy, or in too much of a hurry, to go gather that information.

If you want to find out what the salary is for the kind of job you are being considered for, there is a simple rule: **abandon books, and go talk to people.** Preferably to people who are in the same job *at another company or organization.* Or, go talk to people at the nearby university or college who *train* such people: whatever the department is, where people get trained for this kind of job. These teachers will usually know what their graduates are getting.

Use books only as a *second*, or *last*, resort. I have listed in the footnote below a sampling of the kind of information you can dig up at your local library, using the resources listed in Appendix B and elsewhere.[9] This is for the U.S. Other countries should have similar resources. Ask your local librarian.

Apropos of talking to people, in order to get this information, let's look at some examples:

> First Example: *Working at your first entry-level job, say at a fast-food place.*

You may not need to do any salary research. They pay what they pay. You can walk in, ask for a job application, and interview with the manager. He or she will usually tell you the pay, outright. It's usually *inflexible*. But at least you'll find it easy to

---

9. Some books or journals will give yearly figures; others will give hourly. The yearly figures are roughly convertible to hourly wages, and vice versa. Assume a 40 hour week, and a 50 week year, which is less than some people work, and more than others -- but close enough. Take *however many* thousands the yearly figure is, and divide the number of thousands by two; that will give you the *approximate* hourly wage. Thus, with $30,000 a year, you take the 30, divide by two, and you find it equals (approximately) $15 an hour. Or, to reverse, take the hourly figure, multiply it by two, and add three zeroes. Now, where do you look? In the U.S., the places to look for your information include the Department of Labor's monthly *Employment and Earnings*, ("Household Data, Annual Averages, Median weekly earnings of full-time wage and salary workers by detailed occupation and sex") -- plus its annual *Supplement to Employment and Earnings; Area Wage Surveys* (covers office, professional, technical, maintenance, custodial, and material movement jobs in major metropolitan areas), and individual area bulletins which are available separately, and cover mainly production and non-supervisory workers. Order from the Bureau of Labor Statistics, Publications Sales Center, P.O. Box 2145, Chicago IL 60690. Areas covered include Alexandria-Leesville, Virginia; Ashville, North Carolina; Atlanta; Beaumont–Port Arthur and Lake Charles, Texas; Cedar Rapids, Iowa; Houston; Huntsville; Logansport–Peru, Indiana; Milwaukee; Minneapolis–St. Paul; Monmouth-Ocean, New Jersey; Newark, New Jersey; Norfolk–Virginia Beach–Newport News, Virginia; Northern New York; Northwestern Florida; Oakland, Califonia; Pittsburgh; Portsmouth-Chillicothe-Gallipolis, Ohio; Raleigh-Durham, North Carolina; St. Louis; San Francisco and San Jose, California; Washington DC–Maryland.

Also look in *The Occupational Outlook Handbook* -- it has ballpark figures for a *selected* list of jobs. The job you are interested in *may* be included.

Additional sources: Arsen Darnay, ed., *American Salaries & Wages Survey*. Gale Research, Inc., P.O. Box 33477, Detroit, MI 48232-5477. 1991. It's *expensive;* see your local library.

John W. Wright, *The American Almanac of Jobs and Salaries, revised and updated 1990– 1991 edition.* Avon Books, Dept. FP, 1790 Broadway, New York, NY 10019. This book is revised periodically, but at this writing *this* is the most recent edition. It has a lot of interesting help, but *do* remember that the salary figures are all from 1987, sometimes 1988.

discover what the pay is. (Incidentally, filling out an application, or having an interview there, doesn't commit you to take the job -- but you probably already know that. You can always decline an offer from *any place.* That's what makes this approach harmless.)

> Second Example: *Working at a place where you can't discover what the pay is, say at a construction company.*

If that construction company where you would *hope* to get a job is difficult to research, go visit a *different* construction company in the same town -- one that isn't of much interest to you -- and ask what they make *there.* Or, if you don't know who to talk to there, fill out one of their applications, and talk to the hiring person about what kinds of jobs they have (or might have in the future), at which time prospective wages is a legitimate subject of discussion. Then, having done this research on a place you don't care about, go back to the place that *really* interests you, and apply. You still don't know *exactly* what they pay, but you do know what their competitor pays -- which will usually be *close.*

> Third Example: *Working in a one-person office, say as a secretary.*

Here you can often find useful salary information by perusing the *Help Wanted* ads in the local paper for a week or two. Most of the ads probably won't mention a salary figure, but a few *may.* Among those that do, note what the lowest salary offering is, and what the highest is, and see if the ad reveals some reasons for the difference. It's interesting how much you can learn about salaries, with this approach. I know, because I was a secretary myself, once upon a time.

Another way to do salary research is to find a *Temporary Work Agency* that places secretaries, and let yourself be farmed out to various offices: the more, the merrier. It's relatively easy to do salary research when you're *inside* the place. (Study what that place pays *the agency,* not what the agency pays you.) If it's an office where the other workers like you, you'll be able to ask questions about a lot of things, *including* salary. It's like *summertime,* where the research is easy.

AT HOME
ON THE RANGE

Before you finish your research, before you go in there for your first or final interview, you want more than just one figure. You want *a range.* In any organization which has more than five employees, that range is relatively easy to figure out. It will be less than what the person *who would be above you* makes, and more than what the person *who would be below you* makes.

One teensy-tiny little problem: *how* do you find out the salary of those who would be above and below you? Well, first you have to find out their *names* or the names of their *positions.* If it is a small organization you are going after -- one with twenty or less employees -- finding this information out should be *duck soup.* Any employee who works there is likely to know the answer, and you can usually get in touch with one of those employees, or even an ex-employee, through your contacts. Since two-thirds of all new jobs are created by companies of that size, that's the size organization you are likely to be researching, anyway.

If you are going after a larger organization, then you have our familiar life-preserver to fall back on, namely, every contact you have (family, friend, relative, business, or church acquaintance) who might know the company, and therefore, the information you seek. You are looking for Someone Who Knows

Someone who either is working, or has worked, at the particular place or places that interest you, who therefore has or can get this information for you.

If you absolutely run into a blank wall on a particular organization (everyone who works there is pledged to secrecy, and they have shipped all their ex-employees to Siberia), then seek out information on their nearest *competitor* in the same geographic area. *For example,* let us say you were researching Bank X, and they were proving to be inscrutable about what they pay their managers. You would then try Bank Y as your research base, to see if the information were easier to come by, there. And if it were, you would then assume the two were similar in their pay scales, and that what you learned about Bank Y was applicable also to Bank X.

GETTING THE JOB

With this research in your hip pocket, when you are in the actual job-interview, and the employer mentions the figure *they* have in mind, you are then ready to respond: "I understand of course the constraints under which all organizations are operating in the '90s, but I believe my productivity is such that it would *justify* a salary in the range of . . ." -- *and here you mention a figure near the top of their range.* Hopefully, this will succeed in getting you the salary you want.[10]

During your salary negotiation, do not forget to pay attention to so-called fringe benefits. 'Fringes' such as life insurance, health benefits or health plans, vacation or holiday plans, and retirement programs typically add another 28% to many workers' salaries. That is to say, if an employee receives $800 salary per month, the fringe benefits are worth another $200 per month. You should therefore remember to ask what benefits are offered, and negotiate if necessary for the benefits you want.

---

10. Daniel Porot, in Europe, suggests that if you and an employer really hit it off, and you're *dying* to work there, but they cannot afford the salary you need, consider offering them part of your time. If you need, and believe you deserve, say $25,000, but they can only afford $15,000, you might consider offering them three days a week of your time for that $15,000 (15/25 = 3/5). This leaves you free to take other work those other two days.

Thinking this out ahead of time, of course, makes your negotiating easier, by far. You can prepare the ground during your salary negotiation, by saying: *"If I accomplish this job to your satisfaction, as I fully expect to -- and more -- when could I expect to be in line for a raise?"*

Once all salary negotiation is concluded to your satisfaction, do remember to ask to have it summed up in a letter of agreement -- or employment contract -- that they give to you. It may be you cannot get it in writing, but do try! The Road to Hell is paved with oral promises that went unwritten, and -- later -- unfulfilled.

Many executives unfortunately 'forget' what they told you during the job-interview, or even deny they ever said such a thing.

Also, many executives leave the company for another position and place, and their successor or the top boss may disown any *unwritten* promises: *"I don't know what caused them to say that to you, but they clearly exceeded their authority, and of course we can't be held to that."*

Plan to keep track of your accomplishments at this new job, on a weekly basis -- jotting them down, every weekend, in your own private diary. Career experts, such as Bernard Haldane, recommend you do this without fail. You can then summarize these accomplishments annually on a one-page sheet, for your boss's eyes, when raise or promotion is a legitimate subject for you to bring up.[11]

SUMMARY

Job-hunting always involves luck, to some degree. But with a little bit of luck, the techniques described in these chapters should work for you, even as they have worked for so many thousands before you.

Assuming they do, when you are in that next job -- hopefully your *ideal job* -- you will know the truth of something Dick Lathrop first said over twenty years ago, in his book *Who's Hiring Who:*

---

11. In any good-sized organization, you will often be amazed at how little attention your superiors pay to your noteworthy accomplishments, and how little they are aware at the end of the year that you really are *entitled* to a raise. Noteworthy your accomplishments may be, but no one is taking notes . . . unless *you* do.

There may be others who applied there who could have done the job better than you. But it is true today, and it will ever be true: the person who gets hired is not necessarily the one who can do that job best; but, the one **who knows the most about how to get hired.**

The Pink Pages

Two are better than one;
     for if they fall,
the one will lift up his fellow;

but woe to him that is alone when he falleth,
and hath not another to lift him up.

Ecclesiastes

Appendix A

When Books Are Not Enough
and
You Want A Live Person
To Help You:

Career Counselors
and
Other Resources

LOOK BEFORE YOU LEAP:
How to Choose a Career Counselor,
If You Decide You Need One

It would be nice if the matter of finding a career counselor were relatively simple: look them up in the phone book, choose a name, and go see them. You *can* get a career counselor, that way. But of course you don't just want a career counselor. You want a *good* career counselor. And that's no more easy a task to find than is a *good* doctor or a *good* dentist or a *good* lawyer.

You are, unfortunately, going to have to *work* at this. But there are some things I can tell you that will hopefully make your task simpler and easier.

TYPES OF CAREER COUNSELORS
BY SUBJECT MATTER

If you are seeking help with the job-hunt, you need to be aware that career counselors divide essentially into two types. The first type of counselor is the one whose *primary* expertise is in the area called 'career development' or 'career assessment.' They help people figure out what they want to do with their lives, by way of career choice, etc. They *may* know very little about the actual job-hunt process, so if that's the kind of help you're looking for, this is not the counselor for you.

The second type of counselor is the one whose primary expertise is in the area called 'job-search.' They almost always also know something about 'career development' or 'career assessment,' as above, but their *primary* expertise is in the job-search process.

This latter group of counselors divides, yet again, into two groups. There are those whose primary expertise in the job-search process concerns the *traditional* approach: resumes and interviewing, as described in Chapters 3 and 13 in this book. If you have already given up on that traditional approach, then this is not the counselor for you.

And then there are those career counselors whose primary expertise is in the *creative* process of job-hunting, described in Chapters 9, 10, 11, and 12, as well as 4, in this book. This is the one you want.

'THE PARACHUTE SEAL OF APPROVAL'

Okay, there's a basic overview of the kinds of career counselors. You want a career counselor whose expertise is in the job-search process, and the creative job-search process at that. Well, and good.

Of course, what you're hoping I will offer you at this point is some sort of "authorized list" of names nationwide: people who understand this whole job-hunting process thoroughly, know how to do all the exercises in this book, have been through some kind of careful credentialing process, and received the Parachute Seal of Approval.

Ah, dear reader, how I wish it were so. But, unhappily, there is no such list. First of all, while I do train people once a year, I have only trained 3,000 over the years -- which is *a drop in the bucket,* compared to the number of career counselors that are out there. Moreover, I can't *guarantee* that simply because they've been through my hands, they truly understand. So, publishing a list of *their* names wouldn't answer your problem.

Secondly, there are lots of people out there who understand the whole job-hunting process thoroughly and well, even though they've never been trained by me and may not even (necessarily) have read this book. In most cases, of course, I've never met them, and consequently I don't know who they are or where they are. I simply know *that* they are.

What this adds up to, you've already guessed. You've got to do your own homework, here. Hunting for a decent career counselor is just like hunting for a job. You've got to do your own research, and your own interviewing, in your own geographical area, or you will deserve what you get.

DOING YOUR OWN RESEARCH
IN YOUR COMMUNITY OR NEARBY

What do you want? Let's rehearse what you're looking for. The three things you absolutely want from anyone you're paying good money to, are:
a) a firm grasp of the whole job-hunting process, at its most creative and effective level;
b) the ability on their part to communicate that information lucidly and clearly to you;
c) rapport with you.

This last is the killer. Without that, you can forget the first two. That's why you have to do your own research. No one but you knows whether or not you're going to get along with a particular career counselor. Maybe he's a wonderful man, but unhappily he reminds you of your Uncle Harry. You've always **hated** your Uncle Harry. No one knows that, but you. Or maybe the counselor is a wonderful woman, but unhappily . . . *well, you get the point.*

No one can do this research for you. Because the real question is not "Who is best?" but "Who is best **for you?**" Those last two words demand that it be you who 'makes the call.'

Now, what do you want? Well, you want to find the names of at least three career counselors in your community, you want to go talk with them, and decide which of the three (if any) you want to hook up with.

Where do you look? Where do you find names? Well, the phone book is always a good place to start. They may be listed under a wide variety of titles: career counselors, executive career counselors, executive career consultants, career management teams, vocational psychologists, executive consulting counselors, career guidance counselors, executive advisors, executive development specialists, executive job counselors, manpower experts, career advisors, employment specialists, executive recruitment consultants, management consultants, placement specialists, executive search specialists, vocational counselors, life/work planners, etc. You're going to have to do some hunting.

Outside the phone book, you ask among your friends if any of them have ever used a career counselor. And if so, what did they think of them.

If that doesn't turn up any leads, you look at the Sampler toward the rear of this Appendix, to see if there are any names near you, *with which to start.* They may know how you find out the other names in your community.

One way or another, you want to obtain, as I said, at least three names. Why? Because you're going to be doing comparison shopping.

Of course, you're tempted to skip over that little requirement. *"Well, I'll just call up one place, and if I like the sound of them, I'll sign up. I'm a pretty good judge of character."* Right. I hear many a sad tale from people who adopted that attitude, and all that I can say when it's too late is, "I'm sorry indeed to hear that you had a very disappointing experience; that is very unfortunate, I know, I've been through it myself. But -- as the Scots would say -- 'Ya dinna do your homework.' "[1] Often you could easily have discovered whether a particular counselor was competent or not, before you *ever* gave them any of your money, simply by asking the right questions during this comparison shopping which I'm pleading with you to regard as *essential.*

How do you ask? **You visit in person each of the three places you have chosen.** Don't try to do this over the telephone, *please!* There is so much more you can tell, when you're looking the person straight in the eyes. Remember, these are exploratory visits only. For that reason, be sure and leave your wallet and checkbook at home, please! You are only comparison shopping or information-gathering at this point. You are *not* ready yet to reach a decision. *Please* make this unmistakably clear, when you are setting up the appointment for the interview. And should they ask you to bring in your partner or spouse with you, *beware.* That is a well-known tactic of some of the slickest salespeople in the world, who *want* your spouse or partner there so they can manipulate one *or* the other of you to reach a decision on the spot, while they have you in their 'grasp.'

What do you ask? When you go (by yourself) on this exploratory visit, you ask *each* of the three places you go to, the same questions. Keep a little pad or notebook with you that looks something like this:

---

1. If you are reading this too late, did pay some firm's fee all in advance, and feel you were ripped off, you will want to know about Mr. Stuart Alan Rado. Mr. Rado was a victim of one of the career counseling agencies, and ever since, he has been waging a sort of "one-man crusade" against career counseling firms which take advantage of the job-hunter. Send Mr. Rado your story, together with a self-addressed stamped envelope, and he will send you a one-page sheet of some actions you can take. It may not get your money back, but at least you'll feel better for having done something. His address is: 1500 23rd St., Sunset Island #3, Miami Beach, FL 33140. 305-532-2607.

MY SEARCH FOR A GOOD CAREER COUNSELOR

Questions I Will Ask Them	Answer from counselor #1	Answer from counselor #2	Answer from counselor #3
1. What is your program?			
2. Who will be doing it?			
3. What is your success rate?			
4. How much time will you give me?			
5. What is the cost of your services?			

As you ask the questions at each place, take time to write down direct quotes of their answers, *as* they are answering, please! *Don't* trust your memory. Good counselors will not mind your doing this, in the least. Bad counselors will: *"Do you have to do all that writing as we talk? I find it very distracting."* Too bad. You need to be able to compare, later, *exactly* what each of the three places said.

SOME QUESTIONS, BY MEANS OF WHICH YOU MAY BE ABLE TO SEPARATE THE SHEEP FROM THE GOATS

You can see from the diagram above, that the questions you need to ask *each* place are these:

1. What is your program? Sometimes, their answers to this question will bedazzle you: *we will give you help,* say they, *with evaluating your career history, in-depth analysis of your background, establishment of your job objective, in-depth analysis of your capabilities, writing an effective resume, names of companies, preparing the covering letter, background materials on companies, interviewing techniques, video playback of mock interviews between you and a pretend-employer, help you rehearse for interviews on closed circuit TV, use videotape or cassettes to record your skills or your resume, coach you on salary negotiations, filling out forms, answering ads, aptitude tests, special problems -- unemployment, age, too broad a background, too narrow a background, too many job changes, too*

few job changes, poor references, etc. We will, they say, *open doors for you, tell you which companies are hiring, and so forth and so on.*

But, when all the jargon and the gimmicks are set aside, what are they offering: is it basically "the numbers game" (see Chapter 3 in this book) **or** is it some variation of the creative minority's prescription (see Chapters 9, 10, 11, and 12). If it's the latter, three cheers.

Also, if they give you the feeling that you must do most of the program, with their basically assuming the role of coach, give three more cheers. On the other hand, if you get the feeling that everything (including tests, interpretation of the tests, and decision making about what this means you should do, or where you should do it) will be done *for you* in this program, three warning bells should go off in your head.

2. Who will be doing it? Ask the man or woman you are facing if *they* will be the counselor who works with you throughout the program. If they say *No,* ask to meet the person who will be. If they deny you access to that person, thank them politely for their time, and *walk out.*

Assuming you do get to meet the person whom you will actually be working with, there are a couple of considerations you should weigh:

(a) *Do you like the counselor?* I don't care what their expertise is, if you don't like them, you're going to have a rough time getting what you want. I guarantee it. Rapport is *everything*.

(b) *How long has the counselor been doing this?* It's perfectly legitimate to ask this, and also to ask what training they have had for career counseling. If they get huffy, or try to dodge the questions, politely thank them for their time, and take your leave gently *but firmly.* You might be interested to know that some executive or career counseling firms hire yesterday's clients as today's new staff. Such new staff are sometimes given training only after they're "on-the-job." They are practicing on you. No matter how small or large the fee you would be paying, you have a right to *expertise already acquired.* Incidentally, beware of their summing up their experience in terms of double phrases, such as "I've had eighteen years' experience in the business and career counseling world." What that may mean is: seventeen and a half years as a fertilizer salesman, and one half year doing career counseling. Persist. *"How long have you been with this firm, and how long have you been doing* **formal career counseling,** *as you are here?"*

Don't be hood-winked by 'degrees.' What kinds of degrees will you run into? Well, first of all, B.A., M.A., and Ph.D. You know what they mean. However, *don't* assume that degree is in career counseling. Ask. N.C.C. means "Nationally certified counselor." There are about 20,000 such in the U.S. N.C.C.C. means "Nationally certified career counselor." There are currently about 850 in the U.S. Other initials, such as L.P.C. -- "Licensed professional counselor" -- and the like, often refer to State licensing. There are a number of States, now, that have some sort of regulation of career counselors. In some States it is mandatory, in others it is optional. But, mostly, this field is unregulated.

Much as you might *think* these degrees mean something about the expertise of the counselor in the job-hunt, often they don't. It's much more useful for you to ask, "How many times have you had to go job-hunting yourself, and how many of those times did you use *Parachute*?" That'll tell you more, though again it doesn't always define how expert the counselor is, in the job-search process. The simple fact is: there is no definitive way for you to determine a career counselor's expertise. It's something you'll have to *smell* out, as you go along.

3. *What's their success rate?* If they make it clear that they have had a good success rate, but if you fail to work hard at the whole process, then there is no guarantee you are going to find a job, give them three stars. On the other hand, if they practically guarantee you a job, and say they have never had a client that failed to find a job, no matter what, **watch out.** They're *lying*. I have studied career counseling programs for over twenty years, have attended many, have studied records at State and Federal offices, and I have *never* seen a program that placed more than 86% of their clients *in their best years*. And it goes downhill from there. A prominent executive counseling firm was reported by the Attorney General's Office of New York State to have placed only 38 out of 550 clients (a 93% failure rate).[2]

4. How much time will they give you? At a minimum? At a maximum? This is only a major consideration when you're dealing with *lump-sum-in-advance* firms, who require you to sign a contract (about which, more later).

Anyway, answers like, *"Hey, we work with you until you get a job, no matter how long that takes,"* should basically be distrusted. Try again: "What's the most hours you've ever had to give to a client, in the past?" Believe me, there's got to be a maximum, no matter what they may at first try to tell you. Why? Because every career counselor has, in the past, run into extremely dependent types as clients, who would be visiting them an hour every day of the week, including Saturdays and Sundays, if the counselor or the firm didn't have some policy about time limits. **Press** to find out what that policy is, just so you'll know. How much time *will* they give you? And, **will they put this in writing?** Ah, there's the test that separates the men from the boys, and the women from the girls, in the counseling profession.

5. What is the cost of their services? Is it paid hourly, as you go along, or must it all be paid "up front" before you even start? With **counselors who require you to pay for the entire "program" before you start** -- or shortly after you start -- you will run into an innocent looking instrument: **a contract.** With them, there is **always** a written contract. And you **must** sign it, before they will help you. (Often, your partner or spouse will be asked to sign it, too.) The fee normally ranges from $1,000 on up to $10,000.

---

2. For further details, go to your local library and look up "Career Counselors: Will They Lead You Down The Primrose Path?" by Lee Guthrie, in the December 1981 issue of *Savvy Magazine*, pp. 60ff.

You may *think* the purpose of that firm's contract is that *they* are promising *you* something, that they can be held to. Uh-uh! More often, the main purpose of the contract is to get *you* to promise *them* something. Like, money. Don't . . . do . . . it.

Further, don't let your defenses be lulled by the fact that the contract may allow you to pay the up-front fee *in installments*. If you sign that contract, you **are** obligated to pay the full sum, one way or the other.

You will sometimes be told that, "*Of course,* you can get your money back, or a portion of it, at any time, should you be dissatisfied with the career counselor's services." Nine times out of ten, however, you are told this *verbally*, and it is **not** in the written contract. Verbal promises, without witnesses, are difficult if not impossible for you to later enforce. The written contract is binding.

Sometimes the written contract will claim to provide for a partial refund, at any time, *until* you reach a cut-off date in the program, which the contract specifies. Unfortunately, as many job-hunters have found out *way* too late, and to their sorrow, the cut-off date is often calculated by the counselor or agency in a very different way than you or I would calculate it. Consequently, you are often beyond that cut-off date, and the possibility of any refund, long before *your* calculations tell you you should be.

To make matters worse, many *crafty* fraudulent firms bend over backwards to be extra nice, extra available, and extra helpful to you *until* that cut-off point is reached. So, when the cut-off point for getting a refund has been reached, you let it pass because you are very satisfied with their past services, and believe there will be many more weeks of the same. Only, there aren't. *At fraudulent firms,* once the cut-off point is passed, the career counselor becomes virtually impossible for you to get ahold of. Call after call will *not* be returned. You will say to yourself *"What happened?"* Well, what happened, my friend, is that you paid up in full, they have all the money they're ever going to get out of you, and now they don't want to give you any more time.

You may *think* I am exaggerating: I mean, can there possibly be such *mean* men and women, who would *prey* on job-hunters, when they're down and out. Yes, ma'am, and yes, sir, there are.[3] That's why you have to do this

---

3. If you are **dying** to know more, and your local library has back files of magazines and newspapers (on microfiche, or otherwise) there was a period when bad firms and counselors came under heavy fire (1978–1982) and you can look up some of the articles of that period, as well as those articles which have appeared more recently, to wit:

"A Consumer Guide to Retail Job-Hunting Services," Special Report, reprinted from the *National Business Employment Weekly;* available from Dow Jones Reprint Service, P.O. Box 300, Princeton NJ 08543-0300. A *very* thorough series of articles on the industry, which names *names*, and gives the addresses of Consumer protection agencies in each state, to whom you may complain. **Required reading** for anyone who wants to avoid getting 'burned.'

"'Employment counselors' costly, target of gripes," *The Arizona Republic,* October 8, 1989.

"Career-Counseling Industry Accused of Misrepresentation," *New York Times,* Sept. 30, 1982, p. C1.

"Consumer Law: Career Counselors and Employment Agencies" by Reed Brody, *New York Law Journal,* Feb. 26, 1982, p. 1. Reed was Assistant Attorney General of the State of New York, and more recently Deputy Chief of the Labor Bureau within that State's Department of Law; in this capacity he became the leading legal expert in the country, on career counseling malprac-

preliminary research so thoroughly.

Over the last twenty years, I have had to listen to grown men and women *cry* over the telephone, *all because they signed a contract.* Most often they were executives, or senior managers, who never had to go job-hunting before, and unknowingly signed up with some executive counseling firm that was fraudulent, or at least on the *edge* of legality.

If you want to avoid their tears in your own job-search:

I say, uncategorically, after twenty years of trying to avoid giving this advice; but I've grown weary with the tears of those who got 'taken': if there is a contract involved, don't sign it. It may be innocent, or it may not be. But it will cost you an amount of money that you really can't afford to lose, to find out. If you really like to gamble that much, go to Las Vegas. They give better odds, there.

Fortunately there are other kinds of counselors: **counselors who charge by the hour.** With them, there is no written contract. You sign nothing. You pay only for each hour as you use it, according to their set rate. Each time you keep an appointment, you pay them at the end of that hour for their help, according to that rate. Period. Finis. You never owe them any money. You can stop seeing them at any time, if you feel you are not getting the help you wish.

And what is the going rate? You will find, these days, that the best career counselors *(and some of the worst, too)* will charge you whatever a really good therapist or marriage counselor, in your geographical area, charges for an hour. Currently, in large metropolitan areas, that runs around $100 an hour. In suburbia or rural areas, it may be *much* less.

That fee is for *individual* time with the career counselor. If you can't afford that fee, ask whether they also run *groups.* If they do, the fee will be much less. And, in one of those delightful ironies of life, since you get a chance to listen to problems which other job-hunters in your group are having, similar to yours, the group will *often* give you more help than an individual session would. Not *always;* but *often.* It's always ironic when *cheaper* and *more helpful* run hand in hand.

If the career counselor in question does offer groups, there should (again) never be a contract. The charge should be *payable at the end of each session,* and you should be able to drop out at any time, without further cost, if you decide you are not getting the help you want.

There are, incidentally, some career counselors who run *free* (or almost free) job-hunting workshops through local churches, synagogues, cham-

---

tices, though unfortunately (for us) he now works overseas in Europe, in another profession.

"Career Counselors: Will They Lead You Down the Primrose Path?" by Lee Guthrie, *Savvy Magazine,* Dec. 1981, pp. 60ff.

"Franklin Career Search Is Accused of Fraud In New York State Suit," *Wall Street Journal,* Jan. 29, 1981, p.50.

"Job Counseling Firms Under Fire For Promising Much, Giving Little," *Wall Street Journal,* Jan. 27, 1981, p. 33.

bers of commerce, community colleges, adult education programs, and the like, as their community service, or *pro bonum* work (as it is techically called). I have had reports of such workshops from a number of places in the U.S. and Canada. They surely exist in other places as well. If money is a big problem for you, in getting help with your job-hunt, ask around to see if such workshops as these exist in *your* community.

WHEN YOU'VE FINISHED
YOUR COMPARISON SHOPPING

Having gotten the information *you* want, and therefore having accomplished your purpose for your visit, politely thank them for their time and trouble, and depart.

You then go on to the other two places, and ask the very same questions. Carefully write down their answers in your notebook, *as* they are saying them, please! There should be no charge for such comparison shopping visits as this. Make this clear when you set up the original appointment. If they subsequently bill you, phone them and inquire politely whether or not a mistake has been made by their billing department (good thinking). If they persist in billing you, pay a visit to your local friendly Better Business Bureau, and lodge a nice unfriendly complaint against the firm in question. You'd be surprised at how many firms experience **instant repentance** when the Better Business Bureau phones them. *(They don't want a complaint on their BBB record.)*

Back home now, after visiting the three places you chose for your comparison shopping, you have to decide: a) whether you want none of the three, or b) one of the three and if so, which one.

Look over your notes on all three places. Compare those places. It's time for thought, maybe using some others as a sounding board: partner, spouse, business friend, consultant friend, placement center, buddy, *primary other* or anyone whose judgment you trust.

But remember also to listen to your own intuition, and to your own heart. Did one or more of those places give *any* answer that you didn't like? *Trust your intuition.* Did you dislike your would-be counselor at any of these places? *Trust your intuition.* Did they refuse to let you meet your would-be counselor? *Trust your intuition.* Did one or more of those places have only a package rate, not an hourly rate? *Trust your intuition.* Did one or more of these places have an hourly rate, but seemed to pressure you into taking their 'package' deal? *Trust your intuition.*

Remember, you don't have to choose **any** of the three counselors, if you didn't really care for any of them. If that is the case, then choose three new counselors, dust off the notebook, and go out again. It may take a few more hours to find what you want. But the wallet, the purse, the job-hunt, the life, you save will be your own.

A Sampler

This is not a complete directory of anything. It is exactly what its name implies: a **Sampler.** Were I to list all the career counselors *out there*, we would end up with an encyclopedia. Some states, in fact, have *encyclopedic* lists of counselors and businesses, in various books or directories, and your local bookstore or library should have these, in their *Job-Hunting Section,* under such titles as "How to Get A Job in . . ." or "Job-Hunting in. . . ."

Most of the places listed in this *Sampler* are listed at their own request, and the listing is without charge of any kind. The listing, *of course,* is not an endorsement or recommendation by me of that place. This is a **Sampler**, for you to begin your investigation with -- nothing more. *(If any place misuses their listing, claiming in brochures, ads, or interviews, that we recommend them, or endorse them, or feature them in* Parachute, *implying thereby that they have a sort of Parachute Seal of Approval, that listing gets gently dropped, without further notice.)*[4]

We, of course, display a modicum of caution about listing places. We try to restrict the listing a little bit (but only a little bit), **to counselors and places which claim some expertise in helping readers finish using this book**, since that is what our readers are looking for. So, we ask a few questions along those lines before listing a place. But obviously we are in no position to make any final judgment about a place's expertise, from a distance. That is why you must do your own careful investigation, along the lines I have indicated previously in this Appendix.

I am sure that despite all our cautiousness, some unhelpful places inadvertently got included. If, as you use this *Sampler,* you discover a place that is -- in your opinion -- totally unhelpful, you could be of great service to our other readers by dropping us a line and telling us so. (P.O. Box 379, Walnut Creek, CA 94597.) Let us know also if any place is no longer in existence, or impossible to get ahold of.

On the other hand, some *helpful* places are *not* listed here, either.

---

4. When places or counselors disappear from this Sampler, over the years, it may be for one of several other reasons, as well. Sometimes, it's because they've folded, without a trace. Sometimes it's because, they've moved, without notifying us *where* (so our annual *update card* comes back, stamped: *Addressee Unknown*). Sometimes it's because more than one reader (and former client) has written to complain -- with *details* -- that this place's program or this counselor's counseling skills are for the birds. Naturally, the counselor -- in reply -- always says that his or her program is wonderful, but these are disgruntled people whom any counselor would fail with. In earlier days we tried to be eminently fair by investigating such disputes *at length;* but it took hours, sometimes days, to guess if the counselor was basically sound. I don't have that kind of time anymore. So now we *have* to take the safe route, and cannot continue a list a place that we have been *warned* is unhelpful. That would be unfair to our other readers. Our consolation, in this Solomonic dilemma, is that such places survived before we listed them, and they will survive quite nicely in the future, whether we list them or not. And that if someone has given false witness against them, God will grant that False Witness the life that goes with it.

If you know of such a place, which is very good at helping people with *Parachute* and creative job-hunting or career-change, do send us the pertinent information. We will then ask them a few intelligent questions and if they sound okay, we will then add that place to our next edition. *Don't, however, bother to send us college services which are available only to the students and alumni or alumnae of that college. After many complaints from readers, it is now our policy to no longer list places that thus restrict their clientele. If you discover that we have inadvertently included a place that only serves Their Own, please let us know immediately, and we'll gently drop their listing, from the next edition. Also, we do not list places which employ salespeople as the initial 'in-take' person that you meet. Again, if we have inadvertently included such a place, please let us know.*

As we go to press, this Sampler is as accurate and up-to-date as we can make it. *Unfortunately,* however, there is no way any Sampler can remain up-to-date and accurate, for more than about two days, and six hours. Staff changes. Phone numbers change. Places move, or fold, almost weekly in this field. I apologize for any information or listing that proves to be inaccurate by the time you get to use it. Again, please let me know.

If the listings here aren't helpful for the geographical location where you are, ask everyone you know -- family, friends, and even people you've just met -- if they know any really helpful career counselors in your area.

Try also your telephone book's local Yellow Pages, under the headings (in the index) of *Personnel & Employment,* under *Business and Financial Services.* This index will likely refer you to such entries in the body of the Yellow Pages as: *Aptitude and Employment Testing, Career and Vocational Counseling, Personnel Consultants,* and (if you are a woman) *Women's Organizations and Services.* You will discover, however, that even the Yellow Pages can't keep up with the additional groups that spring up daily, weekly, and monthly -- including job clubs and other group activities. Fortunately, many of these *are* listed in the *National Business Employment Weekly,* on its pages called "Calendar of Career Events." Available on newsstands, $3.95 per issue; or, order an issue directly from: National Business Employment Weekly, 420 Lexington Ave., New York, NY 10170. 212-808-6792, or 800-JOB-HUNT. Among all the listings below, as well as those that you turn up on your own, you will have to pick and choose very carefully.

Some of these people in this **Sampler** are immensely competent; some are not. There is no way to tell, unless you go ask them all the questions I have suggested. I repeat: you must do your own comparison shopping, and do your own sharp questioning before you decide to go with anyone. If you don't, you will deserve whatever you get (or, more to the point, *don't* get). The purse or wallet you save, will be your own.

The listings below are alphabetical within each state, except that counselors listed by their name are in alphabetical order according to their *last* name. To make this clear, only their last name is in **bold** type.

Generally speaking, the places, and counselors, below counsel *anybody*. A few, however, take only women as clients. Ask. If they aren't able to help you, your phone call wasn't wasted, *so long as* you then go on to ask them "who else in the area can you tell me about, who helps with job-search, and are there any among them that you would particularly recommend?"

> *Incidentally, if you are looking for places which specialize in doing career counseling from a religious point of view, these are listed at the end of The Epilogue, "How To Find Your Mission in Life," on page 452.*

ALABAMA

Enterprise State Junior College, P.O. Box 1300, Enterprise, AL 36331. 205-347-2623 or 393-ESJC. Nancy Smith, Director of Guidance Services.

OI/Ronniger, 2027 First Ave. N., Suite 808, Birmingham, AL 35203. 205-324-5030. Michael Tate.

ALASKA

Career Transitions, 2221 East Northern Lights Blvd., Suite 207, Anchorage, AK 99508. 907-278-7350. Deeta Lonergan, Director.

ARIZONA

College PLUS Career Connections, 4540 S. Rural Rd., #P-8, Tempe, AZ 85282. 602-730-5246. Dr. Warren D. Robb, Director.

Debra Davenport Associates, 11446 N. 109th St., Scottsdale, AZ 85259. 602-391-2802. Debra Davenport Fair, M.A., L.C.C.

NewStart Career Counseling Services, 3080 N. Civic Center Plaza, Scottsdale, AZ 85251. 602-947-3311. Sheila Iosty.

Southwest Institute of Life Management, 11122 E. Gunshot Circle, Tucson, AZ 85749. 602-749-2290. Theodore Donald Risch, Director.

Tucson/Pima County Job Club, 110 E. Pennington, Mezzanine Level, Tucson, AZ 85701. 602-884-8280. Stuart R. Thomas.

ARKANSAS

Donald **McKinney,** Ed.D., Career Counselor, Rt. 1, Box 351-A, DeQueen, AR 71832. 501-642-5628.

CALIFORNIA

Alumnae Resources, 120 Montgomery St., Suite 1080, San Francisco, CA 94104. 415-274-4700.

Jill **Andreoni,** 2625 W. Alameda Ave., Suite 514, Burbank, CA 91505. 818-557-0387.

Judy Kaplan **Baron Associates,** 6046 Cornerstone Ct. West, Suite 208, San Diego, CA 92121. 619-558-7400. Judy Kaplan Baron, Director.

Beverly **Brown,** M.A., 809 So. Bundy Dr., #105, Los Angeles, CA 90049. 310-447-7093.

Career Action Center, 445 Sherman Ave., Palo Alto, CA 94306. 415-324-1710.

Career Development Institute, 690 Market St., Suite 402, San Francisco, CA 94104. 415-982-2636.

Career Development Center, John F. Kennedy University, 1250 Arroyo Way, Walnut Creek, CA 94596. 510-295-0610. Susan Geifman, Director. *Open to the public.*

Career Development Life Planning, 3585 Maple St., Suite 237, Ventura, CA 93003. 805-656-6220. Norma Zuber, N.C.C.C., M.S.C., & Associates.

Career Dimensions, Box 7402, Stockton, CA 95267. 209-473-8255. Fran Abbott.

Career Directions, 215 Witham Rd., Encinitas, CA 92024. 619-436-3994.

Career Planning Center/Business Action Center, 1623 S. La Cienega Blvd., Los Angeles, CA 90035. 213-273-6633.

Career Strategy Associates, 1100 Quail St., Suite 200, Newport Beach, CA 92660. 714-252-0515. Betty Fisher.

The **Center for Life & Career Development,**
655 University Ave., Suite 127, Sacramento,
CA 95825. 916-646-3414. Dr. Fran A. Epstein.

The **Center for Life and Work Planning,**
1133 Second St., Encinitas, CA 92024. 619-
943-0747. Mary C. McIsaac, Executive
Director.

Constructive Leisure, Patsy B. Edwards, 511
N. La Cienega Blvd., Los Angeles, CA 90048.
310-652-7389.

Consultants in Career Development, 2017
Palo Verde Ave., Suite 201B, Long Beach,
CA 90815. 310-598-6412. Dean Porter and
Mary Claire Gildon.

Criket Consultants, 502 Natoma St., P.O.
Box 6191, Folsom, CA 95763-6191. 916-985-
3211.

Cypress College, Career Planning Center,
9200 Valley View St., Cypress, CA 90630. 714-
826-2220, Ext. 120.

Margaret L. **Eadie,** M.A., A.M.Ed., WHAT
NEXT Education and Career Consultant,
1000 Sage Pl., Pacific Grove, CA 93050. 408-
373-7400.

Experience Unlimited Job Club. There are
35 Experience Unlimited Clubs in California
at the following locations: Anaheim, Corona,
El Cajon, Escondido, Fremont, Fresno,
Hemet, Hollywood, Lancaster, Monterey, N.
Hollywood, Oakland, Ontario, Pasadena,
Pleasant Hill, Redlands, Ridgecrest,
Riverside, Sacramento midtown, Sacramento
South, San Bernardino, San Diego, San
Diego East, San Diego South, San Francisco,
San Mateo, San Rafael, Santa Ana, Santa
Cruz, Santa Maria, Simi Valley, Sunnyvale,
Torrance, Victorville, and West Covina.
Contact the club nearest to you through
your local Employment Development
Department (E.D.D.).

Mary Alice **Floyd,** M.A., N.C.C., Career
Counselor/Consultant, Career Life Transi-
tions, 3233 Lucinda Lane, Santa Barbara,
CA 93105. 805-687-5462.

Marvin F. **Galper,** Ph.D., 3939 Third Ave.,
Suite 204, San Diego, CA 92103. 619-295-
4450.

Judith **Grutter,** M.S., N.C.C.C., Career
Development Counselor/Consultant, Webb,
Grutter, Helander & Associates, 130 S.
Euclid Ave., Suite #5, Pasadena, CA 91101.
818-795-3883.

Life's Decisions, 1917 Lowland Ct.,
Carmichael, CA 95608. 916-486-0677. Joan
E. Belshin, M.S., N.C.C.C.

Susan W. **Miller,** M.A., 6363 Wilshire Blvd.,
Suite 210, Los Angeles, CA 90048. 213-651-
5514.

Sacramento Women's Center, Women's
Employment Services and Training (WEST)
for income-eligible women, 2306 "J" St.,
Suite 200, Sacramento, CA 95816. 916-441-
4207.

Saddleback College, Counseling Services
and Special Programs, 28000 Marguerite
Pkwy., Mission Viejo, CA 92692. 714-582-
4571. Jan Fritsen, Counselor.

Stoodley & Associates, 1434 Willowmont
Ave., San Jose, CA 95118. 408-448-3691.
Martha Stoodley, M.S., M.F.C.C., President.

The **Successful Job Search Center,** 1700 N.
Broadway, Suite 404, Walnut Creek, CA
94596. 510-283-1776. Marston Watson,
Career Consultant.

Transitions Counseling Center, 171 N. Van
Ness, Fresno, CA 93701. 209-233-7250.
Margot E. Tepperman, L.C.S.W.

Turning Point Career Center, University
YWCA, 2600 Bancroft Way, Berkeley, CA
94704. 510-848-6370. Winnie Froehlich,
M.S., Director.

Caroline **Voorsanger,** Career Counselor for
Women, 1650 Jackson St., #608, San
Francisco, CA 94109. 415-567-0890.

Patti **Wilson,** 15880 Rose Ave., Los Gatos, CA
95030. 408-354-1964.

Women at Work, 78 N. Marengo Ave.,
Pasadena, CA 91101. 818-796-6870.

COLORADO

Samuel **Kirk and Associates,** Central Office,
1418 S. Race, Denver, CO 80210. 303-722-
0717.

Patricia **O'Keefe,** M.A., 350 Cook St.,
Denver, CO 80206. 303-393-8747.

Resource Center, Arapahoe Community
College, 2500 West College Dr., P.O. Box
9002, Littleton, CO 80160-9002. 303-794-
1550.

Women's Resource Agency, 1018 N. Weber,
Colorado Springs, CO 80903. 719-471-3170.

CONNECTICUT

Accord Consultants, Inc., The Exchange,
Suite 305, 270 Farmington Ave., Farming-
ton, CT 06032. 203-674-9654. J. Tod
Gerardo, M.S., President and Director.

Associated Counseling Professionals, Career
Development Div., 415 Silas Deane Hwy.,
Suite 224, Wethersfield, CT 06109-2119. 203-
296-5523 or toll-free in CT, 1-800-654-4320.
John H. Widenheft, M.A., Clinical Director.

Career Choices/RFP Associates, 141
Durham Rd., Suite 24, Madison, CT 06443.
203-245-4123.

Career Services, 94 Rambling Rd., Vernon, CT 06066. 203-871-7832. Jim Cohen, Ph.D., President.

Fairfield Adult Career & Educational Services, Fairfield University, Dolan House, Fairfield, CT 06430. 203-254-4110.

Ilise **Gold Life Management, Inc.** Change management specialists. P.O. Box 2514, Westport, CT 06880. 203-222-9223.

People Management, Inc. See the listing for *Washington State.*

The **Offerjost-Westcott Group,** 263 Main St., Old Saybrook, CT 06475. 203-388-6094. Russ Westcott.

Vocational and Academic Counseling for Adults (VOCA), 115 Berrian Rd., Stamford, CT 06905. 203-322-8353.

DELAWARE

YWCA of New Castle County, Women's Center, 233 King St., Wilmington, DE 19801. 302-658-7161.

DISTRICT OF COLUMBIA

Community Vocational Counseling Service, The George Washington University Counseling Center, 718 21st St. NW, Washington, DC 20052. 202-994-4860. Robert J. Wilson, M.S., Coordinator.

Comptex Associates, Inc., Melwood Shopping Center, 9402 Pennsylvania Ave., Upper Marlboro, MD 20772. 301-599-9222. Mary H. Johnson, President, and Eugene Williams, Sr., Executive Vice President.

George Washington University, Center for Career Education and Workshops, 2020 K St., Washington, DC 20052. 202-994-5299. Abigail Pereira, Manager.

FLORIDA

The **Career and Personal Counseling Center,** Eckerd College, 4200 54th Ave. South, St. Petersburg, FL 33711. 813-867-1166. John R. Sims.

Career Consultants of America, Inc., 2701 W. Busch Blvd., Suite 270, Tampa, FL 33618. 813-933-4088. Michael Shahnasarian, Ph.D., Executive Director.

Center for Career Decisions, 980 N. Federal Hwy., Suite 203, Boca Raton, FL 33432. 407-394-3399. Linda Friedman, M.A., Director.

Centre for Women, 305 S. Hyde Park Ave., Tampa, FL 33606. 813-251-8437. Stacy Clark, Employment Counselor.

Chabon & Associates, 2247 Palm Beach Lakes Blvd., Suite 210, West Palm Beach, FL 33409. 407-640-8443. Toby G. Chabon, M.Ed., N.C.C.C., President.

Challenge: The Displaced Homemaker, Florida Community College at Jacksonville, 101 W. State St., Jacksonville, FL 32202. 904-633-8316. Joan Putnam, Project Coordinator.

Crossroads, Palm Beach Community College, 4200 Congress Ave., Lake Worth, FL 33461-4796. 407-433-5995. Pat Jablonski, Program Manager.

Larry **Harmon,** Ph.D., Career Counseling Center, Inc., 2000 South Dixie Hwy., Suite 103, Miami, FL 33133. 305-858-8557.

Ellen O. **Jonassen,** Ph.D., 10785 Ulmerton Rd., Largo, FL 34648. 813-581-8526.

Life Designs, Inc., 7860 SW 55th Ave. #A, South Miami, FL 33143. 305-665-3212. Dulce Muccio and Deborah Tyson, co-founders.

New Beginnings, Polk Community College, Station #71, 999 Avenue H, NE, Winter Haven, FL 33881-4299 (Lakeland Campus). 813-297-1029.

Resource Center for Women, formerly FACE Learning Center, Inc., 12945 Seminole Blvd., Bldg. II, Suite 6, Largo, FL 34648. 813-585-8155 or 586-1110.

The Women's Center, Valencia Community College, 1010 N. Orlando Ave., Winter Park, FL 32789. 407-628-1976.

WINGS Program, Broward Community College, 1000 Coconut Creek Blvd., Coconut Creek, FL 33066. 305-973-2398.

GEORGIA

Harvey **Brickley,** The Mulling Group, 990 Hammond Dr., Suite 900, Atlanta, GA 30328. 404-395-3131.

Jewish Vocational Service, 1100 Spring St., Suite 700, Atlanta, GA 30309. 404-876-5872. Mark L. Fisher, Executive Director.

St. Jude's Job Network, St. Jude's Catholic Church, 7171 Glenridge Dr., Sandy Springs, GA 30328. 404-393-4578.

Mark **Satterfield,** 5262 Walker Rd., Stone Mountain, GA 30088. 404-469-3462.

HAWAII

No listings.

IDAHO

No listings.

ILLINOIS

Applied Potential, Box 585, Highland Park, IL 60035. 708-234-2130.

Career Path, 3033 Ogden Ave., Suite 203, Lisle, IL 60532. 708-369-3390. Donna Sandberg, M.A., Owner/Counselor.

Career Workshops, 5431 W. Roscoe St., Chicago, IL 60641. 312-282-6859. Patricia Dietze.

Jean Davis, Career Counseling, 1405 Elmwood Ave., Evanston, IL 60201. 708-492-1002

Harper College Community Counseling Center, Building A, Room 347, Palatine, IL 60067. 708-397-3000.

David P. Helfand, Ed.D., N.C.C.C., 250 Ridge, Evanston, IL 60202. 708-328-2787.

Lansky Career Consultants, 500 N. Michigan Ave., Suite 430, Chicago, IL 60611. 312-642-5738.

Midwest Women's Center, 828 S. Wabash, Suite 200, Chicago, IL 60605. 312-922-8530.

Moraine Valley Community College, Job Placement Center, 10900 S. 88th Ave., Palos Hills, IL 60465. 708-974-5737.

Right Livelihood$, 23 W. 402 Green Briar Dr., Naperville, IL 60540. 708-369-9066. Marti Beddoe, Career/Life Counselor.

Jane Shuman, Career Management Consultant, 1S, 283 Danby, Villa Park, IL 60181. 708-916-7754.

Widmer & Associates, 1510 W. Sunnyview Dr., Peoria, IL 61614. 309-691-3312. Mary F. Widmer, President.

Diane Grimard Wilson, 111 North Wabash Ave., Suite 1006, Chicago, IL 60602. 312-201-1142.

INDIANA

Career Consultants, 107 N. Pennsylvania St., Suite 404, Indianapolis, IN 46204. 317-639-5601. Al Milburn, Career Management Consultant.

Sally Jones, Program Coordinator/Developer, Indiana University, School of Continuing Studies, Owen Hall, Room 202, Bloomington, IN 47405. 812-855-4991.

John D. King & Associates, Career Counseling and Consulting, 205 N. College, Suite 614, Bloomington, IN 47404. 812-332-3888.

William R. Lesch, M.S., Career & Life Planning, Health Associates, 9240 N. Meridian St., Suite 292, Indianapolis, IN 46260. 317-844-7489.

IOWA

LifeWorks, 2010 South Ankeny Blvd., Ankeny, IA 50021. 515-964-6710. Michael Anderson, Dennis Mullin, Dr. Ray Martin.

University of Iowa, Center for Career Development and Cooperative Education, 315 Calvin Hall, Iowa City, IA 52242. 319-335-3201.

Suzanne Zilber, 801 Crystal St., Ames, IA 50010. 515-232-9379.

KANSAS

Leigh Branham, The Corinth Group/Mission Assessment, 5300 College Blvd., Suite B, Overland Park, KS 66211. 913-469-9680.

KENTUCKY

OI/Ronniger, Career Consultants, The Summit II, 4360 Brownsboro Rd., Louisville, KY 40207. 502-894-9400. Phillip Ronniger.

LOUISIANA

Career Planning and Assessment Center, Metropolitan College, University of New Orleans, New Orleans, LA 70148. 504-286-7100.

MAINE

Heart at Work, 78 Main St., Yarmouth, ME 04096. 207-846-0644. Barbara Sirois Babkirk, M.Ed., N.C..C., L.C.P.C., Licensed Counselor and Consultant.

Women's Worth Career Counseling, 18 Woodland Rd., Gorham, ME 04038. 207-892-0000. Jacqueline Murphy, Counselor.

MARYLAND

Careerscope, Inc., One Mall North, Suite 216, 1025 Governor Warfield Pkwy., Columbia, MD 21044. 410-992-5042 or 301-596-1866. Ann Sim, Executive Director.

Career Transition Services, 3126 Berkshire Rd., Baltimore MD 21214-3404. 410-444-5857. Michael Bryant.

College of Notre Dame of Maryland, Continuing Education Center, 4701 N. Charles St., Baltimore, MD 21210. 410-532-5303.

Goucher College, Goucher Center for Continuing Studies, 1021 Dulaney Valley Rd., Baltimore, MD 21204-2794. 410-337-6200.

Maryland New Directions, Inc., 2220 N. Charles St., Baltimore, MD 21218. 410-235-8800. Rose Marie Coughlin, Director.

Prince George's Community College, Career Assessment and Planning Center, 301 Largo Rd., Largo, MD 20772. 301-322-0886. Margaret Taibi, Ph.D., Director.

MASSACHUSETTS

Affordable Counseling, 104 Sanborn Ave., Boston, MA 02132. Offices also in Cambridge. 617-327-5343. Carl Schneider. Carl also provides low-cost *group therapy* for up to six months, for unemployed job-hunters who have conflicts that interfere with their job-hunting.

Career Management Associates, 4 Brook St., Suite 18, Scituate, MA 02066. 617-545-7070. Kent Wampler and Marci Mahoney.

Career Management Consultants, Thirty Park Ave., Worcester, MA 01605. 508-853-8669. Patricia M. Stepanski, President.

Career Resource Center, Worcester YWCA, 1 Salem Square, Worcester, MA 01608. 508-791-3181.

Center for Career Development & Ministry, 70 Chase St., Newton Center, MA 02159. 617-969-7750. Stephen Ott, Director.

Center for Careers, Jewish Vocational Service, 105 Chauncy St., 6th Fl., Boston, MA 02111. 617-451-8147.

David J. **Giber,** Ph.D., 80 Waverley St., Arlington, MA 02174. 617-863-4030.

Jewish Vocational Service, Mature Worker Programs, 333 Nahanton St., Newton, MA 02159. 617-965-7940.

Wynne W. **Miller,** 785 Centre St., Newton, MA 02158-2599. 617-527-4848.

Murray Associates, 555 Washington St., Wellesley, MA 02181. 617-235-8896. Robert Murray, Ed.D., Licensed Psychologist.

Neville Associates, Inc., 10 Tower Office Park, Suite 416, Woburn, MA 01801. 617-938-7870. Dr. Joseph Neville, Career Development Consultant.

Radcliffe Career Services (open to the general public), 77 Brattle St., Cambridge, MA 02138. 617-495-8631.

Suit Yourself International, Inc., 115 Shade St., Lexington, MA 02173-7724. 617-862-6006. Debra Spencer.

Women's Educational & Industrial Union, Career Services, 356 Boylston St., Boston, MA 02116. 617-536-5657.

MICHIGAN

Ellman & Associates, 7445 Pebble Point Dr., West Bloomfield, MI 48322. 313-737-7252. Barbara Kabcenell Ellman, M.A., N.C.C., Career Management Professional.

New Options: Counseling for Women in Transition, 2311 E. Stadium, Suite B-2, Ann Arbor, MI 48104. 313-973-0003. Phyllis Perry, M.S.W.

Oakland University, Continuum Center for Adult Counseling and Leadership Training, Rochester, MI 48309. 313-370-3033.

University of Michigan, Center for the Education of Women, 330 East Liberty, Ann Arbor, MI 48104. 313-998-7080.

Women's Resource Center, 252 State St. SE, Grand Rapids, MI 49503. 616-458-5443.

MINNESOTA

Associated Career Services, 1611 West County Road B, Suite 120, Roseville, MN 55113. 612-631-9115. Stanley J. Sizen, Career Counselor.

Career Dynamics, Inc., 8400 Normandale Lake Blvd., Suite 1220, Bloomington, MN 55437. 612-921-2378. Joan Strewler, Psychologist.

Human Dynamics, 3036 Ontario Rd., Little Canada, MN 55117. 612-484-8299. Greg J. Cylkowski, M.A., founder.

Working Opportunities for Women, 2700 University Ave., #120, St. Paul, MN 55114. 612-647-9961.

MISSISSIPPI

Mississippi State University, Career Services Center, P.O. Box P, Colvard Union, Suite 316, Mississippi State, MS 39762-5515. 601-325-3344.

Mississippi Gulf Coast Community College, Jackson County Campus, Career Development Center, P.O. Box 100, Gautier, MS 39553. 601-497-9602. Rebecca Williams, Manager.

MISSOURI

Career Planning and Placement Center, Community Career Services, 110 Noyes Hall, University of Missouri, Columbia, MO 65211. 314-882-6803.

Women's Center, University of Missouri–Kansas City, 5100 Rockhill Rd., 104 Scofield Hall, Kansas City, MO 64110. 816-235-1638.

MONTANA

No listings.

NEBRASKA

Career Management Services, 5000 Central Park Dr., Suite 204, Lincoln, NE 68504. 402-466-8427. Vaughn L. Carter, President.

Olson Counseling Services, 8720 Frederick, Suite 105, Omaha, NE 68128. 402-390-2342. Gail A. Olson, P.A.C.

Student Success Center, Central Community College, Hastings Campus, Hastings, NE 68902.

NEVADA

No listings.

NEW HAMPSHIRE

Individual Employment Services, P.O. Box 917, Dover, NH 03820. 603-742-5616. James Otis, Employment Counselor.

NEW JERSEY

Adult Advisory Services, Kean College of New Jersey, Administration Bldg., Union, NJ 07083. 908-527-2210.

Adult Resource Center, 100 Horseneck Rd., Montville, NJ 07045. 201-335-6910.

Arista Concepts Career Development Service, P.O. Box 2436, Princeton, NJ 08540. 609-921-0308. Kera Greene, M.Ed.

Career Options Center, YWCA Tribute to Women and Industry (TWIN) Program, 232 E. Front St., Plainfield, NJ 07060. 908-756-3836, or 908-273-4242. Janet M. Korba, Program Director.

Loree **Collins,** 3 Beechwood Rd., Summit, NJ 07901. 908-273-9219.

Douglass College, Douglass Advisory Services for Women, Rutgers Women's Center, 132 George St., New Brunswick, NJ 08903. 908-932-9603.

Sandra **Grundfest,** Ed.D., Princeton Professional Park, 601 Ewing St., Suite C-1, Princeton, NJ 08540. 609-921-8401. Also at 11 Clyde Rd., Suite 103, Somerset, NJ 08873. 908-873-1212.

Job Seekers of Montclair, St. Lukes Church, at Union St. and South Fullerton Ave., Montclair, NJ. 201-783-3442. Meets Thursdays 7:30–9:30 p.m.

Lester **Minsuk & Associates,** 29 Exeter Rd., East Windsor, NJ 08520. 609-448-4600.

The **Professional Roster,** 171 Broadmead, Princeton, NJ 08540. 609-921-9561.

W. L. Nikel & Associates, Career Development and Outplacement, 28 Harper Terrace, Cedar Grove, NJ 07009. 201-239-7460. William L. Nikel, M.B.A., Founder.

Women's Center, Princeton University, 201 Aaron Burr Hall, Princeton, NJ 08544. 609-258-5565.

NEW MEXICO

Young Women's Christian Association, YWCA Career Services Center, 7201 Paseo Del Norte NE, Albuquerque, NM 87113. 505-822-9922.

NEW YORK

Academic Advisory Center for Adults., Turf Ave., Rye, NY 10580. 914-967-1653.

Alan B. **Bernstein,** CSW, PC, 122 East 82nd St., New York, NY 10028. 212-288-4881.

Career Agenda, Inc., 180 West 80th St., New York, NY 10024. 212-595-9226. Carol Allen, President.

The **Career Center,** 1525 Western Ave., Albany, NY 12203. 518-869-1311. Thomas J. McKenna, Director.

Career Development Center, Long Island University, C. W. Post Campus, Brookville, NY 11548. 516-299-2251. Pamela Lennox, Ph.D., Director.

Career Development Services, 14 Franklin St., Temple Bldg., Suite 1200, Rochester, NY 14604. 716-325-2274.

The John C. **Crystal Center,** 152 Madison Ave., 23rd Fl., New York, NY 10016. 212-889-8500, or 1-800-333-9003. Nella G. Barkley, President. *(John died in 1988; Nella was his business partner, for many years preceding his death, and now carries on his work. The Center also has offices in Chicago and Los Angeles, run under the aegis of The Crystal-Barkley Corporation. The 800 number above will work for reaching all three centers.)*

Judith **Gerberg Associates,** 250 West 57th St., Suite 1019, New York, NY 10107. 212-315-2322. Judith Gerberg.

Susan **Hadley,** Career and Life/Work Planning Consultant, 59 Jefferson St., Nyack, NY 10960. 914-353-0579.

Hofstra University, Career Counseling Center, 240 Student Center, Hempstead, NY 11550. 516-463-6788.

Kingsborough Community College, Office of Career Counseling and Placement, 2001 Oriental Blvd., Rm. C102, Brooklyn, NY 11235. 718-368-5115.

Janice **La Rouche Assoc.,** Workshops for Women, 333 Central Park W., New York, NY 10025. 212-663-0970.

Livelihood–Network Resumes and Career Services, 60 E. 42nd St., Room. 3404, New York, NY 10165. 212-687-2411. John Aigner, Counselor.

New Options, 960 Park Ave., New York, NY 10028. 212-535-1444.

Orange County Community College, Counseling Center, South St., Middletown, NY 10940. 914-341-4070.

Celia **Paul Associates,** 1776 Broadway, Suite 1806, New York, NY 10019. 212-397-1020.

Personnel Sciences Center, Inc., 276 Fifth Ave., Suite 704, New York, NY 10001. 212-683-3008. Dr. Jeffrey A. Goldberg, Chief Psychologist.

Regional Learning Service of Central New York, 405 Oak St., Syracuse, NY 13203. 315-425-5252.

L. Michelle **Tullier,** Ph.D., Career Counselor. Virginia J. Bush & Associates, 444 E. 86th St., New York, NY 10028. 212-772-3244.

WIN Workshops (Women in Networking), Emily Koltnow, 1120 Avenue of The Americas, Fourth Floor, New York, NY 10036. 212-333-8788.

NORTH CAROLINA

Career Consulting Associates of Raleigh, P.O. Box 17653, Raleigh, NC 27619. 919-782-3252. Susan W. Simonds, President.

Career, Educational, Psychological Evaluations, 2915 Providence Rd., Suite 300, Charlotte, NC 28211. 704-362-1942.

Career Management Center, 3203 Woman's Club Dr., Suite 100, Raleigh, NC 27612. 919-787-1222, ext. 109. Temple G. Porter, Director.

Sally **Kochendofer,** P.O. Box 1180, Cornelius, NC 28031. 704-892-4976.

Diane E. **Lambeth,** M.S.W., Career Consultant, P.O. Box 18945, Raleigh, NC 27619. 919-571-7423.

Life Management Services, 5625 Dillard Dr., Suite 105, Cary, NC 27511. 919-859-4822.

Joyce **Richman & Associates, Ltd.,** 2911 Shady Lawn Dr., Greensboro, NC 27408. 910-288-1799.

Women's Center of Raleigh, 128 E. Hargett St., Suite 10, Raleigh, NC 27601. 919-829-3711.

NORTH DAKOTA

No listings.

OHIO

Adult Resource Center, The University of Akron, Buckingham Center for Continuing Education, Akron, OH 44325-3102. 216-972-7448. Sandra B. Edwards, Director.

Career Initiatives Center, 1557 E. 27th St., Cleveland, OH 44114. 216-574-8998. Richard Hanscom, Director.

Cuyahoga County Public Library InfoPLACE Service, Career, Education & Community Information Service, 5225 Library Lane, Maple Heights, OH 44137-1291. 216-475-2225.

Hill & Hill Consulting, Inc., 393 Hawthorne Lane N.E., Warren, OH 44484. 216-856-4440. Barbara H. Hill, President.

New Career, 328 Race St., Dover, OH 44622. 216-364-5557. Marshall Karp, M.A., N.C.C., L.P.C., Owner.

Pyramid Career Services, Inc., 2400 Cleveland Ave., NW, Canton, OH 44709. Zandra Bloom, Director.

OKLAHOMA

Career Development Services, 5314 Yale, Suite 600, Tulsa, OK 74135. 918-665-1161/1162. William D. Young, Ed.D.

OREGON

Career Development, P.O. Box 5099, Beaverton, OR 97006. 503-357-9233. Edward H. Hosley, Ph.D., Director.

Joseph A. **Dubay,** 1805 NW 34th St., Portland, OR 97210. 503-228-0809.

Marion Bass **Stevens,** Ph.D., 2631 E. Congress Way, Medford, OR 97504. 503-773-3373.

Verk Consultants, Inc., 1441 Oak St., #7, P.O. Box 11277, Eugene, OR 97440. 503-687-9170. Larry H. Malmgren, M.S., President.

PENNSYLVANIA

Career By Design, 1011 Cathill Rd., Sellersville, PA 18960. 215-723-8413. Henry D. Landes, Career Consultant.

Career Management Consultants, Inc., 3207 N. Front St., Harrisburg, PA 17110. 717-233-2272. Louis F. Persico, Career Consultant.

Center for Adults in Transition, Bucks County Community College, Newtown, PA 18940. 215-968-8188.

The **Center for Creative Living,** P.O. Box 8989, Pittsburgh, PA 15221. 412-244-0522. David R. Johnson, Director. Several locations.

Options, Inc., 225 S. 15th St., Philadelphia, PA 19107. 215-735-2202. Marcia P. Kleiman, Director.

Priority Two, P.O. Box 343, Sewickley, PA 15143. 412-935-0252. Five locations in the Pittsburgh area.

RHODE ISLAND

Career Designs, 120 Moore St., Providence, RI 02907. 401-521-2323. Terence Duniho, Career Consultant.

SOUTH CAROLINA

Career Counselor Services, Inc., 25 Woods Lake Rd., Suite 324, Greenville, SC 29607. 803-370-9453. Al A. Hafer, Ed.D., N.C.C.C., N.C.C., L.P.C.

Greenville Technical College, Career Advancement Center, Greenville, SC 29606. 803-250-8281. F. M. Rogers, Counselor.

SOUTH DAKOTA

Career Concepts Planning Center, Inc., 1602 Mountain View Rd., Suite 102, Rapid City, SD 57702. 605-342-5177; toll free: 1-800-456-0832. Melvin M. Tuggle, Jr., President.

Sioux Falls College, The Center for Women, 1501 South Prairie, Clidden Hall, Sioux Falls, SD 57105. 605-331-6697.

TENNESSEE

Career Resources, 2323 Hillsboro Rd., Suite 508, Nashville, TN 37212. 615-297-0404. Jane C. Hardy, Principal/Career Counselor.

Mid-South Career Development Center, 2315 Fisher Place, Knoxville, TN 37920. 615-573-1340. W. Scott Root, President/ Counselor.

S.O.S. (Secretarial Office Services), 314 N. White St., Athens, TN 37303. 615-745-4513. Adelia Wyner, Consultant.

TEXAS

Austin Women's Center, 611 S. Congress Ave., Suite 505, Austin, TX 78704. 512-447-9666. Maydelle Fason, Employment Trainer.

Career Action Associates, 12655 N. Central Expressway, Suite 1012, Dallas, TX 75243. 214-392-7337. Joyce Shoop, Licensed Professional Counselor. Office also at 1325 8th Ave., Ft. Worth, TX 76112. 817-926-9941. Rebecca Hayes, Licensed Professional Counselor.

Catalyst Career Consultants, 2520 Longview, Suite 406, Austin, TX 78705. 512-474-7773. Joia Jitahidi, Senior Consultant.

Richard S. **Citrin,** Ph.D., Psychologist, Iatreia Institute, 1152 Country Club Ln., Ft. Worth, TX 76112. 817-654-9600.

Counseling Services of Houston, 1964 W. Gray, Suite 204, Houston, TX 77019. 713-521-9391. Rosemary C. Vienot, M.S., Licensed Professional Counselor, Director.

Employment/Career Information Resource Center, Corpus Christi Public Library, 805 Comanche, Corpus Christi, TX 78401. 512-880-7004. Lynda F. Whitton, Career Information Specialist.

New Directions Counseling Center, 8140 North Mopac, Bldg. II, Suite 230, Austin, TX 78759. 512-343-9496. Jeanne Quereau, M.A., Licensed Professional Counselor.

New Life Institute, 1203 Lavaca, Austin, TX 78701. 512-469-9447. Bob Breihan, Director.

San Antonio Psychological Services, 6800 Park Ten Blvd., Suite 208 North, San Antonio, TX 78213. 210-737-2039.

Mary **Stedham,** Counseling/Consulting Services, 2434 S. 10th, Abilene, TX 79605. 915-672-4044.

VGS, Inc. (Vocational Guidance Service), 2600 S.W. Freeway, Suite 800, Houston, TX 77098. 713-535-7104. Beverley K. Finn, Director.

UTAH

University of Utah, Center for Adult Development, 1195 Annex Bldg., Salt Lake City, UT 84112. 801-581-3228.

VERMONT

No listings.

VIRGINIA

Career Development Center for Women, The Government Center, 12000 Government Center Parkway, Suite 318, Fairfax, VA 22035. 703-324-5730. Betty McManus, Director.

Golden Handshakes, Church of the Epiphany, 11000 Smoketree Dr., Richmond, VA 23236. 804-794-0222. Jim Dunn, Chairperson; also at Winfree Memorial Baptist Church, 13617 Midlothian Turnpike, Midlothian, VA 23113. 804-794-5031. Phil Tibbs, Volunteer Coordinator.

Hollins College, Career Development Center, Roanoke, VA 24020. 703-362-6364. Evelyn F. Bradshaw, Director.

Life Management Services, Inc., 6849 Old Dominion Dr., Suite 219, McLean, VA 22101. 703-356-2630. Hal and Marilyn Shook, President and Vice President.

Mary Baldwin College, Rosemarie Sena Center for Career and Life Planning, Kable House, Staunton, VA 24401. 703-887-7221.

Psychological Consultants, Inc., 6724 Patterson Ave., Richmond, VA 23226. 804-288-4125.

Virginia Commonwealth University, University Advising Center, Box 2002, 827 W. Franklin St., Rm. 101, Richmond, VA 23284-2002. 804-367-1580 or 367-0200. Marcia F. Zwicker, Director.

The **Women's Center,** 133 Park St., NE, Vienna, VA 22180. 703-281-2657. Virginia C. Marshall, Director of Program Development.

WASHINGTON

Career Management Institute, 8404 27th St. West, Tacoma, WA 98466. 206-565-8818. Ruthann Reim, M.A., N.C.C., President.

The **Individual Development Center, Inc., (I.D. Center),** 1020 E. John, Seattle, WA 98102. 206-329-0600. Mary Lou Hunt, N.C.C., M.A., President.

People Management Group International, 924 First St., Snohomish, WA 98290. 206-563-0105. Arthur F. Miller, Jr., Chairman. Dick Staub, President.

University of Washington Extension, Career Development Services, 5025 25th Ave. NE, Suite 205, GH-21, Seattle, WA 98195. 206-543-3900.

Vecchio & Associates, Career Consultants, 624 Skinner Bldg., 1326 Fifth Ave., Seattle, WA 98101. 206-622-8070. Carol Vecchio, Career Counselor.

WEST VIRGINIA

No listings.

WISCONSIN

Making Alternative Plans, Career Development Center, Alverno College, 3401 S. 39th St., P.O. Box 343922, Milwaukee, WI 53215-3922. 414-382-6010.

David Swanson, Career Seminars and Workshops, 7235 West Wells St., Wauwatosa, WI 53213-3607. 414-774-4755.

WYOMING

Lifetime Career Consultants, P.O. Box 912, Jackson, WY 83001. 307-733-6544. Barbara Gray. Also P.O. Box 1867, Jackson, WY 83001. 307-733-4471. Caryn Haman.

National Education Service Center, P.O. Box 1279, Riverton, WY 82501-1279. 307-856-0170.

University of Wyoming, Career Planning and Placement Center, P.O. Box 3195/ Knight Hall 228, Laramie, WY 82071. 307-766-2398.

USA. -- NATIONWIDE

Forty Plus Clubs. A nationwide network of voluntary, autonomous nonprofit clubs, manned by its unemployed members, paying no salaries, supported by initiation fees and monthly dues. At this writing, there are clubs in the following cities: Buffalo, Chicago, Columbus, Colorado Springs, Dallas, Denver, Fort Collins, Honolulu, Houston, Los Angeles, New York, Oakland (California), Philadelphia, Salt Lake City, Toronto, and Washington, DC. If you live in one of these cities, you can check the white pages of your Phone Book; also you can call Forty Plus of New York, 15 Park Row, New York, NY 10038, 212-233-6086 to get current information about any of the nationwide locations – to see if the club is still there, and what their current address and phone number are.

CANADA

(These are listed by Provinces, from East Coast to West Coast, rather than in alphabetical order.)

Sue **Landry,** Enhancing Your Horizons Consulting, 25 Birchwood Terr., Dartmouth, Nova Scotia B3A 3W2. 902-464-9110.

Robin T. **Hazell** & Associates, 60 St. Clair Ave., E., Seventh Floor, Toronto, Ontario M4T 1N5. 416-961-3700.

Don **McKenzie,** Executive Career Management Centre, 390 Bay St., Suite 2000, Toronto M5H 2Y2, Canada. 416-861-0426.

YMCA Career Planning & Development, 15 Breadalbane St., Toronto, Canada M4Y 2V5. 416-324-4121.

Peat Marwick Stevenson & Kellogg, 130 Dufferin, 12th Floor, Suite 1200, London, Ontario N6A 5R2. 519-663-2660. Brenda Lewis.

Susan **Steinberg,** M.Ed., 74 Denlow Blvd., Don Mills, Ontario M3B 1P9. 416-449-6936.

Des Roches, Wallace, Bond Inc., 360 Albert St., Suite 1701, Ottawa, Ontario K1R 7X7. 613-238-7636. Kenneth Des Roches.

Job-Finding Club, 516-294 Portage Ave., Winnipeg, Manitoba R3C 0B9. 204-947-1948, 947-1996. Connie LeBlanc, Project Manager.

Susan **Curtis,** M.Ed., 4513 West 13th Ave., Vancouver, British Columbia V6R 2V5. 604-228-9618.

See next page for Overseas listing.

OVERSEAS

Cabinet Daniel Porot, 1, rue Verdaine, CH-1204 Geneve, Switzerland. Phone 011 41 22 311 04 38. Daniel Porot, Founder.

Castle Consultants International, 804 Raleigh House, Dolphin Square, London SW1V 3NR, England. Phone 071 798 8804. Walt Hopkins, Founder and Director.

The **Chaney Partnership,** Hillier House, 509 Upper Richmond Rd. West, London SW14 7EE. Phone 081-878-3227. Isabel Chaney, B.A.

Peter **Kessler,** Haus zur Pyramide, Dorfstrasse 55, CH-8715 Bollingen SG, bei Jona-Rapperswil, Switzerland. Phone 055 28 22 80.

Robert J. **Bisdee** & Associates, 22 Allenby Ave., Malvern E., Victoria, Australia 3145. Phone 613-885-4716. Dr. Bob Bisdee, Director.

Judith **Bailey,** Designing Your Life, 10 Nepean Pl., Macquarie ACT 2614, Australia. Phone 06-253-2231.

Centre for WorkLife Counselling, P.O. Box 407, Spit Junction, Australia 2088. Phone 02-969-4548. Paul Stevens, Director.

All of the overseas counselors listed above have attended my two-day workshop.

KPMG Peat Marwick Career Centre, 135 Victoria St., Wellington, New Zealand. (04) 802-1227. Felicity McLennan.

Judy **Feierstein,** M.A., 46/2 Derech Bet Lechem, Jerusalem 93504, Israel. Phone (02) 71 06 73.

Lori **Mendel,** 14/3 Zui Bruk, Tel Aviv 63423. Phone (03) 29 28 30.

Addendum:
IF YOU ARE A CAREER COUNSELOR,
OR WANT TO BE ONE

If you liked the subject matter of this book a lot (and, even more, another book of mine called *The Three Boxes of Life and How to Get Out of Them*), you will of course be thinking about the possibility of becoming a career counselor yourself. Those just getting started in the field of career counseling (inside or outside academia) will, of course, want to read this current edition of *Parachute* from cover to cover, and then **do** all the exercises within it, before they inflict them on their helpless students or clients. *Teaching is Sharing, and Sharing should only follow Experiencing.*

Career-counseling, as you will recall from the beginning of this Appendix, may deal with career development, or with career-change, or with job-hunting -- or any combination of those three. The focus of this book is on career-change and job-hunting; therefore, below I have only listed resources dealing with those subjects, not the much broader field of career development -- which would go on for pages and pages.

Periodicals or Newsletters:

Career Planning & Adult Development Newsletter, published monthly by the Career Planning and Adult Development Network, 4965 Sierra Rd., San Jose, CA 95132. Richard L. Knowdell, Editor.

CNews: Career Opportunities News, Garrett Park Press, Box 190, Garrett Park, MD 20896. Useful news for counselors (and job-hunters) about employment fields, fellowships, new books, etc.

Careers Guidance Index: Sources of Free and Inexpensive Career Guidance Materials. Careers, Inc., P.O. Box 135, Largo, FL 34649-0135. Published monthly. They also have "Occu-Labels," which are over 550 labels addressed to places which have free or inexpensive career and educational materials. Ask them for current prices.

The Journal of Employment Counseling, a professional journal concerned with research, theory, and new and improved job counseling techniques and tools. It does not, in my experience, deal so much with the job-hunt, as with counseling; and the counseling is pretty much along the traditional job-hunting lines. This is the official publication of the National Employment Counseling Association, a division of the American Counseling Association (ACA)[5], 5999 Stevenson Ave., Alexandria, VA 22304. $20 per year.

Resume Pro Newsletter©, A National Newsletter for Professionals, Exploring and Promoting Excellence in Resume Writing. Published quarterly.

---

5. Previously known as the American Association for Counseling and Development (AACD), and -- before that -- as the American Personnel and Guidance Association (APGA).

P.O. Box 3289, Berkeley, CA 94703. Yana Parker, Editor. She has also published a book for professionals, described below.

All the above periodicals or newsletters have a subscription fee. We recommend that you ask them for subscription information and a sample issue, before subscribing.

Books:

Stevens, Nancy Duncan, *Dynamics of Job-Seeking Behavior.* Charles C. Thomas, Publisher, 2600 S. First St., Springfield, IL 62717. 1986. Uses various frameworks (such as Holland's RIASEC theories) to analyze three different job-seeking behavioral patterns.

Azrin, Nathan H., and Besalel, Victoria A., *Job Club Counselor's Manual: A Behavioral Approach to Vocational Counseling.* Pro-Ed, 8700 Shoal Creek Blvd., Austin, TX 78758. 512-451-3246. For any counselor interested in working with job-hunters more than one at a time, this work is *mandatory* reading. Nathan invented the job club idea, and when followed *faithfully* it has a very high success rate (around 86%). Problem is: every technique described in Nathan's book was designed to eliminate some difficulty or obstacle to your client's job-hunt, and each time you try to take shortcuts with his program and cut out *this* technique or *that* (as counselors are *very* wont to do), you *re-introduce* into your client's job-hunt the problem that the technique was designed to eliminate. Therefore, if you're going to use this manual, use it *faithfully.*

The Guide to Basic Skills Jobs, Vol 1. RPM Press, Inc., Verndale, MN 56481. 1986. A catalog of viable jobs for individuals with only basic work skills. This volume identifies 5,000 major occupations within the U.S. economy which require no more than an eighth grade level of education, and no more than one year of specific vocational preparation. Immensely useful book if you counsel that kind of job-hunter.

Career & Job Search Instruction Made Easy, JIST Works, Inc., The Job Search People, 720 North Park Ave., Indianapolis, IN 46202. 1-800-648-JIST.

Job Information and Seeking Training Program Instructor's Guide and Job Seekers Workbook. 1980. JIST Works, Inc., 720 North Park Ave., Indianapolis, IN 46202. 1-800-648-JIST.

Porot, Daniel, *Comment Trouver Une Situation.* Les Editions d'Organisations, 5, rue Rousselet, F-75007 Paris. 1985. If you read French, this is Daniel's approach to the job-hunt. Since he is *the* expert in Europe, it is *of course* well worth reading.

Lathrop, Richard, *The Job Market.* The National Center for Job-Market Studies, Box 3651, Washington, DC 20007. *What would happen if we decreased the length of the job-hunt in America,* and other iconoclastic ideas which are also eminently sensible.

Parker, Yana, *Resume Pro: The Professional's Guide.* Ten Speed Press, P.O. Box 7123, Berkeley, CA 94707. 1993. This book/kit attempts to teach professionals (human resource staff, educators, career counselors, and others) how to go about the writing of resumes. *Extremely* thorough and helpful for those who *like* resumes despite all I've said in Chapter 3.

> *See also the bibliography in Appendix B, for information on books that are related to particular client populations that you desire to counsel.*

Instruments:

This, of course, is a wide world. There are a *million* instruments out there: the Strong-Campbell Interest Inventory, the Holland SDS, the Myers-Briggs, and a host of others -- including my own *Quick Job-Hunting (and Career-Changing) Map: How to Create A Picture of Your Ideal Job or Next Career.*

If you want to know about other instruments available to you, see: Kapes, Jerome T., and Mastie, Marjorie Moran, eds., *A Counselor's Guide to Career Assessment Instruments.* 1988 ed. Published by the National Career Development Association, a division of AGA, 5999 Stevenson Ave., Alexandria, VA 22304.

Film, Audiotape, Videotape:

Sladey, Pat, *Find the job you want . . . and get it!* A four-**audiocassette** program, on the subjects: Find the Hidden Job Market; Sell Yourself in the Interview; Prepare Winning Resumes & Letters; and Stay Motivated During the Search. Available from: Pat Sladey & Associates, P.O. Box 440352, Aurora, CO 80044. *There is also a **videotape** version of this program, on four videocassettes.*

For other videos dealing with the job-hunt, see the 1994 Catalog. Wintergreen Software, Inc., P.O. Box 15899, New Orleans, LA 70175-5899.

Computer Software:

The computer is a wonderful tool. I use one all day long, every day that I work *(for the curious, a Macintosh IIci with color screen).* Nonetheless, my personal opinion is that computer software *for career counselors or job-hunters* is mostly still in the Dark Ages. What help computer software does give with choosing careers is *simplistic;* what help it gives with the actual job-hunt is *elementary* -- except perhaps in the area of resumes, and you know what I think about the effectiveness of resumes. (See Chapter 3.) *However,* for those who wish to explore this arena further, I list here two directories and some *examples* of what is 'out there,' most of which costs less than $150, sometimes much less.

Directories

The 1994 Personnel Software Census. Advanced Personnel Systems, P.O. Box 1438, Roseville, CA 95661. Has sections on 'Career Development,' 'Skills Management/Inventory,' and 'Job Search/Resume Writing.' Lists about 60 programs, altogether, in those areas -- varying greatly in their usefulness. An even more up-to-date listing is available on disk.

1994 Catalog. Wintergreen Software, Inc., P.O. Box 15899, New Orleans, LA 70175-5899. Lists software not found in any other catalog; also videotapes.

Examples of Programs

> *Most of these are for the IBM computer family; rarely, the Macintosh. A listing here is for information only. It is not to be construed as a recommendation, in any sense of the word. Reread the 'Computer Software' section above.*

Jackson, Tom, *The Perfect Resume Computer Kit.* Permax Systems Inc., P.O. Box 6455, Madison, WI 53716-0455. Assists in preparing resumes, based on Tom's very popular book. Enables the user to prepare customized, target resumes. There is both a Personal Version and a Counselor's Version. For IBM computers and compatibles.

Parker, Yana. *ReadyToGo Resumes (Self-Teaching Resume Templates).* Damn Good Resume Service, P.O. Box 3289, Berkeley, CA 94703. 1993. This is a computer disk, and manual, for both Macintosh and IBM computers and compatibles. It is based on her very popular book, *Damn Good Resume Guide.*

Resume Writer. Schonberg Associates, Inc., 2368 Victory Pkwy., Cincinnati OH 45206. A book plus software. Comes in business or student editions. For IBM computers and compatibles.

Easy Working Resume Kit™. Spinnaker Software Corporation, One Kendall Square, Cambridge, MA 02139. 1992. Written only for IBM computers and compatibles. This program has an *excellent* manual, including a long, helpful, and realistic section called *"Beyond Resumes"* -- obviously written by someone who knows what she is talking about, and who is wise and witty to boot. This company also publishes *PFS: Resume and Job Search Pro,* for IBM computers and compatibles. A *Windows* version is also available.

Career Navigator. Drake Beam Morin, Inc., 100 Park Ave., New York, NY 10017. Computer-based training and guidance during one's job-search. For IBM computers and compatibles.

Studner, Peter K., *The Super-Search*™ *System.* Jamenair Ltd., P.O. Box 241957, Los Angeles, CA 90024. A book plus software. The software has the book's resumes on disk, plus databases of contacts, and computerizes one's job-hunt journey. For IBM computers and compatibles.

Training:

By Others: There are countless training opportunities for career counselors in the U.S. and abroad. *Career Planning & Adult Development Newsletter,* mentioned earlier (published monthly by the Career Planning and Adult Development Network, 4965 Sierra Rd., San Jose, CA 95132) maintains a *very good* calendar of these events, and anyone interested in further training would be well advised to be receiving this *Newsletter.*

By Me: Whenever the subject of training comes up, I am asked (endlessly) whether or not *I* do any teaching. We receive hundreds of letters each year asking this. Since I would like to cut down on the mail and also save *you* some trouble, I will give you a summary of the desired information, right here.

In brief, I only do one training or speaking event each year, and that is always in the U.S.A., during the summer, with my esteemed colleague from Europe, Daniel Porot, whose insights you have seen frequently in the main body of this book. We call it:

Fifteen Days of
LIFE/Work Planning
with Vacation

The workshop is always in August, almost always the first Friday through the third Saturday. In 1994, the dates will be August 5–20. **The workshop will not be offered in 1995** (I'm taking a sabbatical that year). In 1996, the dates will be August 2–17.

Since fifteen days is a long time, and people who attend usually do so in lieu of their regular summer vacation, we have deliberately put this workshop, over the years, at a first-class vacation resort. We move it around from time to time. For the past ten years it has been held at the Inn of the Seventh Mountain, a beautiful and popular resort on the outskirts of Bend, Oregon, U.S.A., *which -- as everyone knows -- is in the center of the United States (Honolulu is 3,000 miles to the West, New York City is 3,000 miles to the East).* Prior to that, it was held for many years in Overland Park, Kansas, as well as Madison, Wisconsin, and Colorado Springs.

In fairness you should be told that if you attend this workshop, you won't have *a lot* of time to just 'lay back,' since you will be working *very* hard throughout the fifteen days. But you will have three hours of free time each day, and twenty-two hours off, on the second weekend.

The total training at this workshop exceeds 100 hours. The workshop is led, from beginning to end, by Daniel and myself; we teach as a team. Daniel's expertise and teaching skills are really dazzling.

The hundreds of counselors who have attended since 1974 have found this to be the most thoroughgoing training in the art of career counseling and life/work planning that is available anywhere in the world today. Year after year people say that this was close to the most enjoyable fifteen days of their entire life. *If you decide to attend, be sure to bring your playful self.* In age, participants have ranged from 17 to 74, have embraced all ethnic groups, and have come from all parts of the world: England, Canada, New Zealand, Australia, Indonesia, Brazil, Gabon, the Netherlands, Belgium, France, Switzerland, Germany, Poland -- as well as the U.S., of course. The workshop is limited to the first 60 people who apply, each year.

I should mention that this workshop is open to **people who are not career counselors;** and each year many 'non-counselors' attend -- job-hunters of all ages, career-changers, homemakers, union organizers, CEOs, teachers, people facing a move, people facing retirement, the recently divorced, college students, clergy, and so forth. It is also attended by people from all over the world. Our methodology at this workshop is to have you master the principles of life/work planning by rigorously applying them to *your own life* during the two weeks, rather than discussing the problems of clients or their case histories, etc., as is often the fashion these days. Because of this methodology, **the workshop is useful to anyone.**

The cost of the workshop -- the tuition -- is currently $1,500. This includes all materials and sessions. There is a discount of $500 off this price *if* you register between September 1st and December 15th, in any year, for the following summer.

Room and board costs are **additional,** and vary from year to year, inevitably, depending upon what facility we are at. Currently, as I write, the cost of a room plus breakfast, lunch, dinner, and three refreshment breaks each day averages about $125 per day.

If you wish more information about this workshop, a brochure and registration blank will be sent to you, if you phone or write to:

The Registrar
Fifteen-Day Workshop
What Color Is Your Parachute?
P.O. Box 379
Walnut Creek, CA 94597

Phone No.: 1-510-932-8872 (10 a.m.–Noon, or 1:30 p.m.–4 p.m.,
Monday thru Friday, Pacific Coast Time).
Fax No.: 1-510-932-4864 (twenty-four hours a day).

My son, be admonished:
of making many books there is no end;
and much study is a weariness of the flesh.

Ecclesiastes

Appendix B
Bibliography:

Books and Notes for Job-Hunters and Career-Changers

A SAMPLER
OF INFORMATION SOURCES
for You, as Job-Hunter and Career-Changer,
To Use

Here is a list of *some* of the books which - - from the experience of career-changers and job-hunters before you - - will likely prove useful *at one time or another* during the research phase of your career-search.

Since many of these resources are much too expensive for the average job-hunter to purchase, be grateful for your local public library, or business library, or local college library.

You don't need to use *all* of the books listed below. Just those that will help you with the particular question you're trying to find answers to, at any given moment. Incidentally, the surest way to make certain your trip to the library is a total waste of time, is to be *hazy* about what you're trying to find out. So, please, before you go to the library, each time, write out on a piece of paper, for your own use, "This is the information I am trying to find out *today:* _____." Be specific. Be clear.

Now, let's look at books that may help you with whatever question you come up with, about organizations:

American Men and Women of Science.

American Society of Training and Development Directory: Who's Who in Training and Development, 1640 King St., Box 1443, Alexandria, VA 22313-2043.

Better Business Bureau report on a particular organization that you may be interested in (call the BBB in the city where the organization is located).

Business Information Sources, by Lorna M. Daniels. University of California Press, Berkeley, CA 94720. Annotated guide to business books and reference sources.

Career Guide to Professional Associations. Garrett Park Press, Garrett Park, MD 20896.

The Career Guide: Dun's Employment Opportunities Directory. Covers more than 5,000 major U.S. companies that have indicated they plan to recruit during the publication year. Primarily for college graduates.

Chamber of Commerce data on an organization or field that interests you (visit the Chamber in the appropriate city or town).

Company/college/association/agency/foundation *Annual Reports.* Get these directly from the personnel department or publicity person at the company, etc., or from the Chamber or your local library.

Consultants and Consulting Organizations Directory 1992, 12th ed. Gale Research, Inc., Box 33477, Detroit, MI 48232-5477. Lists over 15,000 firms, individuals and organizations engaged in consulting work. Consultants are usually experts in their particular field, and hence may be useful to you in your information search about that job or career-change that you are contemplating.

Contacts Influential: Commerce and Industry Directory. Businesses in particular market area listed by name, type of business, key personnel, etc. Contacts Influential, Market Research and Development Services, 321 Bush St., Suite 203, San Francisco, CA 94104, if your library doesn't have it.

Corporate and Industry Research Reports. Published by R.R. Bowker/ Martindale-Hubbell, 121 Chanlon Rd., New Providence, NJ 07974. Can be very helpful.

Corporate Technology Directory. 1990, 5th ed. Lists companies by the products they make or the technologies they use. Corporate Technology Information Services, Inc., 12 Alfred St., Suite 200, Woburn, MA 01801-9998.

Dictionary of Holland Occupational Codes.

Dictionary of Occupational Titles.

Directory of American Research and Technology: Organizations Active in Product Development for Business. R.R. Bowker/Martindale-Hubbell, 121 Chanlon Rd., New Providence, NJ 07974.

Directory of Corporate Affiliations. National Register Publishing Co., Inc.

Directory of Information Resources in the United States. (Physical Sciences, Engineering, Biological Sciences) Washington, DC., Library of Congress.

Directory of Special Libraries and Information Centers 1993, 16th ed. Gale Research, Inc., Box 33477, Detroit, MI 48232-5477. Lists 22,000 research facilities, on various subjects, maintained by libraries, research libraries, businesses, nonprofit organizations, governmental agencies, etc. Detailed subject index, using over 3,500 key words.

Dun & Bradstreet's Million Dollar Directory. Very helpful.

Dun & Bradstreet's Million Dollar Directory — Top 50,000 Companies. Very helpful. An abridged version of Dun's *Million Dollar Directory Series.*

Dun & Bradstreet's Reference Book of Corporate Managements.

Encyclopedia of Associations 1993. Vol. 1, National Organizations of the U.S.; Vol. 2, Geographic and Executive Indexes; Vol. 3, New Associations and Projects. Gale Research, Inc., Box 33477, Detroit, MI 48232-5477. Lists 25,000 organizations, associations, clubs and other nonprofit membership groups that are in the business of giving out information. There is a companion series of books: *Regional, State and Local Organizations 1992–1993,* a five-volume set, which lists over 50,000 similar organizations on a regional, state, or local level. There is another companion volume, also: *International Organizations 1993.* This lists 4,000 international organizations, concerned with various subjects. There was still another companion volume, *Association Periodicals,* 1st ed., which listed 12,000 newsletters, periodicals, and journals put out by national associations in particular. It is still available, but no longer updated.

Encyclopedia of Business Information Sources, 9th ed. Gale Research, Inc., Box 33477, Detroit, MI 48232-5477. Identifies electronic, print, and live resources dealing with 1,500 business subjects. Their companion volume is entitled *Business Organizations, Agencies and Publications Directory,* 6th ed., listing over 24,000 entries, such as federal government advisory organizations, newsletters, research services, etc.

F & S Indexes (recent articles on firms).

F & S Index of Corporations and Industries. Lists "published articles" by industry and by company name. Updated weekly.

Fitch Corporation Manuals.

Fortune Magazine's 500.

The Foundation Directory.

Hoover's Handbook of American Business 1994, ed. by Gary Hoover, Alta Campbell, and Patrick J. Spain. Publishers: The Reference Press, 6448 Highway 290E., Suite E-104, Austin, TX 78723. 800-486-8666. Profiles of over 500 major U.S. companies. A special section on the companies that have created the most jobs in the last 10 years and those that have eliminated the most jobs.

Hoover's Handbook of Emerging Companies 1993-1994, ed. by Patrick J. Spain, Alta Campbell, and Alan Chai. Lists and profiles of 250 smaller, emerging companies with high growth rates. Very useful for those seeking employment at smaller companies.

Hoover's Handbook of World Business 1993, ed. by Alan Chai, Alta Campbell, and Patrick J. Spain. Profiles of nearly 200 major European, Asian, Latin American, and Canadian companies who employ thousands of Americans both in the U.S. and abroad.

How to Reach Anyone Who's Anyone, by Michael Levine Price/Stern/Sloan, 360 N. La Cienega Blvd., Los Angeles, CA 90048.

How To Read A Financial Report: Wringing Cash Flow and Other Vital Signs Out of the Numbers, 3rd ed., by John A. Tracy, CPA. John Wiley & Sons, Business Law/General Books Division, 605 Third Ave., New York, NY 10158-0012. Also Chichester, Brisbane, Toronto, and Singapore.

Information Industry Directory 1993. 13th ed. Gale Research, Inc., Box 33477, Detroit, MI 48232-5477. Lists 30,000 computer-based information systems and services, here and abroad. Their companion volume, *Computers and Computing Information Resources Directory,* 1st ed., lists trade shows, conventions, users' groups, associations, consultants, etc., worldwide.

International Business Travel and Relocation Directory, 6th ed. Gale Research, Inc., Box 33477, Detroit, MI 48232-5477. It presents all the relevant details for every country in the world.

Investor, Banker, Broker Almanac.

Macmillan's Directory of Leading Private Companies.

MacRae's Blue Book.

Moody's Industrial Manual (and other Moody manuals).

National Business Telephone Directory. Used to be published by Gale Research, Inc., Box 33477, Detroit, MI 48232-5477. In one single alphabetical listing, contains phone numbers, address, and city for over 350,000 business and industrial establishments that have more than 20 employees. Particularly useful when you know the name of an organization, but not what city or state it is located in. Since this is technically out of print, see if your library has a back copy.

National Directory of Addresses and Telephone Numbers. Concord Reference Books, 240 Fenel Lane, Hillside, IL 60162.

National Recreational Sporting and Hobby Organizations of the U.S. Columbia Books, Inc., 777 14th St. NW, Washington, DC 20005.

National Trade and Professional Associations of the United States and Canada and Labor Unions. Garrett Park Press, Garrett Park, MD 20896.

Newsletters Directory, 6th ed. Gale Research, Inc., Box 33477, Detroit, MI 48232-5477. Detailed entry on 10,000 newsletters in various subject fields, or categories. It includes newsletters that are available only on-line, through a computer and modem.

Occupational Outlook Handbook. Superintendent of Documents, U.S. Government.

Occupational Outlook Handbook for College Graduates. Superintendent of Documents, U.S. Government.

Petras, Kathryn and Ross, *Jobs '93: By Career, By Industry, By Region.* Covers thousands of careers, companies, and associations. Prentice Hall Press, 15 Columbus Circle, New York, NY 10023. 1993.

Professional's Job Finder. This is a wonderful book by Daniel Lauber which lists job-sources such as trade magazines, journals, computerized job-listings, job-matching services, etc., for all the mainline industries and professional occupations. He has done a very thorough research job. Caveat: *some* of the "leads" given here are hideously expensive, so pray your local library has them. Further caveat: in hard times, these places may be as bereft of job leads as anyone else, but they are certainly worth trying. There are companion volumes entitled *Government Job Finder, Non-Profits' Job Finder* among others. If your library doesn't have them, try your local bookstore. If neither has them, write to Planning/Communications, 7215 Oak Ave., River Forest, IL 60305.

Register of manufacturers for your state or area (e.g., *California Manufacturers Register*).

Research Centers Directory 1993, 17th ed. Gale Research, Inc., Box 33477, Detroit, MI 48232-5477. Also: *Research Services Directory,* 5th ed. The two volumes together cover some 13,000 services, facilities, and companies that do research into various subjects, such as feasibility studies, private and public policy, social studies and studies of various cultures, etc.

Standard and Poor's Corporation Records.

Standard and Poor's Industrial Index.

Standard and Poor's Industry Surveys. Good basic introduction, history, and overview of any industry you may be interested in.

Standard and Poor's Listed Stock Reports (at some brokers' offices).

Standard and Poor's Register of Corporations, Directors and Executives. Key executives in 32,000 leading companies, plus 75,000 directors.

Standard Industrial Classification Manual, 1985. Published by the U.S. Government Printing Office. Gives the Standard Industrial Classification code number for any field or industry - - which is the number used by most business references in their indices.

Statistics Sources 1993, 16th ed. Gale Research, Inc., Box 33477, Detroit, MI 48232-5477. Tells you where to find statistics on more than 20,000 specific topics. Key live sources are also featured.

Telecommunications Systems and Services Directory, 1992–1993, 4th ed. Gale Research, Inc., Box 33477, Detroit, MI 48232-5477. Lists over 2,000 national and international firms dealing with communications systems, tele-conferencing, videotext, electronic mail, fax services, etc.

Telephone Contacts for Data Users. Customer Services Branch, Bureau of the Census, 1-301-449-1600, for statistical information on any subject.

Thomas' Register of American Manufacturers. Thomas Publishing Co.

Trade association periodicals.

Trade journals.

Training and Development Organizations Directory, 5th ed. Gale Research, Inc., Box 33477, Detroit, MI 48232-5477. For those of you interested in teaching or training, it lists over 2,500 firms and their areas of interest and expertise.

United States Government Manual.

U.S. Industrial Outlook 1993. Published by the U.S. Department of Commerce, Industrial Trade Administration, Washington, DC 20230. Covers 350 manufacturing and service industries. Gives the trends and outlooks for each industry that you may be interested in. Updated annually.

Value Line Investment Survey, from Arnold Bernhard and Co., 5 E. 44th St., New York, NY 10017. (Most libraries have a set.)

Walker's Manual of Far Western Corporations and Securities.

Ward's Business Directory, 3 vols. (Vol. 1, Largest U.S. Companies; Vol. 2, Major U.S. Private Companies; Vol. 3, Major International Companies). Information Access Company, 1201 Davis Dr., Belmont, CA 94002. Updated yearly. Despite the titles, helpful in identifying smaller companies, as well as large.

Who's Who in Finance and Industry, and all the other Who's Who books. Useful once you have the name of someone-who-has-the-power-to-hire, and you want to know more about them.

Besides these reference books, some periodicals are worth perusing: *Business Week, Dun's Review, Forbes, Fortune,* and the *Wall Street Journal.*

Many public libraries have very efficient database search capabilities, through their computers, and can dig up, copy, and mail to you copies of reports on local companies (for a modest cost). For example, one Pennsylvania job-hunter got the Cleveland (Ohio) Library to send him copies of annual reports on a Cleveland-based company. So, when you get to the point where you're researching organizations, if there's an organization or company that particularly interests you, you might want to try contacting the nearest large public library to their home base, and see what that library can turn up for you.

For help on a question no one seems to know the answer to, try the National Referral Center at the Library of Congress, 1-202-287-5670. Also, you can call the Federal Information Center of the General Services Administration at 1-202-755-8660 to find the names of experts in any field.

Additional Reading

Parachute is designed to give you all that you need for figuring out what you want to do, and then going about the job-hunt successfully. But no one book *(including this one)* can reach every reader's every need. If you find *Parachute* isn't giving you all that you need or want, there are other books that may succeed for you. They are listed immediately below.

It may also be that while *Parachute* is helping, you feel you have special needs in your situation *(your age, sex, background, etc.)* where you need or want more light shed. That section begins on page 396.

RECOMMENDED

Wegmann, Robert, and Chapman, Robert, *The Right Place at the Right Time: Finding a Job in the 1990s.* Ten Speed Press, Box 7123, Berkeley, CA 94707. 1987, revised and updated, 1990. Highly highly recommended. Bob Wegmann, who died January 2, 1991 after a long illness, knew more about what was going on in the world of work than anyone else in the country. His death is a *great* loss, but here are his insights for us to still profit by.

Wegmann, Robert, and Chapman, Robert, and Johnson, Miriam, *Work in the New Economy: Careers and Job Seeking into the 21st Century.* JIST Works, 720 North Park Ave., Indianapolis, Indiana 46202. 1989. Updated. Highly recommended, of course. Bob Wegmann's insights in another form.

Sher, Barbara, *Wishcraft: How to Get What You Really Want.* Ballantine Books, 201 E. 50th St., New York, NY 10022. 1983. A very helpful book; our readers love it.

LeCompte, Michelle, ed., *JOB HUNTER'S SOURCEBOOK; Where to find employment leads and other job search resources.* Gale Research, Inc., P.O. Box 33477, Detroit, MI 48232-5477. 1991. This is a new resource which I think is exceptional, as it tells you how to find sources of information and job-leads for a whole variety of occupations (155, in all). Somebody did their homework well.

Jackson, Tom, *Guerrilla Tactics in the New Job Market* (2nd ed.). Bantam Books, 666 Fifth Ave., New York, NY 10103. 1991. A very popular and useful book, now revised for the '90s. Tom has some great ideas and insights found in no other authors'.

Jackson, Tom, *Not Just Another Job: How to Invent a Career That Works for You—Now and in the Future.* Times Books, a division of Random House, Inc., 201 E. 50th St., New York, NY 10022. 1992.

Figler, Howard E., *The Complete Job-Search Handbook: All the Skills You Need to Get Any Job and Have a Good Time Doing It.* Henry Holt & Co., Inc., 115 W. 18th St., New York, NY 10011. 1988, Revised and Expanded Edition. Identifies the twenty skills the job-hunter needs in order to pull off a job-hunt *successfully.* A very unusual approach to the subject of skills, as well as to the subject of the job-hunt.

Germann, Richard, and Arnold, Peter, *Bernard Haldane Associates' Job and Career Building.* Ten Speed Press, Box 7123, Berkeley, CA 94707. 1981, 1980. A detailed description of how to find a job, *once you know what it is you want to do;* very detailed, and helpful, particularly for executives. Adapted from the well-known program of Bernard Haldane Associates.

Haldane, Bernard, *Career Satisfaction and Success: How to Know and Manage Your Strengths.* Insights from the master himself. Bernard has been in this field longer than anyone I know of. Published by Wellness Behavior, 4502 54th Ave., NE, Seattle, WA 98105. 1988.

Miller, Arthur F., and Mattson, Ralph T., *The Truth About You: Discover What You Should Be Doing with Your Life.* Ten Speed Press, Box 7123, Berkeley CA 94707. 1977, 1989. I like this book a lot. I know of no other book that sets out to do what my friend Arthur has done here: look for *overall patterns* in your choice of jobs -- within the overarching context of *faith.* The process is still an art, not a science, and some readers will be frustrated by that. But the rest will find it suggestive and thought-provoking.

Hirsch, Arlene S., *VGM's Careers Checklists: 89 Proven Checklists to Help You Plan Your Career and Get Great Jobs.* VGM Career Horizons, 4255 West Touhy Ave., Lincolnwood, IL 60646-1975. 1991. Clever format. Primarily a book of job-hunting notes, put in the form of lists. Those who find the previous book too undefined will probably like this book. It should appeal to anyone who likes to be organized, and likes to check things off.

Wallach, Ellen J., and Arnold, Peter, *The Job Search Companion: The Organizer for Job Seekers.* The Harvard Common Press, 535 Albany St., Boston, MA 02118. 1984. Also a book for those who like to get organized. Primarily a book of very useful "forms" for keeping track of your job-search. Intended as a supplement to other job-hunting books.

Irish, Richard K., *Go Hire Yourself an Employer.* Anchor Press, Doubleday, New York, NY. 1987, third ed. An old and popular classic, now reissued.

Campbell, David P., *If You Don't Know Where You're Going, You'll Probably End Up Somewhere Else.* Argus Communications, Niles, IL. 1974. Useful for those who need to be convinced of the need for career planning.

Kojm, Kurt Barnaby, *The Changing Job Jungle: How to Find Your Almost Perfect Career.* About Face Press, 1833 Kensington Ave., Buffalo, NY 14215. 1991. A potpourri of traditional ideas about job-hunting, but some readers will find it suggestive and helpful.

Stevens, Paul, *Stop Postponing the Rest of Your Life.* Ten Speed Press, P.O. Box 7123, Berkeley, CA 94707. 1993. A classic text from Australia, now revised and updated.

OTHER RESOURCES FOR THE JOB-HUNTER OR CAREER-CHANGER BY RICHARD BOLLES

Bolles, Richard N., *How to Create A Picture of Your Ideal Job or Next Career, Advanced Version* (revised) *of the Quick Job-Hunting (and Career-Changing) Map.* Ten Speed Press, Box 7123, Berkeley, CA 94707. 1991, revised. An 8½ x 11 inch 48-page workbook, which expands upon Chapters 9, 10, and 11 in this book; in color. $5.95.

Bolles, Richard N., *The Quick Job-Hunting Map for Beginners.* Ten Speed Press, Box 7123, Berkeley, CA 94707. 1990. A workbook version of the Map for high school students just entering the labor force, and those other job-hunters who may prefer a simpler alternative to the Map above. $1.25.

Bolles, Richard N., "The Anatomy of a Job." A 24 x 36 inch poster, designed as a worksheet to be used with *How to Create A Picture* (above). It lists the families of skills on one side, and has a flower-diagram on the other, that can be filled in. 1991. $4.95.

Bolles, Richard N., *How to Find Your Mission in Life.* Ten Speed Press, Box 7123, Berkeley, CA 94707. 1991. A gift-book edition of the Epilogue in this book. $5.95.

Bolles, Richard N., *Job-Hunting Tips For The So-Called Handicapped or People Who Have Disabilities. A Supplement to What Color Is Your Parachute?* Ten Speed Press, Box 7123, Berkeley, CA 94707. 1991. 61 pages. $4.95.

Bolles, Richard N., *The Three Boxes of Life, and How To Get Out of Them.* 480 pages. Ten Speed Press, Box 7123, Berkeley, CA 94707. 1978. $14.95. 350,000 copies in print.

With other co-authors:

Crystal, John C., and Bolles, Richard N., *Where Do I Go From Here With My Life?* 272 pages. Ten Speed Press, Box 7123, Berkeley, CA 94707. 1974. $11.95. 150,000 copies in print.

OTHER VERSIONS OF PARACHUTE

Italian: Bolles, Richard Nelson, *Ce l'hai il paracadute? Guida pratica per chi cerca o vuole cambiare lavoro.* Translated and adapted by Giuseppe Mojana; preface by Fabrizio Luzzatto-Giuliani. Sperling & Kupfer, Via Borgonuovo, 24, 20121 Milano, Italy. 1992.

Spanish: Bolles, Richard N., *¿De Qué Color Es Su Paracaidas?* Editorial Diana, S.A., Roberto Gayol 1219, Mexico, D.F. 1983.

French: Bolles, Richard N., *Chercheurs d'emploi, n'oubliez pas votre parachute.* Translated by Daniel Porot. Sylvie Messinger, éditrice, 31 rue de l'Abbé-Grégoire, Paris 6e, France. 1983. Also: Bolles, Richard N., *Chercheurs d'emploi, n'oubliez pas votre parachute.* Translated by Daniel Porot. Guy Saint-Jean Editeur Inc. 674 Place Publique, Laval, Quebec H7X 1G1, Canada. 1983.

Dutch: Bolles, Richard N., *Werk zoeken-een vak apart, Een professionele aanpak voor het vinden van een (nieuwe) baan.* Translated by F.J.M. Classens. Uitgeverij Intermediair, Amsterdam/Brussels. 1983.

German: Bolles, Richard N., *Tausend geniale Bewerbungstips: Stellensuche richtig vorbereiten.* Goldmann Verlag, Neumarkterstrasse 18, 8000 München. 1987.

Japanese: Bolles, Richard N., *'87 What Color Is Your Parachute?* (In Japanese) Japan UNI Agency, Inc., Ten Speed Press and Writers House, Inc., NY. 1986.

CAREER BOOKS IN OTHER COUNTRIES AND LANGUAGES

French: Porot, Daniel, *Votre entretien d'embauche: 107 conseils pour le Reussir.* Premiere edition. Les Editions d'organisation, 26, avenue Emile-Zola, F — 75015 Paris. Tel: 45-78-61-81. 1990. Highly, highly recommended, for those who read French.

Danish: Lausten, Torben, *Kan vingerne bære? Håndbog i JOBJAGT og karriereudvikling.* Udgivet af Forlaget Thorsgaard ApS, Frederikssund, Denmark. 1989.

Japanese: Brockman, Terra, *The Job Hunter's Guide to Japan.* Kodansha International/USA Ltd., 114 Fifth Ave., New York, NY 10011. 1990.

Special Situations

Most of you will find that the main body of *Parachute* tells you all you need to know, in order to successfully conduct your job-hunt. However, *if* you are in one of the groups listed below, and you want additional guidance or information, I have made further comments, and listed some additional resources for you, in the remainder of this Appendix.

Job-Hunting Notes

1. ELEMENTARY SCHOOL STUDENTS, HIGH SCHOOL STUDENTS, AND SUMMER JOBS

If you are a high school student looking for work, you already know that you face especial difficulties during your job-hunt. You *can* overcome these difficulties. But you do need to be aware of what they are.

Employers currently are turning down, on average, 5 out of every 6 young people who apply for a job, and some companies report that fewer than 1 in 10 applicants meet *their* skills-needs. What's the problem? In a 1991 Harris Poll,[1] 78% of employers said graduates do not have discipline in their work habits. 90% of all employers felt that high school graduates "do not know how to solve complex problems."

Many also feel high school graduates lack basic skills, like **reading, writing, math** *or typing* (as, on a computer keyboard). In 1945, the written vocabulary of a 6 to 14-year-old American child was 25,000 words. Today it is only 10,000. The average young adult in this country is reading at only a 2.6 level of English proficiency, while current jobs require a proficiency, on the average, of 3.0 *(going up to 3.6 by the year 2000, experts say)*.

If you are still in high school, **get those skills** -- in reading, writing, math, and typing -- while you are there. If you are *out* of high school, but lack these skills, consider seriously going to night school at your local high school or community college, to make up for lost time.

In spite of the difficulties reported above, any high school student who is willing to diligently follow the job-hunting strategies in this book, particularly Chapters 9, 10, 11, as well as 3 and 4, should be able to put themselves well ahead of the pack. The rules are: *Know your skills. Know what you want to do. Talk to people who have done it. Find out how they did it. Do the homework, on yourself and the companies, thoroughly. Seek out the person who actually has the power to hire; use contacts to get in to see him or her. Show them how you can help them with their problems.* Cut no corners, take no shortcuts.

Below are some books that you or your parents and counselors may find additionally helpful (I have begun this listing with some resources proper for elementary school, since some teachers and counselors want to at least broach the subject of *What do you want to do, when you grow up?* during *those* years):

Otto, Luther B., *How to Help Your Child Choose a Career.* M. Evans & Co., 216 E. 49th St., New York, NY 10017. 1984.

Hummel, Dean L., and McDaniels, Carl, *How to Help Your Child Plan a Career.* Acropolis Books, Ltd., Colortone Bldg., 2400 17th St., NW, Washington, DC 20009. 1979.

Litvin, Jay, and Salk, Dr. Lee, *How To Be A Super Sitter*™. VGM Career Horizons, 4255 West Touhy Ave., Lincolnwood (Chicago), IL 60646-1975.

---

1. Reported in the *San Francisco Chronicle,* 9/30/91.

1991. Gives advice to young babysitters about getting jobs, keeping a business going, and how to go about the job.

Mosenfelder, Donn, *Vocabulary for the World of Work.* Educational Design, Inc., 47 W. 13th St., New York, NY 10014. 1985. The 300 words that people entering the work force most need to know.

Kimeldorf, Martin, *Job Search Education.* Educational Design, Inc., 47 W. 13th St., New York, NY 10011. 1985. Worksheets for the young job-hunter. Educational Design puts out a number of different books for elementary and high school students, in addition to the ones listed here, and they have a catalog of such materials, which you can ask for.

The Guide to Basic Skills Jobs, Vol. 1. RPM Press, Inc., Verndale, MN. 1986. A catalg of viable jobs for individuals with only basic work skills. This volume identifies 5,000 major occupations within the U.S. economy which require no more than an eighth grade level of education, and no more than one year of specific vocational preparation.

Henderson, Douglass, *Get Ready: Job-Hunters Kit* (for high school students). This package includes: *Get Ready, Teachers Manual; Get Ready, Students Manual;* and cassette. Done in 'rap' style, with music. Very popular. Get Ready, Inc., a subsidiary of Educational Motivation, Inc., Box 18865, Philadelphia, PA 19119. 1980.

Haldane, Bernard, and Haldane, Jean, and Martin, Lowell, *Job Power: The Young People's Job Finding Guide.* Acropolis Books Ltd., 2400 17th St. NW, Washington, DC 20009. 1980. Undoubtedly the best job-hunting book available for high school students.

Farr, J. Michael, *A Young Person's Guide to Getting and Keeping a Job.* JIST Works, 720 N. Park Ave., Indianapolis, IN 46202. 1990.

Kimeldorf, Martin, *Write Into A Job: Resumes and More.* Meridian Education Corporation, 236 E. Front St., Bloomington, IL 61701. 1990. Written particularly for entry-level or high school job-seekers. Teaches them how best to describe their marketable skills, in resumes or in other forms.

Kennedy, Joyce Lain, and Laramore, Dr. Darryl, *Joyce Lain Kennedy's Career Book.* VGM Career Books, 4255 W. Touhy Ave., Lincolnwood, IL 60646-1975. 2nd ed., 1992. Joyce is probably the most popular and knowledgeable syndicated columnist on the subject of careers, while Darryl has written other books on youth and jobs. Updated for the '90s.

As for **summer jobs,** whether for high school or college students, here are the best-known directories. Most of them are annually updated, and the year of their revision often appears in their title:

Beusterien, Pat, ed., *Summer Employment Directory of the United States.* Peterson's Guides, P.O. 2123, Princeton, NJ 08543. Issued in annual revisions. The year of the revision appears in the title of the book.

Woodworth, David, ed., *Directory of Overseas Summer Jobs.* Peterson's Guides, P.O. Box 2123, Princeton, NJ 08543. Issued in annual revisions.

Hatchwell, Emily, ed., *Directory of Summer Jobs in Britain.* Peterson's Guides, P.O. Box 2123, Princeton, NJ 08543. Issued in annual revisions.

2. COLLEGE STUDENTS

If you are a college graduate or student looking for work, you already know that you face especial difficulties during your job-hunt. You *can* overcome these difficulties. But you do need to be aware of what they are.

The major problem is the illusion we have that there is a job that goes with the degree. *Don't corporate recruiters just come on campus during your senior year, and clamor for you to come work for them?* Well, no, they don't. In 1991, only one in three graduates had jobs waiting for them at graduation time. At some colleges or universities, that figure is reduced to only one in ten, when times are hard.[2] The rest have to hunt -- hard -- after they are out. The situation is likely to improve *some* during the rest of the 1990s, but in most cases it is *you* who are going to have to take charge of your job-hunt. You can no longer rely on corporate recruiters coming to campus (if you ever could). The race for the best jobs belongs not to the strong, but to those who take initiative and know how to conduct their job-hunt themselves.

That leads us to the second problem, which is that job-hunting isn't taught in most colleges, even though it has today become a necessary survival skill. So, you'll have to pick it up on your own -- as you already know, or you wouldn't be looking at this book.

The rules are easy to learn, since they are the same for you as they are for everyone: *Know your skills. Know what you want to do. Talk to people who have done it. Find out how they did it. Do the homework, on yourself and the companies, thoroughly. Seek out the person who actually has the power to hire; use contacts to get in to see him or her. Show them how you can help them with their problems.*

Memorize Chapters 8, 9, 10, 11, 12, 13, and 14 in this book, as well as Chapters 3 and 4, please. And *do* the exercises therein. Cut no corners, take no shortcuts.

Remember that one out of seven students, in some sections of the country, get their job at the place where they interned.[3] So, internships might be an important part of your planning during the four years.

If you want further reading, here it is:

Shingleton, Jack, *Which Niche? Answers to the most common questions about careers and job hunting.* Bob Adams, Inc., 260 Center St., Holbrook, MA 02343. 1989, 1969. A little book, marvelous for its brevity, and its humor. Has many cartoons by well-known San Francisco cartoonist Phil Frank.

Phifer, Paul, *College Majors and Careers: A Resource Guide for Effective Life Planning.* Garrett Park Press, Box 190, Garrett Park, MD 20896. 1987.

Phifer, Paul, *Career Planning Q's & A's: A Handbook for Students, Parents, and Professionals.* Garrett Park Press, Box 190, Garrett Park, MD 20896. 1990.

Books on summer jobs are listed at the end of Section 1, above.

---

2. *USA Today,* 5/1/92.
3. *San Francisco Chronicle,* 5/27/92.

3. IMMIGRANTS TO THE U.S.

If you are newly arrived in this country, and are looking for work, you already know that you face especial difficulties during your job-hunt. You *can* overcome these difficulties. But you do need to be aware of what they are. And, how to overcome them.

Most of what you need to know, on both counts, can be learned in two ways. First of all, by talking to other immigrants, who have been here longer than you have, and have already 'learned the ropes.' And secondly, by reading this book you are holding in your hands, especially Chapters 3 and 4.

The rules are the same for you as they are for everyone else: *Know your skills. Know what you want to do. Talk to people who have done it. Find out how they did it. Do the homework, on yourself and the companies, thoroughly. Seek out the person who actually has the power to hire; use contacts to get in to see him or her. Show them how you can help them with their problems.* Pay particular attention to Chapters 9, 10, and 11. Also study Chapters 3, 4, 12, 13, and 14. Cut no corners, take no shortcuts.

If you want further reading, there is:

Friedenberg, Joan E., Ph.D., and Bradley, Curtis H., Ph.D., *Finding a Job in the United States*. NTC Publishing Group, 4255 W. Touhy Ave., Lincolnwood, IL 60646-1975. 1988, 1986. A guide for immigrants, refugees, limited-English-proficient job-seekers, foreign-born professionals -- anyone who is seeking work in the United States. It contains job information based on the successful experience of job-seekers, plus advice from the U.S. Department of Labor. Includes information about American job customs and laws related to immigration, as well as a systematic plan for job-hunting.

4. WOMEN

Approximately 74% of all women aged 20 to 44 years of age -- that totals over 57 million women -- are in the work force, currently employed or looking for work.

When women first started coming into the world of work in droves, which was in the early 1970s, there was a widespread feeling that they needed special job-hunting techniques -- and that they needed career counselors who catered particularly to women job-hunters. Consequently, books for women job-hunters came out in those days by the bushel basket, and counselors catering just to women *thrived*. That day has passed, and now it is widely recognized that the advice for women who go job-hunting is the same as it is for men: *Know your skills. Know what you want to do. Talk to people who have done it. Find out how they did it. Do the homework, on yourself and the companies, thoroughly. Seek out the person who actually has the power to hire; use contacts to get in to see him or her. Show them how you can help them with their problems. Cut no corners, take no shortcuts.*

Since this realization dawned, there has been a great decline in the number of *women's* job-hunting books -- though a few do still appear each year. In spite of this trend, it is foolish to claim that there are no unique problems to women who are job-hunting. There are. You *can* overcome these problems, but you need to be aware of what they are.

Some problems reside within the myths that still dance in the heads of *some* employers, particularly *male* employers. Some *still* believe, for example, that if they hire a woman, she will be out sick more than a man. (As my mother always used to say when she couldn't believe the ideas some people had: *Honestly, what is the world coming to?*) Well, anyway, if you are a woman going job-hunting, it will be useful to have some statistics at your fingertips. In this instance, the statistics (from the National Center for Health Statistics) are: women average 5.5 lost work days per year while men miss 4.3 days. In other words, women take only one more sick day *per year* than men do. Next?

There are problems that women face *as* they get the job, or *after* they get the job. Salary is a major one. Single women are notoriously underpaid, whether with children or without. The number of single parents in America currently -- most of them women -- is 10.1 million; of these, 2.1 million live in households headed by someone else -- most often, their parents.[4] The reason they do this is overwhelmingly because they can't afford to live on their own. Said one, "I'd have to earn twice my present salary in order to be able to live on my own." Married women don't fare much better, salarywise. True, in roughly one out of every five marriages, the wife is out-earning her mate; but then there are the other four. On average, working wives earned $13,250 in a recent year[5] compared to working husbands who averaged $29,150 that same year.

Part of the inequity is due to the fact that 50% of all working wives only work part-time. Wives working full-time averaged $18,930 in a recent year[6] which is better than the $13,250 cited above -- but still far below husbands' average salary of $29,150. In general, men get paid more than women of equal experience and training, for the same positions. You *can* increase the salary offered you, *if* you know something about salary negotiation, before you go in for the job interview. Be *sure* and study Chapter 14, in this book.

Related to salary is the problem of child care. In a relatively recent year, 1987, it was found, about one-third of the nation's 18.2 working mothers at that time had to pay for child care -- and this cost them between $2,000 and $6,000 annually; the average was $2,305. For the working poor, child care costs represented one-fifth of their income. Needless to say, these costs reduce the *net* amount of their already-low paycheck, considerably. In 1992, the lowest paid child care workers earned $5.08 per hour, while the highest paid earned $8.19 per hour.[7]

Another problem, as the famous Anita Hill/Clarence Thomas hearings on Capitol Hill first drove home to the nation, is that of sexual harassment or abuse in the workplace. While harassment in this crazy topsy-turvy

4. Reported in the *San Francisco Chronicle*, 4/28/92.
5. 1987, the last year for which statistics were available as we went to press.
6. 1987, again.
7. From the Child Care Employee Project, of Oakland, California, as reported in *The New York Times*, 4/18/93, page F-25.

world can sometimes be inflicted by women managers on the men or women they work with, or by males to males, the vast majority of harassment is done by males to females: and the harassment ranges from infinitely subtle to infinitely gross. The crux of the problem lies in *some* men's egos, insecurity, insensitivity, and in their assumption that women basically think like they do. They do not.

One evidence for a wide difference in the way the two sexes think, is the fact that 75% of men in the workplace find sexual advances from the opposite sex *flattering*, while 75% of women in the workplace find them *offensive.*[8]

Again, a similar proportion of men naively see nothing wrong with offering to spend extra **time,** inside or outside of work, helping women clients or women workers whom they happen to like; whereas a like proportion of women increasingly now tend to see this behavior as wrong.

Naive men think this offer of their time to be *'open-hearted,'* while many women *(though not all)* -- because they have had prior experience with such offers from *devious* men, who intended it as a prelude to seduction -- hold such behavior to be always *'unprofessional,'* and *'inappropriate,'* at the least, or *'the beginning of sexual agression,"* at the most.

Clearly, men and women need to educate each other.

When women are asked why they silently put up with harassment, subtle or gross, their universal reply is: "Because I need the job."

The idea of not putting up with it, but instead filing a sexual harassment suit, winning it, thus getting rid of your nemesis, and then being able to continue working in that same organization, is a wonderful vision. But do count the cost. Jobs are not just a series of tasks. They are people environments. Much depends on your having *good* rapport with the rest of the staff. Absent that rapport -- if you are shunned by your co-workers or superiors, in the aftermath of winning your sexual harassment suit -- your *wonderful* job can turn into *'the job from hell'* very quickly.

Moreover, future male employers are often reluctant to hire you if you are (unfairly) viewed as 'a trouble-maker,' based on your having filed this harassment suit; I have had to counsel three women to whom this has happened. Of course, if you limit your future job-hunting to firms run by women, this may not be a factor; on the contrary, they may regard you as a heroine. However, the accent is on the word *may.*

My advice is simple: if you think that filing a harassment suit is not going to fundamentally harm your rapport with the people you have to work with (let us say *everyone* dislikes the person who is your nemesis), and you are not worried about what it will do to your future employability, then seek out some good advice (I mean, from a lawyer), and if it is agreed that a suit is a good idea, by all means go ahead with it.

On the other hand, if you think that filing such a suit *is* going to irreparably damage the people environment for you at that job, and in the future, and you therefore decide not to file it, *don't* just decide to stay at that place and continue to take the abuse. Don't 'knuckle under.' Don't

---

8. According to a survey done in the U.S., in 1992.

let anyone -- even your best friend, partner or spouse -- tell you *"Well, hey, if it's a good job and you like everything else about it, just put up with the sexual innuendos."* A good job, with sexual harassment present, is now by definition a bad job.

What keeps people in bad jobs *(most often)* is lack of confidence in their ability to go find another job, of equal merit. So, take command of your life. Sharpen up your job-hunting skills, *now*. Devour this book. Do all the exercises. When you're confident about your ability to go find another job, go find it. *Then* quit this one. You *don't* need to lose self-esteem for a paycheck.

It's obvious the workplace is still a pretty chauvinist place, despite some limited improvement over the years. This is reflected not merely in sexual harassment, but also in another problem: that of the invisible *'glass ceiling.'* This now well-known phrase refers to the difficulty women have, in getting promoted beyond a certain point. At lower levels, women are doing better than they used to. They now represent 41% of all managers in the U.S., 40% of all managers in Canada, and 40% of all managers in Australia.[9] But when you get to higher levels, it's a different story. *Oops! The glass ceiling!* In U.S. organizations in general, women hold fewer than 11% of high-ranking jobs, and less than 3% of top-level jobs.[10] This explains why so many women are gravitating instead to small organizations, or forming their own companies.

The number of women-owned businesses totaled 6.5 million in 1992.[11] They provide jobs for 10% of all U.S. workers, or close to 12 million people. This is more than the total employees of the 500 largest corporations in America -- 11.7 million. 40% of women-owned businesses have been in business twelve years or longer. If the idea of following in their footsteps interests you, be *sure* and study Chapter 6.

Due partly to the obstacles cited above, partly to the hard times we are in, partly to many mothers' desire to be with their children while they may, partly to women concluding they want more time to smell the flowers, some women are dropping out of the workplace and taking on the role of homemaker. In 1990, the percentage of women in the workforce did not increase over the previous year, for the first time since 1948. In fact, it dropped. So, if you're contemplating dropping out of the workforce, for any of the above reasons, don't feel lonely, as though you were going against the trend. You've got lots of company. Even though this means you will not be going job-hunting, I would still advise you to do Chapters 9, and 10, in order to be clear about how you want to use your energies and skills, in the home and community.

---

9. Reported in *USA Today*, 2/5-7/93, as the result of a survey by The International Labor Organization.

10. *Ibid.*

11. Reported in *The (Bend, Oregon) Bulletin*, 4/19/93, p. A5, quoting Working Woman magazine. For further statistics, see: *Women Owned Businesses: The New Economic Force*, the 1992 Data Report of the National Foundation for Women Business Owners, available from them at 1377 K St., N.W., Suite 637, Washington, D.C. 20005.

If you're moving in the other direction, from the house to the marketplace, there are some *very* helpful resources you may want to get your hands on. The first listing is for either male or female homemakers:

Ekstrom, Ruth B., Harris, Abigail M., and Lockheed, Marlaine E., *How to Get College Credit for What You Have Learned as a Homemaker and Volunteer.* 1977. Project HAVE SKILLS, Education Testing Service, Princeton, NJ 08541. They also publish the: *HAVE SKILLS Women's Workbook, HAVE SKILLS Counselor's Guide,* and *HAVE SKILLS Employer's Guide.* All of these include the famous "I CAN" lists, based upon the pioneering work, in the assessment of volunteer skills and knowledge, of the Council of National Organizations for Adult Education. The preeminent resource for women coming out of the home into the marketplace, who wonder what they can claim about their home experience. It applies to all homemakers returning to the marketplace, regardless of whether or not they wish college credit for what they have learned so far in life. It should also be useful to *househusbands* who want to now return to the marketplace. These workbooks classify the homemaker's skills under the various roles of: administrator/manager, financial manager, personnel manager, trainer, advocate/change agent, public relations/communicator, problem surveyor, researcher, fund-raiser, counselor, youth group leader, group leader for a serving organization, museum staff assistant (docent), tutor/teacher's aide, manager of home finances, home nutritionist, home child caretaker, home designer and maintainer, home clothing and textile specialist, and home horticulturist. *Very* helpful book, with accompanying aids.

Nivens, Beatryce, *Careers for Women without College Degrees.* McGraw-Hill Book Company, 11 West 19th St., New York, NY 10011. 1988. Has some useful information about the skills required for some typical occupations that a woman might be considering.

Doss, Martha Merrill, *Woman's Organizations: A National Directory.* Lists over 2,000 women's organizations nationwide as well as locally, plus much more. Garrett Park Press, Box 190, Garrett Park, MD 20896. 1986.

If you are interested in sales positions, you will want to know about the National Association for Professional Saleswomen, P.O. Box 2606, Novato, CA 94948. They have chapters across the country, and they publish a newsletter, called *Successful Saleswoman.*

If it's daycare that concerns you, there are directories beginning to come out now, such as:

The New York Daycare Directory (includes northern New Jersey and southwestern Connecticut). Bob Adams, Inc., 260 Center St., Holbrook, MA 02343.

The Boston Daycare Directory. Bob Adams, Inc., 260 Center St., Holbrook, MA 02343.

5. MINORITIES (BLACK, HISPANIC, NATIVE AMERICANS, OR ASIAN)

Minorities comprise the coming workforce of the year 2000. Already, one out of every three *new* workers is either Black, Hispanic, or Asian, according to the Bureau of Labor Statistics. One out of every five workers, new or experienced, was from one of these minorities in 1986.

In spite of this, if you are a member of one of the minorities, you already know that you face especial difficulties in looking for a job. You *can* overcome these difficulties. But you need to be aware of what they are.

The principal one is the mental view that others have of the world. I call this *tribalism,* and it is the root of so many troubles throughout the world: in the Persian Gulf region, the Middle East, Yugoslavia, Russia, Africa, and -- *of course* -- *here.* So long as whites remain dominant among employers here, *tribalism* and its bastard offspring, *prejudice,* will be something you have to take into account.

Everyone is familiar with the consequences that this tribalism has had for **blacks:** while the number of affluent black households (a yearly income of $50,000 or more) doubled between 1982 and 1987, nonetheless 33% of the nation's 30.2 million blacks still live in poverty; black unemployment in 1988 averaged 11.7%, versus 5.5% for the nation; the median 1987 income of black families was only 56% of that of white families.

Other minorities run into the same tribalism. Minorities hold fewer than 1% of senior management jobs in this country.[12] So, if you're a member of a minority, that's what you're up against. Now, what can you do about it -- what will help you compete more successfully in the job-market? Answer: *Know your skills. Know what you want to do. Talk to people who have done it. Find out how they did it. Do the homework, on yourself and the companies, thoroughly. Seek out the person who actually has the power to hire; use contacts to get in to see him or her. Show them how you can help them with their problems.* Pay particular attention to Chapters 3, 4, 9, 10, and 11. Also study Chapters 12, 13, and 14, *as though your life depended on it.* Cut no corners, take no shortcuts.

When it comes time to look for sources of information, or contacts, the following may be of help, in your local library, or direct from the publisher:

Minority Organizations: A National Directory. 4th ed. Garrett Park Press, Box 190, Garrett Park, MD 20896. 1992. An annotated directory of 9,700 Black, Hispanic, Native American, and Asian American organizations.

The Black Resource Guide. Black Resource Guide, Inc., 501 Oneida Pl., NW, Washington, DC 20111. 1987. A comprehensive list of over 3,000 black resources or organizations in the U.S.

Johnson, Willis L., ed., *Directory of Special Programs for Minority Group Members: Career Information Services, Employment Skills Banks, Financial Aid Sources,* 5th ed. Garrett Park Press, Box 190, Garrett Park, MD 20896. 1990.

---

12. Reported in *USA Today,* 4/24/92.

6. EXECUTIVES, THE BUSINESS WORLD AND CORPORATE JOBS

If you are an executive looking for work, you already know that you face especial difficulties during your job-hunt. You *can* overcome these difficulties. But you do need to be aware of what they are. And, how to overcome them.

The first is, there are a lot of other executives out there, job-hunting at the same time you are. This most recent recession hit white-collar workers *hard*. In other words, you've got a lot of stiff competition. That's why the average job search period for executives was 6.8 months recently.[13]

Secondly, the length of your job-search will likely be related to your age, and the amount of salary that you are seeking. One large out-placement firm kept records and discovered that if an executive was 25–34 years of age, the average length of their job-hunt was about 20 weeks, but if over 55 years in age, it took almost 30 weeks. They further discovered that for those seeking an annual salary of $40,000 to $75,000, the average length of their job-hunt was about 25 weeks, while for those seeking more than $100,000, the average length of their job-hunt was almost 30 weeks.[14] That's what you're up against.

However, these statistics reflect not only a difficult job-market, but *more importantly* the method of job-hunting that executives traditionally depend upon. Chapter 3, in this book, describes executives' traditional method of job-hunting, mostly because they don't know any better. Avoid that method, like the plague.

Your salvation depends on the same creative job-hunting methods as anyone else: *Know your skills. Know what you want to do. Talk to people who have done it. Find out how they did it. Do the homework, on yourself and the companies, thoroughly. Seek out the person who actually has the power to hire; use contacts to get in to see him or her. Show them how you can help them with their problems.* Pay particular attention to Chapters 3, 4, 9, 10, and 11, *as though your life depended on it.* Also study Chapters 12, 13, and 14. Cut no corners, take no shortcuts.

I you aren't yet an executive, but think you would like to be one, know what you are walking into. According to a 1990 survey by Accountemps, it ain't all glamor: the average business executive reports that he or she spends on average 60 hours a year *on hold* on the phone, and 128 hours a year reading or writing unnecessary memos, and 288 hours a year attending unnecessary meetings. To get a more precise fix on the kind of executive that you'd like to be, in the kind of company that you'd like to work for, go talk to executives who are already there, and ask them what their week is like.

For would-be executive, and experienced executive alike, there are the following additional helps:

---

13. According to Drake Beam Morin Inc., for the year 1990.
14. Reported in the *National Business Employment Weekly,* in the 8/27/89 edition. Statistics were for the year 1989.

Boll, Carl R., *Executive Jobs Unlimited.* Updated edition. Macmillan Publishing Co., Inc., 866 Third Ave., New York, NY 10022. 1979, 1965. **One of the two classics** in the executive job-hunting field.

Drucker, Peter, *Management: Tasks, Responsibilities, Practices.* Harper-Collins, 10 E. 53rd St., New York, NY 10022. 1973. **The other classic** in this field. Should be absolutely required reading for anyone contemplating entering, changing to, or becoming a professional within any organization in the business world.

Burton, Mary Lindley, and Wedemeyer, Richard A., *In Transition: From the Harvard Business School Club of New York Personal Seminar in Career Management.* HarperBusiness, a division of HarperCollins Publishers, 10 E. 53rd St., New York, NY 10022. 1991.

Corporate Jobs Outlook, "The Key to America's Top Employers," P.O. Drawer 100, Boerne, Texas 78006, is a newsletter published bi-monthly, with detailed information about current situations at top corporate employers. Your library may have it, and it is also available online, for those of you who have a computer and subscribe (or want to subscribe) to **NewsNet** (the telephone number is 800-345-1301, except in Pennsylvania or outside the U.S., where it is 215-527-8030). They emphasize that the seven keys to look for in your research of any corporate employer are: financial stability; growth plans; research and development programs; product development or manufacturing -- emerging products, services, or use of new technologies; marketing and distribution methods; employee benefits; and quality of work factors -- continuing training, health programs, childcare, promote-from-within, performance reviews.

Cole, Kenneth J., *The Head-hunter Strategy.* John Wiley & Sons, Inc., 605 Third Ave., New York, NY 10158. 1985.

7. 'RECOVERING PEOPLE' (FROM ALCOHOLISM, DRUGS, OTHER CHEMICAL DEPENDENCIES, CO-DEPENDENCIES), AND OTHER '12-STEP PROGRAM PEOPLE'

You know what I'm going to say: if you are 'in recovery' and looking for work, you may face especial difficulties during the hiring interviews. You *can* overcome these difficulties. But you do need to be aware of what they are. And, how to overcome them.

Any prejudice about your history can be overcome if you: *Know your skills. Know what you want to do. Talk to people who have done it. Find out how they did it. Do the homework, on yourself and the companies, thoroughly. Seek out the person who actually has the power to hire; use contacts to get in to see him or her. Show them how you can help them with their problems.* Pay particular attention to Chapters 3, 4, 9, 10, and 11, *as though your life depended on it.* Also study Chapters 12, 13, and 14. Cut no corners, take no shortcuts.

If you want additional help, there are the following resources:

Tanenbaum, Nat, and Eric A., *The Career Seekers: A Program for Career Recovery.* The Working Press, a division of The Career Center, Inc., P.O. Box 49631, Atlanta, GA 30359. 1988. This book is for people who are actively practicing any 12-step program, or are in counseling for co-dependency; but its principles apply to all who see themselves as 'recovering people.' Very useful supplement to *Parachute.*

Whitfield, M.D., Charles L., *A Gift to Myself.* Health Communications, Inc., Deerfield Beach, FL. 1990. Deals with root emotional issues often blocking job-hunters in recovery.

8. EX-MILITARY

If you are an ex-military person who has decided to look for work outside the military, in the general workplace, you already know that you will have some problems convincing the world you know *anything* except how to wage war. You *can* convince them, but it will take work.

Your major problem is that you speak a different language from those out there in the world. You have been living in a sub-culture within our general culture, and this sub-culture is in many respects like the general job-market, *except* that it has its own unique vocabulary. It is *crucial* that you sit down and inventory the skills you have been using during your time in the military (Chapters 9, 10, and 11 in this book are *mandatory* for you to *do*). Take especial care to take your skills and fields of knowledge out of the military *jargon,* and translate them into language that is understood in the general marketplace.

There are three aids to help you do this: (1) Each service's personnel manual has a section where military jobs and tasks are cross-coded to the civilian *Dictionary of Occupational Titles.* (2) There is also a two-volume Military Occupation Training Data series, available from Defense Manpower Data Center, 1600 Wilson Blvd., Suite 400, Arlington, VA 22209, which does the same thing. (3) Militran, Inc., Box 490, Southeastern, PA 19399-0490, 1-800-426-9954, has a *Militran Guide to Career Opportunities,* published monthly in three editions: one for Army personnel, one for Navy-Marine Corps personnel, and one for Air Force personnel, which not only lists what civilian job title is equivalent to your former military job title, but also lists a considerable number of ads which they have culled from various newspapers around the country, *indexed by those same civilian job titles.*

Militran also operates a free computerized resume database for all military personnel. In any profession, such databases typically are more used by job-seekers than they are by employers, but you may want to try this one, anyway. For information about the database, write to Militrans, 1255 Drummers Lane, Suite 306, Wayne, PA 19087.

If you are or were an officer, you should know that the Retired Officers Association (TROA), 201 North Washington Street, Alexandria, VA 22314-2529, 703-838-8117, has an Officer Placement Service which maintains a comprehensive job-search library, a computerized placement service, and resume critiques for their members. It is, however, open only to officers who become members of TROA.

Officer or not, your salvation depends on the same creative job-hunting -- and career-changing -- methods as anyone else: *Know your skills. Know what you want to do. Talk to people who have done it. Find out how they did it. Do the homework, on yourself and the companies, thoroughly. Seek out the person who actually has the power to hire; use contacts to get in to see him or her. Show them how you can help them with their problems.* Pay particular attention to Chapters 3, 4, 9, 10, and 11, *as though your life depended on it.* Also study Chapters 12, 13, and 14. Cut no corners, take no shortcuts.

An additional book:

Schlachter, Gail Ann, and Weber, R. David, *Financial Aid for Veterans, Military Personnel, and Their Dependents 1990-1991.* Reference Service Press, 1100 Industrial Road, Suite 9, San Carlos, CA 94070. 1990. Outlines over 1,000 programs open to veterans and their dependents.

9. CLERGY AND RELIGIOUS

If you are an ordained person who has decided to look for work outside the church, in the general workplace, you already know that you will have some problems convincing the world you know *anything* except theology. As a matter of fact, you *can* convince them, but it will take work.

Your major problem is that you speak a different language from those out there in the world. Like the military (above), you have been living in a sub-culture within our general culture, which describes your skills and work-experience in its own unique vocabulary. It is *crucial* that you sit down and inventory the skills you have been using during your time in the clergy (Chapters 9, 10, and 11 in this book are *mandatory* for you to *do*), and that you take especial care to *translate* your skills and fields of knowledge out of the clerical *jargon* and into language that is understood in the general marketplace.

The rules for *your* job-hunt, or career-change, are the same as they are for everyone: *Know your skills. Know what you want to do. Talk to people who have done it. Find out how they did it. Do the homework, on yourself and the companies, thoroughly. Seek out the person who actually has the power to hire; use contacts to get in to see him or her. Show them how you can help them with their problems.* Pay particular attention to Chapters 3, 4, 9, 10, and 11, *as though your life depended on it.* Also study Chapters 12, 13, and 14. Cut no corners, take no shortcuts.

In case you want further reading, or counseling, the books and counselors who look at job-hunting and career-changing particularly from a religious point of view are to be found at the end of The Epilogue, on page 450–452.

10. EX-OFFENDERS

If you are an ex-offender, and are looking for work, *of course* you are going to face especial difficulties during the hiring interviews, because of your history. You *can* deal with this problem, if you remember this above all: all employers divide into two groups: those who will be bothered by your incarceration, and those who won't be. Your job is to find the second group of employers, and just thank the first very politely for their time.

With the second, your case will be helped immeasurably if you: *Know your skills. Know what you want to do. Talk to people who have done it. Find out how they did it. Do the homework, on yourself and the companies, thoroughly. Seek out the person who actually has the power to hire; use contacts to get in to see him or her. Show them how you can help them with their problems. Cut no corners, take no shortcuts.*

If you want to start working on this while you are still in prison, devour *this* book. Pay particular attention to Chapters 3, 4, 9, 10, and 11, *as though your life depended on it.* Do all the pertinent exercises therein. Also study Chapters 12, 13, and 14. Cut no corners, take no shortcuts.

You can also obtain a "Pre-Employment Curriculum" from the American Correctional Association, 4321 Hartwick Rd., College Park, MD 20740.

If you decide you want to work on a college degree program while you are in prison, it can be done. See the Appendix entitled,

"Advice for People in Prison," in Bear, John, *College Degrees by Mail: 100 Good Schools that Offer Bachelor's, Master's, Doctorates and Law Degrees by Home Study.* Ten Speed Press, Box 7123, Berkeley, CA 94707. 1991.

Once you're out, and you are job-hunting, Federal/State Employment Offices can often be of particular assistance to ex-offenders. All offices can provide for bonding of ex-offenders, if needed to obtain employment. They also have information on tax breaks for employers who hire ex-offenders. The larger offices even have Ex-Offender Specialists.

For further reading: *A Survival Source Book for Offenders,* from Cega Services, Box 81826, Lincoln, NE 68501.

11. PEOPLE WITH DISABILITIES OR HANDICAPS

If you have a physical, mental, emotional, or other disability, and are looking for work, *of course* you are going to face especial difficulties during the hiring interviews, because of your disability. You *can* deal with this problem, if you remember this above all: all employers divide into two groups: those who will be bothered by your disability, and those who won't be. Your job is to find the second group of employers, and just thank the first very politely for their time.

With the second, your case will be helped immeasurably if you: *Know your skills. Know what you want to do. Talk to people who have done it. Find out how they did it. Do the homework, on yourself and the companies, thoroughly. Seek out the person who actually has the power to hire; use contacts to get in to see him or her. Show them how you can help them with their problems.* Cut no corners, take no shortcuts.

Beyond this, there is much more to be said that is helpful, but unfortunately this requires more space than we have here. I have, therefore, produced a lengthy booklet on this subject, intended to be used with *Paracute,* available in your bookstore, or directly from Ten Speed Press, Box 7123, Berkeley, CA 94707. Its title is *Job-Hunting Tips For The So-Called Handicapped or People Who Have Disabilities. A Supplement to What Color Is Your Parachute.* 1991. 61 pages. $4.95.

If you wish to save this money, you can consult your local library to see if it has a copy of the booklet, *or* a copy of the 1990 or 1991 editions of *Parachute,* since this stuff first appeared as an Appendix in the back of those editions.

12. PEOPLE FACING RETIREMENT
OR ALREADY RETIRED

Now, a word or two about **retirement:** if you work in a company with 20 or more employees, they cannot since 1986 force you to retire just because you reach a specified age, though they can force you to retire for unsatisfactory performance of your job at any age. Does this mean there are a lot more 'older workers' now than there used to be? No, strangely enough, it does not. In 1950, 46% of men over 65 were still in the labor force; and now that percentage is less than 17%. Most women now leave the workforce before they turn 60, and most men before they turn 63. In fact, one-third of all career jobs now end by age 55.

What happens **after** retirement? The percentages, according to a relatively recent study,[15] are that half of the elderly who are out of the workforce are satisfied with their situation, one-quarter are simply *unable* to work (presumably because of health), and one-quarter are very unhappy with the fact that they aren't working. The numbers underlying those percentages are these:[16] 21.5 million Americans are between ages 50 and 65, of whom 13.3 million are working, and 8.2 million are not. Of the latter, 4.7 million don't want to work, 1.6 million are unable to, and almost 2 million would like to be back at work. In fact, one out of three retired **men** does return to the labor force, usually within two years.[17]

If you are retired, and would like to return to work, *of course* you are going to face especial difficulties during the hiring interviews, because of your age. You *can* deal with this problem, if you remember this above all: all employers divide into two groups: those who will be bothered by your age, and those who won't be. Your job is to find the second group of employers, and just thank the first very politely for their time.

With the second, your case will be helped immeasurably if you: *Know your skills. Know what you want to do. Talk to people who have done it. Find out how they did it. Do the homework, on yourself and the companies, thoroughly. Seek out the person who actually has the power to hire; use contacts to get in to see him or her. Show them how you can help them with their problems.* Cut no corners, take no shortcuts.

As you probably already know, your desire to work will be complicated by Social Security requirements, which amount basically to a disincentive to work: in order to continue to receive full benefits, *as of 1992*, you must not earn more than $7,440 a year if you are under 65. You will lose $1 in benefits for every $2 that you earn above that limit. If you are 65 to 69, you must not earn more than $10,200. You will lose $1 in benefits for every $3 that you earn above that limit. After you reach 70, however, there is no limit. Check with your local Social Security office to find out if the limits have been raised, by the time you read this.

If you want to work primarily (or solely) to supplement your retirement

---

15. Reported in *The New York Times*, 4/22/90.
16. Reported in *National Business Employment Weekly*, 2/18/90.
17. Reported in *American Demographics*, 12/90. Statistics for women in retirement are not yet available.

income, the foregoing is a serious disincentive, indeed. On the other hand, if you want to work for the pure joy of working, the economic disincentive will probably not faze you. You can always volunteer your time (see Chapter 5), without cost to the place where you serve. Now, to further reading:

If you want to prepare for your final ten years in the world of work, before retirement, there is:

Bolles, Richard N., "The decade of decisions," in *Modern Maturity* magazine, February-March 1990 issue (see your local library). Discusses the six options you can choose between, during the final ten years of your life in the world of work.

If you're trying to plan what your retirement will be like, even if you don't work, there is:

Chapman, Elwood N., *Comfort Zones: Planning Your Future.* Crisp Publications, Inc., 95 First St., Los Altos, CA 94022, or from Career Research & Testing, 2005 Hamilton Ave., Suite 250, San Jose, CA 95125-9872. 1990, second ed. A very popular and practical guide for retirement planning.

Kouri, Mary K., *Elderlife: A Time to Give -- A Time to Receive.* Human Growth & Development Associates, 6780 S. Adams Way, Littleton, CO 80122-1802.

T. Rowe Price Retirees Financial Guide. A very useful and detailed financial planning guide put out by T. Rowe Price, possessing one other sterling virtue: it is free. 1-800-541-5790. Their address is T. Rowe Price Investment Services, Inc., 100 E. Pratt St., Baltimore, MD 21202. *Naturally,* they hope you'll invest in some funds they list, so you might get some follow-up mail (I did). But it's a fine guide.

How to Plan Your Successful Retirement, AARP Book Publication. AARP, 1909 K St., NW, Washington, DC 20049. 1988.

If you want some guidance about possible places to retire to, in the U.S. there are:

Boyer, Richard, and Savageau, David, *Places Rated a·l·m·a·n·a·c.* Prentice Hall Press, A division of Simon & Schuster, Inc., 15 Columbus Circle, New York, NY 10023. 1989. All 333 metropolitan areas ranked and compared for living costs, job outlook, crime, health, transportation, education, the arts, recreation, and climate. Highly recommended. A knockout of a book. They update it periodically.

Savageau, David, *Retirement Places r·a·t·e·d.* Prentice Hall Press, A division of Simon & Schuster, Inc., 15 Columbus Circle, New York, NY 10023. 1990. 151 top retirement areas ranked and compared for costs of living, housing, climate, personal safety, services, work opportunities, and leisure living. Highly recommended. Tremendously useful. He updates it periodically.

Best-Rated Retirement Cities & Towns, Consumer Guide Publications International, Ltd., 7373 N. Cicero Ave., Lincolnwood, IL 60646. 1988. A review of 100 of the most attractive retirement locations across America.

If you want to know what retired people do, by way of work, after retirement, the classic on this subject is:

Bird, Caroline, *Second Careers: New Ways to Work After 50.* Little, Brown and Company, Boston, Toronto, London. 1992. The subject of this book is not what 'seniors' *ought* to do after age 50, but what in fact they *do* do . . . and why. This book is her 'report to the nation' of her analysis of some 36,000 questionnaires sent in by readers of *Modern Maturity* magazine. Highly recommended.

If your aging is an issue for you, you might want to take out of your local library (or bookstore):

Dychtwald, Ken, and Flower, Joe, *Age Wave: The Challenges and Opportunities of an Aging America.* Bantam Books, 666 Fifth Ave., New York, NY 10103. 1990. The most important book out yet on all the implications of aging.

There's also a book which describes how old some people were, when they did their great achievement. Designed, of course, to inspire you to go and do likewise. It begins with actual achievements, like learning classical Greek, at age three. (Talk about over-achievers!) You'll probably be especially interested in what people did between ages 50 and 96:

Bierlein, J. F., *The Book of Ages.* Ballantine Books, a division of Random House, Inc., 201 E. 50th St., New York, NY 10022. 1992.

Addendum
OTHER CAREER BOOKS

If there's some career-related, or job-hunting, problem that you're dying to find out more about, and none of the above books will do, there are three alternative routes open to you.

(1) Your local **public library,** or nearby community college library. You will of course fly over there and see if they can shed some light. If they have a friendly **reference librarian** by all means ask to see him or her. They can be worth their weight in gold to you. Tell them your problem or interest, and see what they can dig up. They often know of hidden treasures, buried in articles and clippings, as well as books, which could be the answer to your prayers.

(2) Your **local bookstores** -- go there, browse, and see what they have.

(3) **Mail order.** There are a number of places which specialize in career books. Below is a *sampling* (only) of some of those catalogs, which you can write and ask for:

General Catalogs:

The Whole Work Catalog: Resources for Career Direction. The New Careers Center, Inc., 1515 23rd St., P.O. Box 339, Boulder, CO 80306.

Masterco Career Catalog, Masterco, P.O. Box 7382, Ann Arbor, MI 48107.

Catalog of job-quest books, Planning/Communications, 7215 Oak Ave., River Forest, IL 60305.

Job & Career Library. Consultants Bookstore, Templeton Road, Fitzwilliam, NH 03447.

Catalogs Listing Primarily Their Own Publications:

Ten Speed Press Catalog, Ten Speed Press, Box 7123, Berkeley, CA 94707. They often have a listing of just their career-related books. (As I write, it is called *The 1994 Career-Planning, Business Know-How and Skills for Personal Growth List*.)

Writer's Digest Catalog. Writer's Digest Books, 1507 Dana Ave., Cincinnati, OH 45207.

Garrett Park Press Catalog, Garrett Park Press, Box 190, Garrett Park, MD 20896.

Career Development Resources Catalog. Career Research & Testing, 2005 Hamilton Ave., San Jose, CA 95125.

Career Planning and Job Search Catalog. JIST Works, Inc., 720 North Park Ave., Indianapolis, IN 46202.

Peterson's Guides, P.O. Box 2123, Princeton, NJ 08543.

VGM *Career Books 1994*. NTC Publishing Group, 4255 West Touhy Ave., Lincolnwood, IL 60646-1975.

Careers, Inc. Catalog, Careers, Inc., 1211 10th St., SW, P.O. Box 135, Largo, FL 34649-0135.

> *Books and periodicals designed particularly for career-counselors, are listed at the end of Appendix A, beginning on page 379. Some job-hunters or career-changers looking for further insights, may want to browse there, to see if there is anything of interest to themselves.*

Appendix C

How To Survive Financially

Even if you are *not* out of work, this Appendix may be of interest to you. As I mentioned in Chapter 5, during the '90s thus far, over 30% of all adults in the U.S. -- working or not -- describe their financial situation as "shaky." Furthermore, many people who find work -- hopefully a job they love -- may find it only at a reduced salary compared to what they used to make; in which case, they too will need many of the tips in this Appendix, as they learn how to tighten their belts, on a smaller salary than they previously earned.

WHEN MONEY IS SHORT: TIGHTENING THE BELT

If you grew up in a poor family, as I did *(we had to rent our housing and move often, clothes were most often 'hand-me-downs,' we couldn't afford a car, and we only had a very limited food budget)*, you will know how to tighten your belt, without reading this section at all.

But if all of this is new to you, here are a few suggestions about how many people go about this task.

In general, you analyze *everything* you spend, and see how you could do it cheaper, or even do without. It goes like this:

Housing: If you own your house, you will of course stay in it unless the monthly mortgage payments are killing you. In which case, you may consider *buying down* -- selling this house, and buying a much smaller one. This is not, however, a good strategy when times are really hard, as you will likely *take a bath,* or *lose your shirt (or blouse)*, when you sell your house. Still, you may have no choice. If things get *really* bad you may have to sell your home, put your furniture in storage, and go live with your parents or children, nearby or far. This should be considered a short-term *emergency* strategy only, since it discomforts both families -- but, it is preferable to the streets. . . . If you rent, you may consider moving to a house where the rent is cheaper each month. . . . As far as electricity and gas are concerned, your local utilities company usually has a pamphlet on how you can cut down on these monthly obligations. Keeping the house less warm in winter, and wearing a sweater, is a place to begin. Turning off lights in any room where you are not physically present at the moment, is another. . . . Conserving water involves techniques that almost any water company can give you a pamphlet about. . . . If you have multiple telephones, you might consider reducing their number to one. Also, contact your phone company, as they may have a special budget plan available. . . . Garbage removal is usually unavoidable, unless the dump is near and you want to drive your garbage there yourself. . . . If you've been paying for cleaning, maintenance, or repairs of your home, you might start doing all that yourself. There are books; there are also simple strategies *(e.g., if the pull-mechanism for stopping up your bathtub breaks, instead of calling the plumber, buy a simple pancake-shaped rubber stopper at your local hardware store)*. If you find even the simplest home-repairs impossible, then wait to call the plumber, carpenter, or whoever, until you've *saved up* several jobs that you can ask him/her to come and do all at once.

Food: Many people, faced with the necessity to save money on their food, find a little plot of land in their backyard or in a community garden, and grow a lot of their own vegetables and herbs. If that doesn't appeal to you, and even if it does, for the rest you're going to have to plan ahead and buy smart. You were thinking about becoming a vegetarian some day? Now is a good time to start. It's not only good for your body, it's good for your budget. . . . Before going shopping, you lay out your planned meals for an entire week ahead, and shop for the whole week at one time. You'll save, by doing so. And, *of course*, 'generic' brands are usually less expensive than big-name brands, but you already knew that, didn't you? . . . Experts on how to survive when you're poor, say this is what you do. You buy non-fat milk; you buy grains, breads, pasta, beans, and vegetables; you buy dark-green and deep-orange veggies (broccoli, carrots, lettuce, spinach, sweet potatoes, winter squash); you buy (or grow) lots of fresh herbs; and if you're not being a strict vegetarian, you buy canned tuna, chicken, turkey, and fish. . . . You cook pasta, soups, stews, souffles, chicken or turkey pies, filled pancakes/crepes, or meals with nothing but vegetables and rice *(light on the salt, heavy on the herbs -- if you're gonna eat cheaply, you might as well also eat healthy)*. You cook roast chicken, you cook *(if your taste runs to meats)* inexpensive cuts of meats, roasts, marinated or simmered long. . . . As far as eating out is concerned, you may have to give that up for the duration. *But,* for those days when eating out seems an essential pillar of your mental health, you will find that inexpensive meals can be found, in most towns or cities of any size, for under $15 and very often for under $10 per person. There are four routes to such meals: a) eat at ethnic restaurants, if your town has them, such as Indian, Thai, Chinese, Burmese, Taiwanese, Japanese, Middle Eastern, Greek, African, Italian, French and others. Ethnic restaurants aren't *by nature* inexpensive; in fact, sometimes they can be *hideously* expensive -- but search for the ones that aren't. These often offer *fine* food at unbelievably *low* prices. *Always* read over the menu outside the restaurant, or just inside the door before asking to be seated, and *study* the prices. That way, there will be no surprises. b) Make your main dining-out meal a lunch, rather than a dinner, when the same food is priced for less -- sometimes *much* less -- at many if not most restaurants. c) Look in the newspapers for restaurants advertising 'Early-Bird' specials, to those who can come in before 6 p.m. or whenever. Also look for those "All you can eat" restaurants that have sprung up all over the country. d) If none of the above is available in the small town where you are, go to your favorite place and make a large salad your main entree, or if orders are large-sized, split one entree between two of you. Or if you *love* fast-food places (I know a Frenchman who thinks Burger King is *heaven*), by all means go *there*.

Clothing: Most people are pretty savvy about what to do here, to tighten the belt: watching the newspaper ads, and waiting for sales; visiting sales racks, clearance racks, and bargain basements in stores; going to discount stores, factory outlets, warehouses, secondhand stores, and flea markets.

(If you live in any large-size city or metropolitan area, there often are books which tell you exactly where all these places are located -- see your bookstore or library.) *Always* try clothes on, before buying them. With secondhand clothes, check for stains (especially under the armpit), and check for faded coloring in part of the garment (out in the sun too long). With secondhand shoes, check everything inside and out: lasts, soles, heels.

Automobile/transportation: If you currently own a more expensive car than you would like to, under these present circumstances, you might consider going to an auto dealer and *trading down*. One job-hunter I know of, traded his expensive used car, with payments still due, for a less-expensive car that was brand new. The new monthly payments were much more kind to his budget. . . . You might also consider buying a used car, with low mileage, from rental fleets; they often are heavily discounted, and many are still under warranty. . . . Incidentally, some job-hunters have found a car so indispensable to their job-hunt, that when they had no car they have even down-traded on their house, in order to purchase that essential car. . . . As for public transportation, if you need to fly -- say to a job interview -- there are definite savings if you purchase the ticket thirty days ahead of time. Also it is often the case that one airline *is* cheaper than others; the travel section in the Sunday edition of newspapers in major cities across the country lists which airline has the cheapest fare to your destination city. Travel agents, of course, can also discover this information for you, provided that they are not using computers provided by one of the major airlines, programmed to bring up that airline's fares first.[1]

Insurance: It is very tempting, when your budget is tight, to let your insurances lapse, in order to save the payments. This temptation should be avoided at all costs. The fact that you are unemployed or working at a lesser salary than you formerly did, does not mean that no further calamity will strike. Accidents, grave illnesses, fire and flood çan still occur; I have seen it happen many times.[2] Without insurance, this can be devastating. Should it happen to you, and you let your insurance lapse, you will say (too late): *"Worst mistake I ever made."* Penny-wise and pound foolish. Don't be. This is precisely the time of your life when you *most* need protection against calamity.

Medical plan and medical insurance: As indicated in the previous section, this is *very* important to have at all times, but particularly when you are unemployed. If you have a spouse, who is still employed while you are not, and there is a health plan covering your spouse, you ought to inquire whether you are covered under that plan, or can be enrolled. . . . Absent that possibility, if there was a group health plan at the place where you

---

1. Further savings are available on transportation, hotel costs, and car rentals, if you happen to be a senior citizen (62 years and older, in most cases). There are books that describe these, such as, *Unbelievably Good Deals & Great Adventures That You Absolutely Can't Get Unless You're Over 50*, by Joan Rattner Heilman. Contemporary Books, 180 North Michigan Ave., Chicago IL 60601. Revised regularly.

2. The last time I myself was unemployed, I was also burned out of my house during the same time period.

used to work, and that place had twenty or more employees, in the U.S. there is a federal law called COBRA[3] which requires that health plan to give you written notice of your right to continue under that plan for up to 18 months after you are terminated -- *provided* that you are willing to pay the premiums during those eighteen months.[4]. . . Absent that possibility, if you are without insurance you can ask an insurance agent (hopefully a friend) to get in touch with an expert in *impaired-risks,* who can research for you what company will cover you, for the least premium per month. This is particularly advisable if you have some current medical risk. (There should be no charge for this service, because insurance companies pay for that expert's help.)

Schools/Learning: If you decide that you want to go back to school for retraining while you are unemployed, you should look for classes run through the nearest adult education program, or your local community college, since these tend to be the most inexpensive. *However,* you would be well-advised to *first* read Chapters 9, 10, and 11, and do the homework described there. It may be that you will be able to change careers without going back to school at all. That could save you a lot of money, on educational costs. . . . As for your children's education, the ways to cut corners there will already be obvious to you. *(e.g., if they are attending a private college, and you are footing the bills, you will probably need to talk to them about the possibility of transferring to a public college or university, with reduced fees, in your own State.)*

Pet care: I know, you'd rather *starve* than cut back on your pet's lifestyle. Next.

Bills and Debts: If your past debts are over your head, you have two alternatives. The first is, if those debts are the size of a hill but not a mountain, to go to each of your creditors and offer to pay them off on a regular, but reduced schedule. During one period in my life when I was immensely down on my luck, I owed around $50 to each of several department stores. I figured all I could afford to pay each of them, at that time, was $5 a month; so I wrote each of them, told them of my circumstances,

---

3. COBRA stands for **C**onsolidated **O**mnibus **B**udget **R**econciliation **A**ct (you were dying to know that, weren't you?).

4. Under the COBRA coverage you may have to pay up to 102% of the premium, which means both the employer's share *and* your share, but it usually is still cheaper than if you went out and bought your own individual health insurance. Premiums of course vary from health plan to health plan, but to give you *some* guidance of how much this might be: on average, companies paid $3,573 per employee (in 1991) for those still employed at their company, and those employees themselves paid $1,050 for individual coverage or $2,100 for family coverage, for a grand premium total of $4,623 to $5,673. That works out to $385.25 to $472.75 *per month. Study by A. Foster Higgins & Co.* You are eligible under COBRA even if you quit, rather than being fired or terminated. *And,* you have sixty days from your termination to decide whether or not you want the 18-month COBRA extension. (The extension may be 29 months if you left work because you became disabled.) There are some circumstances which can make you ineligible. *For example,* if you were fired for 'gross misconduct.' Or if your health plan is not covered by COBRA (those at employers who have less than 20 employees are not, and neither are those plans that are sponsored by the Federal government, or by certain church-related organizations). If you want more information, and your former health plan doesn't provide it, contact the nearest regional office of the U.S. Department of Labor, and ask for their booklet about COBRA.

and offered to pay them off at the rate of $5 a month. That meant of course that it would take me ten months to pay off each $50 debt, but the stores preferred *that*, to not being paid at all. They all accepted the offer, and I did pay them all off. You may want to follow this same strategy. . . . On the other hand, if your debts are the size of Mount Everest, and you know you have *no* chance of ever paying them off, you may want to file (in the U.S.) for "Chapter 11" bankruptcy. On the positive side, this step takes you out from under crushing debt, gives you a chance to reorganize, and a chance to pay your creditors at least some of what they are owed, over time. On the negative side, it does affect your credit adversely for a time, and makes getting new loans or credit very difficult. And *some* future employers may also regard it as 'a proven record of financial instability,' causing them to be reluctant to hire you. (Other employers, however, will just sympathize with your plight, having been there themselves in the past. You will have to simply excuse yourself when you meet the former kind, and keep going until you find the latter.) It is *very* important that you go talk to some *knowledgeable* financial advisor -- a friend, an officer at your bank, a lawyer, an accountant -- so that you *fully* understand this step, *before* you ever take it. . . . **Now,** let's go on to talk about something infinitely more important than how you deal with *past* debts, and that is: how you avoid piling up more debt *in the future.* 'Out of the fryin' pan, and into the fire' is a fate that you want to avoid at all costs, here. The recipe for casting yourself into the fire while you are unemployed is this: mounting credit card debt *(charging more each month, by far, than your monthly pay-off on that card);* letting your insurances lapse (thus having no protection if a sudden emergency -- *car accident, family member falling ill, etc.* -- pushes your budget over the edge); and chronically living each month beyond your budget. Avoid all these, like the plague. The most important step is probably to take all those credit cards, put them in a bottom drawer, and *never* use them until your hard times are past.

Taxes: If you are going to be owing Federal, State, or local (property) taxes somewhere ahead, figure out *now* what the due date is, how much it will be, and then set aside that money (in monthly installments, or in one lump sum from your savings) so you can meet the obligation on time. Otherwise, your taxes will push you under the heading of 'crushing mounting debt,' above.

Charity Giving/Tithe: This budget category is approached very differently by various people enduring hard times. Some of you will use this category as a place to cut corners, reducing your monthly or annual charitable giving for the duration of your unemployment.[5] Others of you, however, who regard The Tithe as part of your sacred obligation to God, will consider the continued offering of 10% of your income as inviolate and untouchable, regardless of your circumstances. You will find other

---

5. It is interesting to note that during Hard Times charity giving is often on the *rise* from the poor. Apparently, being badly off does stimulate compassion for those who are even *worse* off than we are.

places where your budget can be reduced. In either case, no advice is needed from me. You already know what you are going to do here.

Entertainment: When we are going through hard times, we need to have our minds taken off our plight. That is one of the reasons that the 'Swing Era' of the Big Bands in the '30s occurred during the worst Hard Times this country has ever seen. You don't have to swear off entertainment just because you're enduring hard times, and are on a very limited budget. If you're dyin' to see a movie, for example, remember that some movie theaters have 'Early Bird' specials, where the 5 p.m. showing, for example, is at a much reduced price. Also, plenty of other kinds of free entertainment are available in most major cities, and even some smaller towns.[6] Enterprising souls have put out directories of these, for large metropolitan areas (see your bookstore or library); and you can also ask your local newspaper if they ever publish a directory of such events. If they do, ask if you can buy the back issue which contained that directory.

For further tips on how to tighten your belt, browse your local bookstore or library. There are *always* new books coming out on this subject (often in the business, or financial book racks at your local bookstore.)[7]

Well, so much for tightening the belt. If that only partially solves your problem, then it's time for the next move.

It's time to think about how to bring in more money. There are six strategies for doing this. Let's see what they are.

WHEN MONEY IS SHORT:
(1) TEMPORARY WORK

In these difficult '90s, many many employers are cutting their staff to the bone. Trouble is, as time goes on, some extra work may then come their way, work which their reduced staff can't keep up with.

At that point, employers won't usually hire back the staff they cut, but they will turn to what are called "Temporary Help" agencies, as I mentioned in Chapter 11, for either full- or part-time work. If you have any marketable skills and experience, and are looking for some ways to earn some money, you certainly want to go register at one or more of these agencies.

---

6. San Francisco, for example, has huge free concerts most Sunday afternoons in the summer, at its Stern Grove; and many other major cities have similar traditions.

7. For example:

Linda Bowman, *Free Food . . . & More*. Probus Publishing Company, 1925 N. Clybourn Ave., Chicago, IL 60614, 1-800-PROBUS-1. 1991.

Ellen Kunes, *Living Well or Even Better On Less*. Perigee Books, Putnam Publishing Company, 200 Madison Ave., New York, NY 10016. 1991.

Charles Long, *How To Survive Without A Salary*. Summerhill Press, distributed by Collier Macmillan Canada, Inc., 50 Gervais Dr., Don Mills, Ontario M3C 3K4.

Albert Ellis and Patricia A. Hunter, *Why Am I Always Broke? How to Be Sane About Money*. Carol Publishing Group, 120 Enterprise Ave., Secaucus, NJ 07094. 1991.

Your library may have some older, out-of-print books on this subject, such as:

Joan Ranson Shortney, *How To Live On Nothing*. Pocket Books, A division of Simon & Schuster, Inc., 200 Old Tappan Rd., Old Tappan, NJ 07675. 1971.

Frances Cerra, ed., *Better Times: The Indispensable Guide to Beating Hard Times*. Dolphin Books. 1975.

You realize, of course, that in Hard Times there are many more job-hunters who list themselves, than there are employers who come there looking for help. So, this cannot be your only strategy for finding money. But it is certainly worth a try. If your experience is out of the mainstream, say in environmental engineering, but you know your field well, you can increase your chances of getting employment through a particular agency by compiling *for them* a list of the companies in your field, together with (if you know it) the name of the contact person there. The temporary agency does much of its business through initiating calls to companies, soliciting their business, and you can help your chances a lot by telling the agency which companies to call, and who to ask for.[8]

You will find the agencies listed in the Yellow Pages of your local phone book, under *Employment–Temporary*. Their listing or their ads will usually indicate what their specialties are.

WHEN MONEY IS SHORT:
(2) PART-TIME WORK

If the temporary agencies never call, and you still can't find any full-time job, your next strategy for bringing some money in, is to look for part-time work.

Part-time work takes many forms:

(1) Some temporary agency work is for part-time work, as we just saw.

(2) You can often find part-time work through a study of the help-wanted ads in the newspaper. If they want part-time workers, they will say so. Experience usually dictates that these jobs will either be at places you like, for much less money than you want, or they will be at places you hate, for a lot more money (e.g., toll-booth collectors, check-out people at supermarkets, etc.) The general rule is: the more boring the job, the higher the pay. You decide.

(3) If you discover -- *through newspaper ads, or by whatever means* -- a full-time job that you are interested in, but you really only want to work part-time for now, you have a dilemma. Fortunately, there is a *possible* solution. You can sometimes sell the organization on the idea of letting *two* of you fill that one job *(one of you from 8–12 noon, say, and the other from 1–5 p.m)*. Of course in order to do this, you have to find someone else -- a relative, friend, or acquaintance -- who is also looking for part-time work, *and* is very competent, *and* would be willing to share that job with you. And you have to find them *first*, and talk them into it, before you approach the boss at that place that interests you. This arrangement is called *job-sharing*, and there are a number of books and places you can write to, if you need some further guidance about how to do it, and how to sell the employer on the idea.[9] Incidentally, don't omit larger employers, from this particular search

---

8. I am indebted to one of our readers, Tathyana Pshevlozky, for this idea.

9. Barney Olmsted and Suzanne Smith, *The Job Sharing Handbook*. Ten Speed Press, Box 7123, Berkeley, CA 94707. 1983. How to share a full-time job with another person, if you don't want to work full-time.
   A Selected Bibliography on Work Time Options. 1989. Order from: New Ways to Work, 149 Ninth

just because they would seem to you to be too bound by their own bureau-cratic rules -- *some* of them are very open to the idea of job-sharing. *On the other hand, a lot of them aren't.*

WHEN MONEY IS SHORT:
(3) SELLING STUFF
OUT OF YOUR OWN HOME

Money is getting *real* tight, and you are beginning to look around your apartment or home with a new and jaundiced eye. *Do I really need that extra television set? Wonder how much money I could get for it?* Your possessions all go and huddle in a corner, fearful that they may be next: *She never really liked me, I know it. I'm heading for the auction block.*

Well, being out of work for a long time does that. You begin to reevalu-ate all the *stuff* (as George Carlin calls it), that you own. How much of it is really necessary? You are on the brink of a values crisis, with a profound reordering of your life hanging in the balance.

So, you pick what you feel you can spare, and you organize a garage sale,[10] with little signs, and pointing arrows, plastered to telephone poles or elsewhere, for blocks around (*do remember to go take them down, after the sale is over, please!*).

If the amount of stuff you have to sell is truly pathetic, then you try to sell your neighbors on the idea of going in with you, for a sort of *neighbor-hood garage sale*, so that there will be a lot of varied merchandise. Analo-gous to this idea of the neighborhood garage sale, is the idea of a 'flea market,' a kind of open market which is held in many metropolitan (and some not-so-metropolitan) areas throughout the U.S. You pay a fee, you set up a table, alongside the other 150 vendors, usually on a Sunday, and hope for the best.

If the garage sale or the flea market doesn't work for you, then you'll probably want to put ads in the local newspaper, and/or ask your friends if they need an old *whatever it is,* at a very reasonable price. Ads are especially

---

St., San Francisco, CA 94103. A 42-page listing of various books, articles, etc., about new ways to work.

In addition to New Ways to Work, there are other centers that are dedicated to helping people who want to find flexible work-time options, such as job-sharing. These places often have helpful pamphlets and other publications. Ask.

Association of Part-Time Professionals, Crescent Plaza, Suite 216, 7700 Leesburg Pike Falls Church, VA 22043. 703-734-7975.

Austin Women's Center, 1700 S. Lamar, #203, Austin, TX 78704. 512-447-9666.

Focus, 509 Tenth Ave. E., Seattle, WA 98102. 206-329-7918.

PHR & Associates, 5515 S. Hurricane Ct., Tempe, AZ 85283. 602-839-8284.

Job-Sharing Manuals, Human Resources Dept., City of Lansing, 119 N. Washington Sq., Lansing, MI 48933. 517-483-4479. (*Ask for a list of their publications, and prices.*)

San Diego Center for Worktime Options, 1200 Third Ave., Suite 1200, San Diego, CA 92101. 619-456-4424.

Work Options, 1611 N. Mosley, Wichita, KS 67214. 316-264-6604.

Workshare, 311 E. 50 St., New York, NY 10022. 212-832-7061.

10. For those in other countries, who have never heard this phrase, it is so called because all the items to be sold are usually displayed in an open garage, facing the street. The sale is usually held on a Saturday or Sunday, so that more people will come by.

recommended if it's something large, like a second car, that you're trying to turn into money.

If this works, with one old car or a lot of littler things, like a VCR, you'll get a couple of hundred bucks out of it. Maybe more. Enough to tide you over, temporarily; which is, after all, all that you were looking for. This isn't a permanent solution to your problems. Just a way of plugging up a hole, for the short-term.

WHEN MONEY IS SHORT:
(4) SELLING YOUR HOME

If you are living in one of the sections of this country that has a high cost of living, you may be able to cut *all* your expenses by selling your present home, or clearing out of your present apartment, and moving to another State, where houses are cheaper, as is food, clothing, and most other things.[11]

One thing I would caution you about: if you presently own, or partially-own your home, reject the idea of selling it, if you are not going immediately to buy another one, but are going to rather use up that capital on living expenses, and simply rent a place. *Don't do it.*

Buy another home, a much cheaper home if necessary, in a different part of the country; but buy another home. Once a former home-owner is into rentals, they may never own their own home again, for the rest of their life, because the cost of housing keeps going up and up, ever beyond their reach. Having rented most of my life, I say: Avoid that fate, like the plague, *if you can.*

Richard Boyer and David Savageau's *Places Rated Almanac: Your Guide to Finding the Best Places to Live in America*[12] will tell you where cheaper places are. It ranks 333 metropolitan areas by their cost of living.

Life out in the country is even cheaper than in metropolitan areas, of course. See page141 in Chapter 7, if you want to consider *that* option.

WHEN MONEY IS SHORT:
(5) BARTERING OR SWAPPING

Swapping, or *bartering,* is a system designed to satisfy two people's needs, without using money between them. The essence of bartering is that you offer to someone something you own, or some work you could perform for them, in exchange for something that they own, or some work that they could perform for you -- without any money ever changing hands. If you offer to trade your old car to your neighbor in exchange for his old car, *that* is barter.

Barter is not only a substitute for money, in some cases it is preferred to money. "In Russia, a repairman will yawn if you offer 30 rubles to get your

---

11. Salaries drop too, in these areas, but not as dramatically as the cost of living does. Usually you still come out way ahead.

12. See your bookstore or library. Or order it from Prentice Hall, a division of Simon & Schuster, Inc., 15 Columbus Circle, New York, NY 10023.

car fixed or your ceiling plugged. But if you offer a bottle of vodka, the job gets done."[13]

And you know this also in your own life. If there's something big that you need to have done to your house or apartment, and you haven't a prayer of affording a professional to come in and do it, *but* your next door neighbor-handy-person offers to do it, *if* you'll let her take your new car away for a skiing weekend -- well, you know you'd be tempted to shake hands on the deal.

Over time, the goods or services which get bartered in this country (and around the world) run the gamut from the obvious to the astonishing: food, clothing, housing (where someone handy with electricity, plumbing and carpentry offers to completely fix up a run-down house, if the landlord gives him or her free lodging there), airline seats, toys for your kids, *complete weddings,* auto repairs. If you can think of it, it can be bartered.

The essence of barter is that you make a list of the things you need, and then of the people who have those things. Then you try to decide what it is you could offer each of them in exchange.

Some of you will know how to do this, instinctively. In many cases, you've done it for years, informally. Others of you will be brand new to this idea, and will wonder how you go about it, in any detail. Going to any local 'flea market' on a weekend, and talking to the people behind the booths or tables there, will quickly give you an education about this. Many of them have become *experts* at this, and will gladly share their learnings and experience.

WHEN MONEY HAS *REALLY* RUN OUT:
(6) STOP-GAP JOBS

This phrase, used by many experts, refers to the situation where there is a gap between the time when your money is about gone, and the time when money will start coming in again, after you have found the kind of work you do best and enjoy most. To fill that time gap, meantime, you take *any kind of work you can get.* That fills, or stops-up, the gap -- hence, *stop-gap job.*

The mark of a stop-gap job is simple: it's a short-term job that you would *hate* if it was anything but short-term. It isn't supposed to be anything you really *like* to do. Its only requirement is that it be honest work, and that it bring in some money. It will probably be less money than you are used to making, per hour. It will probably also be hard work; or boring work. *But,* who cares? Its sole purpose is to put some honest money on the table, so you can eat. And pay the rent. And that's *it.*

The way you go about finding a stop-gap job is simple.

If you have the courage to do this sort of thing, you go to your nearest supermarket and stand out near the street with a sign that says something

---

13. Joseph Albright, Cox News Service, in an article appearing in the *San Francisco Chronicle,* 12/30/91.

like: "Out of work temporarily. Willing to work for $8/hour. Will do anything, but will not accept charity" -- the latter phrase to distinguish you from those who have taken this approach merely as a more elegant method of hustling.

This open-sign-at-the-supermarket will not appeal to very many. So, what's the alternative? Well, you get your local newspaper, you look at the help-wanted ads, and you circle *any* and *every* job that you could see yourself doing *for a short time*, simply for the money. Then you go and apply for those jobs.

You also go to employment agencies, and say, "I'll do *anything;* what have you got?"

Unhappily, this spirit is rarer than it ought to be. Many job-hunters refuse to even consider a stop-gap job; they'd rather go on welfare, first. One reason for this financially-suicidal feeling is the conviction that 'such jobs are *beneath* me.' You know: *"I wouldn't be caught* dead *washing dishes."*

I need to state the obvious here: namely, that **any honest hard work neither demeans you, nor makes you less important as a person.** The 'you' who is doing that work, remains the same. Except that it is a 'you' that *needs this money.* I should also add, while I'm at it, that there are many salutary lessons for the soul, to be learned from temporarily taking a stop-gap job. And this is especially true if that job is at a different level and in a different world than you have been accustomed to.[14]

Many of us delay in seeking a stop-gap job for a somewhat higher reason: namely, the conviction that we must have full-time to devote to our job-hunt. Well, that's important, of course; but so is eating. You may want to consider a part-time stop-gap job, in order to address both concerns, fairly. (Also you might want to keep a *time-log* for two weeks, to see just how much time you actually *are* spending on your job-hunt. The easiest person in the world to deceive is *ourselves.*)

A final reason many refuse to seek a stop-gap job is that they are receiving unemployment benefits, which of course would be cut off, if they took a job of any kind. Presently, for those receiving, say, $230 a week in tax-free unemployment benefits, any job that pays $6.50 an hour or less, will cause a *decrease* in their income. And if the cost of commuting and child care is factored in, as it must be for many single mothers, etc., the cut-off figure per hour is even higher than $6.50.

But, of course, unemployment benefits do run out, and should they run out before you have found a job, then it is a very different story. Run, do not walk, to find a job, any job, find it and take it -- as a stop-gap measure . . . only. And keep looking.

For, as the birds say *(I overheard them just the other day):* "A stop-gap job is like a frail branch of a tree: a lovely place to stop and catch your breath, but a lousy place to build a permanent nest."

---

14. At one point in my life, I took a stop-gap job which involved cutting grass, helping lay cement sidewalks, and building retaining walls. It was one of the most educational experiences of my life. It also brought in exactly the money that I so badly needed.

Surviving Financially On Welfare

If none of the above strategies work for you, you will of course want to consider applying for welfare, somewhere down the line. Currently in the U.S. there are 13 million already on welfare, although this total only includes 4 million adults; the rest are children.

Getting into the program is sometimes incredibly difficult; other times it is relatively easy, especially if you have dependent children. But regardless, if things are getting really hairy for you, financially, go down to your local Welfare office and apply, by all means.

How much can you expect to receive, if you are qualified for welfare? Currently, as I write, the monthly nationwide average of payments, for a family of three, is $402. Food stamps raise that average, nationally, to $623. That comes out, of course, to a *weekly* payment of $155.75. *(This is 27% less, in inflation-adjusted dollars, than the average grant in 1972.)* For jobless families who have exhausted all of their money, it isn't enough, but it is the difference between surviving and starving. Moreover, under the 1988 Family Support Act passed by Congress, you may be introduced into a work-training program, which could help your future employability.

Welfare at its best is intended to be a door into employment, or a temporary 'tiding-over' until conditions in the labor-market improve. We do not know how well this goal is achieved in the case of men, but we do know in the case of women. The statistics are that one-half the women who go onto welfare stay on it for less than four years, and never return to welfare the rest of their lives. However, it doesn't always thus function as a doorway. 25% of the women on welfare do stay on it for more than ten years.[15]

Man or woman, if you decide to apply for it, and you succeed in receiving welfare payments, make it your goal to use it *only* as a temporary resting place, until you can find meaningful work that you truly enjoy doing. Doing the homework in Chapters 9, 10, and 11 are -- for you -- *crucial.*

To use this period of your life well, take time to do more than adjust to tighter financial constraints, or hardship. Take time to think out your

15. Statistics from *The New York Times,* The Week in Review, p. 3, 3/1/92

whole relationship with money, and what is essential and non-essential in your life.

Those who are happiest on a reduced income are those who not only seek to become expert on living on less, but who also search for a kind of voluntary simplicity, with a way of life that is outwardly simple but inwardly rich.[16]

> Yesterday is but a dream,
> Tomorrow is but a vision
> But today well lived makes
> every yesterday a dream of
> happiness, and every tomorrow
> a vision of hope. Look well,
> therefore, to This Day.
>
> *Sanskrit proverb*

---

16. *The* textbook for this is: *Voluntary Simplicity: Toward A Way of Life That is Outwardly Simple, Inwardly Rich,* by Duane Elgin. Quill Press, William Morrow, 1359 Avenue of the Americas, New York NY 10019. 1993 (revised edition).

There are other books, out there, that may also be helpful to you, such as: *Your Money or Your Life: Transforming Your Relationship with Money and Achieving Financial Independence,* by Joe Dominguez and Vicki Robin. Viking Penguin, 375 Hudson St., New York NY 10014. 1992.

Introduction

As I started writing this section on "Religion and Job-Hunting," I toyed at first with the idea of following what might be described as an "all-paths approach" to religion. But, after much thought, I decided not to try that. This, because I have read many other writers who tried, and I felt the approach failed miserably. An "all-paths" approach to religion ends up being a "no-paths" approach, even as a woman or man who tries to please everyone ends up pleasing no one. It is the old story of the "universal" vs. the "particular."

Those of us who do career counseling could predict, ahead of time, that trying to stay universal is not likely to be helpful, in writing about religion. We know well from our own field that truly helpful career counseling depends upon defining the **particularity** or uniqueness of each person we try to help. No employer wants to know only what you have in common with everyone else. He or she wants to know what makes you unique and individual. As I have argued throughout this book, the identification and inventory of your uniqueness or *particularity* is crucial if you are ever to find meaningful work.

This particularity invades and carries over to *everything* a person does; it is not suddenly "jettisonable" when he or she turns to religion. Therefore, when I or anyone else writes about religion I believe we **must** write out of our own particularity -- which *starts*, in my case, with the fact that I write, and think, and breathe as a Christian. So, this article speaks from my own personal Christian perspective. I want you to be forewarned.

I have always been acutely aware, however, that this is a pluralistic society in which we live, and that I owe a great deal of sensitivity to the readers of my books who may have convictions very different from my own. I rub up against these different convictions, daily. By accident and not design it has turned out that the people who work or have worked here in my office with me, over the years, have been predominantly Jewish, along with some non-religious and a smattering of Christians. Furthermore, **Parachute's** more than 4 million readers have included Christians of every variety and persuasion, Jews, members of the Baha'i faith, Hindus, Buddhists, adherents of Islam, and believers in 'new age' religions, as well as (of course) secularists, humanists, agnostics, atheists, and many others. Consequently, I have tried to be very courteous toward the feelings of all my readers who come from other persuasions or convictions than my own, *while at the same time* counting on them to translate my Christian thought forms into their own thought forms -- since this ability to thus translate is the indispensable *sine qua non* of anyone who aspires to communicate helpfully with others.

In the Judeo-Christian tradition from which I come, one of the indignant Biblical questions is, "Has God forgotten to be gracious?" The answer was a clear No. I think it is important *for all of us* also to seek the same goal. I have therefore labored to make this section gracious as well as helpful.

R. N. B.

The Epilogue

Religion
and
Job-Hunting:

How to Find Your Mission in Life

How I Came To Write This

Some time ago, a woman asked me how you go about finding out what your Mission in life is. She assumed I would know what she was talking about, because of a diagram which appears a number of times in one of my other books, The Three Boxes of Life:

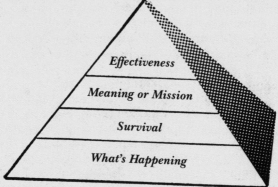

The Issues of the Job-Hunt

As this diagram asserts, the question of one's Mission in life arises naturally as a part of many people's job-hunt.

She told me that what she was looking for was not some careful, dispassionate, philosophical answer, where every statement is hedged about with cautions and caveats -- "It may be . . ." or "It seems to me . . ." Nor did she want to know why I thought what I did, or how I learned it, or what Scriptures support it. "I want you to just speak with passion and conviction," she said, "out of what you most truly feel and believe. For it is some vision that I want. I am hungry for a vision of what I can be. So, just speak to me of what you most truly feel and believe about our mission in life. I will know how to translate your vision into my own thought forms for my own life, when I reflect afterwards upon what you have said. But I want you to talk about this now with passion and conviction -- please."

And so, I did. And I will now tell you what I said to her.

The Motive for Finding
A Sense of Mission in Life

We begin with the fact that, according to fifty years of opinion polls conducted by the Gallup Organization, 94% of us believe in God, 90% of us pray, 88% of us believe God loves us, and 33% of us report we have had a life-changing religious experience (*The People's Religion: American Faith in the 90s. Macmillan & Co. 1989*).

It is hardly surprising therefore, that so many of us are searching these days for some sense of mission. Career counselors are often afraid to give help or guidance here, for fear they will be perceived as trying to talk people into religious belief. It is a groundless fear. Clearly, the overwhelming majority of U.S. job-hunters and career-changers already have their religious beliefs well in place.

But, we want some guidance and help in this area, because we want to *marry* our religious **beliefs** with our **work**, rather than leaving the two -- our religion and our work -- compartmentalized, as two areas of our life which never talk to each other. We *want* them to talk to each other and uplift each other.

This marriage takes the particular form of a search for a Sense of Mission because of our conviction that God has made each of us unique, even as our fingerprints attest. We feel that we are not just another grain of sand lying on the beach called humanity, unnumbered and lost in the 5 billion mass, but that God caused us to be born and put here for some unique reason: so that we might contribute to Life here on earth something no one else can contribute in quite the same way. At its very minimum, then, when we search for a sense of Mission we are searching for reassurance that the world is at least a little bit richer for our being here; and a little bit poorer after our going.

Every keen observer of human nature will know what I mean when I say that those who have found some sense of Mission have a very special joy, "which no one can take from them." It is wonderful to feel that beyond eating, sleeping, working, having pleasure and *it may be* marrying, having children, and growing older, you were set here on Earth for some special purpose, *and* that you can gain some idea of what that purpose is.

So, how does one go about this search?

I would emphasize, at the outset, two cautions. First of all, though I will explain the steps that seem to me to be involved in finding one's Mission -- based on the learnings I have accumulated over some sixty years, I want to caution you that these steps are not the only Way -- by any means. Many people have discovered their Mission by taking other paths. And you may, too. But hopefully what I have to say may shed some light upon whatever path you take.

My second caution is simply this: you would be wise not to try to approach this problem of "your Mission in life" as primarily an **intellectual** puzzle -- for the mind, and the mind alone, to solve. To paraphrase Kahlil Gibran, *Faith* is an oasis in the heart that is not reached merely by the journey of the mind. It is your will and your heart that must be involved in the search as well as your mind. To put it quite simply, it takes the total person to learn one's total Mission.

It also takes the total disciplines of the ages -- not only modern knowledge but also ancient thought, including the wisdom of religion, faith, and the spiritual matters. For, to put it quite bluntly, the question of Mission inevitably leads us to God.

The Main Obstacle in Finding Your Mission in Life: Job-Hunting Compartmentalized from Our Religion or Faith

Mission challenges us to see our job-hunt in relationship to our faith in God, because *Mission* is a religious concept, from beginning to end. It is defined by Webster's as "a continuing task or responsibility that one is destined or fitted to do or specially called upon to undertake," and historically has had two major synonyms: *Calling* and *Vocation*. These, of course, are the same word in two different languages, English and Latin. Regardless of which word is used, it is obvious upon reflection, that a Vocation or Calling implies *Someone who calls*, and that a destiny implies *Someone who determined the destination for us*. Thus, unless one opts for a military or governmental view of the matter, the concept of Mission with relationship to our whole life lands us inevitably in the lap of God, before we have even begun.

There is always the temptation to try to speak of this subject of *Mission* in a secular fashion, without reference to God, as though it might be simply "a purpose you choose for your own life, by identifying your enthusiasms, and then using the clues you find from that exercise to get some purpose you can choose for your life." The language of this temptation is ironic because the substitute word used for "Mission" -- *Enthusiasm* -- is derived from the Greek, *'en theos,'* and literally means "God in us."

It is no accident that so many of the leaders in the job-hunting field over the years -- the late John Crystal, Arthur Miller, Ralph Mattson, Tom and Ellie Jackson, Bernard Haldane, Arthur and Marie Kirn, and myself -- have been people of faith. If you would figure out your Mission in life, you must also be willing to think about God in connection with your job-hunt.

The Secret of Finding Your Mission in Life: Taking It in Stages

The puzzle of figuring out what your Mission in life is, will likely take some time. It is not a *problem* to be solved in a day and a night. It is a *learning process* which has steps to it, much like the process by which we all learned to eat. As a baby we did not tackle adult food right off. As we all recall, there were three stages: first there had to be the mother's milk or bottle, then strained baby foods, and finally -- after teeth and time -- the stuff that grown-ups chew. Three stages -- and the two earlier stages were not to be disparaged. It was all Eating, just different forms of Eating -- appropriate to our development at the time. But each stage had to be mastered, in turn, before the next could be approached.

The Three Stages of Mission:
What We Need to Learn

By coincidence, there are usually three stages also to learning what your Mission in life is, and the two earlier stages are likewise not to be disparaged. It is all "Mission" -- just different forms of Mission, appropriate to your development at the time. But each stage has to be mastered, in turn, before the next can be approached. And so, you may say either of two things: You may say that you have *Three Missions in Life*. Or you may say that you have *One Mission in Life, with three parts to it*. But there is a sense in which you must discover what those three parts are, each in turn, before you can fully answer the question, "What is my Mission in life?" Of course, there is another sense in which you never master any of these stages, but are always growing in understanding and mastery of them, throughout your whole life here on Earth.

As it has been impressed on me by observing many people over the years (admittedly through *Christian spectacles*), it appears that the three parts to your Mission here on Earth can be defined generally as follows:

(1) *Your first Mission here on Earth* is one which you share with the rest of the human race, but it is no less your individual Mission for the fact that it is shared: and it is, **to seek to stand hour by hour in the conscious presence of God, the One from whom your Mission is derived.** *The Missioner before the Mission*, is the rule. In religious language, your Mission here is: *to know God, and enjoy Him forever, and to see His hand in all His works.*

(2) Secondly, once you have begun doing that in an earnest way, *your second Mission here on Earth* is also one which you share with the rest of the human race, but it is no less your individual mission for the fact that it is shared: and that is, **to do what you can, moment by moment, day by day, step by step, to make this world a better place, following the leading and guidance of God's Spirit within you and around you.**

(3) Thirdly, once you have begun doing that in a serious way, *your third Mission here on Earth* is one which is uniquely yours, and that is:

   a) **to exercise that Talent which you particularly came to Earth to use -- your greatest gift, which you most delight to use,**
   b) **in the place(s) or setting(s) which God has caused to appeal to you the most,**
   c) **and for those purposes which God most needs to have done in the world.**

When fleshed out, and spelled out, I think you will find that there you have the definition of your Mission in life. Or, to put it another way, these are the three Missions which you have in life.

The Two Rhythms of the Dance of Mission:
Unlearning, Learning,
Unlearning, Learning

The distinctive characteristic of these three stages is that in each we are forced to *let go* of some fundamental assumptions which the world has *falsely* taught us, about the nature of our Mission. In other words, throughout this quest and at each stage we find ourselves engaged not merely in a process of *Learning*. We are also engaged in a process of *Un*learning. Thus, we can restate the above three Learnings, in terms of what we also need to *un*learn at each stage:

• We need in the first Stage to *un*learn the idea that our Mission is primarily to keep busy *doing* something (here on Earth), and learn instead that our Mission is first of all to keep busy being something (here on Earth). In Christian language (and others as well), we might say that we were sent here to learn how *to be* sons of God, and daughters of God, before anything else. *"Our Father, who art in heaven . . ."*

• In the second stage, "Being" issues into "Doing." At this stage, we need to *un*learn the idea that everything about our Mission must be *unique* to us, and learn instead that some parts of our Mission here on Earth are *shared* by all human beings: e.g., we were all sent here to bring more gratitude, more kindness, more forgiveness, and more love, into the world. We share this Mission because the task is too large to be accomplished by just one individual.

• We need in the third stage to *un*learn the idea that that part of our Mission which is truly unique, and most truly ours, is something Our Creator just *orders* us to do, without any agreement from our spirit, mind, and heart. (On the other hand, neither is it something that each of us chooses and then merely asks God to bless.) We need to learn that God so honors our free will, that He has ordained our unique Mission be something which we have some part in choosing.

• In this third stage we need also to *un*learn the idea that our unique Mission must consist of some achievement which all the world will see, -- and learn instead that as the stone does not always know what ripples it has caused in the pond whose surface it impacts, so neither we nor those who watch our life will always know *what we have achieved* by our life and by our Mission. *It may be* that by the grace of God we helped bring about a profound change for the better in the lives of other souls around us, but it also may be that this takes place beyond our sight, or after we have gone on. And we may never know what we have accomplished, until we see Him face-to-face after this life is past.

• Most finally, we need to *un*learn the idea that what we have accomplished is our doing, and ours alone. It is God's Spirit breathing in us and through us which helps us to do whatever we do, and so the singular first person pronoun is never appropriate, but only the plural. Not *"I* accomplished this" but *"We* accomplished this, God and I, working together . . ."

That should give you a general overview. But I would like to add some random comments on my part about each of these three Missions of ours here on Earth.

Some Random Comments About Your First Mission in Life

Your first Mission here on Earth is one which you share with the rest of the human race, but it is no less your individual Mission for the fact that it is shared: and that is, **to seek to stand hour by hour in the conscious presence of God, the One from whom your Mission is derived.** The Missioner before the Mission, is the rule. In religious language, your Mission is: to know God, and enjoy Him for ever, and to see His hand in all His works.

Comment 1: How We Might Think of God

Each of us has to go about this primary Mission according to the tenets of his or her own particular religion. But I will speak what I know out of the context of my own particular faith, and you may perhaps translate and apply it to yours. I will speak as a Christian, who believes (passionately) that Christ is the Way and the Truth and the Life. But I also believe, with St. Peter, "that God shows no partiality, but in every nation any one who fears him and does what is right is acceptable to him." (Acts 10:34-35)

Now, Jesus claimed many unique things about Himself and His Mission; but He also spoke of Himself as the great prototype for us all. He called himself "the Son of Man," and He said, "I assure you that the man who believes in me will do the same things that I have done, yes, and he will do even greater things than these . . ." (John 14:12)

Emboldened by His identification of us with His life and His Mission, we might want to remember how He spoke about His Life here on Earth. He put it in this context: **"I came from the Father and have come into the world; again, I am leaving the world and going to the Father."** (John 16:28)

If there is a sense in which this is, in even the faintest way, true also of our lives (and I shall say in a moment in what sense I think it is true), then instead of calling our great Creator "God" or "Father" right off, we might begin our approach to the subject of religion by referring to the One Who gave us our Mission and sent us to this planet not as "God" or "Father" but -- *just to help our thinking* -- as: **"The One From Whom We Came and The One To Whom We Shall Return,"** when this life is done.

If our life here on Earth be at all like Christ's, then this is a true way to think about the One who gave us our Mission. We are not some kind of eternal, pre-existent *being*. We are **creatures**, who once did not exist, and then came into Being, and continue to have our Being, only at the will of our great Creator. But as creatures we are both body and soul; and although we know our body was created in our mother's womb, our soul's origin is a great mystery. Where it came from, at what moment the Lord created it, is something we cannot know. It is not unreasonable to suppose, however, that the great God created our *soul* before it entered our body, and in that sense we did indeed stand before God before we were born; and He is indeed **"The One From Whom We Came and The One To Whom We Shall Return."**

Therefore, before we go searching for "what work was I sent here to do?" we need to establish or in a truer sense *reestablish* -- contact with this **"One From Whom We Came and The One To Whom We Shall Return."** Without this reaching out of the creature to the great Creator, without this reaching out of *the creature with a Mission* to *the One Who Gave Us That Mission*, the question **what** *is my Mission in life?* is void and null. The *what* is rooted in the *Who*; absent the Personal, one cannot meaningfully discuss The Thing. It is like the adult who cries, "I want to get married," without giving any consideration to *who* it is they want to marry.

Comment 2: How We Might Think of Religion or Faith

In light of this larger view of our creatureliness, we can see that *religion* or *faith* is not a question of whether or not we choose to (*as it is so commonly put*) "have a relationship with God." Looking at our life in a larger context than just our life here on Earth, it becomes apparent that some sort of relationship with God is a given for us, about which we have absolutely no choice. God and we **were and are** related, during the time of our soul's existence before our birth and in the time of our soul's continued existence after our death. The only choice we have is what to do about **The Time In Between,** i.e., what we want the nature of our relationship with God to be during our time here on Earth and how that will affect the *nature* of the relationship, then, after death.

One of the corollaries of all this is that by the very act of being born into a human body, it is an inevitable that we undergo a kind of *amnesia* -- an amnesia which typically embraces not only our nine months in the womb, our baby years, and almost one third of each day (sleeping), but more importantly any memory of our origin or our destiny. We wander on Earth as an amnesia victim. To seek after Faith, therefore, is to seek to climb back out of that amnesia. Religion or faith is **the hard reclaiming of knowledge we once knew as a certainty.**

Comment 3: The First Obstacle to Executing This Mission

This first Mission of ours here on Earth is not the easiest of Missions, simply because it is the first. Indeed, in many ways, it is the most difficult. All can see that our life here on Earth is a very physical life. We eat, we drink, we sleep, we long to be held, and to hold. We inherit a physical body, with very physical appetites, we walk on the physical earth, and we acquire physical possessions. It is the most alluring of temptations, *in our amnesia*, to come up with just a *Physical* interpretation of this life: to think that the Universe is merely interested in the survival of species. Given this interpretation, the story of our individual life could be simply told: we are born, grow up, procreate, and die.

But we are ever recalled to do what we came here to do: that without rejecting the joy of the Physicalness of this life, such as the love of the blue sky and the green grass, we are to reach out beyond all this to **recall** and recover a *Spiritual* interpretation of our life. *Beyond* the physical and *within* the physicalness of this life, to detect a Spirit and a Person from beyond this Earth who is with us and in us -- the very real and loving and awesome Presence of the great Creator from whom we came -- and the One to whom we once again shall go.

Comment 4: The Second Obstacle to Executing This Mission

It is one of the conditions of our earthly amnesia and our creatureliness that, sadly enough, some very *human* and very *rebellious* part of us *likes* the idea of living in a world where we can be our own god -- and therefore loves the purely Physical interpretation of life, and finds it *anguish* to relinquish it. Traditional Christian vocabulary calls this **"sin"** and has a lot to say about the difficulty it poses for this first part of our Mission. All who live a thoughtful life know that it is true: our greatest enemy in carrying out this first Mission of ours is indeed *our own* heart and our own rebellion.

Comment 5: Further Thoughts About What Makes Us Special and Unique

As I said earlier, many of us come to this issue of our Mission in life, because we want to feel that we are unique. And what we mean by that, is that we hope to discover some "specialness" intrinsic to us, which is our birthright, and which no one can take from us. What we, however, discover from a thorough exploration of this topic, is that we are indeed special -- but only because God thinks us so. Our specialness and uniqueness reside in Him, and His love, rather than in anything intrinsic to our own *being*. The proper appreciation of this distinction causes our feet to carry us in the end not to the City called Pride, but to the Temple called Gratitude.

> What is religion? Religion is the service of God
> out of grateful love for what God has done for us.
> The Christian religion, more particularly, is the
> service of God out of grateful love for what God
> has done for us in Christ.
>
> Phillips Brooks, author of
> *O Little Town of Bethlehem*

Comment 6: The Unconscious Doing of
The Work We Came To Do

You may have *already* wrestled with this first part of your Mission here on Earth. You may not have called it that. You may have called it simply "learning to believe in God." But if you ask what your Mission is in life, this one was and is the precondition of all else that you came here to do. Absent this Mission, and it is folly to talk about the rest. So, if you have been seeking faith, or seeking to strengthen your faith, you have -- willy nilly -- already been about *the doing of the Mission you were given.* Born into **This Time In Between,** you have found His hand again, and reclasped it. You are therefore ready to go on with His Spirit to tackle together what you came here to do -- the other parts of your Mission.

Some Random Comments About
Your Second Mission in Life

Your second Mission here on Earth is also one which you share with the rest of the human race, but it is no less your individual mission for the fact that it is shared: and that is, **to do what you can moment by moment, day by day, step by step, to make this world a better place -- following the leading and guidance of God's Spirit within you and around you.**

Comment 1: The Uncomfortableness of
One Step at a Time

Imagine yourself out walking in your neighborhood one night, and suddenly you find yourself surrounded by such a dense fog, that you have lost your bearings and cannot find your way. Suddenly, a friend appears out of the fog, and asks you to put your hand in theirs, and they will lead you home. And you, not being able to tell where you are going, trustingly follow them, even though you can only see one step at a time. Eventually you arrive safely home, filled with gratitude. But as you reflect upon the experience the next day, you realize how unsettling it was to have to keep walking when you could see only one step at a time, even though you had guidance in which you knew you could trust.

Now I have asked you to imagine all of this, because this is the essence of the second Mission to which *you* are called -- and *I* am called -- in this life. It is all very different than we had imagined. When the question,

"What is your Mission in life?" is first broached, and we have put our hand in God's, as it were, we imagine that we will be taken up to *some mountaintop,* from which we can see far into the distance. And that we will hear a voice in our ear, saying, "Look, look, see that distant city? That is the goal of your Mission; that is where everything is leading, every step of your way."

But instead of the mountaintop, we find ourself in *the valley* -- wandering often in a fog. And the voice in our ear says something quite different from what we thought we would hear. It says, **"Your Mission is to take one step at a time, even when you don't yet see where it all is leading, or what the Grand Plan is, or what your overall Mission in life is. Trust Me; I will lead you."**

Comment 2: The Nature of This Step-by-Step Mission

As I said, in every situation you find yourself, you have been sent here to do whatever you can -- moment by moment -- that will bring more gratitude, more kindness, more forgiveness, more honesty, and more love into this world.

There are dozens of such moments every day. Moments when you stand -- as it were -- at a spiritual crossroads, with two ways lying before you. Such moments are typically called **"moments of decision."** It does not matter what the frame or content of each particular decision is. It all devolves, in the end, into just two roads before you, *every time.* **The one** will lead to *less* gratitude, *less* kindness, *less* forgiveness, *less* honesty, or *less* love in the world. **The other** will lead to *more* gratitude, *more* kindness, *more* forgiveness, *more* honesty, or *more* love in the world. Your Mission, each moment, is to seek to choose the latter spiritual road, rather than the former, *every time.*

Comment 3: Some Examples of This Step-by-Step Mission

I will give a few examples, so that the nature of this part of your Mission may be unmistakably clear.

You are out on the freeway, in your car. Someone has gotten into the wrong lane, to the right of *your* lane, and needs to move over into the lane you are in. You *see* their need to cut in, ahead of you. **Decision time.** In your mind's eye you see two spiritual roads lying before you: the one leading to less kindness in the world (you speed up, to shut this driver out, and don't let them move over), the other leading to more kindness in the world (you let the driver cut in). **Since you know this is part of your Mission, part of the reason why you came to Earth, your calling is clear. You know which road to take, which decision to make.**

You are hard at work at your desk, when suddenly an interruption comes. The phone rings, or someone is at the door. They need something from you, a question of some of your time and attention. **Decision time.**

In your mind's eye you see two spiritual roads lying before you: the one leading to less love in the world (you tell them you're just too busy to be bothered), the other leading to more love in the world (you put aside your work, decide that God may have sent this person to you, and say, "Yes, what can I do to help you?"). **Since you know this is part of your Mission, part of the reason why you came to Earth, your calling is clear. You know which road to take, which decision to make.**

Your mate does something that hurts your feelings. **Decision time.** In your mind's eye you see two spiritual roads lying before you: the one leading to less forgiveness in the world (you institute an icy silence between the two of you, and think of how you can punish them or otherwise get

even), the other leading to more forgiveness in the world (you go over and take them in your arms, speak the truth about your hurt feelings, and assure them of your love). **Since you know this is part of your Mission, part of the reason why you came to Earth, your calling is clear. You know which road to take, which decision to make.**

You have not behaved at your most noble, recently. And now you are face-to-face with someone who asks you a question about what happened. **Decision time.** In your mind's eye you see two spiritual roads lying before you: the one leading to less honesty in the world (you lie about what happened, or what you were feeling, because you fear losing their respect or their love), the other leading to more honesty in the world (you tell the truth, together with how you feel about it, in retrospect). **Since you know this is part of your Mission, part of the reason why you came to Earth, your calling is clear. You know which road to take, which decision to make.**

Comment 4: The Spectacle Which Makes the Angels Laugh

It is necessary to explain this part of our Mission in some detail, because so many times you will see people wringing their hands, and saying, *"I want to know what my Mission in life is,"* all the while they are cutting people off on the highway, refusing to give time to people, punishing their mate for having hurt their feelings, and lying about what they did. And it will seem to you that the angels must laugh to see this spectacle. *For these people wringing their hands,* their Mission was right there, on the freeway, in the interruption, in the hurt, and at the confrontation.

Comment 5: The Valley vs. The Mountaintop

At some point in your life your Mission may involve some grand *mountaintop experience,* where you say to yourself, "This, this, is why I came into the world. I know it. I know it." *But until then,* your Mission is here in *the valley,* and the fog, and the little callings moment by moment, day by day. More to the point, it is likely you cannot ever get to your mountaintop Mission unless you have first exercised your stewardship faithfully in the valley.

It is an ancient principle, to which Jesus alluded often, that if you don't use the information the Universe has already given you, you cannot expect it will give you any more. If you aren't being faithful in small things, how can you expect to be given charge over larger things? (Luke 16:10,11,12; 19:11-24) If you aren't trying to bring more gratitude, kindness, forgiveness, honesty, and love into the world each day, you can hardly expect that you will be entrusted with the Mission to help bring peace into the world or anything else large and important. If we do not live out our day-by-day Mission in the valley, we cannot expect we are yet ready for a larger *mountaintop* Mission.

Comment 6: The Importance of Not Thinking of This Mission As 'Just A Training Camp'

The valley is not just a kind of "training camp." There is in your imagination even now an invisible *spiritual* mountaintop to which you may go, if you wish to see where all this is leading. And what will you see there, in the imagination of your heart, but the goal toward which all this is pointed: **that Earth might be more like heaven. That human's life might be more like God's.** That is the large achievement toward which all our day by day Missions *in the valley* are moving. This is a *large* order, but it is accomplished by faithful attention to the doing of our great Creator's **will** in little things as well as in large. It is much like the building of the pyramids in Egypt, which was accomplished by the dragging of a lot of individual pieces of stone by a lot of individual men.

The valley, the fog, the going step-by-step, is no mere training camp. The goal is real, however large. **"Thy Kingdom come, Thy will be done, on Earth, as it is in heaven."**

Some Random Comments About Your Third Mission in Life

Your third Mission here on Earth is one which is uniquely yours, and that is:

    a) **to exercise that Talent which you particularly came to Earth to use -- your greatest gift which you most delight to use**

    b) **in those place(s) or setting(s) which God has caused to appeal to you the most,**

    c) **and for those purposes which God most needs to have done in the world.**

Comment 1: Our Mission Is Already Written, "in Our Members"

It is customary in trying to identify this part of our Mission, to advise that we should ask God, in prayer, to speak to us -- and **tell us** plainly what our Mission is. We look for a voice in the air, a thought in our head, a dream in the night, a sign in the events of the day, to reveal this thing which is otherwise *(it is said)* completely hidden. Sometimes, from just such answered prayer, people do indeed discover what their Mission is, beyond all doubt and uncertainty.

But having to wait for the voice of God to reveal what our Mission is, is not the truest picture of our situation. St. Paul, in Romans, speaks of a law "written in our members," -- and this phrase has a telling application to the question of **how** God reveals to each of us our unique Mission in life. Read again the definition of our third Mission (above) and you will see: the clear implication of the definition is that God has **already** revealed His will to us concerning our vocation and Mission, by causing it to be **"written in our members."** We are to begin deciphering our unique Mission by studying our talents and skills, and more particularly which ones (or One) we most rejoice to use.

God actually has written His will *twice* in our members: *first in the talents* which He lodged there, and secondly *in His guidance of our heart*, as to which talent gives us the greatest pleasure from its exercise (**it is usually the one which, when we use it, causes us to lose all sense of time).**

Even as the anthropologist can examine ancient inscriptions, and divine from them the daily life of a long lost people, so we by examining **our talents** and **our heart** can *more often than we dream* divine the Will of the Living God. For true it is, our Mission is not something He **will** reveal; it is something He **has already** revealed. It is not to be found written in the sky; it is to be found written in our members.

Comment 2: Career Counseling:
We Need You

Arguably, our first two Missions in life could be learned from religion alone -- without any reference whatsoever to career counseling, the subject of this book. Why then should career counseling claim that this question about our Mission in life is its proper concern, *in any way?*

It is when we come to this third Mission, which hinges so crucially on the question of our Talents, skills, and gifts, that we see the answer. If you've read the body of this book, before turning to this Epilogue, you know without my even saying it, how much the identification of Talents, gifts, or skills is the province of career counseling. Its expertise, indeed its *raison d'etre*, lies precisely in the identification, classification, and (forgive me) "prioritization" of Talents, skills, and gifts. To put the matter quite simply, career counseling knows how to do this better than any other discipline -- **including** traditional religion. This is not a defect of religion, but the fulfillment of something Jesus promised: "When the Spirit of truth comes, He will guide you into all truth." (John 16:12) Career counseling is part (we may hope) of that promised late-coming truth. It can therefore be of inestimable help to the pilgrim who is trying to figure out what their greatest, and most enjoyable, talent is, as a step toward identifying their unique Mission in life.

If career counseling needs religion as its helpmate in the first two stages of identifying our Mission in life, religion repays the compliment by clearly needing career counseling as **its** helpmate here in the third stage.

And this place where you are in your life right now -- facing the job-hunt and all its anxiety -- is the perfect time to seek the union within your own mind and heart of both career counseling (as in the pages of this book) and your faith in God.

Comment 3: How Our Mission Got Chosen:
A Scenario for the Romantic

It is a mystery which we cannot fathom, in this life at least, as to why one of us has this talent, and the other one has that; why God chose to give one gift -- and Mission -- to one person, and a different gift -- and Mission -- to another. Since we do not know, and in some degree cannot know, we are certainly left free to speculate, and imagine.

We may imagine that before we came to Earth, our souls, *our Breath, our Light,* stood before the great Creator and volunteered for this Mission. And God and we, together, chose what that Mission would be and what particular gifts would be needed, which He then agreed to give us, after our birth. Thus, our Mission was not a command given peremptorily by an unloving Creator to a reluctant slave without a vote, but was a task jointly designed by us both, in which as fast as the great Creator said, **"I wish"** our hearts responded, **"Oh, yes."** As mentioned in an earlier Comment, it may be helpful to think of the condition of our becoming human as that we became amnesiac about any consciousness our soul had before birth -- and therefore amnesiac about the nature or manner in which our Mission was designed.

Our searching for our Mission now is therefore a searching to recover the memory of something we ourselves had a part in designing.

I am admittedly a hopeless romantic, so of course I like this picture. If you also are a hopeless romantic, you may like it too. There's also the chance that it just may be true. We will not know until we see Him face-to-face.

Comment 4: Mission As Intersection

There are all different kinds of voices calling you to all different kinds of work, and the problem is to find out which is the voice of God rather than that of society, say, or the superego, or self-interest. By and large a good rule for finding out is this: the kind of work God usually calls you to is the kind of work (a) that you need most to do and (b) the world most needs to have done. If you really get a kick out of your work, you've presumably met requirement (a), but if your work is writing TV deodorant commercials, the chances are you've missed requirement (b). On the other hand, if your work is being a doctor in a leper colony, you have probably met (b), but if most of the time you're bored and depressed by it, the chances are you haven't only bypassed (a) but probably aren't helping your patients much either. Neither the hair shirt nor the soft birth will do. **The place God calls you to is the place where your deep gladness and the world's deep hunger meet.**

Frederick Buechner
Wishful Thinking -- A Theological ABC

Comment 5: Examples of Mission As Intersection

Your unique and individual mission will most likely turn out to be a mission of Love, acted out in one or all of three arenas: either in the Kingdom of the Mind, whose goal is to bring more Truth into the world; or in the Kingdom of the Heart, whose goal is to bring more beauty into the world; or in the Kingdom of the Will, whose goal is to bring more Perfection into the world, through Service.

Here are some examples:

"My mission is, out of the rich reservoir of love which God seems to have given me, to nurture and show love to others -- most particularly to those who are suffering from incurable diseases."

"My mission is to draw maps for people to show them how to get to God."

"My mission is to create the purest foods I can, to help people's bodies not get in the way of their spiritual growth."

"My mission is to make the finest harps I can so that people can hear the voice of God in the wind."

"My mission is to make people laugh, so that the travail of this earthly life doesn't seem quite so hard to them."

"My mission is to help people know the truth, in love, about what is happening out in the world, so that there will be more honesty in the world."

"My mission is to weep with those who weep, so that in my arms they may feel themselves in the arms of that Eternal Love which sent me and which created them."

"My mission is to create beautiful gardens, so that in the lilies of the field people may behold the Beauty of God and be reminded of the Beauty of Holiness."

Comment 6: Life As Long As Your Mission Requires

Knowing that you came to Earth for a reason, and knowing what that Mission is, throws an entirely different light upon your life from now on. You are, generally speaking, delivered from any further fear about how long you have to live. You may settle it in your heart that you are here until God chooses to think that you have accomplished your Mission, or until God has a greater Mission for you in another Realm. You need to be a good steward of what He has given you, while you are here; but you do not need to be an anxious steward or stewardess.

You need to attend to your health, *but you do not need to constantly worry about it.* You need to meditate on your death, *but you do not need to be constantly preoccupied with it.* To paraphrase the glorious words of G. K. Chesterton: **"We now have a strong desire for living combined with a strange carelessness about dying. We desire life like water and yet are ready to drink death like wine."** We know that we are here to do what we came to do, and we need not worry about anything else.

Final Comment: A Job-Hunt Done Well

If you approach your job-hunt as an opportunity to work on this issue as well as the issue of how you will keep body and soul together, then hopefully your job-hunt will end with your being able to say: "Life has deep meaning to me, now. I have discovered more than my ideal job; I have found my Mission, and the reason why I am here on Earth."

For Further Reading

Most, though not all, of the following resources are written from a Judaic-Christian viewpoint, but they should be suggestive and helpful for people of any faith, as you mentally translate these texts into your own thought-forms and concepts of your faith:

Mattson, Ralph, and Miller, Arthur, *Finding a Job You Can Love.* Thomas Nelson Publishers, Nelson Place at Elm Hill Pike, Nashville, TN 37214. 1982. The most useful, I think, of all the books in this section.

Lewis, Roy, *Choosing Your Career, Finding Your Vocation: A Step by Step Guide for Adults and Counselors.* Integration Books, Paulist Press, 997 Macarthur Blvd., Mahwah, NJ 07430. 1990. Particularly helpful for mid-life issues.

Blanchard, Tim, *A Practical Guide to Finding and Using Your Spiritual Gifts.* Tyndale House Publishers, Inc., Wheaton, Illinois.

Moran, Pamela J., *The Christian Job Hunter.* Servant Publications, 840 Airport Blvd., Box 8617, Ann Arbor, MI 48107. 1984.

Edwards, Lloyd, *Discerning Your Spiritual Gifts.* Cowley Publications, 980 Memorial Drive, Cambridge, MA 02138. 1988.

Moore, Christopher Chamberlin, *What I Really Want To Do . . . : How to Discover The Right Job.* CBP Press, Box 179, St. Louis, MO 63166. 1989.

Roskind, Robert, *In The Spirit of Business: Applying the Principles of* A Course in Miracles *to Business.* Celestial Arts, P.O. Box 7123, Berkeley, CA 94707. 1992.

A Center for the Practice of Zen Buddhist Meditation, *That Which You Are Seeking Is Causing You to Seek.* Available from the Center, P.O. Box 91, Mountain View, CA 94042. 1990. A *great* title, and a very interesting book, written -- of course -- from the Buddhist point of view, with one of the contributors being a woman who was dying (and has since died) from cancer.

Staub, Dick; Trautman, Jeff; and Cutshall, Mark, eds., *Intercristo's CAREER KIT: A Christian's Guide to Career Building.* Intercristo, 19303 Fremont Ave. N., Seattle WA 98133. 1985. Booklets (6) and cassette tapes (3) enclosed in binder.

Wehrheim, Carol and Cole-Turner, Ronald S., *Vocation and Calling. Introduction/Hearing God's Call/Sharing Gifts: An Intergenerational Study Guide.* United Church Press, 475 Riverside Dr., 10th fl., New York, NY 10115. 1985.

Rinker, Richard N., and Eisentrout, Virginia, *Called to Be Gifted and Giving: An Adult Resource for Vocation and Calling.* United Church Press, 475 Riverside Dr., 10th fl., New York, NY 10115. 1985.

For Counseling

All counselors in these centers are sincere; many are also very skilled. If you run into a clerical counselor who is sincere but inept, you will probably discover that the ineptness consists in an inadequate understanding of the distinction between career **assessment** -- roughly comparable to taking a snapshot of people as they are in one frozen moment of time -- vs. career **development** -- which is roughly comparable to teaching people how to take their own motion pictures of themselves, from here on out.

Having issued this caution, however, I will go on to add that at some of these centers, listed below, are some simply *excellent* counselors who fully understand this distinction, and are well trained in that empowering of the client, which is what career *development* is all about.

We begin with counseling centers founded primarily to help **clergy** (though in most cases not restricted just to them). No profession has developed, or had developed for it, so many resources to aid in career assessment as has this profession.

THE OFFICIAL INTERDENOMINATIONAL CAREER DEVELOPMENT CENTERS

The Career and Personal
Counseling Service
St. Andrew's Presbyterian College
Laurinburg, NC 28352
919-276-3162
Also at: 4108 Park Rd., Suite 200
Charlotte, NC 28209
704-523-7751
Elbert R. Patton, Director

The Career and Personal
Counseling Center
Eckerd College
St. Petersburg, FL 33733
813-864-8356, Ext. 356
John R. Sims, Director

The Center for Ministry
8393 Capwell Dr., Suite 220
Oakland, CA 94621-2123
510-635-4246
Robert L. Charpentier, Director

Lancaster Career
Development Center
561 College Ave.
Lancaster, PA 17603
717-397-7451
L. Guy Mehl, Director

North Central Career
Development Center
3000 Fifth St. NW
New Brighton, MN 55112
612-636-5120
John Davis, Director

Northeast Career Center
407 Nassau Street
Princeton, NJ 08540
609-924-9408
Roy Lewis, Director

Career Development Center
of the Southeast
531 Kirk Rd.
Decatur, GA 30030
404-371-0336
Robert M. Urie, Director

Midwest Career
Development Service
1840 Westchester Blvd.
Westchester, IL 60154
708-343-6268
Also at: 2501 North Star Rd.
Columbus, OH 43221
614-486-0469
Also at: 754 N. 31st St.
Kansas City, KS 66110
Ronald Brushwyler, Director

Southwest Career
Development Center
Box 5923
Arlington, TX 76011
817-640-5181
William M. Gould, Jr.,
Director-Counselor

Center for Career
Development and Ministry
70 Chase St.
Newton Center, MA 02159
617-969-7750
Stephen Ott, Director.

Clergy wishing to stay within the parish ministry, but wanting help with the search, will want to know about:

Mead, Loren B., and Miller, Arthur F., and Ayers, Russell C., and Bolles, Richard N., *Your Next Pastorate: Starting the Search*. Order #AL122 from The Alban Institute, Inc., 4125 Nebraska Ave., N.W., Washington, DC 20016.

And now, on to centers which are open to anyone, and do career counseling from a spiritual point of view:

ALSO DOING CAREER COUNSELING FROM A RELIGIOUS POINT OF VIEW

(These are listed by general geographical location, from West Coast to East Coast, North to South)

People Management Group International, P.O. Box 33608, **Seattle, WA** 98133, 206-443-1107. Arthur F. Miller, Jr., Chairman. Dick Staub, President.

Bernard Haldane, Wellness Education Council, 4502 54th NW, **Seattle, WA** 98105, 206-525-2205. A pioneer in the clergy career management and assessment field, Bernard teaches *(totally independently of the agency which bears his name)* seminars and training of volunteers (particularly in churches) to do job-search counseling.

Lifework Design, 448 S. Marengo Ave., **Pasadena, CA** 91101, 818-577-2705. Kevin Brennfleck, M.A., and Kay Marie Breenfleck, M.A., Directors.

Olson Counseling Services, 8720 Frederick, Suite 105, **Omaha, NE** 68124, 402-390-2342. Gail A. Olson, P.A.C.

Ministry of Counseling and Enrichment, 1333 N. 2nd St., **Abilene, TX** 79601, 915-675-8131. Mary Stedham, Director.

New Life Institute, Box 1666, **Austin, TX** 78767, 512-469-9447. Bob Breihan, Director.

Institute of Worklife Ministry, 2650 Fountainview Drive, Suite 444, **Houston, TX** 77057. 713-266-2456. Diana C. Dale, Director.

Life/Career Planning Center for Religious, 10526 W. Cermak Rd., Suite 111, **Westchester, IL** 60153, 708-531-9228. Dolores Linhart, Director. Doing work with Roman Catholics.

Life Stewardship Associates, 6918 Glen Creek Dr., SE, **Dutton, MI** 49316, 616-698-3125. Ken Soper, M.Div., M.A., Director.

CareerConcepts, 1451 Elm Hill Pike, Suite 314, **Nashville, TN** 37210, 615-367-5000. Robert H. McKown.

Mid-South Career Development Center, 2315 Fisher Place, **Knoxville, TN** 37920, 615-573-1340. W. Scott Root, Director.

Career and Personal Counseling Center, 1904 Mt. Vernon St., **Waynesboro, VA** 22980, 703-943-9997. Lillian Pennell, Director.

Career Pathways, 601 Broad St., **Gainsville, GA** 30501, 800-722-1976. Lee Ellis, Director. Offers career-guidance from a Christian point of view, through the mails -- based on questionnaires and various instruments or inventories which they send you.

Judith Gerberg Associates, 250 West 57th St., **New York, NY** 10107, 212-315-2322. Judith Gerberg.

Index

Every page of the book, including footnotes and appendices, is indexed except that book titles are included only if they appear in the main text.

Author Index

Other Resources

Additional materials by Richard N. Bolles to help you with your job-hunt:

HOW TO CREATE A PICTURE OF YOUR IDEAL JOB OR NEXT CAREER

This workbook (8½ by 11 inches) is designed to lead the reader through a series of detailed exercises, expanding upon Chapters 9 and 10 in *Parachute*. $5.95

THE ANATOMY OF A JOB

This 24 by 36 inch poster serves as a worksheet to supplement the workbook above *(How to Create A Picture . . .)*. The 'Skills Keys' are on one side, and the 'Flower' is on the other side. $4.95

HOW TO FIND YOUR MISSION IN LIFE

This is a gift book version of the current Epilogue in *Parachute*. Judging by the mail Dick Bolles receives, this is a favorite of readers who want their work to fulfill a purpose and bring more than simply money to their lives. $5.95

THE MISSION POSTER

This colorful 24 by 36 inch poster summarizes the main ideas in the booklet above *(How to Find Your Mission in Life)*. $4.95

JOB-HUNTING TIPS FOR THE SO-CALLED "HANDICAPPED" OR PEOPLE WHO HAVE DISABILITIES

Originally published as an appendix in *Parachute,* this popular material is now only available as a separate booklet. In this work, Dick Bolles uses his unique perspective on job-hunting and career-change to address the experiences of the disabled in doing these tasks. $4.95

To: Ten Speed Press
P.O. Box 7123
Berkeley, CA 94707

I would like to order:

_____ copies of **HOW TO CREATE A PICTURE OF YOUR IDEAL JOB OR NEXT CAREER** @ $5.95 each.

_____

_____ copies of the poster **THE ANATOMY OF A JOB** @ $4.95 each.

_____

_____ copies of **HOW TO FIND YOUR MISSION IN LIFE** @ $5.95 each.

_____

_____ copies of **THE MISSION POSTER** @ $4.95 each.

_____

_____ copies of **JOB-HUNTING TIPS FOR THE SO-CALLED "HANDICAPPED" OR PEOPLE WHO HAVE DISABILITIES** @ $4.95 each.

_____

Subtotal $ _____

Postage is $2.50 for the first item ordered and 50¢ for each additional item.

Postage $ _____

Total $ _____

Check or money order only, please, made out to Ten Speed Press.

Send to: (please print)

Name_____

Organization_____

Mailing Address_____

City, State, Zip_____

Update for 1995

TO: PARACHUTE
P.O. Box 379
Walnut Creek, CA 94597

I think that the information in the '94 edition needs to be changed, in your next revision, regarding (or, the following resource should be added):

_____

_____

_____

_____

_____

I cannot find the following resource, listed on page _____ :

_____

_____

_____

_____

_____

Name _____

Address _____

Please make a copy.
Submit this so as to reach us by February 1, 1994. Thank you.